ROBERT GROSSETESTE

I. GREGORY THE GREAT, MORALIA IN IOB III, §§ 60–62, WITH
GROSSETESTE'S ANNOTATIONS AND INDEXING SYMBOLS

(See pp. x, 121)

MS. Bodley 198, fol. 120ᵛ

ROBERT GROSSETESTE

SCHOLAR AND BISHOP

*Essays in Commemoration of
the Seventh Centenary of his Death*

Edited by

D. A. CALLUS

With an Introduction by

SIR MAURICE POWICKE

OXFORD
AT THE CLARENDON PRESS
1955

Oxford University Press, Amen House, London E.C.4

GLASGOW NEW YORK TORONTO MELBOURNE WELLINGTON
BOMBAY CALCUTTA MADRAS KARACHI CAPE TOWN IBADAN

Geoffrey Cumberlege, Publisher to the University

———

PRINTED IN GREAT BRITAIN

PREFACE

THE seven-hundredth anniversary of the death of Robert Grosseteste could not be allowed to pass by without some tribute to his memory. The diocese of Lincoln on 27 June 1953 commemorated in its Minster one of its greatest bishops by dedicating a new memorial on the very place where his body was first laid. And in the University of Oxford he will be honoured on 21 October as one of her most famous sons and her first chancellor. But it was thought that a volume of essays by leading Oxford and Lincoln scholars would contribute more fully and in a more permanent manner to an adequate appreciation of his manifold activities in the field of learning, in the Church, and in the State.

Grosseteste was a great scholar and a great bishop. The Editorial Committee planned this book to cover both aspects. A glance at the summaries of each chapter—which sufficiently supplies the need of an index—will show that this plan has been amply fulfilled. It was also designed to include an essay on Grosseteste's relations with the newly founded Orders of Friars, who played such an important part in his life. To the regret of the Committee, however, unforeseen circumstances have prevented this.

The papers have been read by the members of the Editorial Committee and by Miss Beryl Smalley. Their unfailing co-operation and generous assistance made the task of the editor a light one. To all I wish to express my deep gratitude, and in particular to the Chairman, Sir Maurice Powicke, for his inspiring leadership and for supplying the introduction, and to the Secretary, Miss Kathleen Major, whose unwearied patience and unsparing help, so kindly and abundantly given, have been most invaluable throughout. To all our contributors for their ready response to our invitation we are very thankful. To the Right Rev. D. C. Dunlop, Dean of Lincoln, for his initiative and continued interest we are all indebted.

Our thanks are due to the Librarian of John Rylands Library, Manchester, and to the Editor of *Oxoniensia*, Oxford, for kindly allowing us to print sections from papers which appeared in their periodicals. We are particularly grateful to the Delegates of the

Clarendon Press for undertaking to publish this book, and to their officers for the care they have taken in seeing it through the press.

I wish to express my respectful and grateful thanks to His Grace Archbishop David Mathew. It was only through his encouraging words that I assumed the editorship of this volume.

D. A. C.

BLACKFRIARS, OXFORD

July 1953

CONTENTS

conception of experimental science: induction and demonstration, 'resolution'
and 'composition', *pp*. 101–3; explanation of the rainbow, *pp*. 103–9; types of
cause, theoretical models, theory of light and colour, *pp*. 105–6, 108–9; intuition,
falsification, uniformity of action, principle of economy, nature of scientific
theories, *pp*. 106–8. (3) Mathematical physics: method, *pp*. 109–11; metaphysics
of light, *pp*. 111–12. (4) Grosseteste's influence: on the physical sciences,
pp. 112–13; on the calendar, *pp*. 113–15. Appendix: Grosseteste's treatise *On
the Heat of the Sun*, *pp*. 116–20.

abuses in the Church and the Roman Curia, *p.* 210; the claims of the Archbishop of Canterbury, *p.* 211; kingship and tyranny, *p.* 212; natural and positive law, *p.* 213; Grosseteste and the cure of souls, *p.* 214.

LIST OF PLATES

The plate shows the lower part of the left-hand column of the page. The indexing symbols are seen in the column next to the text. The three notes at the top
are later additions. The first of Grosseteste's notes is a subject head 'Quomodo
quidam superbiunt comparando se ad alios'. The second 'in se negligi consider-
are quod habet' supplies an omission in the text, and is marked for insertion by
two oblique strokes over the first word, corresponding to two oblique strokes in
the text after 'habet'. The two lowest notes are identifications of biblical quotations 'Jer. Tren. 1' and 'Ps. 34'. It will be seen that Grosseteste used Arabic
numerals. The text of Gregory is printed in Migne, Pat. lat. 75, cols. 629C–
630C. (See p. 121)

ABBREVIATIONS

Angl. Sacr.	*Anglia Sacra*, ed. H. Wharton, 2 vols., 1690–1.
Ann. Mon.	*Annales Monastici* (Rolls Series), ed. H. R. Luard, 5 vols., 1864–9.
Arch. HDLMA.	*Archives d'histoire doctrinale et littéraire du Moyen Age.*
Bacon, *Op. In.*	*Opera quaedam hactenus inedita*, ed. J. S. Brewer (Rolls Series). London, 1859.
Baur, *Die Philosophie*	L. Baur, *Die Philosophie des Robert Grosseteste*, B.G.P.M., xviii. 4–6. Münster i. W., 1917.
Baur, *Die Werke*	L. Baur, *Die philosophischen Werke des Robert Grosseteste*, B.G.P.M., ix. Münster i. W., 1912.
B.G.P.M.	*Beiträge zur Geschichte der Philosophie des Mittelalters.* Münster, i. W.
Brown	*Fasciculus rerum expetendarum et fugiendarum.* London, 1690.
Callus, *Aristotelian Learning*	D. A. Callus, *Introduction of Aristotelian learning to Oxford.* Proceedings of the British Academy, xxix, 1943.
Callus, 'Oxford Career'	D. A. Callus, 'The Oxford Career of Robert Grosseteste', *Oxoniensia*, x, 1945.
Callus, 'The date'	D. A. Callus, 'The date of Grosseteste's translations and commentaries on Pseudo-Dionysius and the Nicomachean Ethics', *R.T.A.M.* xiv. 1947.
Callus, Studies . . . F. M. Powicke	D. A. Callus 'The *Summa Theologiae* of Robert Grosseteste', in *Studies in Medieval History presented to F. M. Powicke.* Oxford, 1947.
C.P.R.	*Calendar of Patent Rolls.*
C. Pap. R.	*Calendar of Papal Registers relating to Great Britain and Ireland*, vol. i, ed. W. H. Bliss, 1898.
C.S.E.L.	*Corpus scriptorum ecclesiasticorum latinorum.*
Eccleston	*Fratris Thomae vulgo dicti de Eccleston Tractatus De adventu Fratrum Minorum in Angliam*, denuo ed. A. G. Little. Manchester, 1951.
E.H.R.	*English Historical Review.*
Ep. Epp.	*Roberti Grosseteste Epistolae* (Rolls Series), ed. H. R. Luard, London, 1861.
Franceschini, *Rob. Grossatesta*	*Roberto Grossatesta, vescovo di Lincoln e le sue versioni latine.* Venice, 1933.
Gir. Cam.	*Giraldi Cambrensis Opera* (Rolls Series), ed. J. S. Brewer, J. F. Dimock, and G. F. Warner, 8 vols. London, 1861–91.
J.T.S.	*Journal of Theological Studies.*
Lanercost	*Chronicon de Lanercost*, ed. J. Stevenson, The Maitland and Bannatyne Clubs, 1839.
Liber Antiquus	*Liber Antiquus Hugonis Wells 1209–35*, ed. A. Gibbons, privately printed 1888.
M.A.R.S.	*Mediaeval and Renaissance Studies.*
Mon. Angl.	*Monasticon Anglicanum*, by Sir William Dugdale, new enlarged edition by J. Caley, H. Ellis, and B. Bandinel, 6 vols. in 8. London, 1817–30.

Mon. Franc.	*Monumenta Franciscana*, ed. J. S. Brewer (Rolls Series). London, 1858.
O.H.S.	Oxford Historical Society.
Paris, *Chron. Mai.*	Matthew Paris, *Chronica Maiora* (Rolls Series), ed. H. R. Luard, 7 vols. London, 1872–4.
Paris, *Hist. Angl.*	Matthew Paris, *Historia Anglorum* (Rolls Series), ed. F. Madden, 3 vols. 1886–9.
Powicke, *Henry III*	*King Henry III and the Lord Edward.* 2 vols. Oxford, 1947.
Powicke, *Rob. Grosseteste*	*Robert Grosseteste and the Nicomachean Ethics.* Proceedings of the British Academy, xvi, 1930.
PMLA	Proceedings of the Modern Language Association.
P.G.	Migne, *Patrologia Graeca.*
P.L.	Migne, *Patrologia Latina.*
R.S.	Rolls Series.
Rotuli Grav.	*Rotuli Ricardi Gravesend diocesis Lincolniensis*, ed. F. N. Davis (Canterbury and York Society, xxxi), Lincoln Record Society, vol. xx.
Rotuli Gros.	*Rotuli Roberti Grosseteste episcopi Lincolniensis*, ed. F. N. Davis (Canterbury and York Society, x), Lincoln Record Society, vol. xi.
Rotuli Welles	*Rotuli Hugonis de Welles Episcopi Lincolniensis*, ed. W. P. W. Phillimore and F. N. Davis (Canterbury and York Society, i, iii, iv), Lincoln Record Society, vols. iii, vi, ix.
R.T.A.M.	*Recherches de Théologie ancienne et médiévale.*
Russell, *Dictionary*	J. C. Russell, *Dictionary of Writers of Thirteenth Century England.* Bulletin of the Institute of Historical Research, Special Supplement III, 1936.
Russell, 'Preferments and Adiutores'	J. C. Russell, 'The preferments and *Adiutores* of Robert Grosseteste' *Harvard Theological Review*, xxvi, 1933.
Russell, 'Richard of Bardney'	J. C. Russell, 'Richard of Bardney's account of Robert Grosseteste's early and middle life', *Medievalia et Humanistica*, ii, 1944.
Russell, 'Phases'	J. C. Russell, 'Phases of Grosseteste's intellectual life', *Harvard Theological Review*, xliii, 1950.
Salimbene	Salimbene, *Cronica* (Monumenta Germaniae Historica, *Scriptores*, vol. xxxii), 1905.
Smalley, *Study of the Bible*	Beryl Smalley, *The Study of the Bible in the Middle Ages.* Oxford, 1952.
Smalley, 'Robert Bacon'	Beryl Smalley, 'Robert Bacon and the early Dominican School at Oxford'. *Transactions of the Royal Historical Society*, 4th ser. xxx, 1948.
Smith, *Church and State*	A. L. Smith, *Church and State in the Middle Ages.* Oxford, 1913.
Stevenson	Francis S. Stevenson, *Robert Grosseteste, Bishop of Lincoln.* London, 1899.
Thomson, *Writings*	Thomson, S. Harrison, *The Writings of Robert Grosseteste.* Cambridge, 1940.
Trivet. *Ann.*	*F. Nicholai Triveti, De ordine Fratrum Praedicatorum, Annales*, ed. Thomas Hog. London, 1845.

INTRODUCTION

IN pre-Reformation days the memory of Robert Grosseteste, of *Lincolniensis*, was alive in the West; it was revived, in certain learned quarters in the seventeenth century, and again in the first considerable biography of him by Samuel Pegge (1793). It naturally received fitting and intelligent recognition during the great historical renascence in the nineteenth century. The life of Grosseteste, published in 1899 by F. S. Stevenson, took account of the new learning; but Grosseteste is really coming to his own in our time, as the true significance of his work as a scholar, notably in the history of scientific method, and as a churchman, is revealed. The definitive life of him has still to be written and can only be written by a very learned, versatile, and penetrating scholar indeed.

I do not mean to suggest any contrast between the man whom we can now see and the man seen more clearly by his contemporaries. I mean that we can now better realize the nature of a man who was felt by all, whether they admired or disliked him, to be a portentous person, a man of universal genius. Grosseteste lived in the open. He was not one of those who have to be discovered, or whose discovery is due to the moods and fashions of an age which is better able to appreciate, and can easily overrate, the merits of genius misunderstood or disregarded while it was struggling to express itself. Grosseteste could not and need not be admired or detested or, except in one regard, be appreciated by us today more than he was in his own day. The exception, indeed, his significance in the history of science, is only an exception because scientists here and there today are becoming more interested in the history of science and can marvel at the clear-headedness and insight of a man outstanding in the medieval schools. Natural science today has nothing to *learn* from him except a better understanding of movements of thought which it has been wont to despise, and a humble sense of gratitude to any fine mind in any age which has helped to produce it. From this point of view the realization that Grosseteste had a truly scientific mind is in itself part of the historical process which sweeps away the mist and prejudice between us and any period in the past. The historian is not concerned to make a hero of Grosseteste or to pick him out to the disadvantage of his fellows: this would be to falsify history. The historian's duty is to make Grosseteste live so clearly that we can better understand the age in which he lived, thought, and strove to make men what he believed they ought to be. He was a man of his age in the sense in which Dr. Johnson or Sir Walter Scott was a man of his age, and like them the more impressive because he never thought of himself as anything else.

Grosseteste's orderly, stern, but gracious spirit was innate in him and directed everything that he did both as a thinker and a director of souls. It was grounded in instinct and habit, yet trained by reason. Above all, it had the quality which was inconsistent with laziness and pomposity. Grosseteste always looked to the end, not the means. He believed in and understood the society in which he found himself, without a trace of easy-going acceptance or prejudice. It never occurred to him to reject the good because it might disturb existing conventions or traditions. Thus he was one of the first to welcome the followers of St. Francis and St. Dominic, not only because he admired them, but also because he saw in them the helpers of whom a bishop who meant business was most in need. He was shocked when he was told that his friend Alexander of Stavensby, of all people, Bishop of Coventry and Lichfield, formerly a teacher who had lectured to St. Dominic and his disciples at Toulouse, had publicly reviled the Franciscans when he heard that they were about to settle in his diocese at Chester. There was room, Grosseteste declared, for both orders in Chester. 'This incredible thing, if it is true, I believe can only have proceeded from some sudden disturbance of your mind, not from deliberate conviction.'[1] Grosseteste always acted with deliberation. That is why his anger could be so terrible.

The letter which I have just quoted was written soon after Grosseteste became Bishop of Lincoln. He was already well over sixty years old. I have always found it hard to believe that the busiest and most active bishop of his time did his hardest work when he was between sixty-five or seven and eighty-three or five years of age. Yet, to use his own words, this incredible thing seems to be true. During these eighteen years he made himself a power to be reckoned with in England, twice visited the papal Court at Lyons, on the second occasion (1250) haranguing the Pope and cardinals, was in touch with everybody, and wrote or supervised much of his literary work. The fact is significant. As a bishop he was reaping the harvest of long experience and mental discipline. He had nothing to fear, a great deal to say, and the virility to act strenuously upon his convictions.

[1] *Ep.*, p. 121.

His career is known with certainty from his appearance in Oxford after the year 1215. Those who have given minute attention to his earlier writings have satisfied themselves that they date from about 1200 onwards and were the outcome of teaching and study at Oxford, and, as no evidence can be adduced to the contrary, we may agree with Father Daniel Callus that Grosseteste lectured in the budding university between 1200 and 1209, left England, like so many other scholars, during the Great Interdict, and returned to Oxford about 1214 after the quarrel between King John and Archbishop Stephen Langton had been composed. It is indeed unlikely that a scholar who became one of the first chancellors of the University, after its formal recognition and the provision of an official head, and whose scientific and philosophical reputation was already so high, had no previous experience of the foremost school in England. Whether, during his absence in France, he was a theological student in Paris and proceeded to the higher degree of master or doctor in theology is uncertain, but the fact that a chancellor in Oxford had to be a master in theology makes it likely that he qualified for the degree there or continued his studies for a year or two in order to qualify for it after his return to Oxford. However this may be, he did not desert his philosophical studies. One of his works, his marginal glosses on Aristotle's *Physics*, was jotted down at the end of his Oxford career (1230–5) in the years when he was acting as *lector* to the lately established house of the Franciscans; but by this time he was especially immersed in the Biblical teaching and expositions required of a theologian. In 1235 he was elected Bishop of Lincoln, the largest diocese in England, stretching from the Humber to the Thames, and comprehending Lincoln in the north and Oxford in the south.

The self-discipline acquired by Grosseteste in the scientific environment of the study of the arts in the Oxford schools helped to form his theological teaching and the studies which he pursued during his brief but important period of office as the first *lector* of the Franciscans at Oxford and after his elevation to the episcopate in 1235. His interest lay in the great texts and led to his translations from the Greek. During fifteen busy years the aged scholar used his scanty leisure as bishop to work with his clerks and translators. His country manors where he stayed, Stow by Lincoln, Buckden on the London road, Fingest in its lovely hollow in the Chilterns, and many other places were the scenes of this congenial relief from the business and troubles of the episcopal day.

Grosseteste's public life as Bishop of Lincoln was informed by two experiences, one his outlook on the universe as a scholar, the other the realization of his duties as a prelate, an experience which, though of slow and steady growth, was doubtless given a more urgent and personal edge by his friendship with the friars at Oxford.

His curiosity about natural things, his scientific accuracy, and his consciousness of a wider world, embracing the celestial hierarchy, directed by an omnipresent God, and sanctioned by an overruling natural law revealed in the Scriptures and claiming the allegiance of the informed will—all this and much more was fostered and defined by his experience as a scholar and a friend of scholars. That no responsible teacher should say anything unless he was sure of it and had studied its ground and implications was a truth to which he often recurred. In one of his earlier books (1231), the *De Cessatione Legalium*, he applies it to the allegorical interpretation of Scripture, in which all truth is contained. The *De Cessatione* attracted attention in the seventeenth century; some of it was printed with an appreciation of its author, in London in 1658; its subject, the relations between the Old and the New Law, as revealed by the Scriptures and interpreted by the wisest doctors, was felt to be of topical interest. A new sign, says Grosseteste, does not necessarily 'evacuate' an old sign. The observance of the Sabbath, for example, is so generally (*communiter*) useful and necessary that it proclaims itself to have been ordained by God, not as temporary but as permanent in the order of the universe. Reason cannot make the supreme reason better. The significance of the observance in the new order, he points out later, requires the most careful regard to the literal texts in the search for their allegorical meaning.

A good teacher does not inform the mind of his disciple by means of the abbreviated word but of the full word, and every scholar of a master or an art knows how to distinguish between the two and finds the master's intention fully and clearly in his perfected and rounded (*integris*) utterances. So the elucidation of Scripture must be based upon the text as a whole, the naked word, not on truncated and casual words.

This instruction is clearly in the Augustinian tradition. St. Augustine tried 'to steer a middle course between literal and allegorical expositions'. Earnest meditation on the text is needed if the interpretation 'which tends to establish the reign of charity' is to be found.[1] Grosseteste explained this tradition in the light of the new scholastic

[1] Beryl Smalley, *Study of the Bible*, pp. 23-24.

method. He was on the way to the canons of interpretation laid down
by St. Thomas;[1] but his point of view is best approached by way of
Roger Bacon, who stood nearer to him and gave high praise to his
expositions of Scripture.

Probably the quickest way to realize how Grosseteste as a Christian
scholar applied his mind to the world about him as part of an ordered
universe under divine direction would be the study of his *Dicta*,
one of the most popular of his works, for this miscellaneous collection of 147 passages, mainly taken from his sermons and lectures,
including the whole of some of the sermons delivered to the clergy
or people while he was a teacher in the schools, was obviously
intended as a work of edification. Unhappily, only twenty-one of the
Dicta have been published. These were printed by Edward Brown
in his valuable *Fasciculus Rerum Expetendarum* in 1690. Professor
Harrison Thomson, in his book on the writings of Grosseteste, has
given a full list with brief indications of their contents (pp. 216–32).
A more satisfactory guide to Grosseteste's mind would be editions
of his sermons and commentaries, especially his moralia on the
Gospels and his work on the Psalter. Thomson has listed ninety-two
sermons which he regards as certainly Grosseteste's, and seventy-
five more, mainly from an early Durham manuscript, which he feels
safe in attributing to him; but only one or two have been published.
Gascoigne in the fifteenth century was emphatic that Grosseteste
commented on all the Epistles of St. Paul, but only one, on the
Epistle to the Galatians, has survived, though another, on the
Romans, may also be his. None of them have been printed. Hence
we have to rely upon the Letters, and fortunately these are full and
comprehensive, and can be supplemented by the numerous letters
written to the bishop by his disciple and friend, the Franciscan
Adam Marsh.

One of the sermons from which extracts have appeared in print[2]
was preached by Grosseteste to the Franciscans in chapter. Its
theme is the ladder of poverty. The preacher characteristically urges
his hearers to avoid the pride latent in humility and always to
remember the end or purpose of their way of life. This Aristotelian
emphasis on the intention of things and the subordination of every
grade in the ordered scale of being to its superior grade is as fundamental to an understanding of Grosseteste's life as a bishop and his
outlook on practical issues as it is in the development of philosophical

---

[1] Ibid., p. 300.   [2] Eccleston, edit. A. G. Little (Paris, 1909), pp. 178–87.

thought in the thirteenth century. The conception, however, implies a scale of values, and, in this case, of theological and cosmological values, which must guide the religious life, whether contemplative or ecclesiastical or parochial, and in particular illuminate the cure of souls. Theology, so he said in one of his *Dicta* (no. 118), turns the syllogism to spiritual uses and catches in its net spiritual fish who are readily caught. Here we come to the influences which clarified the mind and strengthened the will of the elderly scholar in the years which preceded his episcopate.

What made him consent to change his life at Oxford for the duties of a diocesan? And what made him, in contrast to that other great scholar, St. Edmund of Abingdon, who in these same years became Archbishop of Canterbury and found that he could not tolerate the burden, so resolute and forthright a prelate? I do not know, but I suspect that his friendship with and admiration for the new Mendicant Orders had something to do with his decision and his pertinacity. The arrival of the Orders in 1221 and 1224 and their immediate establishment in Oxford had aroused much excitement. Their sense of purpose and their modes of life had created a deep impression. About the time when Grosseteste agreed to supervise Franciscan studies in the humble Greyfriars, Jordan of Saxony, St. Dominic's successor as Master General of the Dominicans, came on a visit to England. He preached on St. Martin's Day (11 Nov. 1229) in Oxford and issued a 'challenge to the prelates assembled there to save the souls of the people throughout England'. Grosseteste, who, in a letter (no. 40) written to the Master General some years later, recalls the intimate and friendly conversations which he had had with him in Oxford, must have heard this sermon. Its text survives in the Durham manuscript which contains the material for Grosseteste's work on the Psalms and many of his own sermons.[1] Brother Jordan, speaking from the texts, Judith viii. 21, 'You are priests in the people of God, from you hangs their soul', and Isaiah xxii. 23, 24, on the nail fastened in a sure place, from which all kinds of vessels hung, exclaimed, 'Oh, my God, where shall be found a cord so long that the people of all the parishes of England may hang on it? Will it come from their prelates residing in Oxford? God knows, I know not. But we do know that if the column falls or the nail gives way, all the vessels which hang on it will fall and be

---

[1] A. G. Little, in *Eng. Hist. Rev.* liv (1939), 1–19, has edited Jordan's sermon and two others preached by him in England.

broken.' And then, turning to the masters in the schools, he warned them against pride and cupidity and the desire for worldly promotion. 'We read in Matthew how the devil lifted the Lord to the pinnacle of the Temple, which signifies the status of the *magisterium*. The Devil has placed many there, all, that is to say, who are so eager to be made or called masters that they may be honoured and advanced in temporal things. There is nothing wrong in being called master; it is the height of pride to wish to be called master.'

About this time Grosseteste became the first lecturer to the Franciscans. Brother Thomas of Eccleston, who wrote the story of the arrival of the Friars Minor in England, put on record their debt to their teacher. 'Under him within a short time', he says, 'they made incalculable progress both in scholastic discussion, and the subtle moralities suitable for preaching.' In 1232 he decided to resign his prebends, including the archdeaconry of Leicester. He retained only his prebend in the Cathedral Church of Lincoln. In a letter (no. 8) to his sister Juetta, who was a nun, telling her of this decision, he says:

You, who wear the habit and have bought the vow of the religious life, must not be at all disturbed or sorry. If I am poorer by my own choice, I am made richer in virtues. If I am more despicable in the eyes of the world, I am more acceptable to the citizens of heaven. If I have given up temporal things for the sake of obedience, only by obedience can I merit heavenly things. You should love more in me the good which you love in yourself, the more closely we are bound together by ties of the flesh.

He seems to have felt some doubt whether Juetta would receive his news with the sisterly and sympathetic understanding that he had the right to expect from a cloistered nun.

Grosseteste's most troublesome problem as a bishop in England was his relations with the dean and chapter of Lincoln. His right of episcopal visitation was challenged. The long and dramatic controversy which ensued had finally to be settled in his favour by the Pope. Early in the dispute (*c.* 1239) he prepared for the dean and chapter a long essay about the relations which should exist between a bishop and his cathedral chapter (Epistle 127). This illustrates perfectly his conception of the Church as an organism. It is based upon arguments made clear by examples—examples taken from the Old Testament, examples drawn from daily life, examples suggested by his almost passionate interest in the nature of light. Moses, as the meaning of his name suggests, is the type of a Christian prelate. When he gave duties to his helpers he did not surrender power but reserved his own rights; just as the sun is no less the source of light when its rays are reflected by a mirror and throw light in places not directly exposed to them. Moses and his helpers correspond to the Pope and the bishops; each bishop in his own diocese is what the Pope is in the whole Church and controls his assistants in the same way, and the dean and chapter have their helpers and so down to the lowest. A bishop's powers may be limited; for example, he cannot visit Cistercian abbeys as each abbot can visit the houses affiliated to his own mother abbey; but every case of this kind depends upon a privilege granted by the Pope. A dean cannot visit his own chapter, for he resides in the cathedral with it, and even if he could, he could not exclude the bishop. The Pope is like the sun, giving light to moon and stars. He imparts power to bishops who impart power to others. Just as the Pope cannot diminish his plenitude of power unless a mandate from Christ approves his action because of its advantage (*utilitatis*), so no bishop can give away any of his authority. Moreover, no civil law or custom can stand in his way, for custom is a positive, not a negative thing, and cannot overrule the exercise of the good. Underlying all this formal argument about structure is the conception of the happiness and freedom which cordial co-operation in the salvation of souls can and should bring to all. All are watchmen, trusting in the watchfulness of their subordinates. All are shepherds anxious for the safety of the sheep. In another memorandum, written eleven years later for the guidance of Archbishop Boniface of Canterbury, Grosseteste likens the hierarchy to the subdivision of an immense flock, 10,000 sheep divided into thousands, thousands into hundreds, hundreds into tens, each group or multiple of groups under its shepherd, feeding and watching the sheep. To revert to the pamphlet for the dean and chapter, Grosseteste argued that here was true liberty, for as Philo-Judaeus wrote: 'The slave is everyone who sins; the freeman is everyone who labours for the good.' And so, throughout this long argument the bishop turns from one aspect of the theme to another, with inexhaustible fertility in Scriptural analogy. It appears to have made very little impression upon the canons. They lived decently and contentedly in an English world of rights, customs, precedents, social distinctions, secular and ecclesiastical. They resented this instruction from a low-born prelate, who brought newfangled mendicant friars into his household to help him to get on with his diocesan job.[1]

Everything that Grosseteste did and said as bishop can be brought within the implications of this document. Neither his view of the universe nor its expression in the details of a reformed ecclesiasticism was new. Some of it was very old, much had been defined in 1215 at the Fourth Lateran Council and again by Stephen Langton at a provincial council at Oxford in 1222, and yet again in episcopal constitutions. The qualities which made Grosseteste so formidable and brought him to the front were the range of his incisive mind, his tireless energy, and the grandeur of his character.

He was a leader from the first years of his episcopate, a propelling force which might be deplored but could not be disregarded. In letters to Archbishop Edmund and the justice William Ralegh he gave the clearest and most orderly statement yet made of the grievances of the clergy and the subordination of the common law to the law of the Church. His constitutions or directions to his clergy were, in Professor Cheney's opinion, more widely adopted than any others were in later episcopal constitutions. His lists of *gravamina* initiated a movement which found periodic expression during the next hundred years. His pertinacity in inquiries into the conduct and character of the laity in his widespread diocese, a form of interference with the king's subjects for which at least twice he was called to account by the royal authority, set an example which could not be disregarded in giving this episcopal duty such effectiveness as it ever had in English medieval life. His insistence that prelates and clergy should not accept secular office found little response, but must, I think, have done much, at a critical time, to set the tradition of clerical independence later expressed in a separate convocation of the clergy, distinct from parliament.

He knew everybody and feared nobody. At King Henry's request he instructed him on the nature of an anointed king, and in so doing courteously reminded him of his responsibility for the maintenance of his subjects in peace and justice and of his duty to abstain from any interference with the cure of souls. He would allow no compromise on matters of principle. The common law of the Church should be applied in the light of equity, the dictate of conscience, and the teaching of natural law, as revealed in the Scriptures,

---

[1] For their reply, recently discovered, and more to the point than their private feelings, see below, p. 173, n. 2.

implicit in the working of a Divine Providence, and conformable to the teaching and guidance of Christ in the Church militant on earth. Hence came his fierce attacks upon legal pedantry and venality in the ecclesiastical courts, notably that of Canterbury, and upon Archbishop Boniface's exaction of procurations on an early visitation which, so the bishops insisted, had a financial rather than a spiritual objective, his hatred of the indiscriminate provision to benefices by the papal Court and the exploitation of parishes by monastic houses, his minute scrutiny of presentations to benefices and dignities, his urgent expostulations in his letters of counsel to all kinds of persons in positions of civil or ecclesiastical authority, and the influence which he could exercise over men like Earl Simon de Montfort. His memory was venerated by like-minded men and was invoked in times of revolt by many who can have had no clear idea of the cause for which he stood, the art of arts, the salvation of souls.

In no matter was Grosseteste more true to himself than in his relations with the papacy. He was a thoroughgoing papalist. The Vicar of Christ was the linch-pin upon which the whole fabric of the Church depended; but he was the Vicar of Christ and woe betide if he fell short of his awful responsibilities. Orthodox minds were more outspoken than they were in post-Tridentian days in their criticism of papal behaviour. The rapid development of the ecclesiastical system under the impulse of the papal plenitude of power was itself a justification of their concern during the century and a half which separate St. Bernard's paternal warnings to his friend Pope Eugenius III from the unseemly relations between Pope Boniface VIII and his cardinals. Some distinguished canonists found a solution in the conception of the Church as a whole, and the college of cardinals in particular, as corporations. Thus Hostiensis worked out the implications of the current view that the cardinals are part of the Pope's body. 'Not the Pope alone but the cardinals also are comprehended in the expression of the *plenitudo potestatis*', which remains with the cardinals during a vacancy in the Holy See. The Pope could certainly act on his own initiative, he was not compelled to adopt the advice of the cardinals, but his decision must not 'tend to subvert the well-being of the Universal Church'. But what if it does? Here Hostiensis went farther than the other leading canonists. He maintained that in matters of faith the ultimate authority is a general council.[1]

[1] See Brian Tierney, 'A Conciliar Theory of the Thirteenth Century', in *The Catholic Historical Review*, xxxvi (Jan. 1951), 415–40.

Grosseteste followed a personal course when he was confronted
by the problem of papal error. He was a theologian, not a profes-
sional canonist. In practice and probably in principle he was not
affected by the legal theory of corporation. He trusted rather to
the mystical union of the Church whose authoritative expression on
earth was the Vicar of Christ. As an English bishop he did not regard
himself, as Hostiensis seems to have regarded all bishops, as bound
to consult his chapter, as the Pope consulted his cardinals. In his
dealings with the papal Curia he kept in touch with friendly cardinals, as all important litigants liked to do, and he was very conscious of the value to be attached to the influence of the Sacred
College;[1] but as a thoroughgoing papalist he could and would
appeal to an erring pope alone, as man to man.

He was prepared, indeed, to support his English episcopal colleagues in deploring the extent of papal exactions and, needless to
say, in appealing for papal support against all kinds of secular interference in the ecclesiastical system, but he was mainly concerned to
emphasize the responsibility of the Curia for the danger to the
pastoral care of a narrow and pedantic insistence on the common
law in Church and State, the demoralizing effect of papal provisions
and Archbishop Boniface's perversion of his right to visit his
province, so different from his own conception of an episcopal
visitation. In 1250, when he was at least eighty years of age, he went
to the papal Court to make his protest. He stood up alone, attended
by nobody but his official, Robert Marsh, who wrote a description
of the scene with a text of the memoranda presented by the bishop
and of the speeches which he made. Pope Innocent IV sat there with
his cardinals and members of his household to hear the most
thorough and vehement attack that any great pope can ever have
had to hear at the height of his power.[2] Three years later, in the
year of his death, Grosseteste, in a letter of protest addressed to a
papal agent and notary against a papal provision of the Pope's
nephew to a benefice, took the extreme step. He refused, in the
name of papal power, to obey the papal mandate. Some scholars,
confining their attention to the letter alone, have rejected it as a
forgery, though it is one of the best authenticated of Grosseteste's
works; but in fact it accords with all his moral and cosmological

---

[1] Cf. *Ep.*, no. 36, for Grosseteste's high view of the Pope with his cardinals as giving
light and beauty to the universe.
[2] Thomson, *Writings*, pp. 141–7.

convictions. Pope Innocent had presented his nephew, explicitly setting aside any obstacles or episcopal privileges of any kind, as a naked act of papal authority. Grosseteste, old, tired, and angry, but in full control of his mental faculties, denounced the papal mandate as an act of sin impossible to the Apostolic See. He went on:

No faithful subject in pure and full obedience to the Holy See, who is not schismatically cut off from the body of Christ and the same See, can be in accord with this or any other mandate of its kind, even though it came from the highest order of Angels. Wherefore, reverend Sir, out of the obedience and fealty by which I am bound, as a child to his parents, to the most Holy Apostolic See and the love I bear to its union with the Body of Christ, filially and obediently I do not obey, I reject, I rebel against the contents of this letter.[1]

That this outburst came from the depth of his being and expressed his inmost conviction is shown very clearly if we place it beside the passage translated by Mr. Pantin from the memorandum presented three years before this date to Pope Innocent and the cardinals.[2] This passage anticipates in some measure the argument in the *Monarchia* where Dante maintains the function and necessity of universal empire as the ultimate end for the universal civil order of mankind, on the ground that 'the work proper to the human race, taken as a whole, is to keep the whole capacity of the potential intellect constantly actualized'. Grosseteste expressed himself in terms natural to a student of natural science and the pseudo-Dionysius, Dante as a reader of Aristotle's *Politics* influenced by Averroistic thought;[3] but the impression conveyed by both is of a great organism working at full strength. The difference between them is this: Grosseteste was afflicted by the incredible fear that the papacy, at the height of its power, might falter in its function as the source of vivifying light; whereas Dante, in a mood of temporary exaltation, saw in the restoration and enlargement of an empire which had ceased to function the only way to unite mankind on earth. Grosseteste was shocked by the possible perversity of a great power whose operations were affecting every Christian soul, Dante, as he came to feel, was (to use a fine phrase of Professor d'Entrèves) confusing the mission of a man with that of the Divine Saviour.

---

[1] *Ep.*, no. 128; cf. Thomson, *Writings*, pp. 212–13.
[2] Brown, *Fasciculus*, ii. 254; see the translation by Mr. W. A. Pantin, below, pp. 214–15.
[3] Cf. A. P. d'Entrèves, *Dante as a Political Thinker* (Oxford, 1952), pp. 47–51.

Each of these great men expected the impossible from the human nature which each, in his own way, desired to save from disorder and corruption. Grosseteste, in his urgency and strong faith in the existing ecclesiastical system, underrated the virile forces at work in the world about him, and the opportunities open to the good no less than to the bad. He may, for all we know, have been a different man in his personal relationships with his flock, but I fear that he was too old, too certain of himself, too tidy-minded, to keep in touch with the souls which he longed to save. I can see few traces of the grace of compassion in his revealing letters. Adam Marsh himself thought sometimes that he was too hard. He and Simon de Montfort had this fault in common. In one of his last letters to his archdeacons (c. 1250–1), a letter which he ordered them to have read throughout his diocese, he writes despairingly about the state of his spiritual subjects. He had even, he says, decided to resign but had been prevented by higher authority. In fact he seems to have relied too much upon the efficacy of injunctions and exhortations and his disciplinary powers. He had not really got to know his sheep as a good shepherd should; not, for example, as one of his successors, Oliver Sutton, Bishop of Lincoln from 1280 to 1299, was to get to know them.[1] Yet, when all is said, he was one of those rare men whose minds and spirits move easily in the universe of things and in practical life do not fear to face the consequences. In 1953 his church at Lincoln venerated him as the greatest of her bishops; and, in my view, the University of Oxford would not be far wrong if she were to honour him as the greatest of her sons.

[1] See Rosalind Hill, *Oliver Sutton* (Lincoln Minster Pamphlets, no. 4, 1950), and her paper on 'Public Penance: Some Problems of a Thirteenth Century Bishop', in *History* for October 1951 (new series, xxxvi. 213–26).

Robert Grosseteste as Scholar

THE central figure in England in the intellectual movement of the first half of the thirteenth century was undoubtedly Robert Grosseteste. Little is known of his life before his elevation to the see of Lincoln in 1235. The collection of his letters is of great value for his episcopate, but contains only a few from the years preceding his accession, and none of these would seem to go beyond 1229. Again, the letters of his friend and helper, the Franciscan Adam Marsh, of the utmost importance for an intimate knowledge of Grosseteste, belong to his later days. We have to rely for our information on scattered evidence gleaned mainly from Matthew Paris, the *Annales Monastici*, and other chronicles, from the episcopal Rolls, and from occasional entries in a deed or a charter. Summing up, all this is extremely meagre and fragmentary.

Of Grosseteste's contemporaries, St. Edmund of Abingdon, Archbishop of Canterbury, St. Richard Wych, Bishop of Chichester, and St. Thomas de Cantilupe, Bishop of Hereford, we possess lives written almost immediately after their death; but no biography of Grosseteste has come down to us.[1] This is the more surprising when we remember that attempts to secure his canonization were made in 1280 and earlier, in 1286, 1288, and 1307.[2] The letters written to the Pope for this purpose by the king, archbishops, bishops, abbots, and magnates yield no new material of any relevance for the early years.

Most historians regard the metrical life, written in 1503 by Richard, monk of Bardney,[3] as, in Stevenson's words, 'a work of fiction, devoid of historical value'.[4] One writer assumes that 'the main part of Bardney's information came from a good source and may be used as a basis for the reconstruction of the early and middle parts of Grosseteste's life'.[5] Although the possibility of such a source

[1] The earliest account is by John de Schalby in the *Lives of the Bishops of Lincoln*, written about 1330, edited by Dimock in *Gir. Cam. Opera*, vii. 204–6; but even this is fragmentary as it has come down to us in a very imperfect copy. A translation with notes has lately been made by Canon J. H. Srawley (Lincoln Minster Pamphlets, ii).

[2] See Kemp, 'The Attempted Canonization of Robert Grosseteste', below, pp. 241–6.

[3] Bardney's Life of Grosseteste is printed in *Anglia Sacra*, ii. 325–41.

[4] Stevenson, p. viii, cf. also p. 4; Luard's Preface to his edition of Grosseteste's *Epistolae*, pp. x, xxxi, and *D.N.B.*, viii, 72 (Oxford ed.).

[5] Russell, 'Richard of Bardney', pp. 45–54.

cannot be ruled out *a priori*, Bardney's late composition—250 years after Grosseteste's death—does not by itself vouch for any assurance of accuracy. Moreover, its fanciful, legendary, and mythical character tends rather to shake than to win our confidence. It does not follow from this that every detail in Bardney's account is necessarily inaccurate, some might in fact be correct, but we can in no way accept his statements unless supported by documentary evidence.

The surname 'Grosseteste' was not as rare as is at times assumed. A master Richard Grosseteste was Archdeacon of Wilts. and rector of Calne in the first decades of the thirteenth century,[1] and a master Ralph Grosseteste was appointed papal judge-delegate by Pope Innocent III;[2] but whether these were Robert's relatives we do not know. All that is known about his family is that he had a sister, Juetta (or Ivetta), a nun, probably at Godstow, to whom one of his letters is addressed.[3] After he became Bishop of Lincoln he promoted to the church of Litchborough,[4] and later to the rectory of Whissendine, Rutland,[5] Master John Grosseteste, and in 1245 he collated to the living of Felmersham the subdeacon Robert Grosseteste.[6] These may well have been his relatives. Nevertheless, that he did not unduly favour his kinsmen is evident from a letter of Adam Marsh, who repeatedly interceded on behalf of two of them who were scholars at Oxford, and, taking the liberties possible to a loyal friend and a faithful adviser, had to remind him in the severe words of St. Paul that 'if any provideth not for his own, and especially his own household, he hath denied the faith, and is worse than an infidel'.[7]

Contemporary authority is, however, unanimous in asserting that Robert Grosseteste was of lowly origin.[8] The traditional place of his birth is in the county of Suffolk, but its exact location is un-

---

[1] Cf. *The Register of St. Osmund*, ed. W. H. R. Jones (R.S.), London, 1884, i. 380; ii. 16, 130, 133; *Charters and Documents illustrating the History of the Cathedral, City and Diocese of Salisbury* (R.S.), London, 1891, pp. 111–13. The editor wrongly changed the name *Ricardus*, which the manuscript has, into *Robertus*, thus causing much confusion. A 'magister Ricardus Grosseteste' occurs as a witness *c.* 1184–9 in the *Cartulary of Oseney Abbey*, ed. Salter (O.H.S. lxxxix), Oxford, 1928, i. 217.

[2] Cf. Russell, *Dictionary*, p. 136, n. 5.

[3] *Ep.* 43–45; cf. Adam Marsh's letters, *Mon. Franc.* i. 95, 164. Stevenson, p. 2.

[4] *Rotuli Gros.*, pp. 164, 166.

[5] Ibid., pp. 172, 225. John witnessed several deeds, cf. pp. 26–27, 165, 184, 186, 351, 401, 406, 407, 452. See Major, below, pp. 229–30.

[6] *Rotuli Gros.*, pp. 330, 332. He appears as a witness on p. 336.

[7] 1 Tim. v. 8. Adam Marsh's letter xxxv, *Mon. Franc.* i. 137.

[8] Paris, *Hist. Angl.* ii. 376; *Chron. Mai.* iii. 528; *Lanercost*, p. 43; Trivet, *Ann.*, p. 242 :'De ima gente Suthfolchiae, Northwicensis dioecesis, originem traxit.'

certain.[1] It is generally stated that he was born between 1170–5;[2] but, as he was already a master in arts not later than 1190,[3] and assuming that he was then in his twenties at the least, it would be fairly safe to advance the date of his birth to 1168 or thereabouts. Thus he would be nearing his seventieth year at his accession to the see of Lincoln, and well over eighty at his death in 1253. ' Along life', in the language of Roger Bacon.

From his early boyhood Grosseteste learned his letters, *a primis annis scolis educatus.*[4] It is possible that he received his first schooling at Lincoln. We cannot say with certainty where he pursued his studies in arts, whether at Oxford, as is more probable, or, like other contemporary youths, at Paris. Thomas Gascoigne unhesitatingly asserts that Grosseteste was master in arts of Oxford, *magister Artium Oxoniae*,[5] but he gives no authority for his statement. Matthew Paris, on the other hand, says simply without specifying the place that he was 'eleganter tam in trivio quam quadrivio eruditus'.[6]

Robert Grosseteste's name appears for the first time in a charter of Hugh, Bishop of Lincoln.[7] Generally ascribed to Hugh of Wells (1209–35),[8] this charter really belongs to Hugh of Avalon (1186–1200).[9] Grosseteste is the last in the list of the witnesses, and is described as *Magister Robertus Grosteste*. Among other witnesses there was Simon of Siwell (Southwell), but he was not yet treasurer of Lichfield, which he became in 1203. But since he left Lincoln and joined the household of Hubert, Archbishop of Canterbury, about

---

[1] For Suffolk see Trivet, above, p. 2, n. 8. At a much later date, on the authority of the *Flores Historiarum*, formerly known as Matthew of Westminster, his native place was described as Stradbroke (cf. Luard, *Epp.*, p. xxxi; Stevenson, 1, 5). But the sentence 'in villa Stradbroke' seems to have been inserted, on his own authority, by Archbishop Parker in his edition, London, 1570, ii. 258. See Luard's Introduction to his edition of the *Flores Historiarum* (R.S.), London, 1890, i, p. xlvi. MS. Corpus Christi College, Cambridge 152, which was once in Parker's hands, contains a copy of Trivet's *Annales*. Mr. R. Vaughan of Corpus Christi College, Cambridge, tells me that 'the passage in Trivet was evidently noticed by M. Parker, because there is a mark in the margin opposite it in his red chalk—but "Stradbroke" certainly did not come from this manuscript'. According to the dubious authority of Richard of Bardney Grosseteste was born in Stow.

[2] Cf. Luard's Preface, *Epp.*, p. xxxii; Stevenson, p. 4.

[3] See below, p. 4.

[4] Paris, *Chron. Mai.* iii. 306.

[5] *Liber de Veritatibus*, MS. Lincoln College 117, p. 246[b].

[6] Paris, *Hist. Angl.* ii. 376.

[7] Dugdale, *Monasticon Anglicanum*, v. 191.

[8] Cf., for instance, Stevenson, p. 25.

[9] See Russell, 'Preferments and *Adiutores*', pp. 162–3; and *Dictionary*, p. 136. Professor Russell was the first to call attention to this fact.

1193,[1] it is reasonable to assume that he signed the charter before that date, that is, while he was still at Lincoln. Accordingly, the charter is earlier than Hugh of Wells's accession in 1209. Again, William de Monte became Chancellor of Lincoln shortly before 1192, but in the charter he appears simply as a canon, not as chancellor; and Roger of Rolveston, in his turn, had not yet been appointed Archdeacon of Leicester, 1189–90. The charter must, therefore, be assigned to a time between 1186, St. Hugh's elevation to the see of Lincoln, and 1189–90.

From a letter of Gerald of Wales we learn that master Robert Grosseteste was in the household of William de Vere, Bishop of Hereford, not later than 1198 (date of the bishop's death). He is praised not only for his remarkable proficiency in the liberal arts and abundant knowledge of literature, but also for his dexterity in handling various affairs and determination of causes and in securing and preserving bodily health.[2] The references to 'the preservation of health' and 'the determination of causes' have with plausible certainty been interpreted as pointing to his knowledge of medicine, as well as of canon, if not civil, law.[3]

His presence at Hereford is attested during William de Vere's episcopate by three of the bishop's charters, and by one of Hubert Walter, Archbishop of Canterbury (1193–1205). He appears among the witnesses as 'master Robert Grossicapitis'.[4]

Of his other pursuits at Hereford we have no record. It may, perhaps, be supposed that he took up teaching in that cathedral school. A contemporary, Simon du Fresne, urging Gerald of Wales to come to Hereford, in a poem written c. 1195–7, describes with enthusiasm the curriculum of studies of the school, how not only the seven liberal arts, the trivium and the quadrivium, were flourishing there, but also astrology and geomancy, and the natural sciences, together with Holy Writ and canon and civil law.[5] This would surely

[1] See C. R. Cheney, *English Bishops' Chanceries*, Manchester, 1950, pp. 13, 79, n. 2, 158; S. Kuttner and Eleanor Rathbone, 'Anglo-Norman Canonists of the Twelfth Century', *Traditio*, vii (1949–51), 326.

[2] *Gir. Cam.* i. 249.

[3] Cf. *Epp.*, p. xxxii, and *D.N.B.* viii. 718; Stevenson, pp. 12–13.

[4] Cartulary of the Benedictine Priory of St. Guthlac at Hereford, MS. Balliol College 271, fols. 21ᵛ, 73ᵛ 97ᵛ, 106ᵛ (modern foliation). See also Russell, *Dictionary*, p. 136, n. 4.

[5] See R. W. Hunt, 'English Learning in the Late Twelfth Century', *Transactions of the Royal Historical Society*, 4th ser., xix (1936), 23. The description of the subjects taught at Hereford is not in Brewer's text (*Gir. Cam.* i. 382), and is published for the first time by Hunt, ibid., 36–37.

appeal to Grosseteste, and perhaps it was here that his bent for mathematics and the natural sciences was first formed.

Nowhere is it stated whether Grosseteste left Hereford on the death of William de Vere, 24 December 1198,[1] or remained there. Although the possibility of his going to Cambridge is not to be altogether excluded, we need a better founded authority than that of Richard of Bardney (early sixteenth century) to render it acceptable. It is more likely that he went to Oxford to teach in the arts school. However this may be, Grosseteste's career at Oxford would be interrupted by the dispersion of masters and scholars which lasted from 1209 to 1214.[2] We have no reason to think that Grosseteste was one of the masters who irreverently persisted in teaching after the secession. It may, on the contrary, be presumed that, like Edmund of Abingdon, John Blund, and other English masters in arts, he migrated to Paris in 1209 to study theology.[3] It was in accordance with an old-established tradition that a master in arts would go to Paris and turn to one of the higher faculties—theology, law, or medicine.

Thomas Gascoigne once again states that Grosseteste was master in theology at Oxford. In his copy of Ranulph Higden's *Polychronicon* (now MS. Balliol College 235), he wrote this marginal note: 'Iste episcopus Lincolniensis magister Robertus Grosteste fuit Doctor Sacre Theologie de Oxonia, ut patet in sermone suo de Levitis, scripto manu propria ipsius Domini Lincolniensis.' (Fol. 181ᵛ.)[4]

There are two sermons which bear the title *De Levitis*; one begins: 'In libro Numerorum scriptum est de levitis, et scient singuli' (Thomson, n. 12, p. 170); the other (n. 31, p. 176) begins: 'Scriptum est de levitis, scilicet, de ministris tabernaculi'; but neither has any bearing on the point at issue. The latter, however, contains a sentence which might have caused Gascoigne to infer that Grosseteste was a doctor in divinity of Oxford: 'primo fui clericus, deinde magister in theologia et presbyter, et tandem episcopus.'[5] In this

---

[1] The bishop's death occurred in 1198, not 1199, as it is generally said. See *Handbook of British Chronology*, ed. F. M. Powicke, London, 1939, p. 150.

[2] The dispersion following the *suspendium clericorum*, 1209–14, though it coincided with the time of the Interdict under which England was placed, is not to be confused with it.

[3] For a discussion of the tradition that Grosseteste studied theology in Paris, see Callus, 'Oxford Career', pp. 49–53.

[4] See also Gascoigne's note in MS. Lincoln College 54, fol. 17ʳᵃ, and a similar one at the end of Grosseteste's *De Cura Pastorali*, MS. Bodley 312 (S.C. 2123), fol. 184ᵛ.

[5] MSS. Bodl. 36, fol. 48ʳᵇ; 801, fol. 197ʳ; Digby 191, fol. 170ᵛᵃ.

sermon, often entitled in the manuscripts *De Confessione*, the bishop is instructing his clergy on their duties in the administration of the Sacrament of Penance. He describes the quality of a good or bad confession, and enumerates the circumstances which should be included. In the words in question he is explaining the first circumstance, *quis*, and illustrates it by an instance, that is, that if a bishop, or a priest, or a master in theology, or a cleric commits a sin, it is not sufficient to say in confession: 'I accuse myself of such a sin', but he must specify his status, whether he is a bishop, or a priest, or a master in theology, or a cleric, or whatever he is.[1] The clause *de Oxonia* does not, and obviously should not, occur there, since, whether one is a master in theology of Oxford or of Paris does not affect the gravity of the sin. In a similar instruction on confession (Thomson, n. 15, p. 172), Grosseteste replaces the qualification of a 'master in theology' by 'Cistercian monk': 'Ego episcopus, vel ego sacerdos, vel ego monachus ordinis Cisterciensis.' (MSS. Bodl. 52, fol. 154ʳ; 830, fol. 170ʳᵇ.) It is significant of the great importance which Grosseteste attached to the mastership in theology, or to the perfection of the state of a Cistercian, that he should require it to be included in confession.

Whether Grosseteste gained his mastership in theology in Paris or took his degree at Oxford after his return is not easy to determine. In the absence of definite evidence I have been unable to substantiate either view. Naturally, a regular course of university studies should normally be crowned by a master's degree. All things considered, Gascoigne's statement, that Grosseteste was 'Doctor Sacrae Theologiae de Oxonia', does not necessarily imply that he obtained his mastership at Oxford, but may simply mean that he was Regent-master in Oxford, a fact which has never been disputed.

That there was a school at Oxford in the twelfth century, which included theological and legal studies, is certain; it is equally certain that the liberal arts were taught at the close of the century, and the 'New Aristotle' was introduced in the first decade of the thirteenth.[2] This seems a clear indication, at the least, of the nucleus of the three faculties—theology, law, and arts. Moreover, as Dr. Rashdall rightly pointed out,[3] the secession of 1209 obviously implies that

---

[1] Russell, 'Phases', pp. 98–100, by interpreting Grosseteste's words in question out of their context, has misunderstood their real meaning.

[2] Cf. Callus, *Aristotelian Learning*, pp. 12–26.

[3] H. Rashdall, *The Universities of Europe in the Middle Ages*. A new edition by F. M. Powicke and A. B. Emden, Oxford, 1936, iii. 47.

there already existed some kind of corporation of masters and scholars; even a rudimentary *universitas magistrorum et scholarium*. But how and when the Oxford school grew into a *studium generale* we can hardly say.

Doubtless, the earliest indisputable evidence of the existence of the University of Oxford is the Legatine ordinance of 1214,[1] which by all accounts may fittingly be regarded as its first charter. With the return of masters and scholars in 1214, lectures were resumed, the office of chancellor was instituted, and academic life gained a new impetus.

Perhaps the most salient point in the Legatine ordinance is the institution of the chancellorship of the University. It strengthened her organization, and gave her unity, order, and stability.

Tradition has it that Grosseteste was the first chancellor. 'That he was chancellor is not a mere legend', as Dr. Salter puts it.[2] Oliver Sutton (1280-99), Grosseteste's successor in the see of Lincoln, attests the fact in a most unequivocal way: Beatus Robertus, quondam episcopus Lincolniensis, qui huiusmodi officium gessit dum in Universitate predicta regebat, in principio creationis sue in episcopum, dixit, proximum predecessorem suum episcopum Lincolniensem non permisisse quod idem Robertus vocaretur cancellarius, sed magister scholarum.[3]

This is a plain and categorical statement; any attempt to find in it a recondite meaning is mere quibbling. It must be accepted or rejected as it stands. If we refuse to admit it, it would be either because we do not believe that Grosseteste did in fact make the alleged statement; or because we take it that Bishop Sutton did not report it accurately. In either case we are assuming that Sutton designedly or undesignedly misrepresented the fact. Naturally, such denial carries with it the burden of proof, and no series of 'possibilities' or 'guesses', however ingenious they may appear, ever amount to valid evidence.

Bishop Sutton's pronouncement contains two formal assertions: (i) that Grosseteste filled the office of chancellor while he was regent in the University; and (ii) that, just after he became bishop, Grosseteste declared that his immediate predecessor in the see of

---

[1] Cf. *Mediaeval Archives of the University of Oxford*, ed. H. E. Salter (O.H.S. lxx), Oxford, 1920, i. 2-6.

[2] H. E. Salter, *Snappe's Formulary* (O.H.S. lxxx), Oxford, 1923, p. 319.

[3] Ibid., p. 52.

Lincoln (Hugh of Wells) had not allowed him to assume the title of chancellor, but of master of the schools.

From the first point it follows beyond question that Grosseteste did truly hold the office of chancellor, and that he occupied this position at the time when he was lecturing in the University, 'dum in Universitate predicta regebat'. It is not stated in which faculty he was lecturing, but it stands to reason that he was regent in theology, since the head of the schools, whether styled rector or magister, scholasticus or chancellor, was without fail a master *in Sacra Pagina*. This was a well-established practice in France and wherever a Divinity school existed; and undoubtedly this custom prevailed equally in Oxford. John Grim, who appears in a deed of 1201 as *magister scolarum Oxonie*,[1] was at the same time *theologiam Oxon' legens*.[2] It is true that later the custom was not so strictly enforced. It may well have been the case that masters in canon law were appointed chancellors of the university.[3] There can, however, be no doubt that Grosseteste was doctor in divinity, not in canon law.

The second statement denotes to some extent Grosseteste's tenure of office. There can be no dispute that the chancellorship was instituted by the Cardinal Legate, Nicholas, Bishop of Tusculum, in 1214 after the return to Oxford of masters and scholars. In his award he declares that a payment of 52*s*. a year should be made for the benefit of poor scholars to be dispensed by the Abbot of Osney and the Prior of St. Frideswide's according to the advice of the Bishop of Lincoln, or the Archdeacon of Oxford or his official, or 'of the chancellor whom the Bishop of Lincoln shall set over the scholars', 'aut cancellario quem episcopus Lincolniensis ibidem scolaribus *preficiet*'.[4] Sending the award to the Bishop of Lincoln, the Legate repeats the same injunction: 'or the chancellor whom you or your successors shall set over the scholars', 'ibidem scolaribus *preficietis*'.[5] This is the first formal mention of a chancellor. There was then an archdeacon of Oxford, but not, as yet, a chancellor,

---

[1] Cf. H. E. Salter, *Snappe's Formulary*, p. 318.

[2] Cf. *Eynsham Cartulary*, ed. H. E. Salter (O.H.S. li), Oxford, 1908, ii. 45.

[3] See Salter, *Snappe's Formulary*, p. 44. Sometime before 1350 it was enacted that the chancellor should be a doctor in theology or in decretis. There were a few exceptions in the fourteenth century, but the practice was still in full force in 1454. In fact, on 19 Nov. 1454 Robert Flemyngs asked the University's grace 'quatinus possit esse capax officii Cancellariatus non obstante quod non est doctor in theologia nec in decretis'. Cf. S. Gibson, *Statuta Antiqua Universitatis Oxoniensis*, Oxford, 1931, p. lxxii, n. 16, and p. 64.   [4] *Mediaeval Archives*, i. 3.   [5] Ibid., p. 5.

who had yet to be appointed by the bishop (*preficiet, preficietis,* in the future tense). Now if the office itself had not yet come into existence, it is not easily conceivable that there could arise a controversy about the title. Accordingly, we may infer that Grosseteste was not chancellor before the secession. Further, in a deed of 1210 a *magister Alardus* appears as 'Rector of the Schools', and it is practically certain that no rector of the schools was nominated during the dispersion of masters and scholars. There is no reason to suppose that 'the "rump" university of 1210 should have elected a head if the previous head had left', not only because this is a gratuitous assumption, nor even because the masters and scholars who refused to disperse lacked the initiative to organize themselves, but especially because the papal mandate of 1210 was addressed to the Prior of Osney, the Dean of Oxford, and 'to Master Alard, rector of the schools', that is, to duly and lawfully appointed ecclesiastical dignitaries, and not to unauthorized persons. This is the more cogent when we consider the severe punishment inflicted on the masters who 'irreverently' persisted in teaching after the secession.[1] On the other hand, the fact that the bishop refused to recognize the title shows assuredly a period of transition when the status of chancellor was not yet definitely settled, in all probability on the occasion of the first appointment to the new office, that is, some time after 1214. But it is not doubtful that by 1221 both office and title were recognized. A letter of Pope Honorius III on 30 March 1221, addressed to the Chancellor of Oxford, *cancellario,* and other judges delegate bears witness to this fact.[2] It is unfortunate that no names are given. Taking one thing with another, we cannot escape the conclusion that Grosseteste's presidency over the schools must be placed not earlier than 1214 nor later than 1221.[3]

When did Grosseteste cease to be chancellor? With the dearth of any positive evidence no definite answer can be given; the more so since no fixed term for the tenure of the chancellorship was assigned in the thirteenth century. It is tempting to surmise that the chancellor to whom Honorius III's letter was addressed was Grosseteste himself; in this case he would still hold the office in 1221, and even perhaps later. But all this is pure conjecture. Certainly, Ralph of Maidstone was chancellor in 1231; but we cannot point to any

---

[1] Ibid., pp. 4, 6.   [2] Ibid., pp. 10–11, 15.
[3] Professor J. C. Russell has misunderstood my meaning in his paper, 'Phases of Grosseteste's Intellectual Life', pp. 94, n. 6, 101, n. 23, 103, n. 30.

evidence that shows when he became chancellor, or whether others were appointed in the interval between him and Grosseteste. Since our knowledge is exclusively derived from casual entries in a deed or a record, it is not surprising that it is so scanty and fragmentary. Of Grosseteste's activities at this time little is known.[1] That he was in Oxford in 1229–30 is recorded in his letter to the second Master General of the Order of Preachers, Jordan of Saxony, in which he reminds him of the cordial friendship shown to him and of the many intimate discussions they held together during his visit to Oxford.[2] On 22 June 1231, at his request and that of the Chancellor of the University, Ralph of Maidstone, and other masters, the king pardoned some students imprisoned for forestry offences.[3] Again, on 23 June 1234, together with the chancellor and the Dominican master Robert Bacon, he was entrusted with the charge of some disciplinary matters.[4]

Of more far-reaching consequence was his appointment as the first reader to the Franciscans. They arrived in Oxford in 1224. 'They were so keen to attend theological lectures and to perform scholastic exercises, that they did not hesitate to go daily to the schools of theology, however distant, barefoot, in bitter cold and deep mud.' To come to the aid of the friars, Agnellus of Pisa, the minister-provincial, 'caused a school of fair dimensions to be built in the place of the brethren, and persuaded Master Robert Grosseteste of holy memory to lecture there to the brethren'.[5] The

---

[1] On 25 April 1225 Grosseteste, while still a deacon, received the living of Abbotsley (*Rotuli Welles*, iii. 48). On an unknown date the bishop collated to him the prebend of St. Margaret, Leicester, which he retained until his accession to the see of Lincoln in 1235 (*Rotuli Grosseteste*, pp. 390–1; *Ep.* 43). Perhaps he held another benefice in 1227, but the entry is only fragmentary (*Rot. Welles*, iii. 54). Certainly he was Archdeacon of Leicester from 1229 to 1232 (ibid. ii. 32, 235, 280–301, 308–21). In 1232 he resigned all his preferments, except the Lincoln prebend, St. Margaret's, Leicester (*Ep.* 43). On no authority whatever he is said to have been Archdeacon of Chester. Similarly, the statement that he was Archdeacon of Wilts. with the rectory of Calne is based on a false assumption. The editor of *The Charters and Documents ... of Salisbury* was so convinced that there was no other Grosseteste at the time except Robert that, against the authority of the document, he changed the name *Ricardus* of the manuscript into *Robertus* (see above, p. 2, n. 1). Nor is there any proof that he ever held the archdeaconry of Northampton, with the prebend of Empingham in Lincoln Cathedral.

[2] *Epp.* 131–2. For the date of Jordan's visit to Oxford, see A. G. Little and Decima Douie, 'Three Sermons of Friar Jordan of Saxony, the Successor of St. Dominic, preached in England, A.D. 1229', *E.H.R.* liv (1939), 1–8.

[3] *Close Rolls, Henry III, 1227–31*, London, 1902, p. 520.

[4] *Close Rolls, 1231–4*, London, 1905, p. 568.

[5] *Fratris Thomae vulgo dicti de Eccleston Tractatus de Adventu Fratrum Minorum in Angliam*, denuo edidit A. G. Little, Manchester, 1951, p. 48, cf. p. 27.

building of the schools was completed about 1229–30, and from that time till his elevation to the see of Lincoln on 27 March 1235 Grosseteste lectured to the Franciscans.[1] 'Under him', says Eccleston, 'within a short time they made incalculable progress both in scholastic disputations and the subtle moralities suitable for preaching.'[2] His interest in their studies and progress continued to the end; he warned them, we are told, that unless they fostered learning and were assiduous in the study of divine law they would be like certain religious orders whom 'we see walking in the darkness of ignorance'.[3] His influence was beneficial, wide, and lasting, and he founded a special tradition of learning which prevailed for several generations in the Franciscan school.[4]

This leads us to a consideration of Grosseteste's writings.

To appreciate duly the extent and versatility of Grosseteste's learning, as well as its significance in the history of thought, it is of primary importance to identify his writings and to distinguish the authentic from the dubious or spurious.[5] Moreover, a consideration of the author's purpose and aims, and an estimate of the definite literary genus to which each book belongs, are all relevant factors for an adequate appreciation of its doctrinal implications. Just as it is not the same thing to write a history and an historical novel, a popular book on animals and a technical treatise on zoology, even if the historical novel is based on history and contains many historical events, or the popular book is written by an expert and includes accurate scientific data; so too, it is not irrelevant to trace and define the purpose and object of the work and the author's peculiar state of mind.

It is of no less consequence for a full understanding of the author's development of thought to determine as exactly as possible, or at least approximately, the time at which each book was written. Deal-

---

[1] *Lanercost*, p. 45, states explicitly that Grosseteste lectured to the Franciscans until he became bishop. Similarly Eccleston: 'Ipso igitur ab cathedra magistrali in cathedram pontificalem providentia divina translato, . . .', p. 48.

[2] Eccleston, ibid.

[3] Eccleston, op. cit., p. 91.

[4] On the Oxford Franciscan school, see A. G. Little, 'The Franciscan School at Oxford in the Thirteenth Century', *Archivum Franciscanum Historicum*, xix (1926), 803–74; and *Franciscan Papers, Lists and Documents*, Manchester, 1943, pp. 55–71.

[5] This fundamental and laborious task has been undertaken by Professor L. Baur in his *Prolegomena* to *Die philosophischen Werke des Robert Grosseteste, Bischofs von Lincoln*, Münster, i. W., 1912; and more completely and systematically by Professor S. Harrison Thomson, *The Writings of Robert Grosseteste Bishop of Lincoln 1235–1253*, Cambridge, 1940.

ing with a master with a long teaching career, we must at the outset
examine whether the work in question belongs to the schools—a
commentary, or a *quaestio*—or is an occasional or independent
treatise. In the latter case, unless external or internal evidence
provides some indications, it is often not an easy matter to assign
the date of its composition. In practice, the dating is always a task
of some delicacy, and requires extreme care and caution. It is unwise
to generalize about dates; each work must be examined and judged
on its own merits.

Grosseteste's works fall roughly into two distinct categories and
periods: to the former belong his commentaries on Aristotle and on
the Bible, and other original treatises; they cover the time from his
mastership in arts to his elevation to the see of Lincoln in 1235; to
the latter, from 1235 to his death in 1253, his translations from the
Greek and the corresponding *notulae*.

There can be no doubt that to his teaching activity in the arts
school are to be assigned the glosses on the *De Sophisticis Elenchis*,[1]
still unprinted, and on the *Analytica Posteriora*.[2] Nicholas Trivet
expressly states that Grosseteste commented on the *Posterior Analytics* while he was master in arts.[3] Although he does not specify the
place or the time, it is reasonable to assume that it was at Oxford
and in the first decade of the thirteenth century. Thus he would
be following in the footsteps of St. Edmund of Abingdon and of
Master Hugh, who, if Roger Bacon writing as late as 1292 is to be
believed, were the first to lecture at Oxford on the *Elenchi* and
on the *Posterior Analytics* respectively.[4]

The commentary on the *Posterior Analytics* is one of the best
authenticated works of Grosseteste. The need for it had long been
felt. Known by the middle of the twelfth century, the *Posterior
Analytics* found its way slowly into the schools. John of Salisbury
tells us that, owing to its manifold difficulties, few masters ever
attempted its interpretation.[5] By the last quarter of the century,

---

[1] Only one manuscript of this work is known, MS. Merton College 280, fols. 3ʳ–37ᵛᵃ.
It is explicitly ascribed to Grosseteste in the colophon: 'Explicit tractatus super librum
Elenchorum datus a magistro Roberto Grostest.'

[2] It was printed several times; first edition Venice, 1494. My citations are from the
Venice edition of 1552, corrected on MSS. Merton College 280, 289. My friend, Dr. R. J.
O'Donnell, C.S.B., of the Pontifical Institute of Mediaeval Studies, Toronto, Canada,
is preparing a critical edition of this work.   [3] Trivet, *Ann.*, p. 243.

[4] *Fratris Rogeri Bacon Compendium Studii Theologiae*, ed. H. Rashdall (B.S.F.S. iii),
Aberdeen, 1911, p. 34.

[5] *Ioannis Saresberiensis Metalogicon*, iv. 6, ed. C. C. J. Webb, Oxford, 1929, pp. 170–1.

however, it was unquestionably taught in the Paris schools; but it was later, if we accept Roger Bacon's statement, that it reached Oxford. At all events, Grosseteste's commentary would be one of the very first, and it became at once a classic of its kind. And it is indeed Grosseteste's monumental work *aere perennius*. It contains, explicitly or implicitly, all his main theses. In it he laid the foundations upon which his philosophical and scientific works are built: sometimes he simply inferred logical conclusions from their principles, as when he applied mathematics to the philosophy of nature; sometimes he expounded his theories more fully, as when he elaborated his teaching on light in the famous treatise *De Luce*. He collated the existing translations and made abundant use of Themistius's commentary; but, as was to be expected at such an early stage, there is no trace in it of his knowledge of Greek.[1] It was through this commentary that his influence, directly or indirectly, was more especially felt, not only in Oxford, but everywhere. Already in his lifetime his younger contemporary, St. Albert the Great, took up the commentary, probing its interpretations and discussing the doctrine in detail, now praising it, now dissenting from it.[2] It is interesting, and most instructive, to watch a joust between the two masters on some delicate point of Aristotelian exegesis: as, for example, when Albert argues against Grosseteste that it is purely Platonic teaching, inconsistent with Aristotle, to maintain that a point, inasmuch as it constitutes materially and substantially a line, is included in the definition of a line, and that a line is included in the definition of a figure.[3] A few years later the commentary gained general acceptance, and was quoted in the schools, no more under the anonymous designation *quidam modernorum*,[4] as in Albert's days, but in its own right, *Lincolniensis super Posteriora*, and continued

---

[1] Stevenson was mistaken in assuming that Grosseteste 'had doubtless used, or at any rate consulted, the original text, in his lectures and commentaries on the *Posterior Analytics*' (p. 224).

[2] *Alberti Magni Opera Omnia. Liber Posteriorum Analyticorum*, I, tr. ii, c. xvii: 'Dicunt tamen satis subtiliter quidam modernorum' (ed. Borgnet, ii. 63). Cf. ibid., cc. v, xii, xv; tr. iii, c. viii; tr. iv, cc. ii, viii, x, &c.

[3] Ibid. I, tr. ii, c. viii (39–40).

[4] Grosseteste is still for Albert the Great *quidam modernorum*, whilst Roger Bacon places him among the *antiqui sapientes*, *Opus maius*, ed. Bridges, i. 73; iii. 88; *Opus minus*, *Op. In.*, 329, 428; *Opus tertium*, ibid. 88, 187, &c. For the distinction between *Antiqui et Moderni*, and its significance in the history of medieval philosophy and theology, see M. D. Chenu, 'Notes de lexicographie philosophique médiévale, *Antiqui, Moderni*', *Revue des sciences philosophiques et théologiques*, xvii (1928), 82–94; cf. for Grosseteste, pp. 87, 92–93.

to exert its influence to the close of the Middle Ages. How Grosseteste himself applied to experimental science the principles and
method of the *Posterior Analytics*, as set forth in his commentary, and of its influence on natural science, is told by Dr. A. C.
Crombie in his book, *Robert Grosseteste and the Origins of Experimental Science*.[1]

Grosseteste's exposition of the *Analytica Posteriora* was not his
first work. Commenting on Book I, ch. xxvi, 'The superiority of
affirmative and negative demonstration to the *reductio ad impossibile*'
(Bekker, 87a 1–30), he refers to an earlier treatise written on the subject: 'Istud plane exposuimus in tractatu quodam de hoc specialiter
composito.'[2]

This is a clear and positive statement. The difficulty is to determine
to which treatise in particular he was alluding. Possibly he had in
mind the immediate context. In this case, considering that he was
striving to bring home the point at issue by an illustration from
geometry, it is not unlikely that the reference is to the *Praxis
Geometriae*, now untraced, which he is said to have written.[3] It is
also possible that the clause, *istud plane exposuimus*, refers to the
whole comment on ch. xxvi. If this is so, it may concern either a
treatise on ostensive demonstration, or one simply on the *reductio ad
impossibile*. In either case it does not seem to be among his known
writings, and consequently we are at present unable to identify it.[4]

Bale, followed by Pits, Tanner, Pegge, Stevenson, and others,
ascribes to Grosseteste a 'Sententias in libros Priorum, lib. ij', with
the *Incipit*, 'Cum omnis scientia sit veri inquisitiva', and a 'Questiones Priorum, lib. i'.[5] Now the former work, as Baur, Powicke,
and others have already remarked, is Robert Kilwardby's well-
known commentary on the *Analytica Priora*, printed in Venice
several times under the name of Giles of Rome. The latter is a work
altogether distinct from the commentary.

The cause of Bale's error is not difficult to detect. It arose out of
a hasty reading of MS. Merton College, Oxford, O. i. 12 (now MS.
280).[6] Bale himself tells us that he knew of both works from a Merton

---

[1] Oxford University Press, 1953.
[2] Venice edition of 1552, fol. 24ʳᵃ.
[3] See Thomson, *The Writings*, 'Lost or Untraced Works', p. 271, n. 7.
[4] There is some possibility that this treatise is still extant.
[5] Bale's *Index*, ed. Poole, p. 378; cf. Thomson, p. 87.
[6] See on this manuscript F. M. Powicke, *The Medieval Books of Merton College*,
Oxford, 1931, pp. 115–16.

manuscript, 'Ex Mertonensi Collegio, Oxon'. In fact Bale's entry in his *Index* reads:

In Elencha, lib. ij, 'De sophisticis autem elenchis';—Sententias in libros Priorum, lib. ij, 'Cum omnis scientia sit veri inquisitiva';—Questiones Elenchorum, lib. i;—Questiones Priorum, lib. i.

This corresponds exactly to the contents of the fly-leaf on fol. 2^v:

Tractatus Lyncolniensis super libro Elenchorum;—Sententie ipsius Culuerdebis super libro Priorum;—Item questiones bone super eodem libro;—Item tractatus Lyncolniensis super libro Posteriorum;—Item questiones bone eiusdem libri.

Identifying 'Culuerdebis' with 'Lincolniensis', Bale took 'ipsius' as referring to Grosseteste, and attributed to him Kilwardby's *Sententie* on the *Priora*. Next, he interpreted the 'Questiones bone super eodem libro' as meaning 'Questiones Elenchorum'; and lastly, by another oversight not noticing the 'Tractatus Lyncolniensis super libro Posteriorum', he ascribed to him the 'Questiones bone eiusdem libri', with the wrong title of 'Questiones Priorum'. Thus his error passed to all those who, without checking on the manuscript, copied his misleading account.

So, too, with the Erfurt MS. Amplon. Q. 328. Folios 94–161^v contain Kilwardby's commentary with the same *Incipit* and *Explicit* as in other manuscripts. Moreover, the text is twice fully ascribed to Kilwardby at the end of each book: on fol. 138, 'hoc de primo libro priorum a magistro Roberto Killurbie (*sic*)', and in the colophon on fol. 161^v, 'Expliciunt scripta supra librum Priorum Aristotelis edita a magistro Roberto de Killurbi (*sic*) dicto'. Despite this positive testimony Amplonius entered it in his catalogue as the work of Grosseteste.[1] If, therefore, 'the tradition that Grosseteste was the author of some kind of commentary on the *Prior Analytics*' rests exclusively on these authorities, it has no foundation whatever.

A fifteenth-century manuscript in the Estense Library, Modena, cod. lat. 54, contains on fols. 1–48^v, according to Thomson, a commentary on the *Prior Analytics* explicitly ascribed to Grosseteste. This text, however, does not seem to possess all the guarantees of authenticity, and its attribution to Grosseteste needs further investigation.

Be that as it may, to his early scholastic activity at Oxford we may

---

[1] Cf. W. Schum *Verzeichnis d. Amplonianischen Handschriften-sammlung zu Erfurt*, Berlin, 1887, pp. 563 and 795.

assign a brief tract in praise of the liberal arts.[1] Perhaps Grosseteste's earliest work, it is an *Introitus*[2] to the arts course, not a
special treatise. 'For a threefold cause', he says, 'error and imperfection obtrude themselves upon human actions: because the mind
is darkened by ignorance; because the affections stop short of, or by
excess advance beyond, the limits of what is right; and because the
motive powers on account of the corruption of the flesh are feeble
and imperfect instruments of the body. But now in whatever operation error and imperfection originate, we need guidance and help to
purge away error and supply deficiencies.'

In truly neo-Platonic fashion—the only explicit citation is from
Macrobius—he goes on to show how the seven liberal arts, which
alone amongst all branches of philosophy are called arts, cleanse
human operation from error (*purgationes erroris*) and so lead on to
perfection.

Whatever actions are within our power, they consist, one and all,
either in the gaze of our mind (*in mentis aspectu*), or in its affectivity
(*in eiusdem affectu*), or in bodily activities, or in modifications of those
activities. Gazing (*aspectus*) gives us the first grasp; next comes a
verification of what we have contemplated or known; and when the
mind is satisfied about what is attractive or noxious, then our affection (*affectus*) yearns to embrace what is attractive or withdraws
within itself in flight of what is noxious.

The trivium provides directives and assistance, and sets right
and guides to perfection both the *mentis aspectus et affectus*. The
function of Grammar is to understand rightly and, by expressing
correctly what is rightly grasped, to convey it to others properly.
Logic in its turn judges what is rightly grasped, and discusses this
according to the three operations of reason. But to Rhetoric especially belongs the setting in motion of our affections, the rousing up of
torpid spirits, the correction of the unruly, the encouragement of the
faint-hearted, the assuaging of the truculent.

If from the trivium we turn to the quadrivium, we perceive at once
that Music gives the proper measure and tone to all corporeal movements. Music in Grosseteste's opinion is a kind of universal art
directing all knowledge. It deals in fact not only with the proportions
and melody of sounds, with the modulation of human voice and

---

[1] Baur, *Die Werke*, pp. 1–7.
[2] See on the *Introitus*, R. W. Hunt, 'The Introductions to the "Artes" in the Twelfth
Century', *Studia Mediaevalia in honorem . . . R. J. Martin*, pp. 85–112.

expression of gestures, with musical instruments, and with the harmony of things celestial and non-celestial, but also with the harmony of times and of every movement. And since the concordance of times, and the composition and harmony of the inferior world, and of everything composed of the four elements, are dependent on the movements of the celestial world, it follows that to Music pertains the investigation of the inner structure of things composed of the four elements, and even of the elements themselves.

But since by our movements we mean something else besides mere moving, we either divide what is united, or unite what is separated, or we order or place or extract figures. To do this rightly we need Arithmetic and Geometry. Further, to these three arts we must add Astronomy, which by means of the movements of the stars teaches us to discern the place of the world and the space of times.

The seven arts are attendants (*ministrae*)—he does not say *ancillae*, handmaids, but *ministrae*—on the philosophy of nature and on ethics. Grammar and Logic because they provide other sciences with true reasoning; Rhetoric is particularly helpful to moral philosophy, whose purpose is to teach how to strive after good and to shun evil. Moral science should, therefore, be taught by rhetorical ornament in order to produce and mould human conduct. But other sciences, inasmuch as they seek only after truth, do not need any rhetorical persuasion. Thus Music is as useful to natural philosophy as it is to medicine. He who knows the due proportion of the elements in the human body, and the concord of the soul with the body, can restore any lack of harmony to its proper state by the modulation of sound and tone and the melody of musical instruments. Philosophers indeed believe that even wounds and deafness may be cured by musical modulations. Nevertheless, the philosophy of nature needs the aid of Astronomy more than that of the other arts. There is hardly any operation in the realm of nature or of our own, such as the planting of vegetables, or transmutation of minerals, or cure of diseases, which does not need the help of Astronomy. For inferior nature does not act save as celestial virtue moves it and turns it from potentiality to act. The physician, accordingly, to free himself from error should observe the hours when nature is moved by the celestial virtue, and choose the right time in the preparation of medicine and its administration to the sick.

One point strikes the eye in this oration on the usefulness of the liberal arts: the little attention paid to arithmetic and geometry,

Grosseteste's absorbing interests in later days. Whilst grammar, logic, rhetoric, music, and astronomy have the lion's share, both arithmetic and geometry are dismissed with scarcely a glance. I do not mean that mathematics is altogether disregarded—it is, of course, implied in the disquisition on numbers—but, perhaps, in view of the important role Grosseteste was later to assign to it in the study of natural philosophy, we should have expected more explicit treatment. It may be that he was then too heavily under the spell of music—his fondness for music became proverbial[1]—and of its wonderful efficacy in the cure of diseases, and of the marvellous power of astronomy in the transmutation of metals, turning them into their original state, gold—since, 'according to nature's intention all metals should be gold'—if only one knows the exact time, season, and position of the stars when such an operation should be accomplished. Or possibly, he was too intently fixed on the niceties of the *Ars dictaminis* to feel any attraction to such dry subjects as arithmetic and geometry. At all events, this short treatise (or should I say, fragment?) is a precious gem, typical and representative of Grosseteste. This is why I have dwelt on it at some length, though not as fully as it deserves. It should be quoted in full, and minutely analysed to estimate aright all its implications, to follow the logical sequence, the development of thought, the flow of one idea from another in perfect order, the balance and ease of the clauses with their rhythmic succession. But above all, it gives us a glimpse, as it were, of Robert Grosseteste as we imagine him at Oxford as a young master in arts at the close of the twelfth or the beginning of the thirteenth century; or as Giraldus Cambrensis knew him at Hereford, skilled in medicine, remarkably proficient in manifold learning, 'built upon the sure foundation of the liberal arts and an abundant knowledge of literature', possessing natural gifts of mind and heart and much industry, as befitting a young clerk in the household of a great and distinguished bishop.

To do justice to the merit of Grosseteste's *Introitus* to the arts course, it is not enough to admire its lucidity and literary power—though, surely, the qualities of style and form should not be overlooked. To convey an accurate impression of its full and unsuspected richness, it should be placed in its proper setting, analysed in all its implications, and related to what went before it.

It will suffice here to give one or two instances. Let us take first

---

[1] See Stevenson, pp. 334–5.

the opening section which I have quoted.[1] To the three causes of our errors and imperfections Grosseteste contrasts the three remedies and helps supplied to us to overcome them. These remedies and helps are the seven liberal arts. Now the main idea of the threefold cause of error with its tripartite remedy has a long tradition, coming down from Hugh of St. Victor, through the twelfth-century grammarians,[2] until it reached Grosseteste.

Further, Grosseteste assigns to grammar the function of teaching how 'to understand rightly'. This too presupposes highly technical disquisitions in the twelfth-century grammar schools. Its development may be traced thus. Grammar, dialectic, and rhetoric were looked upon as three branches of logic. The aim of grammar is *intellectum facere*; of dialectic, *fidem*; or rhetoric, *persuasionem*. Petrus Helias had said that words were invented in order that 'men might show their will (*voluntas*) to one another'; but before the end of the twelfth century we notice the relevant substitution of *intellectus* for *voluntas*: words were invented 'that we might have a means of expressing our concepts (*intellectus*) and of showing them to others'.[3] The next step was to include in the definition of grammar the clause, 'to understand rightly'.[4] Nevertheless, some still retained the notion transmitted by William of Conches, 'recte scribere et recte pronuntiare scripta'.[5] Alexander Nequam, in fact, argues impatiently against those who describe grammar as 'the art of teaching how to write correctly and how to pronounce properly', since they omit the most significant part of the definition, that is, 'how to understand rightly'.[6] Common agreement was reached by the beginning of the thirteenth century; the definition generally accepted in the schools, frequently attributed to Priscian, was: 'the art of writing correctly, of understanding what is written rightly, of uttering what is understood properly'.[7] Grosseteste's description comes

---

[1] See above, p. 16.

[2] Cf. Hunt, 'Introductions to the "Artes"', p. 100, n. 2.

[3] See Hunt, 'Studies on Priscian in the Twelfth Century', *M.A.R.S.* ii (1950), 32.

[4] 'Grammatica est scientia recte scribendi, recte pronunciandi, et recte intelligendi gnara.' Gloss on Priscian *Tria sunt*. See on this gloss Hunt (to whom I am indebted for this and other references), 'Studies on Priscian', pp. 11–23.

[5] *De Philosophia mundi*, xli, in *P.L.* clxxi. 100C (cf. Hunt, ibid., p. 21).

[6] 'Ex hiis patet quod grammatica est ars intelligendi, unde insufficienter describunt gramaticam qui dicunt: Gramatica est ars recte scribendi et recte proferendi. Omittunt enim quod potissimum est in arte. Addere igitur debent: et recte intelligendi.' Alexander Nequam, *Corrogationes Promethei* (P. Meyer, *Notices et extraits*, xxxv. 2, p. 660).

[7] 'Secundum Priscianum grammatica est scientia recte scribendi, recte scripta intelligendi, recte intellecta pronunciandi.' From a gloss on the *Doctrinale*. C. Thurot,

very near to this definition; he not only sums up the whole tradition, but by further refinements surpasses it. He substitutes 'logic' for 'dialectic', and for 'the art of writing correctly' he substitutes 'correct understanding and enunciation so as to make correct impression upon another'.[1] The emphasis is on the function of the intellect (*intelligere, intellecta, enuntiando*) rather than on correctness of speech and writing.

There are solid reasons to believe that the treatise *De Generatione Sonorum*[2] should be assigned to the same period as the *De Artibus Liberalibus*. They are so closely connected that the former seems to be an integral part of the latter; or, perhaps, it is a further development of some points raised but not fully discussed previously. On this assumption I regard both treatises as one work. It deals with the physiological aspect of phonetics and the physiological notation of sounds, and their bearing on the formation of letters, vowels, and consonants. The shape of the letter *A*, for instance, in Latin, Hebrew, and Greek, and also in Arabic, is a triangle. So too the fashioning of the letter *R* corresponds in every language to the vibrant sound produced by the throat and by the tongue, which we call guttural; and so on of all the letters of the alphabet. He brings in Priscian's statement,[3] that vowels are like souls (*animae*) and consonants like bodies (*corpora*). The soul is moved by itself, and moves the body, whilst neither can a body be moved without the soul, nor move the soul, but it is moved by the soul. So too the vowels are moved by themselves and move the consonants to make a syllable, but consonants without vowels are immovable. Grosseteste is at pains to show that this statement is not against his own theory, since it simply means that a consonant is not audible without a vowel, but not that a consonant does not possess by itself a certain imperceptible sound in the mouth. In support of his interpretation he adduces the authority of St. Isidore of Seville.[4]

The significance of the *De Generatione Sonorum* lies not only in its bearing on the study of Priscian, but also in showing thus early that meticulous care for detail and that interest in grammar and

---

Extraits de divers manuscrits latins pour servir à l'histoire des doctrines grammaticales au Moyen Age, Paris, 1869, p. 122.

[1] 'Officium grammaticae est recte intelligere, et recte intellecta recte enuntiando apud alterum recte formare.' Baur, *Die Werke*, p. 1.

[2] Edited by Baur, ibid., pp. 7–10.

[3] Priscianus, *Institutiones Grammaticae*, I. xvii (ed. Hertz, i. 13).

[4] *Isidori Etymologiae*, I. iv. 4 (*P.L.* lxxxii. 78; ed. W. M. Lindsay, Oxford, 1911).

linguistics which Grosseteste was later to develop with such advantage in the *notulae* which he appended to his translations from the Greek.

As in the case of the *De Artibus Liberalibus*, this tract has a late manuscript tradition, which makes one somewhat hesitate to ascribe them to Grosseteste with absolute certainty. Yet in spite of that, as Baur has shown,[1] there is such a striking similarity, both in thought and wording, between these two writings and the commentary on the *Analytica Posteriora* as to render Grosseteste's authorship morally certain. Moreover, the main idea that pervades the whole work *On the Liberal Arts* may be summed up in the phrase *mentis aspectus et affectus*, with its counterpart *purgatio erroris*. Now Grosseteste was so fond of dwelling on this expression that we find it almost everywhere, in the commentaries on the *Posterior Analytics* and on the *Physics*, in the *Hexaemeron*, in his letters, sermons, and *Dicta*; he was never tired of bringing it in wherever he could, in season and out of season. For instance, in *Dictum II* he recurs to it to illustrate the need of preaching, that by the word of doctrine and preaching the *mentis aspectus* may be enlightened towards true faith and knowledge, and its *affectus* rectified towards justice.[2] Or again, in the *Hexaemeron* he applies the same notion to explain that the mind (*mentis aspectus*) can never be free from error (*erroris purgatio*) and from the illusions of the imagination and gaze into purely intellectual concepts unless its affections (*mentis affectus*) are purified from the love of earthly things.[3] The ultimate reason for this impossibility had been explained years before in his commentary on the *Posterior Analytics*. The *affectus* and the *aspectus* of the soul are not divided from each other, for the *aspectus* only reaches that which is reached by love and affection.[4] Evidently this corresponds perfectly well with

---

[1] Baur, *Die Werke*, pp. 57*–59*.

[2] 'Ut per sapientiam illuminetur eius *aspectus mentis* ad veram fidem et scientiam, et rectificetur eius *affectus* ad iustitiam. Hec autem illuminatio *aspectus* et rectificatio *affectus* per verbum doctrine et predicationis eveniunt.' *Dictum II*, MS. Bod. 798, fol. 1ᵛᵃ–2ʳᵃ.

[3] 'Unde et huius *erroris purgatio* non potest esse nisi per hoc quod *mentis affectus* purgetur ab amore temporalium, ut *mentis aspectus*, immunis a phantasmatibus, possit transcendere tempus et intelligere simplicem eternitatem, ubi nulla est extensio secundum prius et posterius, et a qua procedit omne tempus.' *In Hexaemeron*, MS. Bod. lat. th. c. 17, fol. 197ʳᵃ. See Smalley, below, pp. 87–88.

[4] 'Causa autem quare obnubilatur visus animae per molem corporis corrupti, est quod affectus et aspectus animae non sunt divisi, nec attingit aspectus nisi quo attingit amor et affectus.' *In Post. Anal.* I, ch. xiv, t. 81 (fol. 18ᵛ). The source of this theory is St. Augustine, *Soliloquia*, I. vi (*P.L.* xxxii. 875–6) and pseudo-Augustine, *De Spiritu et Anima*, x (*P.L.* xl. 781, 785).

the theme of the *De Artibus Liberalibus*. Such persistent use seems to argue to a single author of the *On the Liberal Arts* and other authentic writings. And since both the *De Liberalibus Artibus* and the *De Generatione Sonorum* are closely linked, they fall or stand together.

It would not, perhaps, be irrelevant to note that the pair *aspectus–affectus* caught the attention of a contemporary regent-master, the Dominican Richard Fishacre. In the prologue to his commentary on Book I of the *Sentences* (written *c.* 1240–3) he stresses the point that moral instruction should precede theological questions, since one's inclination (*affectus*) should be fashioned by good conduct before letting the mind (*aspectus*) struggle over difficult questions about the faith: failing this little or no progress can be made.[1]

Father Pelster[2] discovered in 1926 two *quaestiones* in Assisi, MS. Biblioteca Comunale 138. One, *De subsistentia rei*, is duly ascribed in the margin: *Magister R. Grosseteste* (fol. 262rb); the other, through a misreading of the master's name in the title, was also attributed to Grosseteste. Thomson accordingly listed it among the authentic works.[3] On the authority of Pelster and Thomson the *quaestio* has lately been edited by Professor E. Franceschini[4] under the title: 'An unprinted Text of Robert Grosseteste.' Undoubtedly, it was worthwhile publishing, since it is an early important *quaestio* from the Oxford school, but certainly it is not by Grosseteste, though in all probability belongs to one of his circle, Adam Marsh. The note in the margin runs without any shadow of doubt: 'Quaestio de fluxu et refluxu maris a magistro A. [*misread*, R(oberto)] Oxon [*not* Exon] in scolis suis determinata.'[5]

Grosseteste did not write a *Summa* of philosophy, in which he

---

[1] 'Prius est ut affectus informetur sacris moribus quam aspectus desudet in quaestionibus circa fidem difficilibus, alioquin parum aut nichil proficiet.' (MS. Balliol College 57, fol. 4va.) See Smalley, *Study of the Bible*, p. 279, n. 3. For further evidence of influence on Fishacre and Richard Rufus of Cornwall, see below, pp. 29–30. Cf. also Robert Kilwardby, *De Natura Theologiae*, ed. F. Stegmüller (Opusc. et Textus, xvii). Münster i. W., 1935, pp. 8, 34. Moreover, the theme of Kilwardby's *De Ortu Scientiarum* is based on the pair *aspectus-affectus*.

[2] F. Pelster, 'Zwei unbekannte Traktate des Robert Grosseteste', *Scholastik*, i (1926), 572–3. In *R.T.A.M.* v (1933), 388, n. 38, Pelster corrected his reading from *R* to *N*, or possibly *A*.   [3] Thomson, *Writings*, p. 89.

[4] E. Franceschini, 'Un inedito di R. Grossatesta', *Rivista di Filosofia neo-scolastica*, xliv (1952), 1–11.

[5] Père Doucet of Quaracchi has very kindly favoured me with a microfilm of both *quaestiones*. F. M. Henquinet, *Archivum Franciscanum Historicum*, xxv (1932), 552, has rightly pointed out that it should be read *A* and not *R*, and *Oxon* and not *Exon*. Hence he ascribes the *quaestio* to Adam Marsh. Cf. Doucet, *Summa Theologica Alexandri de Hales*, iv, *Prolegomena*, Quaracchi, 1948, p. cxli; and Callus, 'Oxford Career', pp. 47–48.

would have expounded his theories and developed his philosophical system; nor did he leave a series of *quaestiones*, which would have given him an opportunity to discuss fully the more debated problems of his day. His philosophy has to be gleaned, and, as it were, extracted piece by piece from various scattered writings, and often from *obiter dicta*. Thus his philosophy remains fragmentary, and his thought is sometimes more implicit than completely explicit. Nevertheless, we possess enough data to enable us to gather the general lines of his trend of thought, to value the contribution he made to the growth of ideas, and to assign to him the position he held in the intellectual movement of his time.

Obviously, a thorough investigation of Grosseteste's philosophy[1] cannot be attempted here. I would only touch upon one or two points in order to give an idea of the trend of his thought.

His theory of light is perhaps the most original part of his teaching, and has attracted most attention from philosophers[2] and scientists. Although it is a blend of neo-Platonist elements derived from St. Augustine, pseudo-Augustine *De Spiritu et Anima*, St. Basil's *Hexaemeron*, pseudo-Denis, the *Liber de Causis*, Avicenna, Avicebron's *Fons Vitae*,[3] his genius gave order, cohesion, and unity to these scattered members. It pervades the whole of his philosophy as well as his theology, and is applied by him to every being, from God to inanimate things. God is *the* Light, the source of light; all other beings simply participate in that light. In the scale of created beings, a thing is more or less perfect according to its greater or less participation in light. Thus at the summit are the *Intelligentiae*, the angels, wholly luminous. Next comes the human soul, whose apex, *acies intellectus*, is akin to the *Intelligentiae*. Light is the bond which unites and keeps together the soul, pure spirit, with the human body. Through light the soul acquires knowledge from the senses, and

[1] For a general estimate of Grosseteste's philosophy, see Baur, *Die Philosophie*; D. E. Sharp, *Franciscan Philosophy at Oxford in the Thirteenth Century*, Oxford, 1930, pp. 9–46.

[2] Cf., for example, L. Baur, 'Das Licht in der Naturphilosophie des Robert Grosseteste', *Abhandlungen aus dem Gebiete der Philosophie und ihrer Geschichte, eine Festgabe z. 70. Geburtstag Georg Freiherrn v. Hertling*, Freiburg i. B., 1913. The *De Luce* has lately been translated into English by C. C. Riedl, *Robert Grosseteste On Light*, Milwaukee, Wisconsin, 1942.

[3] Although Avicenna and Avicebron are not mentioned by name by Grosseteste, their influence on his philosophy is great. Cf. Avicenna, *Sufficientia*, 1. ii (ed. Venice, 1508), fol. 14ʳ; *Metaphysics*, v. iii (88ʳ); Avicebron, *Fons Vitae*, v. 33–35 (ed. Baeumker, 318–21).

through an irradiation of divine light the truth of things is perceived. Aristotle's *intellectus agens*[1] is utterly ignored. Light is a simple substance, and at the same time is the first corporeal form, which some call corporeity. At the beginning God created formless matter and light, the first form in the first matter. Light, through its infinite multiplication in all directions, extended matter on all sides, and thus brought into being the first body, the firmament, and the other spheres of this visible world.

This leads us to a consideration of matter and form, potentiality and actuality. Grosseteste begins his treatise *De Potentia et Actu* with the statement, 'everything that is, is either actually a being, or only potentially a being'.[2] At first sight this seems in complete agreement with Aristotle, and appears as the equivalent of 'potentia et actus dividunt ens'.[3] But we realize at once the gulf which separates the two concepts when Grosseteste proceeds to explain that a thing is actually, if it has reached its full completion, whereas it is only potentially, if it has not yet acquired the completion which it is possible to have. Potentiality and possibility are often confused, and actuality is regarded as the fullness of all perfections. Potentiality is 'not that which has no actuality whatever, but that which is not totally actual'. According to Aristotle, on the contrary, potentiality is neither bare nothingness nor mere privation of a given perfection, and it is more than sheer possibility—it is true capacity really existing in the subject *qua capacity*; but in itself is purely passive without any actuality whatever.

So, too, with the corresponding notions of matter and form. Although sometimes Grosseteste refers to matter as 'passive', and to form as 'that whereby a thing is what it is', he is far from implying the pure potentiality of Aristotle, since 'both corporeity and matter are simple substances'. Matter has a certain, though slight, actuality of its own, a certain activity, which the form brings to its full completion and perfection. Matter is regarded more like the *rationes seminales* of the Stoics and of St. Augustine than Aristotle's underlying principle *from* which a thing comes to be and is essentially constituted. And though nowhere is the problem of plurality of

---

[1] According to Roger Bacon, Grosseteste identified the *intellectus agens* with God (*Op. In.*, pp. 74–75). Grosseteste, however, nowhere states this theory *ipsis verbis*. He mentions the *intellectus agens* only once in a different connexion; otherwise he ignores it. Cf. E. Gilson, *Arch. HDLMA*, i (1926–7), 90–99.

[2] Baur, *Die Werke*, pp. 126–9.

[3] Cf. Thomas Aquinas *QQ. DD. De spiritualibus creaturis*, a. i.

forms professedly discussed by Grosseteste, the theory of plurality is necessarily contained in his principles. It is obvious that all this is entirely un-Aristotelian; under cover of Aristotelian terminology a doctrine comes to be formulated which is completely foreign to Aristotle.

Still, Grosseteste's originality and real greatness manifest themselves in other ways.

Roger Bacon tells us that Grosseteste utterly disregarded the books of Aristotle and their method, and went his own way in search of scientific learning relying on his personal experience and other authorities. This statement has been interpreted, or rather misinterpreted, in many ways. Nevertheless I venture to say that, taken in its context, it seems clear and unquestionable. It means that Grosseteste's method of expounding the *libri naturales*—since the point at issue regards mainly this branch of philosophy, as Bacon's words make it manifest—was different from the one generally used in the schools. In his treatises on the formation of the universe, on stars and comets, on colour, sound, and heat, on the rainbow and tides, Grosseteste did not follow the fashion of contemporary masters of paraphrasing Aristotle's text, or commenting on it comma by comma, inserting here and there digressions and excursuses, but engaged in the study of Aristotelian wisdom ('negotiatus est in sapientialibus Aristotelis') through a new line of approach, by relying on his personal experience, on other authorities and other sciences.

Assuredly, there is nothing in all this which implies either a condemnation of Aristotelianism or of logic and metaphysics, as often has been assumed. Nor did Bacon himself mean to condemn Aristotelian studies which, in his opinion, are the foundations of all wisdom[1] and the glory of his time.[2] The point at issue was to bring home, by accumulating argument to argument, the utter badness of Latin translations. He was so haunted by this fixed idea that he could not see anything good in them; he would have them consumed by fire, if he could (*si haberem potestatem*). He praises Grosseteste, not because 'in regard to the physical sciences he found it necessary to depart from the teaching of Aristotle', but because, neglecting 'the perverse translations', he discovered a new method of investigation in pursuing the study of Aristotle.

[1] 'Labores Aristotelis sunt fundamenta totius sapientiae.' Bacon, *Op. In.*, p. 469.
[2] 'In quibus [*sc.* naturalis philosophia et metaphysica Aristotelis] est tota gloria studii modernorum.' Ibid., p. 326.

His bold originality consists exactly in this, that he undertook to explain problems connected with Aristotelian *Physics*, the *De Caelo et Mundo*, *Meteorologica*, by applying the principles of the *Posterior Analytics*, as set forth in his commentary on that book, and by positing in mathematics the groundwork for a deep knowledge of natural philosophy. 'The science of lines, angles and figures', he says, 'serves to explain to us the very nature of physical things, of the universe as a whole, and of each part of it, of movement, of activity and passivity with regard to matter and with regard to the sense of sight and the other senses.'[1] Without this science we may know the bare existence, the *quia*, of the natural phenomena, but we can never understand the inner reason, the *propter quid*, concerning them. On these foundations a keen observer can by the power (*potestate*) of geometry account for the causes of all natural phenomena.[2] Grosseteste was convinced that mathematical reasoning provides the human intellect in its present state with the greatest certitude, since the understanding of mathematical entities is helped by images perceived by the sense of sight ('ad quas comprehendendas nos iuvant phantasmata imaginabilia visu recepta'). Consequently error seldom occurs in mathematics, for mathematical entities are clearly visible to the mind. This certainty is in a sense greater than that of metaphysics, and is only inferior to that of divine things attained by a pure intellect *secundum statum suum optimum*.[3]

There was current amongst the Oxford Franciscans a tradition, handed down to us through William of Alnwick in his *Determinationes* (*c.* 1316), that Grosseteste's writings fall into two categories: (*a*) the *authentica*, those polished works accurately written with much study and mature deliberation; and (*b*) the *dissute scripta*, that is, disconnected notes jotted down in the margin of his books, or on small pieces of parchment, on the spur of the moment, just as some noteworthy idea struck his mind, without much elaboration, *non studiose nec complete*; rather drafts than finished writings. To the former class belong the commentaries on the *Posterior Analytics* and on pseudo-Denis, and the *Hexaemeron*; to the latter the glosses on Aristotle's *Physics* and most of his sets of notes for sermons and lectures.[4]

[1] *De Lineis, Angulis et Figuris*, Baur, *Die Werke*, pp. 59–60.
[2] *De Natura Locorum*, ibid., pp. 65–66.
[3] *In Poster. Analyt.* 1, ch. xvii (ed. Venice, 1552, fol. 24^r).
[4] MS. Vat. Palat. lat. 1805, fol. 10^v, cited by Pelzer, 'Les Versions latines', p. 398 n. Cf. Callus, 'Oxford Career', pp. 45–47.

The notes, written by Grosseteste with his own hand in the margin of his copy of the *Physics*, which Alnwick had seen in the Franciscan library at Oxford, came down to us, not exactly in the same manner in which they were written, but consecutively in the form of a commentary. They are preserved in two Oxford manuscripts, MS. Merton College 295 (fols. 120–31^v, 136–45ra) and MS. Digby 220 (fols. 84–105ra).[1] It is significant of the deep devotion to Grosseteste and of the high esteem in which his writings were held that his notes and jottings should be later collected, arranged, and transcribed methodically, as we have them in the copy of the *Physics*. The accuracy of Alnwick's description is borne out by the contents. In contrast with the commentary on the *Posterior Analytics*, these glosses give the impression of hasty and somewhat disconnected annotations rather than of a systematic, careful, and finished exposition; they provide a summary drawn up in propositions with occasional explanatory matter, particularly on topics to which he had a decided leaning, such as space, vacuum, time, the infinite, and so on. One of these, on the non-eternity of the world, which is the concluding section on Book VIII, very slightly abridged, found its way quite early as a separate treatise under the title *De Finitate Motus et Temporis*.[2]

It is plain that this work does not represent Grosseteste's lecture-notes while regent in arts. On the contrary, the citations from Averroes, translated into Latin and put in circulation about 1230,[3] the parallels with the *Hexaemeron*, already noted by Baur, and the development of thought, suggest a later period of philosophical speculation than the first decades of the thirteenth century. It is hardly possible to assign a precise date; the work went on, perhaps, for several years; none the less, it is certainly later than 1230. Moreover, it follows from this that it is rash to assume that Grosseteste after 1229 had lost all his interest in philosophical investigations. The glosses on the *Physics* and his scientific treatises written about this time show him without fail at the height of his experiments and of his philosophical activity.

There can be no doubt that Grosseteste's theological career began

---

[1] Cf. Baur, *Die Werke*, pp. 16, 30. A third manuscript is extant in Venice, S. Marco, vi. 222 (fols. 2^r–30va). See Thomson, *Writings*, p. 82.

[2] The *De Finitate Motus et Temporis* has been published by Baur, *Die Werke*, pp. 101–6. An edition of the *Physics* is in preparation in America.

[3] Cf. R. de Vaux, 'La Première Entrée d'Averroës chez les Latins', *Revue des sciences philosophiques et théologiques*, xxii (1933), 193–245.

long before he was entrusted with the readership to the Franciscans in 1229 or 1230; it is, therefore, highly arbitrary, and even misleading, to limit it to the years 1229–35. It was a period of very great intellectual activity indeed. Together with his regency in theology and the absorbing duties as Archdeacon of Leicester until 1232, he retained all his interests in philosophy and the natural sciences; the glosses on the *Physics*, as we have seen, and the majority of his scientific treatises were all written after 1230.

The duties of a medieval master in theology were *legere, disputare, praedicare*, to teach, to hold disputations, to preach.

Legere meant to interpret the Scriptures. In medieval universities the Bible was the alpha and the omega, the beginning and the end, of the whole theological course. That Grosseteste as a master-regent in theology lectured upon the Scriptures is not doubtful. Some of his commentaries, such as that on Galatians, the *Moralitates super Evangelia*, and the glosses on Psalms i–c, are still extant; but of his *Expositio* on the other Pauline Epistles we have only fragments preserved by Thomas Gascoigne in his *Liber de Veritatibus collectis*.[1] So too the glosses on Psalms i–lxxix came down to us in the form of irregular and fragmentary annotations. It is natural to assume that commentaries and glosses represent the substance of his *lectiones ordinariae*. None the less, taking into account the long period of his theological career, these are by far too few, particularly on the Old Testament; a good number must have been lost, or are still untraced. The *Hexaemeron*, as William of Alnwick has it, is a *scriptum authenticum*. It is not a commentary, but an elaborate and systematic treatise dealing with the *Six Days of Creation*. Although, as it stands, it does not represent his lectures, surely materials from his lecture-notes must have been incorporated in it. But with the Biblical works it will be dealt later in a special chapter by Miss Beryl Smalley.[2]

Disputare, to hold disputations.

Very few, if any, of Grosseteste's *quaestiones disputatae* remain. We may without much hesitation assign to his teaching period the *De Libero Arbitrio, De Ordine emanandi causatorum a Deo, De Veritate*,

---

[1] MSS. Lincoln College 117, 118.

[2] Further examination has shown that there is not sufficient evidence to warrant the attribution to Grosseteste of the Prologue and glosses on Wisdom and Ecclesiasticus and on Romans ('Oxford Career', pp. 57, 63). See Smalley, below, pp. 70–97.

De Veritate Propositionis, *De Scientia Dei*, and the *quaestiones theologicae* extant in MS. 28 of Exeter College, Oxford. But whether they represent *quaestiones* actually disputed in the schools is a more complex problem.

The form in which they came down to us suggests a technique rather of a treatise than of a *quaestio disputata*. Yet, the structure of the arguments against and in favour of the thesis, and certain phrases scattered here and there, which are easily traceable, may possibly hint at disputations. In all probability these opuscules originated from questions raised or disputed in the course of his theological teaching, which were later arranged and set into a definite shape as we now have them.

Admittedly, these tracts, with the exception of the *De Libero Arbitrio*, give the impression of incompleteness, of mere fragments jotted down in view, perhaps, of further elaboration. Even a cursory inspection shows that they are closely related to each other; possibly they are sections of a larger work. It is most probable that Grosseteste had planned and set himself to compose a *Summa Theologiae* in four books within the framework of Peter Lombard's *Sentences*. If this be so, this great work was never brought to completion.[1] These tracts belong undoubtedly to Grosseteste's early years, and are representative of the late twelfth- and early thirteenth-century theological speculation. They corroborate the tradition of his pursuing his theological studies in Paris.

The *De Libero Arbitrio*, on the contrary, shows marks of more mature elaboration. Its influence was felt in Oxford from the early years of its publication, and continued through the centuries; it was deeper in the Merton school from Bradwardine to Thomas Buckingham and Wyclif. The first two commentaries on the *Sentences* written in Oxford in Grosseteste's lifetime, one by the Dominican Richard Fishacre, the other by the Franciscan Richard Rufus of Cornwall (*c.* 1250), preserve the echo of the discussions in the schools on the notion of free will. It is noteworthy that the point cross-examined turned chiefly on the pair *aspectus–affectus*. Both Fishacre and Rufus accept Grosseteste's identification of *aspectus* with reason and *affectus* with the will; but whilst the former, maintaining the distinction between reason and will and stressing the part of reason, disagrees in the long run with Grosseteste's

---

[1] For a full discussion on this question see Callus, *Studies . . . F. M. Powicke*, pp. 180–208.

conclusion and propounds an original theory of his own,[1] the latter, emphasizing the part of the will, makes Grosseteste's view his own.[2]

Praedicare, to preach.

Grosseteste's sermons have been described in great detail by Professor Thomson.[3] They are based upon texts taken from the Scriptures, and follow the technique of mid-thirteenth century sermons. In the *recapitulatio* of his *Dicta* Grosseteste refers to his sermons preached to the clergy and to the people while he was still lecturing, *in scolis*. But, as is to be expected, the majority of the sermons which came down to us belong to the years of his episcopacy. They show him at his best in full exercise of his pastoral duties. Preaching became his great preoccupation, and he never missed any opportunity of bringing it home to his clergy. He maintained all his interests in philosophy and the sciences, and in his sermons often dwells on philosophical or scientific topics; but with advancing age the emphasis shifted more and more towards the importance of preaching and the study of theology. His youthful enthusiasm, which we have admired in the *De Artibus Liberalibus*, gave way to more mature reflections. He did not deny or minimize the wondrous effects of the arts, but looked upon them from a totally different angle. His main attention was now directed to the salvation of souls. He became aware that ecclesiastics, forgetful of their duties, were giving all their time to the study of the sciences, and this for gain and riches, for vainglory and love of being admired. We may illustrate his line of action from some of the works which belong to this period.

In his *Moralitates super Evangelia*, which is undoubtedly to be assigned to his theological teaching at Oxford, the seven liberal arts are represented by the well of water dug by Isaac, called *Esdon*, that is, 'contention', for they are full of strife and contention, particularly dialectics: hence they should be greeted only in passing. But his indignation is sadly aroused by the *scientiae lucrativae*, such as medicine, civil and canon law, and other diabolical sciences sought after exclusively for gain and cupidity, symbolized by the bottomless

---

[1] 'Sufficienter dividitur anima in aspectum et affectum: et affectus est voluntas et aspectus ratio.' MS. Balliol College 57, fol. 128va.

[2] MS. Balliol College 62, fols. 160vb–162rb. On the influence of Grosseteste on Rufus see O. Lottin, *Psychologie et Morale aux XIIe et XIIIe siècles*, Louvain, 1942, i. 183–97.

[3] Thomson, *Writings*, pp. 160–91.

pit called *Satan*, that is, 'enmity': 'puteus, qui vocatur Sathan, quod est nomen diaboli'.[1]

This same train of thought is found in one of his *Dicta*, which contain treasures of practical wisdom. Overwhelmed with grief for the need of good preachers, Grosseteste deplores that many learned clerics (*plurimi litterati*) are neither versed in the art of preaching nor have any inclination to preach. They run after, instead, and follow with eagerness those sciences which, in their opinion, will make them rich or famous. One would devote himself to the study of medicine, so that he may cure the sick and, as it were, bring the dead to life; thus he becomes wealthy or is regarded as a prodigy. Another would by alchemy learn how to turn lead into gold, and by ablutions and sublimations how to purify, clarify, and endow almost with the qualities of the heavenly bodies these terrestrial, impure, dark corporeal substances. Others, still, would master music, and by musical modulations transform men mentally affected, and often snatch them from serious diseases. There are others who would delight in the pursuit of philosophy in order to know the movements and the revolutions of the stars, and by what impulse they are set in motion; the impetuosity of winds, the terrors of lightning, the anger of beasts, the nature of stones and trees. And so others would be attracted to the study of those things knowledge of which causes wonder, and thus they would appear wonderful in the sight of men. Yet, he convincingly concludes, if only those, who are thus so fascinated by these and similar marvels, would dedicate themselves to the study of theology, they would know far better, more nobly, and more readily all these things and many besides, and they would even grasp all the transformations which either nature or art's skill can produce.[2]

Greed and pomposity were equally abhorrent to Grosseteste. In his eyes learning is one of the highest, noblest, and almost sacred pursuits of mankind. It is a perversion to seek learning for mercenary motives. Nothing would have seemed more loathsome to him than to sell learning for base gain or ephemeral glory. Assuredly, he was not against secular studies; but he would not have the clergy follow

---

[1] MS. Lincoln College 79, fols. 96ʳ–97ʳ; MS. Balliol College 35ʙ, fol. 61ʳᵇ⁻ᵛᵃ; MS. Cambridge, University Library, Kk. ii. 1, fol. 218ʳᵛ. For the *Moralitates super Evangelia*, see Smalley, below, pp. 71–74.

[2] MS. Bodley 798, fol. 2ʳ. Cf. E. J. Westermann, 'A Comparison of some of the Sermons and the *Dicta* of Robert Grosseteste', *Medievalia et Humanistica*, iii (1945), 63–64.

them to the detriment of the study of Holy Scripture. The Sacred Page should be learnt from early youth, and not when one is already enfeebled and well advanced in years: 'virgo seni antiquo non sine animi lesione maritatur'.

Moreover, he was exceedingly concerned with the lack of good preachers; and he was convinced that it is impossible to have good preachers unless they are well versed in Biblical studies.[1]

As a bishop, he solved the problem of the want of preachers by calling on the friars, Dominicans and Franciscans. Nevertheless, to the end of his life he insisted in season and out of season on the strict duty of pastors of souls to preach the word of God to their flocks. In one of his last sermons, feeling very old and sick (vetus sum et aeger), taking leave of his clergy, 'nescio utrum redeam ad vos', he examines one by one the arguments brought forward by those who were unwilling to fulfil their obligation. On no account would he accept any excuse. To those of noble birth, or to the magni clerici—e.g. those who had ruled in arts or medicine—who claimed exemption from their obligation because they could not preach with such subtlety and brilliance as suited their high status, he replies drily that they have no alternative—either they must undertake their duty without fail, or demergantur in profundum inferni. To the less proficient in letters, those who were truly unable to preach, he roundly asserts that the proper remedy was to resign their benefice. He would, however, deal with them more leniently, mitius remedium dicam. Accordingly, he gives them the paternal and practical advice that they should attempt during the week to learn the Sunday Gospel and preach it to the faithful. After all, the Gospel is Christ's word, and the Lord Himself preached to the people in a very simple manner. But if they were so deficient in Latin that they were even unable to do this, well, then, they ought to seek the help of a neighbouring priest, and with his assistance to prepare a set of sermons on the Sunday Gospels, in the following year on the Epistles, and in the third year on the lives of the saints—after that to start the cycle again.[2]

Grosseteste was always all of a piece, consistent with himself. If as a master in theology he showed little sympathy with the clerics who spent their time in the study of Justinian, adhaerens scientiae Iustinianae, as a bishop he opposed with all his might the employ-

---

[1] Moralitates super Evangelia, MSS. et loc. cit.
[2] Oxford, Bodleian Library, MS. Digby 191, fol. 168va-b

ment of ecclesiastics in the office of itinerant justices or in other secular functions.[1]

Although invectives against excessive attachment to profane learning were almost a commonplace in contemporary and earlier sermons, especially since the time of the *Decretum* of Gratian—the main inspiration of this kind of literature—Grosseteste's sincerity is beyond doubt. It was in 1232, about the same time that his *Dicta* were written, that, to confirm his teaching on the contempt for worldliness and wealth by his example, he renounced his archdeaconry of Leicester and all his preferments, retaining only his prebend at Lincoln. A few years earlier, his friend and fellow regent-master in theology at Oxford, Robert Bacon, resigned his living and entered the Dominican Order.[2] Again, his lifelong friend, John of St. Giles, once a famous physician and now a rich master in theology, on 22 September 1230, in the course of a sermon he was preaching on poverty at Saint-Jacques in Paris, abandoned all his possessions and became a Dominican.[3] He too inveighs in his sermons against those who *student in scientiis lucrativis*, against the false prophets who teach how they may acquire to themselves prebends, honours, and riches.[4] And a few years later another friend of Grosseteste, a celebrated English master in Paris, Alexander of Hales, a very rich man and, in Roger Bacon's words, 'a great archdeacon', gave up all his wordly greatness and a large income and joined the Friars Minor. How far these four masters in theology influenced each other we can never know; but we can lawfully surmise that the breath of the Holy Spirit blew through this circle of friends to make them poor in the eyes of the world and rich in Christ.

The tradition that Grosseteste translated several works from the Greek and promoted Hebrew studies is well attested. It is early and definite, and therefore trustworthy. Nicholas Trivet sums up this tradition thus:

Doctor vero in triplici lingua eruditus, Latina, Hebraea, et Graeca, multa de glossis Hebraeorum extraxit, et de Graeco multa transferri

---

[1] Cf. for example, *Epp.* 105, 108, 205, 262, &c. See below, pp. 165–8, 181, 199–200.

[2] See on Robert Bacon, Beryl Smalley, 'Robert Bacon and the Early Dominican School at Oxford', *Transactions of the Royal Historical Society*, 4th ser., xxx (1948), 1–19; W. A. Hinnebusch, *The Early English Friars Preachers*, Rome, 1951, pp. 360–3.

[3] N. Trivet, *Annales*, pp. 211–12; cf. Hinnebusch, op. cit., pp. 358–60.

[4] Cf. M. M. Davy, *Les Sermons universitaires parisiens de 1230–1231*, Paris, 1931, pp. 271–97, particularly pp. 275–6, 286, 292.

fecit, ut puta Testamentum duodecim Patriarcharum et libros Dionysii, quorum novam translationem perlucide commentavit.[1]

But Grosseteste did not stop at the bare translation of texts; he added, wherever possible, a version of a commentary on the text. Thus, his translation of the *Nicomachean Ethics* is accompanied by the expositions of Michael of Ephesus, Eustratius, and of two anonymous commentators. He added to the *De Caelo et Mundo* a version of the commentary of Simplicius, at least of Book II; and to the pseudo-Dionysian *corpus* the scholia of St. Maximus the Confessor. Moreover, to render the greatest possible assistance to students, he himself contributed numerous *notulae* or glosses.

These works may be classified according to their subject-matter into three groups: theological, philosophical, and glossarial. To the first group belong the writings of St. John of Damascus and pseudo-Denis with St. Maximus's Prologue and scholia, the Epistles of St. Ignatius, the *Testaments of the Twelve Patriarchs*, and the *De Vita Monachorum*; to the second, Aristotle's *Nicomachean Ethics* with the Greek commentators, Aristotle's *De Caelo* (Book I to the beginning of Book III) with Simplicius's commentary, the pseudo-Aristotelian *De Virtute* and *De Lineis Indivisibilibus*, and the pseudo-Andronicus *De Passionibus*; to the third group, extracts from the *Lexicon Suidae*.

But before we say more about these translations, it will be well to discuss a preliminary, but vital, question: Grosseteste's proficiency in Hebrew and Greek.

Matthew Paris[2] repeatedly asserts that Grosseteste was profoundly learned in Latin and Greek; Nicholas Trivet,[3] as we have seen, adds to this accomplishment a knowledge of Hebrew, and to substantiate this he adduces that 'multa de glossis Hebraeorum extraxit'. On the other hand, according to Roger Bacon,[4] 'the Lord Robert, on account of the length of his life and for the wonderful methods he used, was

---

[1] Trivet, *Ann.*, p. 243. The fundamental work on Grosseteste's translations is E. Franceschini, *Roberto Grossatesta, vescovo di Lincoln, e le sue traduzioni latine*, Venice, 1934.

[2] Paris, *Chron. Mai.* iv. 232: 'Vir in latino et graeco peritissimus'; cf. v. 284.

[3] Trivet, *Ann.*, p. 243. See above, p. 33.

[4] Bacon, *Op. In.*, p. 472. Stevenson, p. 23, has confused the Latin text with the Hebrew. Roger Bacon does not state (p. 329, not 330) that both Grosseteste and Adam Marsh 'used the Hebrew text', but that they used to lecture on the text, that is, on the Bible, in contrast to Alexander of Hales and others who lectured on the book of the *Sentences*. Of course, Bacon meant the Latin Biblical text, not the Hebrew, cf. p. 330. We are not, therefore, entitled to infer from this passage Grosseteste's knowledge of Hebrew.

the only one (*solus*) above all men (*prae aliis hominibus*) to know the sciences'; however, 'he was not proficient enough in Greek and Hebrew to translate by himself, but he had many helpers (*multos adiutores*)'.

Let us take the case of Hebrew first. Modern scholars are rather sceptical about Grosseteste's knowledge of Hebrew. Professor Thomson[1] thinks that this tradition does not rest on solid ground. He may have known the Hebrew alphabet, and, in the abstract, the principles of Hebrew syntax and morphology, or have had any such general information, but 'as for any actual use of the language, it must be concluded that all available evidence is negative' (p. 38). Mr. Raphael Loewe of the University of Leeds tells me that, although he has made by no means an exhaustive investigation of Grosseteste's writings, he has found nothing to controvert Thomson's statement. For my part, I have no special competence to determine the question; nevertheless, I would venture to submit one or two suggestions which may, perhaps, help to shed some light on the point at issue.

It is true that 'we have no real proof' of Grosseteste's knowledge of Hebrew; that neither in his sermons nor in his letters is there any indication of any such interest or achievement; moreover, it is wiser 'to maintain a thorough-going scepticism on the subject' when positive evidence is lacking. Still, it seems that the sceptical view put forward by these scholars is not absolutely convincing. In all fairness it should be added that Professor Thomson had no knowledge of the *Superscriptio Lincolniensis*, which was brought to light by Dr. Beryl Smalley (as we shall see) after his book was published. Moreover, the Biblical commentaries, particularly on *Hexaemeron* and on the Psalms, belong to his scholastic career, and it is well known that only later in life, during his episcopal period, did he seriously give himself to the study of languages. Nor are his later sermons or letters a sure indication, since—though this kind of literature may at times be revealing—it does not always offer an opportunity for a display of such erudition.

Be that as it may, it still remains to explain Bacon's and Trivet's statements. Bacon's words, 'non scivit sufficienter ut per se transferret', are definite. They can only mean that Grosseteste had some knowledge of Hebrew, even if he were not so well versed as to be able to translate by himself without the assistance of others. No less

---

[1] Thomson, *Writings*, pp. 37-39.

categorical is Trivet, himself a Hebrew scholar, who was well aware
of the facts and ascribed to Grosseteste *multa* drawn from glosses of
the Hebrew. What exactly these *multa* were which he extracted *de
glossis Hebraeorum* we have, at present, no means of ascertaining.
But surely we would not be far wrong if we were to identify them
with the *Superscriptio Lincolniensis*, so well described by Miss
Smalley, which she connects with Grosseteste.[1] Trivet knew it and
quoted it as *Iudaeus dicit* among the variant readings in his work on
the Psalms.[2] It is also known that Grosseteste ordered a translation
of the Psalter from the Hebrew, and 'had it written over the Hebrew
of his Psalter, "where three or four Psalters" were "contained together
in one" (*simul coniunctim*). It is quoted by a later commentator (the
Franciscan Henry Cossey, d. *c.* 1336) as the *Superscriptio Lincolniensis.*'[3] Grosseteste was a man who would not spare himself, even
in his old age, any labour, however wearisome, to acquire more than
a smattering of Hebrew in order to supervise intelligently a translation which he ordered. We may rest assured that he had collaborators; but that William of Arundel, Archdeacon of Huntingdon,
'was doubtless one of the scholars who assisted Grosseteste when
he "multa de glossis Hebraeorum extraxit" ', as Russell[4] asserts, is
not so certain. There is no definite evidence either for or against it.
Professor Russell suggests also the Franciscan, William de Mara, as
a probable assistant to Grosseteste in his Hebrew labours.[5] William's
profound knowledge of Hebrew is beyond doubt; he was, however,
by far too young at the time, and it is more than doubtful that he
could really have aided him in that capacity.[6]

I am well aware that this is but a preliminary treatment of the
matter. A definitive conclusion can only be reached after a thorough
investigation of the *Superscriptio Lincolniensis* and other connected
problems. This will be given by Mr. Raphael Loewe (who is preparing an edition of the *Superscriptio*) in his forthcoming book on the
study of *Hebraica* and *Iudaica* in England.

With Grosseteste's knowledge of Greek we are on more solid
ground. There can be little doubt that he contributed more than any

---

[1] B. Smalley, *Hebrew Scholarship among Christians in XIIIth Century England*; and
Study of the Bible, pp. 342–7.

[2] Smalley, ibid., pp. 345–6.   [3] Ibid., p. 343.

[4] Russell, *Dictionary*, p. 183; cf. 'Preferments and *Adiutores*', p. 170. See Thomson,
Writings, p. 38.

[5] Russell, 'Preferments and *Adiutores*', p. 171; *Dictionary*, p. 195.

[6] Cf. Thomson, *Writings*, p. 38.

other person to the introduction of Greek learning into thirteenth-century England.[1] Roger Bacon, who never wearied of repeating the same thing over and over again, tells us that all the wise men of old—many of whom he had seen and some still survived in his own time—knew the learned languages. In addition to the Lord Robert, he mentions by name two only, Thomas the venerable Bishop of St. Davids now deceased, and Friar Adam Marsh.[2] Surely, it is not insignificant that both belonged to Grosseteste's circle. Moreover, Bacon's insistence on the importance and necessity of the study of languages is a commonplace; none the less, others before him had unobtrusively but firmly expressed the same point of view. Adam Marsh stressed almost in identical words the necessity of a knowledge of Hebrew and Greek for the study of the Bible.[3] It would not be far-fetched to see in this a trace of Grosseteste's influence not only on Marsh, but even on Bacon himself who had access to the bishop's as well as to Adam Marsh's writings.

If we accept Roger Bacon's testimony, Grosseteste began to learn Greek late in life. As a matter of fact, whilst no trace of any marked familiarity with this language is noticeable in his early works, by 1230-1 he surely must have known more Greek than the statement of Roger Bacon would lead us to believe. It is not unlikely that during his convalescence after a severe illness, which befell him in these years, he occupied his leisure in Greek studies.

At all events, in his glosses on St. Paul's Epistles[4] to the Galatians written about 1230-1, and in the *De Cessatione Legalium*, of not much later date, we have proofs of his interest in Greek learning. Again, in his commentary[5] on Psalms lxxx-c, expounded in the last years of his theological regency at Oxford, between 1231-5, he shows already a good knowledge of the Greek Fathers unparalleled at that time. The Greek versions of Aquila, Theodotion, and Symmachus are discussed, Greek words or readings are adduced, and the *Graeca lectio* is often preferred. This is in complete contrast to the first part of his notes on Psalms i–lxxix, dated a few years earlier. There

---

[1] See R. Weiss, 'The Study of Greek in England during the Fourteenth Century', *Rinascimento*, ii (1951), 210–24.

[2] Brewer, p. 88; Bridges, iii. 88. In the *Compendium Studii Philosophiae*, Bacon mentions with Bishop Thomas and Adam Marsh also Robert Marsh, William Lupus, and William de Schyrwood, but they are connected with learning in general and not expressly with the study of languages. Robert Marsh, of course, was of Grosseteste's *familia*.

[3] I am indebted to Dr. Hunt for this reference, see below, p. 126.

[4] On the Biblical commentaries see Smalley, below, p. 70–97.

[5] Cf. M. R. James, *J.T.S.*, xxiii (1921-2), pp. 181–5.

is no trace of Greek learning in these, except an occasional etymology, which he could have got second-hand, and the authorities quoted are exclusively the Latin Fathers, Augustine, Jerome, Gregory the Great, Cassiodorus, Rabanus, and Bernard. A more extensive use of Greek sources is shown in his *Hexaemeron* written about this time. His knowledge of Greek is also apparent in a manuscript,[1] newly acquired by the Bodleian Library (MS. Lat. th. c. 17), containing the *De Cessatione Legalium* and the *Hexaemeron*, in which a few Greek words and sentences are written in Grosseteste's own hand (fols. 159, 192^{r-v}, 193^r). To an earlier date may possibly belong a few Greek words written in his own hand in his copy of Boethius, *De Consolatione Philosophiae*.[2]

Yet it was later in life, in his episcopal period, that Grosseteste made his most valuable contribution to Greek learning. While still in the schools, grappling with his Greek text of the Septuagint or of the Fathers, he would have realized, on the one hand, the need of procuring Greek codices, and, on the other hand, that his linguistic attainment was as yet not quite adequate. As bishop of the largest and one of the wealthiest dioceses in England, he had the means to overcome both difficulties. And he did. Roger Bacon assures us that Grosseteste invited Greeks into England, caused Greek manuscripts to be brought from Greece and elsewhere, amongst which there were Greek grammars, and that he himself learnt the Greek language, though not with such proficiency as to translate without the assistance of others.[3] Bacon was never tired of stressing this last point.

Now this statement needs further clarification.

It will make things plainer if we try to determine the exact meaning he attached to the expression *scire sufficienter*, 'to possess sufficient knowledge'. Here Bacon comes to our aid. He distinguishes three degrees in the knowledge of learned languages (*linguae sapientiales*), Greek, Hebrew, Arabic, and Chaldean. The first degree consists in mastering the language with as much perfection as one's own maternal and native tongue, 'ut nos loquimur Anglicum, Gallicum et Latinum'. The next, in being able to translate correctly from one language into the maternal tongue, that is, into Latin. For the last degree one need only have such knowledge of grammar and vocabu-

---

[1] See on this manuscript R. W. Hunt in the *Bodleian Library Record*, ii (1948), 226–7; and below, p. 133.

[2] Now MS. Trinity College, Oxford, 17; see Hunt, below, pp. 121–2, 133.

[3] R. Bacon, *Opus Maius*, iii. (ed. Bridges, i. 67); *Op. In.*, pp. 33, 91, 434, 471, &c.

lary as to understand without great difficulty a Greek or Hebrew text. This could be attained with the greatest ease with the assistance of a teacher ('tertius gradus . . . facillimus est habenti doctorem'), even within three days.[1] Every cultured student should arrive at this minimum achievement ('oportet quemlibet Latinum studentem scire ea quae ad tertium gradum spectant'); otherwise he would be a dullard destitute of all wisdom and learning.[2]

Having this in mind, we may now proceed to consider the qualifications required by Bacon in a good translator. Two factors should concur for a faultless (*vera*) translation: (i) a full mastery of both languages, from which and into which the translation is made; and (ii) a thorough familiarity with the subject-matter. But, with the exception of Boethius who alone knew the languages to perfection (*solus scivit linguas sufficienter*), no translator fulfilled both conditions. Even the Lord Robert failed to stand the test; since although he was unequalled in the mastery of the sciences, and knew enough Greek and Hebrew to understand the saints, the philosophers, and the wise men of old, he did not progress sufficiently far to be able to translate by himself, except at the end of his life, when he summoned the Greeks, and gathered Greek grammars. Roger Bacon in dealing with the study of languages mercilessly contrasts Boethius and Grosseteste: to the former he ascribes the primacy in linguistic attainment, to the latter the supremacy in the knowledge of the sciences; but he allots to him no more than a minimum in the proficiency of languages.[3] Accordingly, we cannot escape the conclusion that in his eyes Grosseteste's knowledge of Greek and Hebrew never reached beyond the third degree, except, perhaps, towards the end of his life.

Roger Bacon's verdict cannot stand without qualification.

That Grosseteste had 'helpers', and that some of them came from Greece (or rather from *Magna Graecia*, southern Italy or Sicily) is a proved fact; of their precise task or number, however, we have no record. Bacon asserts that they were many (*multi adiutores*), some

---

[1] *Compendium Studii Philosophiae*, *Op. In.*, pp. 433–4; cf. *Opus Tertium*, ibid., pp. 65–66, 89.

[2] 'Et ideo cogimur necessario ad debitam notitiam linguarum, aut erimus asini et vacui omni sapientia et doctrina.' Ibid., pp. 434, 435.

[3] 'Nullus scivit linguas nisi Boethius de translatoribus famosis, nullus scientias nisi dominus Robertus, . . . simul cum hoc quod tantum scivit de linguis quod potuit intelligere sanctos, et philosophos, et sapientes antiquos. Sed non bene scivit linguas ut transferret nisi circa finem vitae suae . . .'. *Opus Tertium*, ibid., p. 91; cf. p. 33; and *Compendium Studii*, ibid., pp. 471–2; *Opus Maius* (ed. Bridges, i. 67), &c.

of whom were still living at the time he was writing (*c.* 1272).[1] Two, at least, are known to have been in the diocese of Lincoln at the time; but possibly there were others. One of them, *Magister Robertus Graecus*, occurs twice in Grosseteste's *Rotuli*,[2] but he is no more than a mere name for us; of the other, *Magister Nicolaus Graecus*, a Greek born and bred, we know a little more.[3] He became a canon of Lincoln, belonged to the bishop's *familia*, and after Grosseteste's death was sent to Rome as proctor of the chapter to promote his canonization.[4] He died on 4 December 1279, and in all probability was one of the survivors mentioned by Roger Bacon. If this is so, he must have been of Italian-Greek origin, since Bacon expressly connects the remaining Greeks in England with Italy.[5] W. L. Lorimer[6] and Franceschini[7] have discussed the possibility of identifying Nicholas the Greek with *Nicolaus Siculus*, the translator of the pseudo-Aristotelian *De Mundo*, and Dr. Minio-Paluello has brought forward good evidence to make such identification almost certain.[8] Similarity of method and technique links Nicholas the Sicilian with Grosseteste's circle, and his remarkable skill not only in Greek but in Latin too makes it clear that he was of Italian-Greek descent.

John of Basingstoke, Archdeacon of Leicester, who died in 1252, is also associated with Grosseteste's Greek studies. Deeply versed in Latin and Greek literature, he returned to England from Athens with a load of Greek manuscripts, and composed a Greek grammar called the *Greek Donatus*. He brought to Grosseteste's notice certain things unknown to the Latins, *quaedam Latinis incognita*, which he had seen and learnt at Athens from Greek doctors, particularly about the existence of a famous book entitled the *Testaments of the Twelve Patriarchs*. The bishop sent messengers to Athens and secured a copy, which he later rendered into Latin.[9]

---

[1] 'Aliqui in Anglia usque ad haec tempora sunt superstites.' *Op. In.*, p. 434. Roger Bacon by Greece generally means *Magna Graecia*, that is, southern Italy and Sicily, not Greece proper; cf. *Op. In.*, pp. 33, 351, 434, &c.

[2] *Rotuli Gros.*, pp. 247, 300. Cf. Powicke, *Robert Grosseteste*, p. 22, n. 2; Weiss, op. cit., p. 211, n. 1.

[3] See below, Major, p. 229; and Russell, 'Preferments and *Adiutores*', pp. 169–70; *Dictionary*, p. 89; Weiss, pp. 211, 214.

[4] See below, Kemp, p. 244.   [5] Bacon, *Op. In.*, p. 434.

[6] W. L. Lorimer, *De Mundo* (Aristoteles Latinus, XI. 1–2), Rome, 1951, pp. 10–13.

[7] Franceschini, *Roberto Grossatesta*, pp. 15, n. 1, 71, n. 1.

[8] L. Minio-Paluello, 'Note sull'Aristotele latino medievale', *Rivista di Filosofia neoscolastica*, xlii (1950), 432–6.

[9] Paris, *Chron. Mai.* v. 284–5; cf. Russell, 'Preferments and *Adiutores*', pp. 168–9, and *Dictionary*, pp. 54–55; Weiss, pp. 213–14. See below, pp. 61–62.

Baur[1] includes among Grosseteste's collaborators Thomas the Welshman. Member of the bishop's *familia* and, according to Roger Bacon, learned in Greek and Hebrew, it is within the bounds of possibility that he assisted Grosseteste in his Greek studies, but no evidence has so far come to light to support the surmise that he had any actual part in the translations.[2]

By papal privilege it was granted to Grosseteste to have permanently with him two Dominicans and two Franciscans, learned in the Scriptures, skilled in canon and civil law, zealous for the salvation of souls. They were doubtless his constant, faithful, and trusted counsellors in all matters theological and moral, and in the many ecclesiastical and ministerial problems which faced him in the administration of the diocese.[3] He would, as Trivet assures us,[4] have discussed with them many a philosophical question, difficult points of exegesis arising from Biblical, patristic, or Aristotelian texts, and similar topics. But whether they, or any of them, did actually assist him in his Greek studies, we do not know. Such possibility cannot, of course, be ruled out *a priori*; none the less, it seems more likely that, apart from theological, Biblical, or legal affairs, their assistance was chiefly concerned with apostolic and pastoral work, such as preaching and hearing confessions.[5]

At all events, surviving evidence makes it clear that Adam Marsh's claims deserve special attention. His association with the bishop in intellectual activities is beyond doubt. The *incipit* of the 'Concordance of the Bible and of the Fathers' bears witness that he had a part in its compilation: 'Incipit Tabula magistri Roberti Lincolniensis episcopi cum additione fratris Ade de Marisco.'[6] His letter to Thomas Gallus, the famous Abbot of St. Andrew at Vercelli, concerning the commentaries on pseudo-Denis, and his references to the

---

[1] Baur, *Die Werke*, p. 42*, n. 1.

[2] On Thomas Wallensis see Major, below, p. 239; Little, 'Franciscan School at Oxford', pp. 810-11; J. Conway Davies, *Episcopal Acts and cognate Documents relating to Welsh dioceses*, i (1946), 378-91; ii (1948), 558-61.

[3] Cf. the letters to the Generals of the Dominicans and Franciscans, *Epp.* 131-4, to Alard and the Provincial Chapter of the Dominicans, 59-61, 304-5, to John of St. Giles, 62-63, to Adam Marsh, 69-71, &c. See Luard's *Preface*, pp. xxi-xxiii; Stevenson, pp. 78-87; Hinnebusch, *The Early English Friars Preachers*, pp. 448-53.

[4] Trivet, *Ann.*, p. 243: 'Hic fratres ordinis, tam Praedicatorum quam Minorum, sincera caritate amplectens, eos habuit continue in comitiva sua, delicias computans cum eis de Scripturis conferre.'

[5] Cf., for example, Grosseteste's circular letter to his archdeacons, *Epp.* 317-18.

[6] Cf. Thomson, *Writings*, pp. 122-4; Hunt, below, pp. 123-6, 141-5.

Nicomachean Ethics in two of his letters to Grosseteste,[1] indicate, at
least, his interests in these translations. His knowledge of Greek and
Hebrew, and his insistence on the indispensable necessity of the
study of both languages for the understanding of the Scriptures—
these and similar considerations lead us to surmise his association
with Grosseteste's achievements in Greek. But we cannot exactly
assess his part in the actual work of translation. One is rather inclined
to think that it consisted mainly in that invaluable, though often
indefinable, assistance resulting from friendly talks and scholarly
discussions, from criticisms, advice, suggestions: in a word, in that
help that scholars nowadays acknowledge in the preface to their
books.

If we could sift Grosseteste's work from that of his collaborators,
and assign to each his respective share, we would be in a better position to assess Grosseteste's proficiency in Greek.

Stevenson believed that it is possible to distinguish 'the translations which he effected, when unaided, (from) those which he carried
out without the assistance of others'. In the former, for instance in
the *De Vita Monachorum*, he extracted as best he could the meaning
of the words, and added what was necessary to elucidate their meaning. His later translations, which he effected with aid of others working under him, are, on the other hand, extremely literal, *verbo ad
verbum*.[2] However, granted such a criterion, in no way could Grosseteste be held personally responsible for any of the translations
attributed to him, since all of them are *de verbo ad verbum*, 'almost
painfully literal'.[3]

Professor Franceschini,[4] whose views in this connexion carry
great weight, has justly remarked that the uniformity of method and
technique in all the translations argues in favour of unity of purpose
and execution. This is amply shown by the philological *notulae*
found consistently throughout the whole work. These illustrate
delicate points of Greek grammar and syntax, of orthography and
phonetics, of the different meanings and connotations of the same
word, on the analogy or diversity between Greek and Latin. Now
it is difficult to conceive that these and similar observations, and the
minute, critical explanations which pervade the whole text, were

---

[1] *Mon. Franc.* i. 206–7; 112, 114. For the bearing of these letters on the translation
of pseudo-Denis and the *Ethics*, see Callus, 'The Date', pp. 188 ff., 208–9.
[2] Stevenson, p. 225.   [3] Cf. Franceschini, *Roberto Grossatesta*, p. 16.
[4] Ibid., pp. 17–18.

undertaken to illustrate and explain not his own but others' translations, even if planned and supervised by him. The contribution
of his assistants must have been exclusively oral. In this way they
helped him to translate Greek texts, discussing with him problems
of grammar, syntax, and pronunciation, and supplying other useful
information about the Greek language and usage. As Sir Maurice
Powicke rightly puts it, 'it was he, and no colleague, who used the
first person in explaining his use of terms. The pleasure which he
took in the discourse of etymological points is thoroughly characteristic.'[1] The tradition which ascribes to him a body of translations is
too convincing to be set on one side. With justice, then, his versions
became known throughout the Middle Ages under the title *Translatio Lincolniensis*, whilst his associates remained anonymous.

From the foregoing it logically follows that Grosseteste was fully
versed in Greek. An examination of his translations and of the
numerous *notulae* with which he enriched them shows unmistakably
that he had a very considerable knowledge of Greek. No one could
have given the explanations on Greek grammar and syntax, on the
characteristic structure of the language, on the composition of Greek
words, and on other minute points that we find everywhere, unless
he had full mastery of his subject.[2]

In conclusion, Roger Bacon's statement, that Grosseteste had
assistants to help him in his translations, is found substantially
correct, although he may have exaggerated their number, as he did
indeed overrate their contribution. Grosseteste himself at the close
of his comment on the *Angelical Hierarchy* refers explicitly to his
helpers: 'Tanta autem et a me *et a coadiutoribus meis* ad explana-
tionem huius libri de Angelica Ierarchia dicta sint.'[3] Moreover,
Grosseteste did not arrive at that mature technique which we admire
in his later translations, in the *Ethics* for instance, all at once. His
earlier works, such as John of Damascus, look in fact as if he were
still feeling his way towards a surer and more precise method, and
probably he had to rely more heavily on his assistants. But when all
this is said in support of Bacon's words, the undisguised fact remains
that Bacon has greatly minimized Grosseteste's proficiency in Greek
and his efforts in the field of translations.

No one would deny Roger Bacon's linguistic attainment, great

---

[1] Powicke, *Robert Grosseteste*, p. 21.
[2] Franceschini, op. cit., pp. 12, 18.
[3] MS. Merton College 86, fol. 85vb; cf. Franceschini, op. cit., p. 13.

indeed for his time;[1] but he reached the summit (his first degree) painfully and only with utmost difficulty ('tota difficultas consistit in primo gradu, ut nos qui talibus insistimus experimur').[2] He would not have it, that Grosseteste could even master the second degree so as to be able to translate unaided; hence he assigned to him the third, that is, the lowest grade in the knowledge of languages, just enough to read and understand a Hebrew or a Greek text. With the exception of Boethius, he finds fault in varying degrees with all the translators, from St. Jerome to his contemporaries. He blames the Church for not having promoted translations of the Fathers, and praises the 'Lord Robert' for rendering into Latin John of Damascus, Denis, and some other Doctors. Again, he extols him for inviting Greeks and causing Greek manuscripts to be brought into England; but, at the same time, he remarks that after all he and his associates did very little (*sed isti pauca transtulerunt*).[3] Further, he utterly ignores Grosseteste's Aristotelian versions;[4] nowhere is even a bare mention found of the *Nicomachean Ethics*, or of the *De Caelo et Mundo*, or of the other philosophical treatises. Perhaps Bacon's memory failed him, or his information was wanting. It certainly deserted him when he roundly asserted in 1272, or thereabouts, that there was no other Latin translation of Aristotle's *Metaphysics* but an imperfect and incomplete one in ten books.[5] This is indeed surprising in a man who judged with unmitigated severity all existing versions and chastised with a heavy hand the shortcomings of everyone on earth. Or perhaps he regarded Grosseteste's efforts so unworthy that he included them in the general condemnation, and out of devotion to his memory passed them over in utter silence.

It is time to turn our attention to the translations themselves.

Among the Greek manuscripts which Grosseteste caused to be brought from Greece and elsewhere, there must have been not only

---

[1] See, however, Hastings Rashdall's remark in the Introduction to the edition of *Fratris Rogeri Bacon Compendium Studii Theologiae* (B.S.F.S. iii), Aberdeen, 1911, p. 23: 'Bacon was no doubt somewhat inordinately proud of the little Greek which he knew, and found it convenient to pretend that what he objected to in the current scholasticism could not really lay claim to the great authority of Aristotle.'

[2] Bacon, *Op. In.*, p. 434.

[3] Ibid., p. 91.

[4] See the pertinent remarks of S. D. Wingate, *The Mediaeval Latin Versions of the Aristotelian Scientific Corpus, with special reference to the Biological Works*, London, 1931, pp. 112 ff.

[5] 'De metaphysica non legunt Latini, nisi quod habent de decem libellis, cum multi alii sint, et de illis decem deficiunt in translatione quam legunt multa capitula et quasi lineae infinitae.' *Compendium Studii Philosophiae, Op. In.*, p. 473.

grammars, as Roger Bacon tells us, but also dictionaries. Grosseteste refers more than once, in fact, to Greek glossaries ('sicut in partionariis Graecorum invenitur'). He made constant use of the Lexicon of Suidas in explaining Greek words, and drew from it in varying degree in his *notulae* on the Epistles of St. Ignatius, pseudo-Denis, the *Nicomachean Ethics*, and the *De Caelo et Mundo*. It is reasonably certain that MS. Leiden, Vossianus fol. 2, containing the Lexicon of Suidas, was owned by Grosseteste.[1] We have definite evidence that he rendered into Latin at least seventy-one sections from Suidas, mainly of historical and biographical interest, such as *De probatione virginitatis Beatae Mariae*, which became so popular as to be translated into Anglo-Norman.[2]

The main characteristic of medieval translations from the Greek is their extreme literalness, *verbum de verbo*. Each word had to be represented by a Latin equivalent. The translators claimed that in doing so they were treading in the steps of St. Jerome and Boethius. They followed this method of set purpose, not from ignorance of the Greek language, *pace* Roger Bacon, but out of respect for their 'authorities', lest the meaning of their words should be altered. John Sarracinus, sending his version of the *De Angelica Hierarchia* to John of Salisbury, complains of the poverty of the Latin tongue, of the impossibility of rendering phrases introduced by the article, of the difficulty of expressing compound terms, and of the impossibility of following the strict order of the words. To obviate these obstacles and to keep at the same time the precise meaning of his text, he had to translate as best as he could, sometimes literally but sometimes more freely.[3] His contemporary, Burgundio of Pisa, in his dedicatory letter of his translation of St. John Chrysostom's Homilies on St. John's Gospel, is at pains to explain that he was striving to introduce nothing of his own but to give the very words of John Chrysostom. Conscious of his great responsibility, he kept faithfully to his text, rendering it word for word, only avoiding barbarisms, grammatical faults, and similar irregularities.[4]

Grosseteste's rule was close adherence to the Greek. Like

---

[1] See on this manuscript Hunt, below, p. 135.

[2] Cf. Franceschini, *Rob. Grossatesta*, pp. 63–67; Thomson, *Writings*, pp. 63–65; R. J. Dean, *PMLA*, li (1936), 607–20.

[3] *P.L.* cxcix. 143–4, *inter Epp. Ioan. Sares.* Cf. G. Théry, 'Documents concernant Jean Sarrazin', *Arch. HDLMA*, xviii (1950–1), 51–54.

[4] This preface is printed by C. H. Haskins, *Studies in the History of Mediaeval Science*, Cambridge (Mass.), 1924, p. 151, n. 36.

Sarracinus he contrived to coin compound terms, but unlike him he did not give a free rendering of the text; in a sense he was more in line with Burgundio. Grosseteste had certainly read his translation of John Chrysostom's Homilies on John,[1] and we may presume that he had pondered on the *Preface* before he made his own attempts at translation. None the less, his translations are even more literal than Burgundio's, holding fast to the exact order of the words and representing the Greek in every detail, to the extent of disregarding Latin idiom and syntax. He expounded and justified his method and technique in the countless *notulae* which he added to his versions, particularly in his glosses on pseudo-Denis.[2]

Few of the translations ascribed to Grosseteste are new translations in the strict sense. Like other medieval translators, if a book had already been translated, he did not start work afresh, but tried rather to improve the existing version by revising and correcting it. His first attempts at translation were in this direction.

Grosseteste's authorship of the version of the *De Fide Orthodoxa* of John of Damascus is attested by Salimbene,[3] Roger Bacon,[4] and two thirteenth-century manuscripts (MSS. Pembroke College, Cambridge, 20 and 34). Cross-references, stylistic and literary characteristics make it clear that it was one of his earliest efforts at translating. We find a reference to it in his commentary on the *De Angelica Hierarchia* of pseudo-Denis (1239–40): 'Iohannes Damascenus in quodam capitulo *Sententiarum* suarum',[5] and further, an explicit citation taken verbatim from his own translation.[6] Moreover, the *De Hymno Trisagion*, which is intimately connected with the *De Fide Orthodoxa*, is twice mentioned in the same commentary as having been already translated.[7] Now in his *Hexaemeron* and in the glosses

---

[1] Grosseteste quotes the Homilies on St. John in his glosses on Psalms, see MS. Eton College 8, fol. 91[ra], &c.   [2] Cf. Franceschini, *Rob. Grossatesta*, pp. 74–85.

[3] *Chronica Fratris Salimbene, Monumenta Germaniae Historica*, SS. xxxii. 233.

[4] Bacon, *Op. In.*, p. 474; cf. *Opus Maius* (Bridges, i. 70; iii. 84).

[5] MS. Merton College 86, fol. 68[ra]. Cf. Franceschini, *Rob. Grossatesta*, pp. 42–43. For the date of the *De Angelica Hierarchia*, see Callus, 'The Date', pp. 188–99.

[6] 'De hac autem re et maxime a nostra modicitate et insufficientia nil temere diffiniendum, cum beatus etiam Iohannes Damascenus de angelis loquens fateatur se hoc ignorare, insinuans insuper quemlibet alium eadem detineri ignorantia, dicens quod angelice "substantie speciem et terminum solus qui creavit noscit". Et paulo post: "Sive equales secundum substantiam sive differentes ab invicem, nescimus; solus autem qui fecit ipsos, Deus, scit."' MS. Merton 86, fol. 31[vb] (cf. Franceschini, op. cit., p. 43, n.). For Grosseteste's version I have consulted MS. Ashmole 1526, fol. 129[rb]; fol. 129[va]; and for Burgundio's MSS. Laud misc. 268, fol. 48[rb]; e Museo 134, fol. 382[va]; Canon, *P.L.* 97, fol. 7[rb].

[7] MS. Merton College 86, fol. 44[va], and fol. 68[ra]. Cf. Franceschini, op. cit., p. 43, n.

on the Psalms,[1] composed while he was still in the schools, not later than 1235, his quotations of John of Damascus are from Burgundio's version. We may, therefore, infer that his work as translator, as Roger Bacon states, was not begun before his episcopate. But since the translation is cited in the *De Angelica Hierarchia*, which belongs to 1239–40, it logically follows that the *De Fide Orthodoxa* was not translated before 1235 nor after 1239. The significance of this translation lies in this, that it shows, as it were, Grosseteste at work, while he was still feeling his way as a translator.

A small section of the *De Fide Orthodoxa* (Bk. III, i–viii) was translated in Hungary before the middle of the twelfth century.[2] A few years later, *c.* 1148–50, Burgundio of Pisa, at the command of Pope Eugenius III, made a complete translation. We do not know whether Grosseteste was acquainted with the Hungarian version. At all events, being in possession of some Greek manuscripts, he undertook a new recension, correcting and revising Burgundio, supplementing several passages therein omitted, and adding to it explanatory notes introduced with the words 'From the Greek'. This is concisely borne out by the title in MS. 20 in the Library of Pembroke College, Cambridge (fol. 1rd): 'Incipit liber Iohannis Damasceni secundum *correctam* translationem Roberti Lincolniensis Episcopi', and more precisely by the colophon at the end of the list of chapters in the same manuscript:

> Expliciunt capitula libri Iohannis Damasceni numero centum et unum. Correxit autem dominus R. Grosseteste Lincolniensis episcopus veterem translationem, et inseruit etiam multa que transtulit ex greco exemplari, que in veteri translatione non habentur. (Fol. 1rd.)[3]

A good number of these additions, to which the words *ex graeco* are prefixed, are found in British Museum, MS. Royal 5 C. iv at the end of the *Logica Iohannis Damasceni*, which follows immediately Burgundio's *De Fide Orthodoxa*.[4] More important still is MS. Royal

---

[1] For the *Hexaemeron*, see Smalley, below, p. 78; for the Psalms, cf. MS. Eton College 8, fol. 90[ra-b], and below, p. 52.

[2] R. L. Szigeti, *Translatio latina Ioannis Damasceni* (*De Orthodoxa Fide, l. III, c. 1–8*) *saeculo XII in Hungaria confecta*, Budapest, 1940; E. M. Buytaert, 'The Earliest Latin Translation of Damascene's *De Orthodoxa Fide*, III, 1–8', *Franciscan Studies*, xi (1951), 49–67. Cf. J. de Ghellinck, *Le Mouvement théologique du XIIe siècle*, Bruges, 1948, pp. 385–404.

[3] Cf. M. R. James, *A Descriptive Catalogue of the Manuscripts in the Library of Pembroke College, Cambridge*, Cambridge, 1905, p. 17.

[4] G. F. Warner and J. P. Gilson, *Catalogue of Western Manuscripts in the Old Royal and King's Collections*, i. 107.

5 D. x.[1] It contains Burgundio's version, and, written in the centre of the page between the two columns, several of the conventional signs used by Grosseteste for his subject-index of Biblical, patristic, and other writings, though not in his own hand. The margin of the text of the *De Fide Orthodoxa* is heavily annotated with the prefix *in graeco*.

The marginalia are twofold: (*a*) For the most part they set out the divergence between Burgundio's translation and a Greek text which was in the hands of the annotator. To give one or two instances, on fol. 85[rb], ch. iii, against Burgundio's *secundum quam hec machina*, the marginal note reads, *in greco: hoc omne*; or again, in ch. iv, Burgundio's *informabile* is corrected by *in greco: infigurabile*; in ch. xiii, the *et avertimus* of the text is set right in the margin, 'in greco non est: et avertimus'. (*b*) Other marginalia contain either extracts, translated from the Greek, illustrating references to the text, or explanatory notes, mainly etymological. It would seem that the annotator (*or* the copyist?) became increasingly familiar with Greek, since in the margin of the first pages he transliterated Greek words into Latin script, but later he used Greek script itself. However that may be, the annotations in this manuscript raise many problems which call for further investigation.

The extent of Grosseteste's revision and his method are more clearly and more completely illustrated in the text written, not in the margin of Burgundio's translation, but consecutively. It is extant in eleven manuscripts.[2] A collation of the six copies preserved in England, all written in the thirteenth century, has shown their close relationship. MS. Pembroke College 20, the most carefully written, is far superior to the others, and, if not actually written under Grosseteste's supervision, it was certainly transcribed from a copy very near the archetype. The translation, as in MS. Pembroke College 34 which seems to be derived from it, is explicitly ascribed to Grosseteste. These manuscripts cover not only the full text of Grosseteste's revision, but include also all the additions of MS. Royal 5 C. iv, and many others besides; but unlike the Royal manuscript each addendum is inserted in its proper place.[3] The margins are copiously

---

[1] I am greatly obliged to Dr. R. W. Hunt who has kindly called my attention to this manuscript. For its description, see Hunt, below, p. 126.

[2] Cf. Thomson, *Writings*, pp. 48–50.

[3] In MS. Lambeth Palace 151 the alternative readings are very often inserted in the text itself, e.g. fol. 181[ra], at the very beginning, we have: 'Deum nemo *seu nullus*'; or again: 'immutabilis *seu invertibilis*'; 'sine semine *seu inseminaliter*'; fol. 181[rb]: 'ordine

annotated in such a way as to provide a critical apparatus, as perfect as it could be in that age. The variant readings of Greek manuscripts are examined, alternative renderings of Greek words are carefully noted, different translations discussed, philological, historical, or theological explanations are added. All this shows abundantly Grosseteste's meticulous patience in revising and correcting his text.

There can be no doubt that the marginal notes, which accompany the text, originated from the translator himself. They form part and parcel of the whole work. The use of *seu* in introducing alternative meaning is typical of Grosseteste's method. In the *Praefatio* to his commentary on the *De Angelica Hierarchia* he takes the precaution of explaining it fully, thus: 'Advertat preterea lector expositionis nostre qualiscumque, quod ubi dicimus: hoc seu hoc, non res diversas, sed eiusdem nominis greci interpretationes diversas intendimus dicere ad maiorem mentis auctoris dilucidationem.'[1] Moreover, not a few of these notes are met with in other works which are recognized as certainly genuine, as, for example, the distinction between *dynamis*, meaning 'power' or 'faculty', and *arete* (ἀρετή), which he translates by 'moral virtue', occurs twice in the comment on the *De Angelica Hierarchia*, twice in the comment on the *De Divinis Nominibus*, and again in his *notulae* on the *Nicomachean Ethics*.[2] In addition, four of these notes are expressly ascribed to him with the designation *episcopus* in MS. Pembroke College 20 (fols. 2vb, 10ra, 17rb, 24ra).

In his studies, as in his actions, Grosseteste was in the habit of taking the greatest care over every detail. A man of firm principles, he always acted with deliberation, and would not leave unchallenged anything of which he did not approve. But as a true philosopher, he would search for the cause, and assign the reason for all his actions. It is extremely interesting to watch him at work. Frequently he keeps the reading of Burgundio, but suggests in the margin an alternative meaning, e.g. at the very beginning he retains *nemo*, but gives *nullus*

---

seu lege'; whereas in the other manuscripts 'seu nullus', 'seu invertibilis', 'seu inseminaliter', &c., are written in the margins. This manuscript, which came from the Franciscan convent, Gloucester (cf. N. R. Ker, *Medieval Libraries of Great Britain*, p. 51, and Hunt, *Bodl. Lib. Rec.*, iv (1953), pp. 248, 252), has also other peculiarities.

[1] MS. Merton College 86, fol. 2ra; cf. M. Grabmann, *Mittelalterliches Geistesleben*, Munich, 1926, i. 466; Franceschini, *Rob. Grossatesta*, p. 75.

[2] MSS. Ashmole 1526, fol. 123va; Pembroke College, Cambridge, 20, fol. 2ra; cf. Franceschini, op. cit., pp. 109–10.

as an alternative; or *intellectualia*, but in the margin *seu: intelligibilia*; often, on the contrary, he substitutes another word in his text, e.g. *obviemus* for Burgundio's *deveniamus*, but after all he agrees with him by adding, *seu: deveniamus*. There are cases where Burgundio either misread his text, or his codex had a different reading; in such cases Grosseteste defends his own rendering by appealing to Greek manuscripts, for example:

Aliquis liber latinus habet: 'canticum quod solvitur', ubi nos posuimus: 'spiramentum quod solvitur'. Sed greca exemplaria habent 'asthma', quod est 'spiramentum', non 'asma', quod est 'canticum'.[1]

Or again:

Episcopus. Non sicut aliqui latini posuerunt hic, 'impossibile'; habetur in greco, 'sed impassibile'. Non enim est ibi 'adynaton', sed 'apathes'. Solus enim Deus nec generando nec creando patitur. Et propter hoc utrumque est in eo non 'impossibile' sed 'impassibile'.[2]

Wherever he introduces changes or something new he is at pains to explain why he does so. Thus, although he was well aware that ch. xxiv, 'On Seas', and ch. xxv, 'On Winds', were wanting in several Greek manuscripts, he included them in his text. As a matter of fact, Le Quien, the famous editor of the writings of John of Damascus, remarks that a section in the chapter 'On Winds' is omitted *in omnibus fere codicibus*, whilst the chapter 'On Seas' is either wanting in Greek manuscripts or written separately.[3] It is in fact a later addition. Obviously, it never occurred to Grosseteste that these two chapters might have been a later interpolation; instead he tried to account both for their omission in Greek manuscripts and for including them in his recension.

They were omitted [he says] because some might, perhaps, have thought that such questions on seas and winds were not matters of great relevance to theology. Nevertheless, truly wise men know for certain that every glimpse of truth is useful for the interpretation and understanding of theology. Since, therefore, they were included in his Greek copy, he would by no means leave them out. It stands to reason that such an excellent author (*tantus auctor*) would never have written them, unless he were convinced of their usefulness for the study of Holy Scripture.[4]

---

[1] MSS. Pembroke College 20, fol. 2[va]; Ashmole 1526, fol. 124[rb]; Cambridge, Univ. Libr., Kk. iii. 19, fol. 200[vb]. Cf. *P.G.* xciv. 808B.
[2] MSS. Pembroke College, fol. 2[vb]; Ashmole, fol. 124[vb]. Cf. *P.G.* xciv. 813A.
[3] Cf. *P.G.* xciv. 901, 905.
[4] MSS. Pembroke College, fol. 8[rb]; Ashmole, fol. 135[va]; Royal 5 C. iv, fol. 93[vb].

In the chapter 'On the Stars', he enters the sign proper to each of the seven planets and of the twelve zodiacal constellations, which were not inserted by Burgundio. Further, he includes a diagram, transcribed from the Greek, noting its correct place in the book, and with unmistakable delight tells us that these signs owe their origin to the Greeks, who, especially in their mathematical writings, for brevity's sake indicate things by means of a symbol instead of writing their names in full.[1] Or again, in a note marked 'Episcopus' in the Pembroke manuscript, he goes out of his way to inform us that chapters xci and xcii, on 'Images' and 'Scripture', are not strictly speaking separate chapters, nor are indeed so numbered in the Greek, but rather they are sections of the same chapter 'On the Cult of Saints and their Relics'. And this is quite correct, since we read about the cult due to the Saints in the words of the Scriptures, and this is again expressed by their Images.[2]

Moreover, it is characteristic of Grosseteste's thoroughness that in the midst of textual and grammatical disquisitions on phonetics, spelling, pronunciation, and other niceties of the Greek language, he should bring in a theological *quaestio*. It is suggested by a remark in chapter xxxviii, that 'God takes no counsel: those only take counsel who lack knowledge'. These words, it is argued, prove that God does not take counsel. 'On the contrary', replies Grosseteste, 'we read in the Psalms: "The counsel of the Lord standeth for ever" (Ps. xxxii. 11). Further, St. Gregory says: "The sentence of God changes, but not his counsel."[3] Now, according to Tullius, counsel implies three things: truth, searching, reason; for counsel is a reason to do or not to do something which is truly thought out. Thus the solution of the question is manifest.'[4]

In the last years of his regency in theology at Oxford, commenting on the words of Psalm lxxxii. 4: 'Super populum tuum malignaverunt consilium', Grosseteste had come across the same problem, and had to face the same argument from John of Damascus. He arrived at the same conclusion, that 'God takes counsel', but his

---

[1] MSS. Pembroke College, fol. 6ʳ; Ashmole, fol. 131ᵛᵃ; Cambridge, University Lib., fol. 204ᵛᵃ; Royal 5 D. x, fol. 89ʳᵃ; Magdalen College 192, fol. 166ʳ: 'Hec figura ex greco scripta congrue ponitur post vicesimum quintum capitulum de ventis.'

[2] MSS. Pembroke College, fol. 24ʳᵃ; Ashmole, fol. 162ʳᵇ.

[3] *Moral.* XVI. x: 'Deus etsi plerumque mutat sententiam, consilium nunquam' (*P.L.* lxxv. 1127B).

[4] MS. Ashmole 1526, fol. 139ᵛᵃ. I have not succeeded in identifying the quotation from Cicero.

approach this time is different. In the commentary, his Biblical authority is taken from the book of Job: 'He hath counsel and understanding' (xii. 13), and St. Gregory's contribution is, of course, from the same *Liber Moralium*, but from a different context, that is, from the comment on the words of Job cited as his Biblical authority (*Moral.* xi. viii, *P.L.* lxxv. 958C). The proof from Tullius is omitted, but instead he brings forward long quotations from the *De Fide Orthodoxa* taken from Burgundio's translation, a clear indication that he had not yet made his own version. On the whole, his answer to the question in his comment on the Psalms is more theologically precise. Counsel is truly ascribed to God, but not in the same sense that is attributed to man; in man counsel implies a previous inquiry, but such inquiry has no place in God.[1]

To sum up, Grosseteste's references to 'alius liber', 'aliud exemplar', 'exemplaria graeca', point to the fact that he was working on several Greek manuscripts; and some of these, at least, contained a glossed text. It was from the glossed copies that he extracted the additions and annotations marked *ex graeco*.

If we could trust our three types of manuscripts as faithful copies of Grosseteste's original model, and assign their differences to him and not to chance, it would be possible to distinguish three stages in the process of revision. MS. Royal 5 C. iv, with its fewer marginalia and with the additions written separately at the end, would represent the first stage, at a time when the work was not yet clearly planned. Grosseteste was comparing Burgundio's translation with a Greek text and adding in the margin the divergent readings. This is indeed in accordance with his customary practice, since it is well known that he used to jot his reflections in the margin of his books. The second stage is reached in MS. Royal 5 D. x. The minute corrections and the additional notes inserted in the margin of the text of Burgundio's version bear witness to a more elaborate revision. The complete and definitive work, including recension, annotations, and additions, not inserted in the margins of Burgundio's version, but collected and transcribed in orderly form in the body of a book, a polished copy standing, as it were, on its own, is represented by the handsome MS. Pembroke College, Cambridge, 20 and its derivatives.

Considering the great number of marginalia in the existing manuscripts, after as careful a collation of both works as I could make, I was surprised to find that the changes introduced by Grosseteste

---

[1] MS. Eton College 8, fol. 90^{ra–b}.

were not as numerous as I had expected. There are long chapters where there are scarcely any innovations. If Grosseteste was making his revision on the text of Burgundio's translation, adding his corrections in the margins, as we have it in MS. Royal 5 D. x, it is much easier to explain why, after all, he retained so much of Burgundio's text, and inserted so little new of his own.

The purpose underlying all the changes which Grosseteste made in the revision of Burgundio's version was a closer and more literal rendering of the Greek. In this respect his recension is more involved than Burgundio's, and at times less successful. On the other hand, it cannot be denied that very often it shows a marked improvement; many of the changes are felicitous, and a good number of them are of real importance not only for a more precise understanding of the text, but also for their doctrinal implications.[1] Significantly it was labelled in the Pembroke MS. *correcta translatio*. Yet, in spite of its intrinsic value, Grosseteste's recension did not earn much currency outside the Oxford schools, nor did it ever replace Burgundio's translation, which continued to be in favour everywhere during the Middle Ages. It was doubtless read, but its use was restricted to the purpose of comparison with Burgundio's, or to marginalia in Peter Lombard's *Sentences*, as an alternative reading, *alia lectio secundum Lincolniensem*.[2] It has been remarked that not even such an admirer of Grosseteste as Salimbene took his quotations of the *De Fide Orthodoxa* from his recension, but from Burgundio's version.[3]

It is the merit of Professor Thomson to have called our attention to the *Prologus Translatoris*, and to have pointed to the *Logica* and to the *De Haeresibus* as forming a trilogy with the *De Fide Orthodoxa*.[4] In the manuscript tradition they are often included under the same colophon: 'Explicit liber Logices, Heresum et Sententiarum Iohannis Damasceni.' Accordingly, it may be well to ascribe to Grosseteste, in addition to the *De Fide Orthodoxa* and the *De Hymno Trisagion*, the translation of the *Logica*, in its 'Shorter Form' (this work came down to us, as is well known, in two recensions, a *forma brevior* and

[1] The pertinent remarks of Hocedez, 'Les Trois premières traductions du *De Orthodoxa Fide*', *Le Musée Belge*, xvii (1913), 109–23, on Bk. III, i–viii, may be extended to the whole translation.

[2] Cf. J. de Ghellinck, *Le Mouvement théologique*, pp. 386–93.

[3] Cf. H. Dausend, 'Johannes Damascenus in der Chronik des Salimbene', *Theol. Quartalschrift*, cxviii (1937), 173–92; E. Hocedez, 'La Diffusion de la *Translatio Lincolniensis* du *De Orthodoxa Fide*', *Bulletin d'ancienne Littérature et d'Archéologie chrétiennes*, iii (1913), 188–98. I have been unable to see this last paper.

[4] Thomson, *Writings*, pp. 45–50.

a *forma longior*), of the *De Haeresibus*, of the *Introductio Dogmatum elementaris*, and also of the *Prologus*. Thomson is under the impression that 'most of the prologue is Grosseteste's own'.[1] But, as Le Quien has remarked, this tract was originally written in Greek, and the Latin is simply a translation. It follows, therefore, that the passage quoted by Thomson from the Prologue (pp. 45–46) does not refer to Grosseteste's translation of the trilogy, but to John of Damascus's composition of the three works.

The attribution to Grosseteste of the translation of the four apocryphal letters of St. Ignatius is explicitly attested by at least one manuscript, Tours, MS. Bibliothèque municipale 247, fol. 483: 'Has epistolas transtulit de greco in latinum Magister Robertus Grossa testa Lincolniensis episcopus.' If the extant manuscripts (well over fifty) are a sure indication, these letters must have enjoyed considerable popularity in the Middle Ages. The translation of the genuine letters of the Middle Form, on the contrary, do not appear to have been much read, particularly outside Oxford. It was preserved in two manuscripts only, of which one is now lost.[2] Apart from a few quotations by the fourteenth-century Oxford masters, John Tyssington, William Woodford, and Wyclif, it would seem that this translation fell into utter oblivion, since the rare Ignatian citations which we encounter here and there were all taken from the Long Recension.

The Latin version of the Ignatian letters of the Middle Form was rediscovered by Archbishop Ussher in the seventeenth century, and attributed by him with great plausibility to Grosseteste.[3] Ussher's view, elaborated and corroborated with fresh evidence by J. B. Lightfoot,[4] won general acceptance, and Grosseteste's authorship now obtains among such scholars as Hilgenfeld,[5] de Ghellinck,[6] and

---

[1] Thomson, *Writings*, p. 81. The *Prologus* is published in Migne, *P.G.* xciv. 489–98. See MS. e Museo 134 (S.C. 3614, p. 701).

[2] The lost manuscript, *Montacutianus*, from the library of Richard Mountague or Montacute, Bishop of Norwich, was in Ussher's hands, but it has since disappeared. The other is MS. 395 in Gonville and Caius College, Cambridge. There are also two seventeenth-century transcripts, MS. 445 G. & C. College, and MS. D. 3. 11 Trinity College, Dublin.

[3] I. Ussher, *Polycarpi et Ignatii Epistulae una cum veteri interpretatione*, Oxford, 1644, p. xv.

[4] J. B. Lightfoot, *The Apostolic Fathers. P. II. S. Ignatius. S. Polycarp*, London, 1889, i. 76–86. The text is edited, iii. 13–72.

[5] A. Hilgenfeld, *Ignatii Antiocheni et Polycarpi Smyrnaei Epistulae et Martyria*, Berlin, 1902, pp. xv–xvii. Text, pp. 71–105.

[6] J. de Ghellinck, 'Patristique et argument de tradition au bas moyen âge', *Aus der Geisteswelt des Mittelalters* (*B.G.P.M.*, Suppl. III. 1). Münster i. W., 1935, pp. 410, n. 31, 414, n. 46; *Le Mouvement théologique du XIIe siècle*, Bruges, 1948, pp. 386–7, 408.

Franceschini,[1] but is strongly contested by Thomson.[2] The question needs further investigation.

I agree with Thomson that the rubric in the Tours MS. assigning the translation to Robert Grosseteste refers to the four spurious letters, and not, as Lightfoot contended, 'to the preceding epistles' which have now disappeared. Accordingly, it does not prove the authorship of the genuine but of the apocryphal letters. It is equally true that 'there is no MS. authority for ascribing the translation of the "middle" recension to Grosseteste', and that 'arguments from style are not in themselves determinative'. But even so, there are other cumulative indications which are telling.

An examination of this version shows all the characteristics of Grosseteste's translations, and confirms the conclusions reached by Lightfoot and Franceschini. We have here similarity of method and technique: the same extreme literalness; the marginal notes,[3] in which the words of the translation are compared with the original Greek, due certainly to the translator himself; the use of unusual Latin words introduced to correspond as exactly as possible to the original; the particles scrupulously reproduced in violation of Latin idiom; the order of the words in Greek rigidly followed without any regard for Latin usage; and above all the use of the infinitive with the preposition *cum*, and the explanatory note that the government of the infinitive by *cum* follows the Greek rule.[4] Franceschini has justly remarked—and it can be seen throughout the whole body of Grosseteste's versions—that Grosseteste invariably abides by this construction. In spite, therefore, of lack of external evidence, we are inclined to see in this translation Grosseteste's hand.

The difference in style between this version and that of the *Testaments of the Twelve Patriarchs*, observed by Funk,[5] though real, is not to be exaggerated. Doubtless this latter translation is less literal and is more polished than the others; Grosseteste, perhaps, relied here more heavily than usual on his assistant Nicholas the Greek, as Matthew Paris[6] seems to suggest: 'coadiuvante magistro

[1] Franceschini, *Rob. Grossatesta*, pp. 21–26.

[2] Thomson, *Writings*, pp. 58–62; *Spuria*, p. 251, No. 26.

[3] One of these marginal notes on *incus percussa* is significant, since it betrays the nationality of the author: 'Incus est instrumentum fabri; dicitur anglice *anfeld* [anvil].' (*Letter to Polycarp*, ed. Lightfoot, iii, p. 19. l. 10); cf. vol. i, p. 76.

[4] For particular instances, see Lightfoot, op. cit., i. 79–80; Franceschini, op. cit., pp. 25–26.

[5] F. X. Funk, *Die Echtheit der Ignatianischen Briefe*, Tübingen, 1883, pp. 142–4.

[6] Paris, *Chron. Mai.* iv. 232.

Nicolao Graeco, clerico abbatis S. Albani'. It should not, consequently, make us unduly hesitant in accepting Grosseteste's authorship. In all probability the translation of the letters of St. Ignatius was one of the first undertaken by the bishop, very likely soon after the completion of John of Damascus, but certainly before the pseudo-Dionysian *corpus*, since it is cited in his commentary on the *De Ecclesiastica Hierarchia*[1] (*c.* 1240).[2] The value of this translation for critical purposes in establishing the Greek text has been adequately shown by Lightfoot. The manuscript used by Grosseteste was evidently superior to the existing manuscripts of the Greek; it is free from later interpolations, and in several instances gives words and clauses which have through inadvertence dropped out of the Greek manuscripts.

Grosseteste's reputation as translator is principally associated with his translation of the pseudo-Dionysian *corpus*, which he enriched with valuable commentaries. Their genuineness is beyond doubt; in William of Alnwick's words, they were regarded in the schools, together with the exposition on the *Posterior Analytics* and the *Hexaemeron*, as 'authentic' works. Cross-references serve to demonstrate that a single author was responsible for the translation of the two *Hierarchies*, the *Angelical* or *Celestial* and the *Ecclesiastical*, the *Divine Names*, the *Mystical Theology*, of the so-called Scholia of St. Maximus, and for the comments which accompanied them. That both translation and commentaries ran simultaneously is clearly attested by their internal structure and by Grosseteste himself, who twice brings them together as one whole at the close of his explanation on the *Divine Names*:

> In fine autem huius mee qualiscumque translationis et expositionis dico concorditer sanctissimo patri Dionisio quod vere minor sum et deficiens a certa et diligenti interpretatione et expositione angelice et ecclesiastice, et maxime huius supreme hierarchie, et derelictus plurimum a precedentibus interpretibus et expositoribus.[3]

Moreover, this same passage provides us with a sure indication of the chronological order in which the work was carried out: first the

---

[1] 'Est enim Eucharistia, secundum Beatum Ignatium, caro Salvatoris nostri Iesu Christi pro peccatis nostris passa, quam benignitate Pater resuscitavit.' Cf. *Comm. in Eccles. Hier.*, c. 3 (MS. Merton College 86, fol. 106rb); *Ignatius to the Smyrneans*, vi (ed. Lightfoot, iii. 15).

[2] For the date of the *De Eccles. Hier.* see Callus, 'The Date', p. 198.

[3] MS. Merton College 86, fol. 276^{va-b}. The text reads *derelictis* for *derelictus*, but see Franceschini, *Rob. Grossatesta*, p. 30, and below, p. 58, n. 1.

Angelical Hierarchy, next the *Ecclesiastical*, and then the *Divine Names*. Obviously the *Mystical Theology* is not included, since it was not yet translated and commented upon. Three explicit references in it to the commentary on the *Divine Names* place it beyond any reasonable doubt that the *Mystical Theology*[1] followed, instead of, as Baur believes, preceding the *Divine Names*.

An unexpected light on the approximate date[2] of the *Angelical* and *Ecclesiastical Hierarchies*, and by inference of the other two works, is obtained from a letter of Grosseteste's close friend the Franciscan Adam Marsh to the Abbot of St. Andrew at Vercelli, Thomas Gallus, the famous commentator on pseudo-Denis. At the abbot's request, Adam Marsh sent him together with his letter[3] a copy of the *Expositiones super Angelicam Hierarchiam*, etc. The *etc.* in the text and the plural *Expositiones* clearly imply that in addition to the *Angelical*, he also dispatched a copy, at least, of the *Ecclesiastical Hierarchy*. The letter falls between the edition of the abbot's *Explanatio super Mysticam Theologiam*, written not later than 1241, which is mentioned in the letter as 'just finished', and that on the *Divine Names* on which he was still engaged, *in praesentiarum tractatis*, and completed on 27 April 1242. Now if we allow the necessary time to Grosseteste for the completion of both works, we may without much hesitation assign the date of the two *Hierarchies* to the years 1239–41. But, as the *De Divinis Nominibus* and the *Mystica Theologia* followed the *Angelical* and the *Ecclesiastical Hierarchies* at short intervals, we are fully justified in assigning the translation and exposition of the four books to the years 1239–43.

Grosseteste did not attempt a new translation of Denis, but, as in the case of John of Damascus, revised and corrected pre-existing versions. Yet in spite of this, there were some, it would seem, who, dissatisfied with his labours, took exception to his innovations, disagreed with the way in which the work was carried out, and found his explanations obscure, lengthy, and valueless. In reply to his critics, Grosseteste again and again seeks to justify himself, and spares no efforts to defend and explain his method and his technique. He emphatically asserts that he did indeed strive to retain

[1] Cf. U. Gamba, *Il Commento di Roberto Grossatesta al 'De Mystica Theologia' del Pseudo-Dionigi Areopagita*, Milan, 1942, pp. 63, 66 (twice).

[2] I have discussed fully the question of date in *Recherches de Théologie ancienne et médiévale*, xiv (1947), 186–200.

[3] *Mon. Franc.* i. 206–7. I have corrected Brewer's text, which is manifestly faulty, on B.M., MS. Cotton, Vitellius C. VIII, fol. 45ʳ; see 'The Date', pp. 209–10.

the wording of earlier translators as best he could, putting in the text the phrases now of one, now of another, and rarely (*raro*) inserting anything of his own, except when it was needed for a better understanding of the author's mind. His aim in fact was to render into Latin the exact meaning of the Greek, and to preserve unaltered the author's thought and the beauty of his diction ('mens auctoris et venustas eius sermonis'). If he was so bold as to introduce either in the text or in his explanations something which was not included in the profound and excellent commentaries of his predecessors, he did it because he believed that it should not be taken ill that he too should contribute something, though slender and mean (*modicum et vile*), from the poverty of his talents. After all, even those who contribute a little, are not ousted from those who carry the great luminaries, but are received readily, more especially if they cannot lay their hands on something bigger (MS. Merton College 86, fol. 3ra).

At the end of the commentary on the *Angelical Hierarchy*, he returns to answer those who found his work too lengthy and too involved. If we have overstepped the measure, he says, and, at the same time, if our words are obscure and unrefined, we confess that it is quite true. We are indeed incapable of explaining such deep matter in a concise, lucid, and ornate fashion. If, however, there is such a one, or anyone else on that account (*ille vel quis alius*), who knows how to say these things more briefly, better, more clearly and more elegantly, let him be amongst my very best friends, and my sayings be mere food to fire, but his be most good to souls loving and fashioned like God (fol. 85vb).

At the close of his commentary on the *Divine Names* he asks once more indulgence for his shortcomings and inadequacy in translating and expounding this supreme Hierarchy, since in this he lacked the guidance of previous translators and commentators that he had in the *Angelical* and *Ecclesiastical Hierarchies*.[1] He begs for benevolent correction, that whatever is faulty may be set right, any deficiency may be made up, what has erred from the path of truth may be brought back thereunto. After such pleading he significantly concludes: 'Yet in all this none should carp at anything whatever with

---

[1] It is in this sense that I understand the 'derelictus plurimum a precedentibus interpretibus et expositoribus'. See the text, above, p. 56. I follow Franceschini's reading *derelictus* (quoting MS. Florence, Laur. Plut. XIII dext. iii, fol. 247vb). MSS. Merton College 86, fol. 276v, and Dublin, Trinity College 164, fol. 262v, have the difficult reading *derelictis*.

envy or maliciously, nor put it to scorn with ridicule, but forbear with charity my insufficiency.'[1]

Who were Grosseteste's critics we do not know. The phrase *si autem habet ille*, though it may refer to the indefinite *si autem quis* of the preceding passage, seems to point to a particular person. At any rate, we shall not be far wrong if we identify them with the critics of whom he speaks at the opening of the *Angelical Hierarchy*, who, unfamiliar with Greek (*ignari graecae linguae*), claimed none the less to be able to interpret Denis correctly and acutely, and placed themselves above those who were versed in the language. He retorted rather sharply that without a knowledge of Greek it is impossible to penetrate the real and true meaning of the author. Then with fine irony, he added: It may be that sometimes their utterances are correct, but it would be a mere guess and conjecture ('subtiliora divinare et conicere valentes'); their explanations may appear subtle but only to simple sciolists (fol. 2[ra]). Whoever the critics were, they were not in a position to appreciate Grosseteste's work. It was natural that they should find his translation obscure and involved, and his comments lengthy; the philological niceties had no value for them, and his numerous linguistic disquisitions would appear to them utterly out of place in the midst of doctrinal explanations.

That Grosseteste was greatly grieved is plain from his reaction. His words, 'insufficiency' and 'deficiency', are not the usual rhetorical protestations, but genuine and sincere expressions of one whose sensibility has been deeply wounded by caustic criticism. They recall to our mind the pitiful letters he wrote to his sister and to Adam Marsh in 1232 after he had resigned his benefices.[2] Now, as then, he felt very strongly the adverse and sharp censure of an action which in his view was above reproach. We are also reminded of Albert the Great who in his commentaries on Denis castigates without mincing his words those who condemned the use of philosophy in theological speculation.[3]

It must, however, be admitted that the criticism is not entirely groundless, and Grosseteste himself was fully conscious of this fact. His translation is far from running smoothly. Fascinated by the

---

[1] 'Nec quicquam in hiis invide vel malitiose carpat, vel derisorie subsannet, sed caritative mee compatiatur insufficientie.' MS. Merton College 86, fol. 276[va-b].

[2] *Epp.* 43–45, 45–47. See above, p. 10, n. 1, and p. 33.

[3] *Alberti M. Opera Omnia*, ed. Borgnet, xiv. 910; cf. at the end of his commentary on Aristotle's *Politics*, viii. 803–4.

idea of rendering the *mens auctoris* and the *venustas sermonis* of the Greek, he utterly disregarded Latin idiom, and, as Professor Franceschini has rightly remarked, there are passages which contain no more than a sequence of almost unintelligible words.[1] His comments too are somewhat prolix and digressive, and at times confused. Nevertheless, in spite of these defects, his translation has great merits and his comments are invaluable not only for their linguistic content, but particularly for their contribution to philosophical, mystical, and theological thought. It was, perhaps, with an eye on his critics that Nicholas Trivet praised Grosseteste's work with the words, 'libros Dionysii quorum novam translationem perlucide commentavit'. Much has been done, and very well indeed, by Professor Franceschini and his pupils in the philological field, but the doctrinal aspect has not yet received the adequate treatment which it deserves.

The first half of the thirteenth century witnessed a great revival in Dionysian studies. In 1238, one year before Grosseteste set to work on his translation and commentaries, his friend, and perhaps his teacher in Paris, Thomas Gallus, brought to completion his *Extractio*, a kind of paraphrase of Sarracinus's version of Denis. In the University of Paris a Dionysian *corpus* was then compiled containing not only the complete treatises and letters which went under the name of St. Denis the Areopagite, but in addition an apparatus of glosses and commentaries, the results of four centuries of Dionysian study among the Latins, together with the Greek scholiasts.[2] Grosseteste's *corpus* was also a remarkable piece of workmanship; it came, however, rather too late to make any effective contribution to the study of Denis by the great Schoolmen.[3] St. Albert the Great, so eager to turn to profit any new text, was unacquainted with Grosseteste's work. The few citations, which were supposed to come from it, have been found on examination to be later interpolations introduced in the printed editions.[4] Neither St. Bonaventure nor St. Thomas ever made use of it, nor, so far as it is known, did Gerard d'Abbeville or Henry of Ghent. Even in Oxford it made its way very slowly. The Franciscan Richard Rufus of Cornwall, who wrote his commentary on the *Sentences* at Oxford

---

[1] Franceschini, *Rob. Grossatesta*, pp. 77 ff.
[2] H. F. Dondaine, *Le Corpus Dionysien de l'Université de Paris au XIIIe siècle*, Rome, 1953, pp. 20–21.
[3] Dondaine, op. cit., p. 34.
[4] Ibid., pp. 105 ff., 116, n. 128.

in the mid-thirteenth century, quotes Denis from the version of Sarracinus or from the *Extractio* of Vercellensis; the same is true of the Franciscan John Pecham. On the other hand, we may trace citations of both translation and commentaries in such early masters as Thomas of York. More frequent use is found in late thirteenth- and early fourteenth-century Franciscans, in whose library Grosseteste's writings were preserved, such as Roger Marston, William de la Mare, John Duns Scotus, William of Alnwick, and William of Nottingham (minister provincial 1316–30). This influence was not restricted to the Oxford schools; translation and explanations became known by the end of the thirteenth century for instance to Peter John Olivi and to others. Their success gained impetus by the middle of the fourteenth and in the fifteenth centuries, particularly among the mystics. To give only one instance, Rudolph de Biberach in his *De Septem Itineribus Aeternitatis*[1] quotes passage after passage from Grosseteste, who thus becomes everywhere and for all the *Lincolniensis commentator.* Manuscript tradition and printed editions often join together the commentaries of Grosseteste and Thomas Gallus, and posterity rightly bestowed upon them the title of *Expositores* κατ᾽ ἐξοχήν.

Matthew Paris tells us how Grosseteste came into possession in 1242 of a Greek copy of the *Testamenta XII Patriarcharum* (now MS. Ff. i. 24 in the University Library, Cambridge),[2] and how it was rendered into Latin with the assistance of Nicholas the Greek.[3] This text purported to be a version from the Hebrew, and originally an authentic part of the Hebrew Bible. It was believed to contain 'most evident and most beautiful messianic prophecies',[4] and it was thus hailed as a powerful apologia in favour of the Christian religion against the Jews. Hence it is not surprising that it captured the attention and the admiration of all. Vincent of Beauvais, a few years after its publication, inserted extracts from it in his *Speculum Historiale*[5] (1253), and it is the only translation mentioned explicitly, in addition to Denis, by Salimbene and Nicholas Trivet. Its wide

[1] Printed among St. Bonaventure's *Opera Omnia*, ed. Rome, vii. 145–96; Vivès, viii. 393–485; see Vivès's edit., pp. 422, 426, 438, &c.

[2] See on this manuscript Hunt, below, p. 134.

[3] See above, pp. 40, and 55–56.

[4] 'Haec sunt testamenta XII Patriarcharum, in quibus sunt apertissimae atque pulcherrimae prophetiae de Christo, quas transtulit magister Robertus, dictus Grossa Testa, vel Grossum Caput, Lincolniensis episcopus, de Graeco in Latinum.' Paris, MS. Bib. Nat. lat. 2042 (*olim* Colbert 80), fol. 88. Cf. Vincent of Beauvais, below, n. 5.

[5] Vincent of Beauvais, *Speculum Historiale*, I. cxxv (ed. Venetiis, 1591, fol. 16ᵛᵃ).

popularity is shown by the early translations into the vernacular, by numerous manuscripts, and by many printed editions.[1] The translation, as it has already been remarked,[2] runs more smoothly, and the adherence to Greek construction is less apparent than in other versions. Franceschini,[3] however, has rightly pointed out that one should not rely too confidently on Migne[4] or other printed texts, since a collation with the extracts edited by Vincent of Beauvais has made it clear that the original version has been modified and polished.

However popular the translations of the *Testaments of the Twelve Patriarchs* and of Denis may have been, the most important and the most influential of Grosseteste's translations after that of pseudo-Denis was undoubtedly the *Nicomachean Ethics*. What moved him to turn his efforts at translation from the Greek Fathers to Aristotle, we have no means of ascertaining. But whether the change was caused by the severe criticism to which he was subjected, or because he was able to obtain Greek codices containing Aristotelian treatises, it is beyond doubt that he devoted the last extremely busy years of his episcopate to translating Aristotle, or texts that went then under his name.

Grosseteste's work is accurately described by Herman the German, a contemporary and himself an active translator at Toledo, as a more complete version of Aristotle's *Nicomachean Ethics* from the original Greek, accompanied with Greek commentaries and Grosseteste's own *notulae* or glosses. In fact, a partial translation from the Greek, including the first three books, had already appeared before the close of the twelfth century; Books II and III were generally termed *Ethica vetus* and Book I *Ethica nova*. Moreover, fragments of Books VII and VIII have been lately discovered by Mgr. A. Pelzer in MS. Vatican Borghese 108, known now under the designation of *Ethica Borghesiana*.[5] It is also possible, as Dr. Minio-Paluello has tentatively suggested, that there was a complete translation from the Greek, of which the *Ethica vetus*, the *Ethica nova*, and the *Ethica Borghesiana* were originally parts.[6] Further, Herman the German

---

[1] See R. Sinker, *A Descriptive Catalogue of the Editions of the Printed Text of the Versions of the Testamenta XII Patriarcharum*, Cambridge, 1910, and Thomson, *Writings*, pp. 42–44.   [2] See above, p. 55.

[3] Franceschini, *Rob. Grossatesta*, pp. 46–47, n. 3.   [4] *P.G.* ii. 1037–1150.

[5] See *Aristoteles Latinus*, codices descripsit G. Lacombe in societatem operis adsumptis A. Birkenmajer, M. Dulong, A. Franceschini. Rome, 1939, i. 67–71.

[6] 'Note sull'Aristotele latino medievale', vii, *Rivista di Filosofia neo-scolastica*, xliv (1952), 486, n. 3. Dr. Minio-Paluello has reason to believe that the same translator was responsible for the three parts, ibid.

translated from the Arabic in 1240 the *Liber Nicomachiae*, a para-phrase of Averroes's 'middle' commentary, and in 1243 or 1244 the *Summa Alexandrinorum*, which is an Arabic epitome of the ten books of the *Ethics*. So there is point in calling Grosseteste's work 'a more complete version from the Greek'.

He approached his task by revising and correcting with an eye on the Greek those parts which were already translated, just as he had done in his previous translations. But whether he was in possession of a *complete* Latin version, and consequently whether he translated anew, or only revised, the last seven books (with the exception of the Borghesian fragments which he probably had in hand), we shall be in a position to say only if and when a complete text comes to light. In all probability, if there had ever been a 'complete' translation, either it was lost or fell into oblivion. Albert the Great, who between 1244 and 1246 quotes the *Ethica Borghesiana* in his *De Quatuor Coaequaevis*, the *Summa de Bono*, and in the com-mentary on *Sentences*, Books II and III, definitely states that he was not drawing from a complete version but from excerpts: 'Aristoteles in VIII Ethicorum qui *totus* non pervenit ad nos, sed *excerpta* eius vidimus.'[1] His citations correspond exactly to, and do not go beyond, the Borghesian fragments, and, what is still more significant, he seems to have been, with the possible exception of Grosseteste, the only scholar who was familiar with it.[2]

Grosseteste's authorship of the translation of Aristotle's text and of the Greek commentaries with the additional *notulae*, as described by Herman and as preserved in several manuscripts, has been firmly established by two generations of scholars, such as Pelzer,[3] Sir Maurice Powicke,[4] E. Franceschini,[5] S. H. Thomson,[6] and there is no need to labour the point here. About 300 of the *notulae* have now

---

[1] *Alberti Magni Opera Omnia. De Bono.* Monasterii W., 1951, xxviii, tr. III, q.v, a. 2, p. 197; cf. p. 206.

[2] See the important study of Dom O. Lottin, 'Saint Albert le Grand et l'Ethique à Nicomaque', *Aus der Geisteswelt des Mittelalters* (B.G.P.M., Suppl. III. 1), Münster i.W., 1935, pp. 611–26.

[3] A. Pelzer, 'Les Versions latines des ouvrages de morale conservés sous le nom d'Aristote, en usage au XIIIe siècle', *Revue néo-scolastique de philosophie*, xxiii (1921), 336–8, 378–412. A most important work on the whole question of the Latin versions.

[4] F. M. Powicke, *Robert Grosseteste and the Nicomachean Ethics*, Proceedings of the British Academy, xvi, London, 1930.

[5] Franceschini, *Rob. Grossatesta*, pp. 51–56.

[6] Thomson, *Writings*, pp. 65–66, 85–86; and *The 'Notule' of Grosseteste on the Nico-machean Ethics*, Proceedings of the British Academy, xix, London, 1933. See also the Bibliography cited in these works.

been identified. The work was carried out in its tripartite form as a whole and simultaneously, though the text of the *Ethics* was later transcribed by itself, separately from the Greek commentators and from Grosseteste's annotations. He took in hand the work after the completion of Denis. Assuredly, such a vast and arduous undertaking could not have been achieved in a short time, the more so since the bishop had not much leisure at his disposal. It may well be that the task went on for several years. Nor is it conceivable that the text with its threefold matter could have been transcribed in a few weeks or even months. In the light of the evidence in our possession, we may safely say that the complete work was not circulated before 1245–6, and even more probably not before 1246–7.[1]

To render greater assistance to students and to be as complete as possible, Grosseteste compiled a *Summa*, or summary of the contents of the *Ethics*, generally called *Tituli*. Each book is divided into chapters, and the contents of each chapter are condensed in such a fashion as to convey in a concise form the sum and substance of its salient points. These summaries were meant to facilitate the understanding of the text and to help to fix it in the mind. In Grosseteste's circle Adam Marsh supplied with analytical chapter-headings the *De Doctrina Christiana* of St. Augustine and other books;[2] and this same method, though in a more refined form, was later used by Robert Kilwardby in his *Intentiones*, or *Conclusiones* of St. Augustine and other ecclesiastical writers.[3] In addition, Grosseteste translated two short treatises, the *De Virtutibus et Vitiis*, which was then generally ascribed to Aristotle, and the pseudo-Andronicus *De Passionibus*.[4] It was doubtless his intention to furnish students with a full collection of texts necessary for the right understanding of ethics. This

---

[1] The question of the date of the *Ethics* has been fully discussed elsewhere; see 'The Date', pp. 200–9.

[2] See on this topic, Hunt, below, pp. 125–6; and 'Manuscripts containing the Indexing symbols of Robert Grosseteste', *Bodl. Library Record*, iv (1953), pp. 244 ff.

[3] Cf. D. A. Callus, 'The "Tabulae super Originalia Patrum" of Robert Kilwardby, O.P.', *Studia Mediaevalia R. J. Martin*, Bruges, 1948, pp. 243–70; and *Dominican Studies*, ii (1949), 38–45.

[4] Although there is no manuscript evidence for the attribution of this treatise to Grosseteste, Pelzer has suggested that, since it is included in MS. Peterhouse, Cambridge, 116, which contains a full body of Grosseteste's translations, it may very probably be ascribed to him ('Les Versions', p. 323). Franceschini is also disposed to accept Grosseteste's authorship (p. 61, n. 1); but Thomson, *Writings*, pp. 233–4, lists it amongst the doubtful works. L. Tropia has recently brought good reasons in support of its attribution to Grosseteste and has given us a critical edition, see 'La Versione Latina Medievale del ΠΕΡΙ ΠΑΘΩΝ dello Pseudo-Andronico', *Aevum*, xxvi (1952), 97–112.

group of writings is neatly represented in a Cambridge manuscript, Peterhouse 116. As Sir Maurice Powicke puts it, 'it is impossible to resist the conclusion that in the Peterhouse manuscript we have a carefully arranged body of material—summary of contents, text, commentaries, subsidiary texts—originating in the same quarter, and that we are justified in tracing this to the household of Grosseteste'.[1]

The success of the *Ethics*, in striking contrast to his previous versions, was immediate and far-reaching. Its need was certainly long felt. The *Liber Nicomachiae* and the *Summa Alexandrinorum*, though they included the ten books, did not fulfil the masters' expectations. St. Albert was but voicing the pressing demand of the schools when he complained that a complete translation of the *Ethics* was lacking.[2] Grosseteste provided them, with no sparing hand, not only with a full translation, but with a *corpus* of Aristotelian ethics. Its importance was recognized as soon as it appeared. In all probability St. Albert was the first to make use of it. Scarcely two years after its publication, he cites the translation as well as the commentators in the *In Quartum Sententiarum*, completed in 1249, and in a *quaestio* 'On special Justice' (extant in MS. Merton College 283), which he added to his *Summa de Bono*.[3] Furthermore, in his lectures upon the *Ethics* at Cologne (1248–52), taken down by his pupil Thomas Aquinas, he quotes in addition the two supplementary treatises, whilst the *notulae* were used to great advantage and with consummate skill both by him and by Aquinas. About the same time Robert Kilwardby utilized the commentaries in his *De Ortu Scientiarum*,[4] and a little later St. Bonaventure cites the *Summa* or chapter-headings. Grosseteste, it is true, is seldom, if ever, mentioned; his name was soon forgotten, but his work became the common inheritance of all. It opened new horizons to theology, ethics, and sociology, and inaugurated a new era in the study of moral philosophy.

References to a *translatio Lincolniensis*, written in the margins of MS. Vat. lat. 2088 against William of Moerbeke's version of Aristotle's *De Caelo*, led scholars to the conclusion that Grosseteste

---

[1] *Robert Grosseteste*, p. 11.
[2] See above, p. 63.
[3] *Summa de Bono*, ed. cit., pp. 300–7; cf. p. xiii.
[4] *De Ortu Scientiarum*, chaps. xli and following. MS. Balliol College 3, fols. 42[vb] ff. Cf. Pelzer, op. cit., pp. 403–4; F. M. Powicke, *Robert Grosseteste*, p. 20; D. A. Callus, *The 'Tabulae'*, p. 247.

must have translated at least the first two books of this Aristotelian treatise.[1] Further evidence brought to light by Mr. D. J. Allan[2] has shown this inference to be correct. He has established beyond any reasonable doubt that Grosseteste did translate the first two books of the *De Caelo*, and, what is more, that we have it in its entirety for Book II in MS. Balliol College 99; furthermore, that, as was customary with him, he did not content himself with the bare translation of the text, but added to it the commentary of Simplicius and his own explanatory annotations. The Aristotelian text of the Balliol manuscript quoted in Book II, hitherto believed to be Moerbeke's version, is in fact and in every respect identical with the text quoted as 'Lincolniensis' by the marginal annotator of the Vatican manuscript. Grosseteste's authorship of the Balliol text is further proved by the stylistic idiosyncrasy and other characteristics which we associate with his method and technique. Taking into account the references to Book I in the margins of the Vatican text, we may unhesitatingly conclude that it was translated as well, although its full text has not yet come to light. None the less, this version was never finished. We have it once again on the authority of the Vatican marginalia, *Huc usque dominus Robertus*, that it was cut short at the opening of Book III, ch. i (Bekker 299ᵃ 12). With it Grosseteste's career as a translator from the Greek came to a close.

It was a magnificent achievement. Considering the grave responsibilities and the heavy labours involved in the administration of the largest diocese in England, this period must have been for the Bishop of Lincoln one of overwhelming activity. Before 1239 he had already edited the *De Fide Orthodoxa*, the *De Logica*, the *De Haeresibus*, the *Introductio Dogmatum Elementaris* and the *De Hymno Trisagion* of St. John of Damascus, and also the Epistles of St. Ignatius. Between 1239 and 1243 he rendered into Latin and expounded the two *Hierarchies*, the *Divine Names*, and the *Mystical Theology* of pseudo-Denis, to which he added the translation of the *Prologus* and of the *Scholia in Opera Dionysii* attributed to St. Maximus the Confessor. In 1242 appeared the version of the *Testamenta XII Patriarcharum*, followed shortly by the imposing *corpus* of Aristotelian Ethics,

---

[1] The marginalia in the Vatican manuscript were discovered by Mgr. Lacombe, see *Aristoteles Latinus*, pp. 53, 129; Franceschini, *Rob. Grossatesta*, pp. 57–60; Thomson, *Writings*, pp. 66–67.

[2] D. J. Allan, 'Mediaeval Versions of Aristotle, *De Caelo*, and of the commentary of Simplicius', *Mediaeval and Renaissance Studies*, ii (1950), 82–120.

completed not later than 1246-7. The *De Caelo*, left incomplete, was his last work.

It has been truly said that 'it is hard to believe that, in his last very busy years as bishop, when he was wearied by advancing age and harassed by disputes', he could have found opportunity for so many literary occupations. On the other hand, it is equally true that his task was greatly facilitated, not only by his *adiutores* whose assistance though real was mainly oral, nor because a good number of his translations were merely a revision of pre-existing versions, but especially by his skilful working-method; each Greek word or phrase was tabulated with its proper and alternative, or different meaning; grammatical, syntactic, historical, and similar explanations were accurately arranged in such an order as to be at hand whenever they were required. An examination of his translations shows without fail that the same Greek word is consistently rendered by the same Latin equivalent, and the same explanation occurs invariably in different writings wherever the opportunity presents itself. Such and similar methods, whilst lessening in a great measure the fatigue, shortened considerably the time taken by his work. Grosseteste must have been 'the accomplished scholar', methodical, thorough, meticulous in the extreme, furnished with a sound working-system, with his authorities well sifted, classified, indexed, ready to hand. But, above all, his was a work 'of love'; it was the pride and the joy he took in his enterprise that lightened for the most part the weariness of his labours. We have an excellent instance in the letter to the abbot and convent of Bury, where he went for a quiet week, but having come across a Greek work on the monastic life, he spent a day in translating it for their benefit.[1]

It would be idle, perhaps, to speculate why the *De Caelo* was not completed. It is possible, and it seems obvious, that it was interrupted through his last illness and death. It is, however, also possible to surmise that other interests absorbed the very last years of a long and busy life. It would be pleasant to think that his time was devoted to the study and revision of the Hebrew Psalter, the famous *Superscriptio Lincolniensis*, which seems to belong to this period. Aristotle, the Fathers, and the Bible were through all his life the

---

[1] *Ep.* lvii. 173-8. This work is now generally called *De Vita Monachorum*. The Greek original on which it was based has not yet been identified. See Baur, *Die Werke*, pp. 42*-43*; Franceschini, *Rob. Grossatesta*, pp. 46-51; Thomson, *Writings*, pp. 70-71; and Stevenson, pp. 165-7.

absorbing interests in his intellectual activity; this thought pervades
all his writings, but particularly his letters. When as bishop he had
to write to the king or to the cardinals, to the primate or to his fellow
bishops, to his dean and chapter or to Master Martin, the papal
nuncio, he stresses his point with unmistakable delight by citing
side by side with the 'irrefragable authority of Holy Scriptures', the
sacred truth of the Fathers, and the ancient wisdom of the 'Philosopher'.

It is often said that the characteristic note of Oxford thought, as
distinct from that of Paris, consists in a preference for Augustinian-
Platonism; a bent for mathematics and the natural sciences; and a
study of languages. Should this be true, then the best representative
of such tendencies is assuredly Robert Grosseteste. In the eyes of
Roger Bacon he was one of those few privileged and very wise
beings ever to reach that perfection of philosophy known to Solomon,
and after him to Aristotle in his own time, and later to Avicenna.
He attained this eminent distinction and was perfect in all wisdom,
because he set at the basis of philosophy and every science the
knowledge of mathematics. Like Boethius, he was learned in
languages and a great translator. His training, his tendencies, the
undeveloped state of Aristotelianism, led him to give his allegiance
to the Augustinian-Platonic tradition. He strove after Aristotelian
learning, and when he applied mathematics to explain physical
phenomena, he meant to render service to Aristotelian philosophy.

Grosseteste's contribution to the growth of ideas is of great
significance. His influence was wide and lasting, but naturally was
not equally strong in all fields. As teacher of the *artes* he made his
mark by his commentary on the *Posterior Analytics* and by his tracts
on mathematics and optics. These are works which belong to the
history of European thought, and we are gradually learning how
great a contribution Grosseteste made.[1] As a theologian his influence
ran on different lines from that of his Parisian contemporaries. He
left no important work on speculative theology, and his immediate
influence as teacher of Biblical studies was confined to a limited
circle.[2] It was only a few short pieces of pastoral theology, especially
the *Templum Domini*, which circulated in England widely and continuously until the end of the fifteenth century. It was by his
translations that he made his most fruitful and in the end most
influential contribution to theological study. We have seen, for

[1] See Crombie, below, pp. 98-116.   [2] See Smalley, below, pp. 70-97.

instance, how his teaching on mystical theology as expounded in his commentaries on pseudo-Denis, applied first by him in his conception of Church and State and their intimate relationship,[1] exerted beneficial influence upon the Flemish, German, and Austrian mystical schools in the fourteenth and fifteenth centuries. The steps by which his other theological works, the *Dicta*, the Sermons, and certain of the letters achieved wide popularity in the fourteenth and fifteenth centuries are not yet clear. Just as Grosseteste himself never ceased to grow in intellectual stature, so his posthumous fame grew in the Middle Ages. His linguistic attainments, minimized by Roger Bacon and despised by the humanists, but highly praised by Oxford and Paris masters, such as John Tyssington and Gerson,[2] are recognized even by modern scholars[3] as great not only for his age but for every age. Finally, his Augustinian-Platonic ideas were found both congenial and acceptable among Oxford Franciscans.

Robert Grosseteste, one of the greatest glories of the University of Oxford, and her first chancellor in the crucial years of her formation, hailed in late thirteenth-century Paris by Godfrey of Fontaines as 'a man great in sanctity of life and splendour of doctrine',[4] the *Lincolniensis*[5] of the Schools and 'The great clerk Grostest' in English literature, deserves an honourable place in the history of thought. Great with all the marks of true greatness, he gave a powerful impetus in every department of intellectual activity in which he himself excelled, and left behind him a tradition of learning which was destined to grow, increase, and deepen throughout the centuries.

D. A. CALLUS, O.P.

---

[1] See Pantin, below, pp. 178-215.

[2] Tyssington's saying is a commonplace: 'Expone tu Graecum, si melius noveris quam Lincolniensis' (*Fasciculus Zizaniorum*, p. 152). For Gerson cf. A. Combes, *Jean Gerson commentateur Dionysien*, Paris, 1940, p. 200, n. 5.

[3] Cf. A. Pelzer, 'Les Versions latines', pp. 389-94; S. Troilo, *Due Traduttori dell'Etica Nicomachea: Roberto di Lincoln e Leonardo Bruni* (Atti del R. Istituto Veneto di Scienze, Lettere, Arti, xci), 1932, pp. 275-305; Franceschini, *Rob. Grossatesta, passim*.

[4] *Le Huitième Quodlibet de Godefroid de Fontaines*, ed. J. Hoffmans (Les Philosophes Belges, iv. i), Louvain, 1924, p. 94.

[5] For Salimbene Grosseteste is 'unus de maioribus clericis de mundo', but for the schools he is *Lincolniensis, par excellence*, although William de Montibus was sometimes called also *Lincolniensis*; see, for example, a note in MS. Peterhouse, Cambridge, 255 (after fol. 34), edited by De Ghellinck, *Le Mouvement théologique au XIIe siècle*, pp. 389-90, n. 2: 'Sed quando allegatur alicubi *Lincoln*. absolute, innuitur Robertus grossum caput, qui fuit precipuus omnium.'

The Biblical Scholar

THE usual way to treat a subject of this kind is first to describe the man's writings and then to discuss their influence on his successors. Grosseteste is a law unto himself. Individual and untypical, he does not fit into any pattern. Our knowledge of his Biblical scholarship depends to a surprising extent on a revival of interest in him in the later Middle Ages. He meant little in the thirteenth century, but much to Wyclif and Gascoigne and presumably to students of the fourteenth and fifteenth centuries who had his works copied. In his case, therefore, one must see the beginning in the light of the end. One must keep the major problem before one, while tackling the host of minor technical problems that tease the student of Grossetestiana. When we ask, of each work separately, what its nature is and when it was written, we must add the question 'who read it?' The answer to this last question should give us a sketch of Grosseteste's medieval public. Then we shall examine the contents in the light of that public. We shall try to answer the question why he failed in one age and succeeded in another, wherein lay his appeal to later medieval scholars. Next we shall look at him with modern eyes to see what interest he has for present-day students. The last question to be answered is: 'What place does Grosseteste fill in the whole history of scholarship?'

We have notes or comments by Grosseteste on the *Hexaemeron* (the six days of creation), the first hundred Psalms, the Gospels, and the Pauline Epistles, the last in a fragmentary state apart from a commentary on Galatians. There are also two treatises which deal with Biblical subjects, the *De Decem Mandatis* and the *De Cessatione Legalium*.[1]

Two overlapping stages in his career may help to put the Biblical

[1] My information, unless another source is mentioned, comes from two fundamental studies, Thomson, *Writings*, and Callus, 'Oxford Career', pp. 42–72. Three items (15, 17, 19 in his list) ascribed to Grosseteste by Thomson have to be rejected. 15 and 19, glosses on Wisdom, on Ecclesiasticus, and on the *Great Gloss* by Peter Lombard on the Psalter, were ascribed to him on palaeographical evidence. Further study of Grosseteste's handwriting has made possible a more critical use of it in establishing authenticity. 17, a commentary on Romans, is not by Grosseteste, but only contains a quotation from him, see below, p. 76. Thomson himself is rather doubtful about 85, the *Correctorium totius Biblie*, a guide to the pronunciation and spelling of Biblical words. It seems better to omit the *Correctorium* here, while leaving the question of its authenticity open.

works in order, his lectorship to the Franciscans, 1229/30 to 1235, and his study of Greek, which seems to have begun in the years 1231-5, and which he continued as Bishop of Lincoln. His lectorship would oblige him to expound the Bible. His choice of books for study, the *Hexaemeron*, Psalter, and Pauline Epistles, gives the impression that his notes and commentaries go back to his lectorship and that they sprang from his teaching duties. The Psalter and the Pauline Epistles held a favoured place in medieval teaching for liturgical and theological reasons. The *Hexaemeron* came next to the Psalter as a favourite in the Old Testament, since it raised problems of philosophy and cosmology. It was the custom at Paris, and probably also at Oxford, for the regent-master in theology to run lecture courses on a book of the Old and a book of the New Testament concurrently. Neatly as they agree with this scheme, not one of his works belongs to the easily recognizable class of *reportationes* (lecture notes taken by students and circulated with or without revision by the master). What became of Grosseteste's *reportationes*, if they ever existed, we do not know. It is a coincidence that no lectures of Adam Marsh have survived, although he had almost as high a reputation for learning as Grosseteste.[1] The early Franciscan school at Oxford, as Eccleston's chronicle describes it, was run in a makeshift way. The friars' poverty may have precluded a proper system of reporting and copying.

Fortunately Grosseteste's own papers remained, when his lectures were either unreported or lost. He was one of those scholars who make copious notes and afterwards work them into literary form. He went on writing as bishop. A busy man will seldom succeed in writing up all his notes and his marginalia; so it was with Grosseteste. William of Alnwick in the early fourteenth century remarked that his writings fell into two classes, the rough notes on one hand, the finished, authoritative product on the other.[2] Hence any one of his scriptural works may spill over from his professorship into his episcopate. We shall get more guidance in dating them from the stages of his progress in Greek. A work which shows no Greek influence at all is likely to derive from his early teaching period.

Early works on this assumption are the notes on St. Paul and on Psalms i–lxxix and the *Moralitates in Evangelia*. The *Moralitates* will

[1] D. L. Douie, 'Adam de Marisco, an English Franciscan', *The Durham University Journal*, xxxii (1940), 90.
[2] Callus, 'Oxford Career', pp. 46, 57.

be considered first: it bears the clearest marks of its classroom origin and it suggests no interest in Greek. The medieval *moralitates* or *moralia* had its prototype in St. Gregory's *Moralia in Iob*. It became a common literary genre; we have scores of examples from the twelfth and thirteenth centuries. The *moralitates* generally originated in some university lecture course. The master would expound the text to his pupils according to the literal and the spiritual sense (allegorical or moral). The spiritual exposition would then be excerpted from his commentary and copied and circulated separately. It served a double purpose, providing both an ethical and religious training for the student and a stock of themes which he would use when he was promoted to teaching and preaching in his turn. *Moralitates* were homiletic in content, resembling the sermons for which they supplied material.[1] Grosseteste's *Moralitates in Evangelia* conforms to type. It consists of lectures, not sermons. Comparison with a set of real sermons on the Gospels and Epistles for the year by an older contemporary, John of Abbeville,[2] which became very popular, will bring out the difference in form. John of Abbeville says in his preface that he is writing *rudibus rudi sermone*, not for scholars.[3] He is always referring to 'this Sunday' or to 'today's feast'. He gives a simple address on the prescribed passage. Grosseteste, on the other hand, goes straight through the text of the Gospels.

Eccleston, describing Grosseteste's lectures to the friars at Oxford, says: 'Under him, within a very short time, they made incalculable progress both in scholastic discussion and in subtle moralities suitable for preaching.' Dr. Callus has pointed out that the *Moralitates in Evangelia* 'fits Eccleston's description fairly well. There is such a wealth of subtle moralities and of *exempla* suitable for preaching that it counterbalances abundantly the scantiness of scholastic discussion.' The absence of scholastic discussion need not surprise us, since this belonged to the literal exposition of the text. Grosseteste's literal exposition of the Gospels has disappeared, as often happened, leaving only the *Moralitates*. There has also been a slight reworking of the original material. Grosseteste or perhaps an editor has divided

---

[1] B. Smalley, 'Robert Bacon'.
[2] Ibid., pp. 4–7.
[3] MS. Brit. Mus. Royal 2 E. ix, fol. 1ʳ. See P. Glorieux, *Répertoire des maîtres en théologie de Paris au XIII*ᵉ *siècle* (Paris, 1933–4), no. 113a, for a list of manuscript copies of the *Sermones de tempore* of John of Abbeville.

the *Moralitates* into four parts, each part subdivided into chapters according to the subject matter. The exposition of John i. 1, for instance, forms a chapter headed 'De verbo Dei et de verbo hominis'. A prologue, which may have been extracted from a prologue to a complete commentary on the Gospels, states that the whole work deals with virtues and vices. The content typifies the genre. The author scolds the various ranks of society for their respective sins. We see how a technique of exegesis, the spiritual exposition, which began as an attempt to transform the apparently ridiculous into the sublime, ended by doing the opposite. Grosseteste's comment on the words of the Fourth Gospel, *In him was life* (i. 4), is an attack on women's use of make-up![1]

The *Moralitates* has most interest as a measure of Grosseteste's influence at Oxford. How far was it used by later Oxford writers on the Gospels? One would expect to find it quoted, if anywhere, in 'William of Nottingham on Clement of Lanthony'. Clement of Lanthony, who died about 1190, composed a Gospel harmony which many regarded as the best of its kind. Friar William of Nottingham, a friend and possibly a pupil of Grosseteste, had the harmony, with Clement's long commentary on it, copied for the benefit of the friars in his province. Then his namesake, Friar William of Nottingham II, who was lector at Oxford about 1312, made a commentary on the harmony of Clement which became a classic.[2] This book had taken shape in the Franciscan school at Oxford. The choice of Clement's harmony as a basis went back to the provincialate of William of Nottingham I, 1240–54. Yet the commentary of William of Nottingham II does not seem to contain any trace of quotations from the *Moralitates*. William of Nottingham II knew Grosseteste as a translator of pseudo-Dionysius; so it is all the more surprising that he did not use the *Moralitates in Evangelia*. Did Grosseteste suggest the choice of Clement's harmony to William of Nottingham I? We draw a blank even here. Grosseteste based his commentary on the Gospels on a harmony; he is expounding some kind of conflated text, not each Gospel separately. But the harmony is not Clement's.[3]

---

[1] MS. Lincoln College lat. 79, fol. 12ᵛ.

[2] B. Smalley, 'Which William of Nottingham?' *Mediaeval and Renaissance Studies*, iii (1954).

[3] The sequence of events is quite different in Grosseteste's *Moralitates* and in Clement's harmony. Grosseteste may have been using the harmony of Zachary of Besançon, which was composed about 1150–2, *P.L.* clxxxvi. 11–620. See D. Van de Eynde on Zachary's identity and dates, 'Les *Magistri* du Commentaire "Unum ex

One turns next to Wyclif's university lectures on the Gospels. He quotes the *Dicta Lincolniensis* frequently,[1] but not the *Moralitates*. It seems clear, therefore, that the *Moralitates* failed to establish itself as a standard text in the schools. Only one quotation is known and that belongs to the early fifteenth century. Alexander Carpenter in his *Destructorium Viciorum* quotes an *exemplum* or moral story from 'Lincolniensis super evangelia', giving an exact reference to the part and chapter and copying verbally.[2] The story tells of a kind lady who received a leper against her husband's orders and was rewarded by a miracle. It makes its first known appearance in the sermons of James of Vitry, a contemporary of Grosseteste, whence it passes into the stock collections of *exempla*.[3] Carpenter must have admired Grosseteste, since he quotes extensively from other writings, and he evidently felt that the bishop's authority would give weight to a familiar tale.[4]

The manuscript tradition of the *Moralitates* corroborates the evidence of the quotations. We have two thirteenth- and two fifteenth-century copies. The last two witness to a post-Wyclif cult of Grosseteste, which led to a revival of interest in his lesser-known commentaries. The lack of both quotations and manuscripts from the fourteenth century suggests a long period of neglect.

Thomas Gascoigne, the scholarly Oxford chancellor of the mid-fifteenth century,[5] tells us most of what is known about Grosseteste on the Pauline Epistles. Gascoigne saw and used some notes which

quatuor" de Zacharias Chrysopolitanus', *Antonianum*, xxiii (1948), 1–32, 181–220. Grosseteste follows the same order as Zachary, but there were other harmonies and the relationship between them has yet to be studied.

[1] B. Smalley, 'John Wyclif's *Postilla super totam Bibliam*', *Bodleian Library Record*, iv (1953), 198.

[2] *Destructorium Viciorum*, part iv, cap. 2: 'Istud intelligens quedam nobilis domina de qua narrat Lincolniensis super evangelia, parte iii, capitulo xxxv, quod totis visceribus propter amorem Dei pauperes diligebat infirmos. . . .'; MS. Lincoln College lat. 79, fol. 134ᵛ: 'Quedam matrona in Gallia leprosos totis visceribus diligebat. . . .' The rest of the quotation is verbal. On Alexander Carpenter see G. R. Owst, *The Destructorium Viciorum of Alexander Carpenter* (London, S.P.C.K., 1952). Carpenter was said to be 'of Oxford', but we have no records of him there.

[3] See J. Th. Welter, *Le* Speculum Laicorum, Paris, 1914, pp. 64, 136; *La* Tabula Exemplorum, Paris, 1926, pp. 33, 110. Where the story is not anonymous it is ascribed to James of Vitry, who certainly used it; see T. F. Crane, *The* Exempla *of Jacques de Vitry*, London, 1890, pp. 44–45, 174–5. Grosseteste gives a few individual details in his version of the tale.

[4] There may be other quotations from the *Moralitates* in the *Destructorium Viciorum*. It is a vast and unindexed work. I have only looked through the first half of it.

[5] W. Pronger, 'Thomas Gascoigne', *English Historical Review*, liii (1938), 606–26; liv (1939), 20–37.

Grosseteste had written in the margins of a glossed copy of St. Paul. This manuscript, studied by Gascoigne in the library of the Friars Minor at Oxford, must have corresponded to a modern interleaved book. The Bible text with its Gloss (the *Glossa Ordinaria*) had been spaced in such a way as to leave ample margins for Grosseteste to make his annotations. He annotated part of the text, but not all, and certain passages of the Gloss, but not all. Gascoigne calls the exposition *particularis*, because it dealt with disjointed passages, *particulae*. He also uses the adjective *particulariter* when describing it: '. . . which exposition of the lord bishop of Lincoln is not on the text of the apostle but particularly on diverse texts of the apostle, and he also expounds diverse phrases of the common gloss or common exposition on the epistles of St. Paul.'[1] Gascoigne quotes Grosseteste's notes so copiously that much of the commentary could be reconstructed from his *De Veritatibus Collectis*. The notes, as quoted by Gascoigne, show no evidence of an interest in Greek, though perhaps the selection may be misleading.

The autograph copy described by Gascoigne has now disappeared. We know that Grosseteste wrote up his notes on at least one of the Epistles into a proper commentary. He alludes twice to his 'little exposition' of Galatians in the *De Cessatione Legalium*.[2] We have one fifteenth-century copy of this commentary in MS. Magdalen College 57. Dr. Callus has verified the ascription to Grosseteste by identifying Gascoigne's quotations from Grosseteste on Galatians. It looks as though he delivered this commentary as lectures in the schools. It contains a formula which was current in the classroom: after raising a series of questions, he says that it will be better to treat them in disputation than in lecturing and expounding.[3] By the time he was working up his notes on Galatians his Greek studies had begun. He compares the Latin Vulgate text with the Greek, referring specifically to a Greek codex. He also mentions an *expositor grecus*.[4] The term 'expositor' is technical. It meant a commentary, either composite or by a single author, which a master would use as

---

[1] MS. Lincoln College 118, p. 10. On the *Gloss* see B. Smalley, *Study of the Bible*, pp. 52–56, 215–19, 228–30, 271.

[2] MS. Bodl. lat. th. c. 17 (to be referred to henceforward as B), fols. 167vb, 185va. The first cross-reference is an allusion to reasons adduced for the solving of the ceremonial precepts of the Old Law by Christ, on Gal. ii. 15–21, the second to Grosseteste's views on the discussion between Jerome and Augustine on the Antioch controversy, on Gal. ii. 1–14: MS. Magdalen College 57, fols. 5^v–8^v.

[3] Ibid., fol. 6^v.

[4] Ibid., fol. 13^r.

his reference book when he lectured on Scripture.[1] It seems likely that Grosseteste was using a *catena* or chain of extracts from the Greek Fathers. His Greek *expositor* consisted of the text plus a commentary. Similarly, when he translated the *Ethics* he translated a commentary as well as the text.

We have one quotation of Grosseteste on Romans from the thirteenth century. An anonymous commentary on Romans v-xvi in the compilation that forms MS. Gonville and Caius College 439, written in an English hand about the middle of the thirteenth century, has 'Lincolniensis' in the margin beside the comment on Rom. vi. 12. The commentary consists mainly of a chain of quotations from authors whose names are noted in the margin. Grosseteste seems to be the only contemporary mentioned. Unluckily Gascoigne does not quote him on this particular text of Romans; so we do not know whether the unknown commentator was using the notes written by Grosseteste in the margin of his glossed copy of the Epistles or some other record of his teaching.[2] Hence nothing survives of Grosseteste's work on St. Paul, save this one quotation, Gascoigne's selection from his notes, and the fifteenth-century copy of his commentary on Galatians.

The commentary on Psalms i–c falls into two parts. The scribes of the two manuscripts that we possess have not distinguished them, but they are quite different in character. The commentary on Psalms i–lxxix belongs to the earliest years of Grosseteste's teaching since the prologue and comments on the first psalms are also found in a Durham collection, MS. A. III. 12, which has been dated about 1231. The prologue has also been used in an early thirteenth-century set of notes to Peter Lombard's *Magna Glosatura* on the Psalter in MS. Bodl. e. Mus. 15. This part of the commentary suggests a transcript of notes on *particulae*, of the type described by Gascoigne

---

[1] G. Paré, A. Brunet, P. Tremblay, *La Renaissance du XIIe siècle*, Paris–Ottawa, 1933, pp. 230–1.

[2] The Librarian of Gonville and Caius College very kindly allowed me to use the manuscript in Bodley. A comparison of Gascoigne's copious quotations from Grosseteste on Romans and parallel passages in this anonymous commentary showed no similarity at all. Grosseteste cannot have been the author, as used to be thought. Only the few lines marked 'Lincolniensis' can be ascribed to him. Dr. Callus has given a short description of the commentary, 'Oxford Career', pp. 54, 63–64. He shows that the master was addressing 'a mixed audience of seculars and religious' in the schools; we do not know where. Perhaps it represents a lecture by Adam Marsh or another of the earliest Franciscan masters at Oxford. Dr. Callus had doubts about the authenticity of this commentary and suggested that I should investigate it.

for the Pauline Epistles. A hasty study of it leaves the impression
that it is typical of lectures given on the Psalter in the late twelfth
and early thirteenth centuries at Paris. I have not been able to find
Grosseteste's basic source nor does he resemble his friend Edmund
Rich in his commentary on the Psalter.[1] A more thorough study
might be very rewarding. If we could discover the basic source, we
would probably also have discovered the identity of Grosseteste's
master in theology. So many commentaries on the Psalter have
survived from the period of his student days that the quest would
be quite a hopeful one.

The exposition becomes fuller after Psalm lxxix and the commentator begins to use Greek sources. Just as he wrote up a part
of his notes on St. Paul, so he may have written up a part of his
notes on the Psalter. In each case he did so in the light of his new
knowledge. He evidently had a *catena* of Greek Fathers as well as the
LXX and he may have translated into Latin himself as he wrote.[2]
The importance of his quotations from Greek may be gauged from
the fact that a great modern patristic scholar is studying them as
evidence for the originals.[3] As yet Grosseteste's sources are limited
in number and his attitude to them is passive; he transcribes rather
than discusses. This has led modern scholars to date the commentary
on Psalms lxxx–c to the years 1231–5, the early stage of his Greek
studies.

There are two surviving manuscripts of the commentary on
Psalms i–c; both are English. One of them, now at Bologna, was
copied from an exemplar at Oxford about 1325; the other, which
belongs to Eton College, is fifteenth century. Gascoigne saw two
manuscripts of it in the Franciscan library at Oxford, one autograph, the other with an ascription to Grosseteste. No one so far has
compared Gascoigne's quotations with the existing manuscripts.
Another problem which has still to be solved is the relation between
the Psalter commentary and the *Dicta*, a collection of edifying
thoughts and themes for sermons made by Grosseteste.

We shall break our chronological order for a moment to describe
his other work on the Psalter. He had a new Latin translation from
the Hebrew written between the lines of a Hebrew Psalter, so that

[1] B. Smalley, 'Robert Bacon', p. 4.
[2] M. R. James, 'Robert Grosseteste on the Psalms', *J.T.S.* xxiii (1922), 181–5.
[3] His Eminence Cardinal G. Mercati, Librarian of the Vatican, told me that he was
using the Bologna manuscript of Grosseteste on Psalms lxxx–c for this purpose when
I visited the Library in 1949.

the Latin word should correspond exactly with its Hebrew equivalent. A prologue in our earliest manuscript of this new version explains its purpose and compares certain texts of the Latin and Hebrew. This prologue may well have been written by Grosseteste or at least inspired by him. The translation was probably organized during his episcopate, at a time when he had facilities for patronizing scholars and for arranging team-work. He does not refer to it in any of his writings, Biblical or otherwise, as far as is known. This makes it likely that Hebrew studies came late in his career. Further investigation of the manuscripts may decide whether he was responsible for a similar translation of other Old Testament books found in English libraries.

Two thirteenth-century copies of the Hebrew–Latin Psalter survive and others are known from quotations. Two English scholars of the early fourteenth century, Nicholas Trivet O.P. and Henry Cossey O.F.M., knew and used the new translation.[1]

The commentary on the *Hexaemeron* takes us to the end of Grosseteste's lectorship or even to the earliest years of his episcopate. It is a straightforward commentary of the full, academic type, containing both literal and spiritual exposition of the text and beginning with an author's prologue, followed by his commentary on the prologues of St. Jerome. But the form is literary. Grosseteste divides it into sections and addresses his reader,[2] as he would not do if he were lecturing instead of writing. This again suggests a working up of his notes. A study of his Greek sources by Fr. Muckle and Dr. Callus has made it fairly certain that he was working either in or soon after 1235. His more critical approach to them indicates a rather later stage in his development than either the commentary on Galatians or that on Psalms lxxx–c. It seems that Grosseteste was just getting into his stride as a Greek scholar and exegete when he was promoted to Lincoln. A few more years at Oxford might have resulted in mature and exciting work. As it was, he learned Greek too late in his teaching career to use it fully in his scriptural commentaries. His *Hexaemeron* gives a tantalizing vision of what we have missed. We see him supplementing the traditional Latin commentators by new Christian sources on the one hand, new pagan sources on the other. He used Greek Fathers in existing translations,

---

[1] Smalley, *Study of the Bible*, pp. 342–7.
[2] B, fol. 200rb: 'Unde noverit lector huius scientie . . .'; fol. 203vb: '. . . diligentie lectoris ad presens relinquimus . . .'.

with one possible exception; but this material, though not quite unknown to contemporaries, needed popularizing; it had not yet been applied to the text. Stephen Langton, for example, teaching at Paris about 1180 to 1206, had used only the Latin Fathers in his lectures on Genesis, apart from such very old translations as Origen in the Gloss. Grosseteste does not only transcribe his sources. He claims to add something of his own, which he means to be suggestive, not dogmatic, and his original comments, though rare, are interesting.[1] The freshness of his sources compelled him to some kind of mental effort. Differences of opinion in Greek and Latin tradition, principally in St. Basil as opposed to St. Augustine, imposed comparison and discussion. He had strong views of his own on certain questions and had to reconcile them with his authorities.

Even graver problems arose for the Christian scholar from the reception of new pagan sources. Aristotle's *Libri naturales*, with their Jewish and Arabic commentators, presented a view of the universe which clashed fundamentally with Scripture. In the early stages of reception Latin scholars still hoped to harmonize their pagan and Christian authors. The incompatibility of the two bodies of doctrine took some time to come into the open.[2] Grosseteste is more honest and uncompromising than many of his contemporaries. He takes the bull by the horns and contrasts as sharply as possible the ancient philosophers' view that matter was eternal with the Christian belief in creation *ex nihilo*. One cannot water down the philosophers, he says, nor pretend that Aristotle was a Christian. Those who christianize Aristotle only make themselves heretics. Elsewhere he calls the philosophers' theories mere cobwebs.[3]

The *Hexaemeron* attracts modern scholars more than any other Biblical work by Grosseteste: his study of Greek is more serious and his commentary illustrates the reception of new ideas on cosmology. Hence the prologue and a few extracts have been edited.[4]

[1] B, fol. 207va-b: 'Volo autem sciri quod si que(dam) non ex auctenticis verbis scribendo intersero, non enuntiativo modo eadem profero, sed exercitii loco auditoribus intimo, coniecturis quibusdam atque indiciis veritatis persequens vestigia.' Grosseteste has shown his reverence for authority by putting even this modest disclaimer into the words of St. Gregory of Nyssa in the *De Creatione Hominis* (*P.L.* lxvii. 375). He does not mention the name here, but acknowledges his source when quoting the same passage in the *De Cessatione Legalium*, B, fol. 183rb: '. . . unde Gregorius Nisenus ait de se . . .'.
[2] F. Van Steenberghen, *Siger de Brabant*, Louvain, 1942, ii. 357–497.
[3] B, fol. 205ra. Grosseteste borrowed the simile from St. Ambrose on the *Hexaemeron*, i. 7, *C.S.E.L.* xxxii. 6.
[4] G. B. Phelan, 'An unedited Text of Robert Grosseteste on the Subject-matter of

In the Middle Ages, too, it was the best known of his Biblical commentaries. We possess one thirteenth-century copy with notes in his own hand; they include some words of Greek, which are written in Greek letters. This manuscript has only just come to light. It had been unknown to modern scholarship until the Bodleian Library acquired it in 1947.[1] Apart from this one manuscript, closely associated with the author, we have only much later copies, three of the fourteenth, two of the fifteenth centuries. Four of the five are English. The fifth is at Prague, which had many ties with England in the later Middle Ages. Quotations from Grosseteste on the *Hexaemeron* begin in the early fourteenth century. The Paris master, Henry of Ghent, does not mention or quote him in his lectures on the *Hexaemeron*, given between 1276 and 1293.[2] Grosseteste would have been relevant to his work, since Henry set out to make a systematic comparison between pagan philosophy and Christian teaching on Genesis. William of Alnwick, on the other hand, mentions Grosseteste on the *Hexaemeron* in the early fourteenth century.[3] Duns Scotus quotes from the prologue.[4] Wyclif knew the inside of the book; he quotes Grosseteste's definition of man from his comment on the sixth day of creation,[5] and in another place a passage from the spiritual exposition.[6]

We turn next to the Biblical treatises. They are both of them in literary form. They could not have derived from lecture notes and they show no evidence of an interest in Greek, which would hardly have been relevant to their purpose. It is difficult to date them even

Theology', *Revue néoscolastique*, xxxvi (1934), supplement dedicated to M. de Wulf, pp. 172–80; D. E. Sharp, *Franciscan Philosophy at Oxford in the Thirteenth Century*, Oxford, 1930, pp. 15–46; J. T. Muckle, 'The *Hexaemeron* of Robert Grosseteste', *Mediaeval Studies*, vi (1944), 151–74; 'Robert Grosseteste's Use of Greek Sources', *Mediaevalia et Humanistica*, iii (1945), 33–48.

[1] *Bodleian Library Record*, ii (1941–9), 226–7. It also contains Grosseteste's *De Cessatione Legalium*. There are two parts bound together. Fols. 1–115 contain treatises by William of Auvergne and belonged to Roger de Plimpt(on), rector of Enbourne, Berks., 'perhaps to be identified with the Roger de Plumpton, who was proctor of the University of Oxford in 1267'. There is no evidence for the history of the second part of the volume. The Bodleian Library bought it at Sotheby's, 28 Oct. 1947. It had come from Naworth Castle.

[2] Smalley, 'A Commentary on the *Hexaemeron* by Henry of Ghent', *Recherches de Théologie ancienne et médiévale*, xx (1953), 60–101.

[3] Callus, 'Oxford Career', p. 46.

[4] *Ioannis Duns Scoti Opera Omnia*, Rome, 1950, i. 119. See Phelan, op. cit.

[5] *De Benedicta Incarnatione*, ed. E. Harris, London, 1886, p. 128.

[6] Smalley, 'John Wyclif's *Postilla super totam Bibliam*', *Bodleian Library Record*, iv (1953), 198.

approximately. We do not know whether Grosseteste intended them to go together, though they often pair in the manuscripts.

The title of the *De Cessatione Legalium* has given rise to misunderstanding. Matthew Paris tells us that Grosseteste, when Bishop of Lincoln, translated the *Testaments of the Twelve Patriarchs* from Greek into Latin 'in support of the Christian faith and for the greater confounding of the Jews'.[1] This suggested the idea that the *De Cessatione Legalium* also had a missionary purpose. The next step was to connect it with the plan of 1231 for founding a home for Jewish converts. And so the treatise has been firmly ascribed to the year 1231.[2] A more careful reading puts it in a different perspective. It contains one reference to contemporary Jews towards the end in a subordinate clause.[3] Grosseteste wrote for the student rather than the missionary. A manual of theology of the period would include a section headed *De Cessatione Legalium* or *Quando circumcisio amisit vim suam* or words to that effect.[4] Here would be discussed the reasons why the ceremonial precepts of the Old Law ceased to be binding and the precise moment when they were superseded by the New Law. Grosseteste took his theme from a contemporary sentence-book or *Summa* and vastly elaborated the argument. It was not 'the Jewish problem' that fascinated him, but the mentality of Judeo-Christians in the apostolic era. The Epistle to Galatians must have roused his interest in the subject; he refers back to his commentary on Galatians on this very point. The *De Cessatione Legalium* is therefore less topical than used to be thought. It compensates for loss of interest in this respect by showing us Grosseteste's mind at work on problems of Biblical history that exercised him continuously. The date must be rather later than 1231. The *terminus post quem* is the commentary on Galatians, which, as we have seen, belongs to the period 1231–5. The *terminus ante quem* is indicated by a quotation

---

[1] *Chron. Mai.*, s.a. 1242, iv. 233.

[2] Stevenson thought that 'the primary object of the work' was 'to supply, in a connected and closely reasoned form, material which might be used in controversy with the Jews'; it was a 'thirteenth-century Epistle to the Hebrews'. His references to Matthew Paris in support of his statements send us to passages where Matthew Paris mentions neither Grosseteste nor the *De Cessatione Legalium*; see Stevenson, pp. 104–5. Grosseteste's letter to the Countess of Winchester advising her on the treatment of the Jews on her estates (*Ep.* 5) encouraged the belief that Grosseteste was preoccupied with 'the Jewish question'.

[3] B, fol. 184vb. Grosseteste is arguing that to observe the legal ceremonies under the Christian dispensation would imply the expectation of a new Messias, 'as the infidel Jews still do'.

[4] See, for example, the *Sentences* of Peter Lombard, lib. iv, dist. iii, cap. 8.

from the *De Ecclesiastica Hierarchia* according to the translation of John the Scot. Grosseteste would have used his own translation had it been ready. This belongs to the years 1239–43.[1] The *De Cessatione Legalium* would fit into the end of his lectorship very well.

The Decalogue also had its place in the chapter-headings of a medieval *Summa theologica*. From there it penetrated into more popular works. Ability to explain the Commandments to his flock was part of the minimum required of a parish priest. Grosseteste himself as bishop republished an earlier diocesan statute:

> Since observance of the Decalogue is necessary to the salvation of souls, we exhort you in the Lord, firmly enjoining that every pastor of souls and every parish priest shall know the Decalogue, that is the Ten Commandments of the Law of Moses, and shall frequently preach on them and expound them to the people in his charge.[2]

So scholars of the thirteenth century were multiplying popular manuals, intended to help the less educated parish clergy. The Oxford Dominican, Simon of Hinton, for instance, explained the Decalogue twice, the first time in an academic treatise, which may have been planned as part of a *Summa theologica*, the second time in a short and simple *exposé*, which became popular under the title *Summa Iuniorum*.[3] The *De Decem Mandatis* must have been written for just this purpose. It is less speculative and more practical than the *De Cessatione Legalium*. The author shows himself anxious to combat superstition, about the new moon for example: some people, when they see the new moon, bow to it, bless themselves, say the Lord's Prayer, turn round thrice and kiss the first person they meet, thinking that this will ward off danger for the month.[4] He offers

---

[1] B, fol. 187[va]: 'Dionisius quoque in libro secundo ierarchiarum ait: pulchre mundo post antiquiorem traditionem novum testamentum predicatur, divina et ierarchia ordinatione illud extimo declarante quod ipsa quidem dixit futuras Iesu divinas operationes. Hoc vero illud perficit.' This corresponds verbally with John the Scot (*P.L.* cxxii. 1083), the only two exceptions are *aestimo* for *ex(is)timo* and *quomodo* for *quod*. Grosseteste's version has *convenienter* for *pulchre*, *ostendente* for *declarante*, *quod hec quid(em)* for *quod ipsa quidem*, and *perfecit* for *perficit* (MS. Lincoln College 101, fol. 109[v]). On the date of Grosseteste's translations see Callus, 'The date', *R.T.A.M.* xiv (1947), 186–210. There is a quotation from the *De Fide Orthodoxa*, iv. 6 on fol. 176[va] (cf. *P.G.* xciv. 1111); but unfortunately it is not exact enough to show whether Grosseteste was using the translation of Burgundio of Pisa or his own.

[2] *Ep.* 52, 155. See C. R. Cheney, *English Synodalia of the Thirteenth Century*, Oxford, 1941, chap. v.

[3] Smalley, 'The *Quaestiones* of Simon of Hinton', *Studies in Medieval History presented to F. M. Powicke*, Oxford, 1948, pp. 209–22.

[4] MS. Laud. misc. 524, fol. 85[ra]: '. . . ut qui conspecta nova luna ad ipsam se inclinant

advice to parents on educating their children and on other practical matters. There is only one scholastic *quaestio* and that on a problem which might well have troubled an unlearned preacher: Why should the sins of the fathers be visited on their children? Grosseteste considers the question at length, but in simple, untechnical language. The date of the *De Decem Mandatis* is uncertain. He could have composed it either as lector or as bishop.

The *De Decem Mandatis* and the *De Cessatione Legalium* belong to the best-known group of all Grosseteste's writings. Seventeen copies of the *De Cessatione Legalium* have survived. Two were written in the thirteenth century, including the annotated copy recently acquired by the Bodleian. Four are fifteenth-, all the rest fourteenth-century copies. The *De Decem Mandatis* survives in twenty-three copies, all fourteenth-century, apart from an abridgement, written about 1300. Wyclif quoted both treatises copiously and Alexander Carpenter used the *De Decem Mandatis*.[1] Edward Brown published a synopsis of the *De Cessatione Legalium* in the late seventeenth century.[2]

A clear picture of Grosseteste's reading public is emerging. The works we have classified and listed as 'Biblical' belong to very different types; yet all have a similar history. They are neglected at first and studied later. The majority of manuscripts come from the fourteenth and fifteenth centuries. Quotations start in the fourteenth century, in most instances with Wyclif. Even in the early part of the century Robert Holcot, the Oxford Dominican, famous for his wide range of quotations, cites only a sermon of Grosseteste in his commentaries on Scripture.[3] Of course there may well be other quotations waiting to be discovered. If so, they are more likely to occur

---

et cruce Christi se signant et orationem dominicam dicunt et tunc ter in girum vertunt et eum qui primo occurrerit eis osculant, credentes se per hoc toto mense a periculo liberari'.

[1] *Destructorium Viciorum, passim.* The *De Cessatione Legalium* is said to have 'influenced' a treatise of the same name by John Baconthorpe, an English Carmelite, who died in 1348. But Baconthorpe's treatise must have been a part of his commentary on the *Sentences*, circulating separately. In all his great volume of works he quotes Grosseteste only as a commentator on Aristotle and pseudo-Dionysius; see F. M. Xiberta, 'De magistro Iohanne Baconthorpe, O. Carm.', *Analecta Ord. Carm.* vi (1927), 90–92, 101.

[2] Edward Brown, *Fasc. Rerum Expetendarum et Fugiendarum*, ii (1690), 246–7.

[3] *Lect. in Sap.* vi, cap. 84 (Bâle, 1586), p. 291. Holcot's commentary on Ecclesiasticus (Venice, 1509) does not seem to quote Grosseteste at all. Holcot could not have quoted him on the actual text, since he did not expound Wisdom or Ecclesiasticus. On the other hand, Holcot quotes many authors on many subjects, Albertus Magnus on the Gospels for instance. On his connexion with Oxford see J. Wey, 'The *Sermo finalis* of Robert Holcot', *Mediaeval Studies*, xi (Toronto, 1949), 219–24.

in writers of the later Middle Ages; English scholars of the later thirteenth century have on the whole been more intensively studied than their successors. Roger Bacon, as is well known, admired Grosseteste as a Biblical scholar and dinned his praise in people's ears. But to talk about a man and say how great he was is a different thing from quoting him. Finally we have the striking fact that the biggest Grosseteste 'fan' of all time was Thomas Gascoigne in the mid-fifteenth century. Quite the reverse seems to have happened to the Biblical commentaries of Stephen Langton. He invites comparison with Grosseteste, since he too was an outstanding English churchman and scholar. Langton's commentaries, reported from his lectures at Paris between about 1180 and 1206, won enormous popularity at once. They were often copied and quoted for about the first three-quarters of the thirteenth century.[1] Then they ceased to count. And this is a much more typical history than that of Grosseteste's commentaries.

How can we explain the contrast between Langton and Grosseteste? The difference in the form of their writings will supply an obvious answer. The Langton *reportationes* could serve immediately in the study or the classroom. They conformed to a type which was familiar to all masters and students. Grosseteste on the contrary left no body of writings which could be used readily for teaching purposes. Only an undaunted admirer could make anything of his rough notes and jottings. Of his more literary products not one was suitable as a reference book or manual. But this, by itself, would be a superficial reason. A study of the content of his writings is necessary to a really satisfying explanation. I suggest that Grosseteste was out of step with his contemporaries. As Aristotle said, 'men desire the good and not merely what their fathers had'; but they often admire their ancestors. There are fashions in books. If Grosseteste struck thirteenth-century schoolmen as outmoded, he may have had all the more interest for Wyclif and Gascoigne.

Grosseteste was behind the times in his attitude to Bible study. It has been argued that he probably 'migrated to Paris in 1209 to study theology'. Oxford in the early thirteenth century was tributary to Paris in any case. If we remember his years, we shall not be

---

[1] This is my impression from a study of Langton manuscripts. For an account of his influence in the thirteenth century see *Study of the Bible*, pp. 272, 299, 305. I have not found any quotations from him in fourteenth-century writers. Neither Wyclif nor Gascoigne quotes him.

surprised to find that he always kept the mentality of Paris theologians of the decades on either side of 1200. By the 1230's such a
mentality 'dated' him. He believed, as his masters must have
believed, in associating theology and exegesis very closely. Doctrine
and theological speculation, on this view, ought to be kept within
a scriptural framework; they should be taught in lectures on the
Bible. Grosseteste recommended to the regent-masters in theology
at Oxford that the Bible should be their only teaching book; lectures
on it should take place in the morning when minds were at their
freshest. 'This', he wrote, 'is the custom of our elders, from which
we must not depart.'[1] The newer idea was to separate the two
disciplines of theology and exegesis. The *Sentences* of Peter Lombard replaced the Bible as a text for the study of theology. Specializa-
tion made for progress in both subjects. Oxford masters accepted it
eventually, though later than their opposite numbers at Paris.[2]

Grosseteste sponsored the older view of an all-embracing study of
Scripture. He gave high priority in this study to the spiritual exposition. It was part and parcel of his view of life. He stood, as Langton
had stood before him, for the reformation of society by a reformed
clergy. The spiritual exposition of Scripture enabled preachers to
call for this reformation with the authority of God's word. Grosseteste comments on the spiritual sense of Genesis i. 4, *He divided the
light from the darkness*; this extract from his *Hexaemeron* puts both
programme and method into a nutshell; it is both traditional and
characteristic:

> Allegorically the light of the Church is wise and spiritual prelates, who
> shine with the knowledge and love of truth and with the outer splendour
> of good works. The darkness is their subjects, wrapped in the darkness
> of ignorance and brutish and carnal. Light comes when the carnal (i.e.
> literal) sense of Scripture bursts forth into the spiritual sense.[3]

Grosseteste filled his letters with proof-texts of this sort. He used
them to support whatever application of the reforming ideal he
might have in mind; he might be defending the canon against common law or his right to visit his cathedral chapter. His letter to his

---

[1] *Ep.* 123, pp. 346–7. See Callus, 'Oxford Career', p. 56.
[2] Smalley, *Study of the Bible*, pp. 275–81.
[3] B, fol. 203rb: 'Item allegorice lux ecclesie sunt prelati sapientes et spiritales, qui
lucent veritatis cognitione et amore et bonorum operum exteriori splendore. Tenebre
vero sunt subditi, tenebris ignorantie involuti et animales et carnales. Item lux fit cum
sensus carnalis scripture erumpit in sensum spiritualem.'

archbishop, protesting against an attack on ecclesiastical liberties, has a long string of 'proofs'. Pharaoh, standing for the secular power, released to Abraham, who prefigures the Church, his wife Sarah, that is ecclesiastical liberties, to enjoy freely; the King of England ought to follow Pharaoh's example, and so on. He ends confidently: 'There are countless other such proofs from Scripture witnessing to the liberty of the Church and of Churchmen.'[1]

The modern reader will dismiss such arguments as an inept form of Bible-punching. Grosseteste found them convincing and logical. He would have justified them as follows: the role of the Church in society formed part of the divine plan; God's plan for men was mirrored in his word; he had entrusted the interpretation of his word to the Church; the right and duty of interpretation devolved particularly on 'masters of the sacred page'. Grosseteste was both master and prelate. He had a strong sense of mission and a firm intention to publish the fruits of his Bible studies. The Bible, as he read it, outlined his full programme of ecclesiastical reform.

The spiritual exposition receded into the background in the second half of the thirteenth century. Leaders of Christian thought in the universities began to lay greater emphasis on the literal sense. Then the conflict between Boniface VIII and the King of France with its spate of polemic caused the old arguments for clerical privilege to be reconsidered. Anticlericals[2] exposed the weakness of moralized proof-texts as arguments. Clericals realized that they would have to withdraw from this particular line of defence. Allegories and moralities kept their place in sermon literature, but they became marginal rather than central in political controversy. So Grosseteste by his innermost conviction belonged to a tradition which had passed its high-water mark when he died. In his view of what Biblical studies were for, the discovery of the spiritual sense of the Bible, he represented the past.

Nor was he quite *au courant* with modern techniques. The Fathers and early medieval commentators had divided their text into *lemmata* of greater or lesser extent and had expounded them successively. A study of Aristotelian logic suggested to exegetes a new

---

[1] *Ep.* 72, pp. 214–15.
[2] Even orthodox anticlericals; they only needed to apply a principle of St. Thomas Aquinas that the spiritual sense could not be used in theological argument. See J. Leclercq, *Jean de Paris et l'Ecclésiologie du XIIIe siècle*, Paris, 1942, ch. ii. Dante carried the attack on the use of the spiritual sense in political argument further, *De Monarchia*, iii.

method of division and sub-division, first of the whole book, then of each chapter. The present system of chapter division was being imposed on the text in the first quarter of the thirteenth century. A standard system of chapters made this kind of analysis practicable. It began very simply. The aim was to give students a survey of the contents of the whole book or chapter before they heard the master explaining its parts. Hugh of St. Cher used it in his postills, produced at Paris 1230–5. It spread like wildfire. Like many techniques, it defeated its own purpose eventually by over-elaboration. One master of the early fourteenth century is threatening to divide his text *usque ad indivisibilia.* For good or ill Grosseteste did not use it either in his Biblical or in his pseudo-Dionysian commentaries, but kept to the old method of expounding continuously by *lemmata.*

He differed still more from his contemporaries by keeping his dialectic and his scholarship in separate compartments. Their passion for logic led schoolmen to settle almost any question by means of verbal distinctions. The method suited an abstract science like speculative theology, but sterilized those Biblical problems which call for a study of history and textual criticism. Grosseteste, it is hardly necessary to say, had no idea of historical development in a modern sense. He had, however, a deep interest in human situations. He tackles his problems by putting them into their context and sketching all the factors involved. He reconstructs the event to the best of his ability. Never satisfied to condemn men as wrong, he wants to know why they went wrong. What gave rise to error in their minds? The ancient philosophers erred in supposing the universe to be uncreated and eternal. Grosseteste explains why they thought so:

Know that what deceived the ancients into positing no beginning to the universe was that false fancy especially which drove them to fancy before all time yet more time, as the imagination pictures outside all place yet more place and outside all space yet more space and so to infinity. This error can only be purged by way of the purgation of the mind from worldly affections, in order that the mind's eye, freed from phantasies, may transcend time and may understand simple eternity, which has no extension in time and whence all time proceeds.[1]

[1] B, fol. 197ra: 'Sciendum est autem quod illud quod decepit antiquos, ut ponerent mundum sine initio, fuit precipue falsa imaginatio, qua coacti sunt imaginari ante omne tempus tempus aliud, sicut imaginatur fantasia extra omnem locum locum alium, et extra omne spatium spatium aliud, et hoc usque in infinitum. Unde et huius erroris purgatio non potest esse nisi per hoc quod mentis affectus purgetur ab amore temporalium, ut mentis aspectus, immunis a fantasmatibus, possit transcendere tempus et intelligere simplicem eternitatem, ubi nulla est extensio secundum prius et posterius et

They were deceived also by an argument from causality, which led them to suppose that the effect must always be coexistent with the cause. God is the first cause of the universe. Therefore, they reasoned, the universe must necessarily be coeternal with him.[1]

Grosseteste treats humble superstition in just the same spirit as he treats the great philosophies of antiquity. In the *De Decem Mandatis* he shows that superstitions about the moon go against the commandment not to worship false gods. How have such heathen practices persisted into Christian times? He explains them as relics of the pagan worship of heavenly bodies. Some of the pagan converts to Christianity probably would not drop their cults altogether, just as Jewish converts continued to observe the ceremonies of the Old Law. Children have a habit of imitating their parents and so the bad custom has been handed on from father to son until today. Ask a man why he bows to the new moon; he can only answer that he saw his elders do so. It is likely that when such customs as bowing and turning round thrice were transmitted from heathen times to Christian, some sort of Christian colour was given to them by adding the signing of one's forehead with the cross and the repetition of the Lord's Prayer. Similarly pagan spectacles and shows were continued into Christian times, unchristian as they were.[2] Grosseteste leaves the subject, satisfied that he has fathomed it.

The *De Cessatione Legalium* shows him painting his problems on a canvas of universal history. First he analyses the mentality of Judeo-Christians, those 'false brethren' mentioned by the apostle, who taught that Christians should observe both the ceremonies of the Old Law and the Gospel sacraments together. Grosseteste makes

a qua procedit omne tempus.' Dr. Callus writes in explanation of this rather difficult passage: '*Phantasia* is equivalent to *imaginatio* or *vis imaginativa*, one of the so-called interior senses. "Fantasia imaginatur", i.e. the imagination fancies,—it is pictured by the imagination, or is an illusion of the imagination. The contrast is between the notions we have in our minds, conceived by the intellect, and the images we picture to ourselves, drawn by the imagination. The ancients were deceived because they confused the images of the *phantasia*, sheer fancies, with the concepts of the mind, *intellectus*. In a word: their mind was overwhelmed by their imagination. Grosseteste's theory of knowledge is purely "Augustinian"; that is why the error is purged by the *mentis affectus* etc.'

[1] B, fol. 197ra: 'Decepti erant quoque argumento illo quo dicebant tota et plena causa cui nullam oportet adicere conditionem ad hoc ut agat existente, necessarium esse totum et plenum effectum eiusdem cause simul semper cum ea coexistere. Deus autem talis causa est, quia omnipotens est cui nulla accidit nova conditio vel potentie vel sapiente vel voluntatis, sed semper uniformiter et uno modo se habet, quapropter non mundus ab eo factus est; semper simul cum eo coextitit, et ita mundus sicut et ille sine principio est.'

[2] MS. Laud. misc. 524, fol. 85^{r-v}. I have slightly abridged the argument, which would be too long to reproduce here.

out a case for the Judeo-Christians, putting forward all possible reasons that occur to him, with the modest rider that other, even more cogent ones, may have eluded his poor ingenuity.[1] The Judeo-Christians get the credit for a good education; their arguments include an appeal to the *Timaeus*. Plato says that the stars are incorruptible and immortal, being disposed according to reason and having no principle of contrariety in their being. The Law must have seemed to its adepts to fulfil both conditions for immortality.[2] In answering these arguments, Grosseteste insists, it is no use to quote the apostles. The Judeo-Christians were arguing with these very men and did not accept their words as authoritative. No: we have to substitute ourselves for the apostles and propound only those arguments which we can support by irrefutable reason or plain authority from the Old Testament or the Gospels, which the Judeo-Christians accepted. But we meet an attack on two fronts. Some men condemned the Old Law as wrong or unnecessary from the beginning. Manichees and Marcionites rejected the Old Testament as the work of the devil. Grosseteste remembers the arguments of his various heretics in the course of his book and replies to them severally as his story unfolds. His plan for refuting them is to give a large-scale demonstration that the ceremonies of the Old Law had been necessary for the Jewish people, that they became hurtful and superfluous in the time of grace, and further that the law of nature fittingly preceded both the written Laws.

The project involves a world history, presented from the point of view of law. Grosseteste's version of it justifies the ways of God with men and angels. He brings his imagination to bear on the revolt of Lucifer in connexion with the question whether God gave any law to the angels, corresponding to his command to Adam not to eat the fruit. The authorities yielded no information on the subject: Grosseteste had a flair for hypothetical questions, on which, for good reason, his predecessors kept silence.[3] He conjectures in this

---

[1] B, fol. 159ra: 'Hiis itaque et huiusmodi rationibus et forte multo cogentioribus, que mei ingenii parvitatem latent, potuerunt pseudo-apostoli suam assertionem astruere de observandis legalibus cum sacramentis evangelicis.'

[2] B, fol. 158va, from *Timaeus*, 41a. Grosseteste makes verbal quotations from the translation of Chalcidius, ed. I. Wrobel, *Platonis Timaeus interprete Chalcidio*, Leipzig, 1876, p. 43.

[3] Another example is his long discussion of the question whether God would have become man, even though man had not sinned and so needed redemption. He decides tentatively that the Incarnation would have been vouchsafed in any case (B, fols. 176ra–178va).

case that a law was probably given, but that the good angels were released from it as part of their reward for combating Lucifer. The discussion again illustrates Grosseteste's interest in situations. The persuasions of Lucifer and the strain they put on the good angels' loyalty are graphically described; so graphically indeed as to evoke for a modern reader not *Paradise Lost*, but Grosseteste's Europe, with its chronic tension between king and magnates and its feudal risings. The natural philosopher shows himself when Grosseteste explains why the Old Law had to be written and not always entrusted to man's memory as it was to the patriarchs'. Early men lived longer and had more strength and natural energy than their successors. Hence they must have had better memories. When man's memory degenerated he needed to have the Law in writing, especially as the precepts were multiplied.[1]

Parts II and III of the *De Cessatione Legalium* deal with the advent of Christ and with the gospel story. Part IV broaches the main problem: When exactly was the Old Law superseded as regards its ceremonial precepts, all, that is to say, which was not subsumed in Christianity, as the moral precepts were? There was general agreement that this happened at the passion of Christ. Yet St. Paul circumcised Timothy (Acts xvi. 3) and took the vow of the Nazarites (xviii. 18); St. Peter incurred a reproach from St. Paul for conforming to the Old Law 'fearing them who were of the circumcision' (Gal. ii. 12–13). The discrepancy in the conduct of the apostles had its counterpart in another difficulty, which had equal importance for a medieval scholar: the Fathers were almost on a level with Scripture for him. St. Jerome and St. Augustine had disputed on the Antioch controversy by letter. It was a burning question in patristic apologetic. Some account of the dispute must be given so that we may consider its treatment by Grosseteste.[2]

---

[1] This is hardly an original idea, but Grosseteste works it out in a way that shows he has thought about it; B, fol. 162ra: 'Non enim est scriptura nisi propter supplementum memorie defectus. Homines autem primi temporis habuerunt multam memorie vivacitatem qua potuerunt legem sine oblivione retinere. . . . Quod habuissent tamen comparatione nostri temporis multam sensuum interiorum et exteriorum firmitudinem et vivacitatem patere potest ex eorum longevitate et corporali robure. Longevi enim fuerunt ex bonitate virtutis vitalis et virtutis motive, sed harum virium bonitas esse non potest absque bonitate virtutum sensitivarum. Sicut igitur illi nobis erant longeviores, sic erant nobis operationibus virium naturalium vivaciores.'

[2] Epp. 112 of St. Jerome, 82 of St. Augustine, ed. J. Schmid, *SS. Eusebii Hieronymi et Aurelii Augustini Epistulae mutuatae* (Florilegium patristicum, xxii, Bonn, 1930), pp. 53–93. An account of the whole correspondence and summary of the Antioch controversy according to its different interpretations is given in the Introduction.

Jerome disposed of the whole affair by claiming that the apostles only pretended to observe the Law. The Antioch controversy was a put-up job, which they staged between them for propaganda purposes. He compared it to mock contests in the Roman schools of rhetoric that he had attended as a boy. This explanation horrified Augustine. He regarded Jerome as 'a master of lies'. For his part, he distinguished an intermediate stage in the history of the Law. In the apostolic age it resembled a corpse awaiting burial, which ought to be respected and honoured. To observe its ceremonies in this period was not sinful, provided that one did not hope for salvation by doing so. The apostles observed it out of pity for the weakness of Jewish converts and to demonstrate its superiority to heathen rites. Augustine held that St. Peter had really been at fault and that St. Paul had really reproved him. He erred not in his own observance of the Law, but in compelling 'the gentiles to live as do the Jews' (Gal. ii. 13). Jerome retorted by accusing Augustine of supporting the Ebionite heresy: it had never been permissible, after Christ's passion, for a Christian to observe the ceremonies of the Law. If St. Paul did so, then he fell into the Jewish error himself and had no right to criticize St. Peter. Therefore he must have been pretending. The Latin Church accepted the more realistic view of Augustine on the Antioch controversy; but medieval commentators disliked admitting a mistake in their authorities and felt that the two doctors must somehow be reconciled.

We shall be in a better position to appreciate Grosseteste if we compare his attempt at reconciliation with a crude contemporary effort to reach the same end by means of dialectic. William of Auxerre discusses the problem in his widely circulated *Summa Aurea* which appeared about 1220.[1] He begins by putting the dilemma as starkly as possible. Jerome and Augustine contradict each other; therefore one of them was in error, 'quod est inconveniens in doctoribus sacre scripture'. The error, moreover, concerned a matter of doctrine; therefore whichever was in error was sinning against the faith. He replies by distinguishing between the meanings of 'noxious'. Jerome said that the precepts of the Old Law were noxious in the time of grace. He meant noxious not *universaliter*, but only to those who trusted in them for salvation, as did the Ebionites. Augustine agreed. So there was no real controversy between them, nor did the apostles sin when they observed the

[1] Ed. Paris, 1500, fols. 246ᵛ–247ʳ.

Law. On the question of 'dissimulation', William distinguishes two kinds, good and bad. The bad kind is hypocritical, the good kind medicinal. The latter is illustrated by the engaging example of a physician who pretends not to eat beef, to encourage his patient to diet. The apostles' dissimulation, as presented by Jerome, was of the medicinal type. Augustine and Jerome put forward two different reasons for the apostles' action. Both reasons may have been correct. An alternative solution would be that Augustine understood the word *dissimulatio* in a different sense from Jerome. On the question whether St. Peter actually sinned, we can choose between Jerome and Augustine. On Jerome's view, St. Peter laid himself open to criticism because 'he did not consider all the circumstances that it would have been useful to consider'. If we follow Augustine we may say that St. Peter sinned but that his sin was venial. William of Auxerre, it may be noted, has helped out St. Jerome by tacitly passing over his view that the whole Antioch controversy was faked. The controversy is genuine, though according to Jerome it is about pretending to keep, not actually keeping the Law.

Grosseteste had not gone into the subject very deeply in his commentary on Galatians. He contented himself with a full, clear statement of the two opinions and argued in the course of it that they were not contradictory. Augustine and Jerome agreed in that each found an explanation of the apostles' conduct. Each proved that neither apostle sinned when he observed the legal ceremonies.[1] In the *De Cessatione Legalium* the treatment of the problem is much more ambitious. It is notable, however, that in both works Grosseteste avoided any use of the *Summa Aurea*. He had drawn on it freely in his *Quaestiones* (if they are really his).[2] The whole spirit of the discussion is different. Perhaps the change marks a development in his thought. In his exegesis he no longer depended on the standard theological sources, but found his feet and tried new ways of harmonizing his authorities.

The discussion in the *De Cessatione Legalium* begins with a long, poetic rhapsody on the theme of *concordia discors*. Here, he says eventually, we have manifest discord. If there be harmony, it is hidden and needs diligent inquiry to bring it out. Perhaps the Holy Spirit did not dictate everything to these two doctors, but left them

---

[1] MS. Magdalen College 57, fols. 5ᵛ–6ʳ.
[2] Callus, *Studies... F. M. Powicke*, p. 193. The fragments of this *Summa* do not include any *quaestiones* on the Old Law. See above, p. 29.

to their own devices in some things, in order that their disagreement might bear useful fruit. It must also be remembered that the Fathers did not always make dogmatic statements but indulged in hypotheses. They often seem to differ when in fact they are only speaking of possible or probable. Someone might object that if there were hidden agreement between Jerome and Augustine, they themselves ought to have seen it. The answer is that each one scrutinized the other's argument as that of a man, not as inspired by the Holy Spirit.

After this introduction the conflicting opinions are put forward, Grosseteste speaking for each of the contending parties. Every possible point of view is allowed for. In his solution he shows himself to be aware that the two men were corresponding over a vast distance and that they may have been talking at cross purposes. Thus Jerome suspected Augustine of favouring the Ebionite heresy, which was far from the case. I quote Grosseteste's conclusion:

Hence Jerome did not contradict Augustine's true mind and opinion, but the false opinion that he had formed from Augustine's words and which those words suggested on a superficial reading, having reached Jerome without explanation so far. Augustine agreed with Jerome in his opinion nor did Jerome contradict him, for Augustine's true opinion had not reached Jerome, as has been said. Had it reached him, he would easily, as I think, have agreed to it. It seems to me also that Augustine did not understand Jerome's meaning on the subject of dispensation to simulate. He thought that Jerome meant to say that deceit was permissible by dispensation. Hence he disputed against Jerome as a defender of lying and deceit and as though he had admitted the existence of a lie in holy writ.

Finally, Grosseteste observes that the controversy stimulated the disputants and moved them to an inquiry 'which has saved us from many an error'.[1]

The story of the Jerome–Augustine correspondence with its mishaps and its lost letters does not reduce the difference between them as completely as Grosseteste thought. Nevertheless his attempt to use history rather than dialectic by way of explanation throws light on his own mental processes. Elsewhere he tried still another tack. Gascoigne saw Grosseteste's copy of the letters of St. Jerome in the Franciscan library at Oxford. It had a marginal note by

[1] B, fols. 183ra–185va. Grosseteste may be referring to St. Gregory on the value of the doubts of the Apostle St. Thomas, *P.L.* lxxvi. 1201, n. 7.

Grosseteste stating that Jerome did not give his own view on the Antioch controversy; he was merely quoting from Origen on Galatians. Writing to Augustine, Jerome testified that he had said nothing original on the subject. Hence those who saw disagreement between the two Fathers in Grosseteste's opinion were mistaken.[1] It was acute and correct to point out Jerome's debt to Origen,[2] though even this explanation was not wholly valid: Jerome had borrowed the Greek view of the Antioch controversy, but had adopted it and could hardly evade responsibility. The interesting point is Grosseteste's preference for scholarship to dialectic.

In this respect he was individual and not merely old-fashioned. Twelfth-century Paris commentators had been just as fond of dialectic as were Grosseteste's contemporaries or successors. If he is reverting to an earlier tradition, it is much earlier; he is going back to the pre-logical ethos of the Benedictines or the Victorines. One gets the same impression from his style. Grosseteste is a warm and personal writer, though too diffuse to be forceful. He has no sense of proportion or form and will say anything about anything. His *De Decem Mandatis* is a lop-sided affair, reminding one of a lecturer who looks suddenly at the clock and crams half his paper into the last five minutes. Grosseteste likes a mixture of sentiment and reason. It was becoming customary in his period to treat questions of theology and casuistry in a technical and analytical way, without letting sentiment enter in. Even the Franciscans, who specialized in unction, distinguished the academic treatise or commentary from the sermon or homily. Grosseteste was incapable of making such a separation. He introduces religious topics into his literal exegesis. One sees this all through his notes on St. Paul. The *De Decem Mandatis*, which by tradition should have dealt mainly with casuistry, breaks into a glow of devotion at the end. The Christian's chief concern, Grosseteste says, must be love 'ordered to' God, which 'renews the soul and reforms it to the image and likeness of the Creator, that is, of perfect beauty. This love is a fire, consuming away the rust of sin. . . . This love is the most pleasant thing, for love only can make things pleasant, and without it all things displease.'[3] These are the last words of his commentary

---

[1] MS. Lincoln College 117, p. 473.

[2] J. Schmid, op. cit., pp. 16–22; A. Souter, *The Earliest Latin Commentaries on the Epistles of St Paul*, Oxford, 1927, pp. 111–12, 116–24.

[3] MS. Laud. misc. 524, fol. 110ᵛᵇ: 'Amor quippe ordinatus est qui renovat animam et reformat ad imaginem et similitudinem creatoris, summe scilicet pulchritudinis. Hic

on the Commandments. To the tidy mind of a thirteenth-century schoolman they might seem out of place and more suitable in a purely devotional setting. To a later generation, repelled by the dryness of scholasticism, they might seem as welcome as water in a desert.

Many external reasons must have led Wyclif to cultivate Grosseteste. Here was an Englishman who taught at Oxford, a doctor who reduced theology to Bible study, a reformer who criticized papal provisions, a bishop who devoted himself to pastoral care. Admiration does not always induce study; it can remain purely Platonic. Wyclif's did not. He quoted and knew very well a great variety of Grosseteste's works—the commentaries on the *Posterior Analytics*, pseudo-Dionysius and *Hexaemeron*, the sermons and *Dicta*, some pastoral and devotional treatises, the *De Decem Mandatis* and the *De Cessatione Legalium*. He used the two last as his standard books in his own treatise on the Decalogue and in that section of his *De Veritate Sacrae Scripturae* which deals with the relationship between Old and New Laws (chapters xxviii–xxxi). He used them with scrupulous fairness. They do not serve a polemical purpose. In one passage of the *De Veritate*, where he is explaining the spiritual significance of the precept against eating meat with blood in it, he turns it into an attack on ecclesiastical endowments. Since he has just been quoting Grosseteste, he hastens to add that Grosseteste had a different opinion: 'aliam autem sententiam tangit Lincolniensis'.[1] So Grosseteste was no mere legend to him nor a mouthpiece for his own views, but a source of genuine mental satisfaction.

Grosseteste's appeal for Wyclif is easy to understand. He relished the blend of Biblical theology and moral exhortation. He held that Scripture had 'its own logic', distinct from the changing logic of the schools.[2] Grosseteste must have impressed him as a specialist in this scriptural logic. He approved of Grosseteste's application of the rules for exegesis laid down by St. Augustine.[3] Wyclif also appreciated John of Abbeville, an older contemporary of Grosseteste; he quotes exactly from one of John's Sunday sermons.[4] These two scholars of the late twelfth and early thirteenth century represented

---

est ignis consumens rubiginem peccatorum. . . . Hic amor est res suavissima, quia nulla nisi per amorem sunt suavia et sine illo omnia sunt amara.'

[1] Ed. R. Buddensieg, London, 1907, iii. 197–8.
[2] Ibid. i. 47–54, 194–8, 309, 384, 387–8; ii. 20.
[3] Ibid. iii. 139–40.
[4] Ibid. i. 90. He quotes the sermon on the fourth Sunday after Epiphany, MS. Royal 2 E. ix, fols. 40va–42rb. On John of Abbeville see above, p. 72, n. 3.

to Wyclif a period when the teaching of theology had been simpler and more serious than it was in his own day. Their remoteness from contemporary methods in itself aroused his admiration.

Gascoigne differed from Wyclif in being passionately orthodox; but he shared Wyclif's belief in preaching as a cure-all. His programme for the universities was a patristic revival. This, he felt, would produce the reformed and preaching clergy which the Church needed. Whereas Wyclif had exalted Augustine, Gascoigne almost worshipped 'the celestial doctor', St. Jerome. He thought that the combination of scholarship and spiritual interpretation in Jerome's exegesis was ideal and that it ought to be imitated.[1] The over-elaborate technique of division and sub-division of the text prevented an understanding of its meaning. Jerome had expounded the text as a whole, thus bringing out the sense as a whole.[2] Grosseteste came as close to a reincarnation of Jerome as Gascoigne could have hoped for in modern times. We have seen that Grosseteste did not divide his text. The positive qualities that appealed to Gascoigne come out in his abundant quotations from Grosseteste on the Pauline Epistles. He liked their long extracts from the Fathers. Above all it is the moral tone in Grosseteste that comes through his quotations. Of the many possible examples let us choose a short one. Gascoigne quotes a few lines from Grosseteste on 1 Corinthians x. 13: *Let no temptation take hold on you, but such as is human*: ' "Human temptation" is when one sees no escape from danger by man's help, and suffers it humbly for God's sake, confiding in his help.'[3]

The wheel had come full circle. The archaic, unscholastic strain in Grosseteste had repelled his contemporaries. It brought him a late but warm recognition in his own university.

A modern student of the Middle Ages will see him rather as a forerunner of Erasmus. His linguistic science ran far ahead of his times. He learned enough Greek to study the Greek text of Galatians and Genesis and to translate the Greek Fathers. The new translation from the Hebrew Psalter organized by Grosseteste shows that he realized the need for study of both Biblical tongues; but Greek was his first love and the sphere where he made his most original contribution. Unlike most medieval scholars he never fell under the spell

[1] The *Liber Veritatum* teems with praise of Jerome; see especially MS. Lincoln College 117, pp. 443-4, 457-60.
[2] Ibid., p. 442.
[3] Ibid., p. 468.

of Hebrew and rabbinics to the neglect of Greek. Allusions to Hebrew lore and tradition are conspicuously absent from his Biblical works. He was in a tiny minority in his preference.

The medieval impression of Grosseteste as a scholar seems to pick out the essentials. Salimbene calls him 'one of the greatest clerks of the world'. The reason for his greatness, according to Salimbene, was his translations: 'Second after Burgundio, he translated Damascene and the Testament of the Twelve Patriarchs and many other books.'[1] This conveys a picture of Grosseteste and of his writings as they appeared to an Italian friar, the composite portrait of a scholar which forms itself on the fringe of academic circles. He was remembered less as an original thinker than as a translator. He made his deepest mark on the Middle Ages in a humble but necessary role. He belonged to the band of men whose patience and enterprise made Greek sources available to Latin-speaking Christendom.

BERYL SMALLEY.

[1] *Cronica*, M.G.H. Scriptores, xxxii. 233.

Grosseteste's Position in the History of Science

'ALL the wise men of antiquity', Roger Bacon wrote in the fourth book of his *Opus Maius*, 'worked in mathematics so that they might know all things, as we have seen in some scholars of our own times, and as we have heard of in others who learned all knowledge through mathematics, which they knew well. For there have been some famous men, such as Robert, Bishop of Lincoln, and Brother Adam Marsh and many others, who have known how, by the power of mathematics, to unfold the causes of all things and to give a sufficient explanation of human and Divine phenomena. This is assured by the writings of these great men, for example by their works on the impression [of the elements], on the rainbow, on comets, on the generation of heat, on the investigation of the places of the world, on celestial things, and on other questions appertaining both to theology and to natural philosophy. And so it is obvious that mathematics is absolutely necessary, and useful, to the other sciences.'

It was characteristic of thirteenth-century science as a whole, but especially of that part of it showing Grosseteste's direct influence, to stress the importance of scientific method. The works cited by Roger Bacon as evidence of the effectiveness of the mathematical method, respectively *De Impressionibus Elementorum*, *De Iride*, *De Cometis*, *De Calore. Solis*, *De Natura Locorum*, and *De Sphaera*, contained some of Grosseteste's most interesting contributions to mathematical physics. Bacon claimed in his *Compendium Studii* that 'before all other men' Grosseteste 'wrote about science'. For the historian of science Grosseteste's special importance is that he seems to have been the first Western writer to go systematically into the problem of the role of experiment in scientific inquiry. It was for his conception of experimental and mathematical science that his followers, both in Oxford and on the Continent, chiefly valued his work. The main purpose of this essay will be to show what innovations Grosseteste introduced into the conception of scientific method inherited from the Greeks and Arabs, how he used his method to investigate some specific physical problems, and what influence he had upon his immediate followers and upon the later history of science in the West.[1]

For about half a century before Grosseteste was born (*c.* 1168), one of the most important activities of Western scholars interested in science had been to translate Greek and Arabic scientific writings into Latin. Grosseteste himself took part in this work, encouraging the study of Greek and Hebrew, both at Oxford and at Lincoln, and including among his own translations from Greek at least part of Aristotle's *De Caelo* and of Simplicius's commentary on it, and the pseudo-Aristotelian *De Lineis Indivisibilibus*. By the year of Grosseteste's death (1253), Latin versions had been made of most of the important Greek and Arabic scientific works of which knowledge has survived. All these were not available to him, but certainly his greater knowledge of Greek and Arabic science was one of the reasons for the marked superiority of his own scientific work over that of his immediate predecessors, for example that of Alexander Nequam and Alfred of Sareshel in England. Belonging to an earlier generation when the work of translation was far less complete, these writers were still concerned largely with putting the orginal texts into Latin and with mastering their contents. Grosseteste's was the earliest generation in a position to put this new literary knowledge to original scientific use on any considerable scale. He stands out from his contemporaries as something more than a translator and encyclopaedist because he, before anyone else, was able to see that the major problems to be investigated, if science was to progress, were those of scientific method.

The corpus of translations known in Grosseteste's time contained scientific writings of two main types. First, there was a large number of purely practical treatises, for example on the astrolabe, the calendar, and other astronomical subjects, on surveying, chemistry, and medicine. The West had been the scene of considerable technical activity at least since the ninth century, when the new wheeled plough and new methods of harnessing draught animals came into use. These were followed by further improvements in power-driven machinery; water-mills and windmills were used for numerous industrial purposes, from corn-grinding and fulling to mining and the working of bellows for metallurgy. Chemistry, medicine, surgery, practical mathematics, and other technical subjects closely related to

[1] I have given a fully documented account of these subjects in my book, *Robert Grosseteste and the Origins of Experimental Science*, Oxford, at the Clarendon Press, 1953.

science developed considerably during the thirteenth century; the compass and astrolabe were improved, spectacles and the mechanical clock invented. Scholars took an active interest in various aspects of this new technology and, from the middle of the twelfth century, the technical subjects in school and university courses began to be elaborated. As a result, scholars began to develop a mentality interested in finding exact experimental answers to practical questions.

There is ample evidence to show that many scholars in the twelfth century observed things for themselves and were conscious of the need for experiment. But for a long time their methods remained *ad hoc* and rule-of-thumb, aimed at dealing only with a particular problem. They had no conception of how to generalize problems and how to establish general proofs and explanations. A good example is the use, in works on surveying, of the conclusions of Euclid's theorems, which the authors were quite incapable of proving.

The conception of generalized scientific explanation, with definite canons for accepting one explanation and rejecting another, was introduced into science from the second type of scientific writing to be translated into Latin during the twelfth century. For the present discussion, the main works falling into this category are Euclid's *Elements*, first translated in full in 1126 by Adelard of Bath, who used an Arabic original, and Aristotle's logical writings, especially the *Posterior Analytics*, translated in three versions during the second half of the twelfth century. At first these books had little effect on science itself, but they completely revolutionized philosophy and philosophical theology, and law. Philosophers learnt from them to recognize the distinction between experimental knowledge of a particular fact, and 'rational' or 'scientific' knowledge of the cause of the fact. By this they meant some prior principles from which the fact could be deduced. For example, surveyors could discover experimentally that a triangle inscribed in a semicircle was right-angled. Euclid provided the 'explanation' of this fact by proving that it followed by deduction from his axioms, postulates, and definitions. For twelfth-century philosophers like Peter Abelard, mathematics became the model science; they attempted to formulate theological arguments according to the mathematical-deductive method. Aristotle gave them a generalized account of the method, and showed that there were definite rules for distinguishing between valid and invalid syllogisms. Gratian used the same logical method to reform canon law.

The application of the new conception of rational, or scientific, explanation to natural science was simply the last of the achievements of a general intellectual movement of the twelfth century. By the end of the century the formal structure of the new method had been filled in by material examples from the many specialized scientific writings translated from Greek and Arabic. Prominent among those who discussed these new texts were some English scholars working in centres in which Grosseteste was himself to work: Roger of Hereford, Daniel of Morley, and, possibly, Alfred of Sareshel in Hereford; Alexander Nequam, a Master Hugh, John of London, and John Blund in Oxford. There is evidence to show that Grosseteste studied not only mathematics and philosophy, but also medicine, and perhaps law. Certainly his writings show a wide grasp of contemporary science, ranging from the logic of science and pure mathematics, through theoretical speculations about cosmology and the nature of light, to the application of scientific theories to such practical problems as the reform of the calendar and the improvement of sight. Thus he was well equipped for the role for which he was cast in the history of science, that of the founder of the Oxford school, whose major achievement was its contribution to the modern conception of experimental method.

(2)

Grosseteste's conception of the logic of science, of the goal of a scientific inquiry, and of the explanation that was the achievement of the goal, was based in the first place on Aristotle's *Posterior Analytics*. He gave the most systematic account of his ideas on scientific method in his commentary on this work. It is almost certain, both from specific references in his other writings and from their contents, and from references to external events, that this commentary was written before his treatises on optics and astronomy and other special scientific problems. He seems first to have worked out a methodology applicable to the physical world, and then to have applied it in the particular sciences. This methodology may be considered under two headings: first, induction and experiment; and secondly, mathematical physics.

Grosseteste's conception of the role of induction and experiment in scientific inquiry was based on the conception of scientific explanation expounded by Aristotle. The aim of a scientific inquiry, Aristotle asserted, was to discover premisses from which something already known as a fact could be deduced or 'demonstrated'. When this had been done, the investigator had acquired knowledge not only of 'the fact' (τὸ ὅτι), but also of 'the reason for the fact' (τὸ διότι). These two types of knowledge were distinguished in medieval Latin by the terms, respectively, *demonstratio quia* and *demonstratio propter quid* (or *quare*). The whole effort of Greek natural science had been directed towards getting knowledge of the physical world such that propositions about observed facts could be demonstrated from general principles or theories, in just the same way as the conclusions of Euclid's theorems were demonstrated from his axioms, postulates, definitions, and the conclusions of prior theorems. The principal defect of the Greek consideration of the logic of science was that it did not go deeply into the problems of how to discover true premisses for 'demonstrated knowledge' of observed facts, and of how to test their truth. The Greeks certainly made many observations and some excellent experiments, as did the Arabs; both made fruitful use of mathematical and physical theories. But neither consciously formulated a conception of the roles of induction and experiment in scientific inquiry. To do so was the achievement of Grosseteste and the Oxford school.

A scientific inquiry began, Grosseteste followed Aristotle in asserting, with an observed phenomenon, 'the fact'; the purpose of the inquiry was to discover 'the reason for the fact'. Taking up a discussion in the first chapter of Aristotle's *Physics*, Grosseteste said, in his commentary on this work, that the phenomena perceived through the senses were composite. The first stage of an inquiry was to break up the composite phenomenon into the principles or elements of which it was formed. This process he called induction, or 'resolution'. Having isolated the separate principles involved, the next stage of an inquiry was, by recombining them, to reconstruct the phenomenon theoretically. This process he called 'composition'. The truth of the principles was tested by comparing the composite of theory, deduced from them, with the composite of observation.

A scientific inquiry thus proceeded by the alternation of the argument in two opposite directions, one going inductively from effect to cause, the other deductively from cause to effect. Aristotle had described the argument from effect to cause as a process of abstraction going from composite observed phenomena 'more knowable to us' (πρὸς ἡμᾶς γνωριμώτερα), to abstract principles prior in the order of nature but at first less knowable to us. In his commentary on Aristotle's *Physics*, Grosseteste described the procedure as follows:

> The natural way for us to arrive at knowledge of principles is to go from . . . whole objects which follow from the principles themselves, to the principles themselves. . . . The way of knowledge is . . . from confusedly known whole complete objects . . . into the parts themselves by which it is possible to define the whole object itself, and from the definition to return to determinate knowledge of the whole object.

The essentials of the method of 'resolution and composition' for discovering and defining the causal principles, or 'forms', from which the observed phenomena could be deduced, were briefly described by Aristotle in the thirteenth chapter of the second book of the *Posterior Analytics*. Grosseteste made the method the centre of his logic of inductive inquiry. In effect, the definition of the form stated the conditions necessary and sufficient to produce the phenomenon. The first problem was to investigate as exhaustively as possible the various correlations of happenings present in the phenomenon, so that their 'common formula' could be discovered; that is, so that they could be expressed as a generalization, or statement of a regularity. Grosseteste gave a formal description of the method in his commentary on the *Posterior Analytics*, and applied it to some specific problems. For example, he showed that 'all scammony of its nature withdraws red bile'. About a phenomenon mentioned by Aristotle, he reached the following conclusion:

> If, therefore, we wish to define this accidental natural thing, 'having horns', we will say that 'having horns' is 'not having teeth in the upper mandible in those animals to which Nature does not give other means of preservation in place of horns', and we reach this definition by the division of the accidental natural thing into co-accidents.

The method of 'resolution and composition' can best be illustrated by means of research into the cause of the rainbow, begun by Grosseteste, carried on by Albertus Magnus, Roger Bacon, and Witelo, and completed in the first decade of the fourteenth century by Theodoric of Freiberg, who put forward the 'Cartesian' explanation. The first three writers were directly influenced in their method by Grosseteste, the last at least indirectly.

The inquiry began with a 'resolution' of different kinds of spectrum, including the colours seen in the rainbow, into their elements, so that their 'common formula', or formulae, could be discovered.

A large number of examples of coloured spectra were examined and classified according to their common attributes. For example, the spectra seen in rainbows, in the spray made by mill-wheels, by the oars of a rowing-boat, and by squirting water from the mouth, and in sunlight passed through a spherical glass flask full of water on to a screen, all shared the attributes of being associated with transparent spheres or drops in which, it was found, the different individual colours were refracted through different angles and the colours always formed a circle or part of a circle. Members of a second group, the spectra produced by sunlight shining through a glass prism or hexagonal crystal, shared the common attribute of being formed by colours refracted through different angles, but differed from the members of the first group by not being circular. Members of a third group, the spectra produced by different kinds of iridescent feathers, shared the common attributes of being formed by reflected, not refracted, colours, which changed in a special manner with changing incidence of light: these attributes distinguished the members of this group from those of the preceding ones. The 'common formula' of the first two groups was: 'colours of the spectrum produced by differential refraction'. The common formula of all these groups was furnished by an hypothesis supposing that both refraction and reflection by a dense medium weakened white light; according to the angle through which it was bent, it absorbed different degrees of darkness from the medium, and thereby became differentiated into the colours of the spectrum: 'colours of the spectrum produced by the weakening of white light'.

To the question: What are the conditions necessary and sufficient to produce a rainbow? the investigator had now given a partial answer by defining the species of spectrum to which the rainbow belonged, and by distinguishing this from the species to which it did not belong. From the separate elements, or attributes, discovered by 'resolution', the rainbow could then be reconstituted theoretically by 'composition'. This genus, 'colours of the spectrum', of one species of which the rainbow was a member, was divided according to successive *differentia*, and those applicable to the rainbow combined to form an aggregate defining the rainbow itself. As Grosseteste said in his commentary on the *Posterior Analytics*: 'the whole aggregate becomes convertible with [i.e. equivalent to] the thing to be defined, though each of the parts of that aggregate has a wider application'. For example, the genus was divided according to whether the colours were produced by refraction or reflection; colours produced by refraction were then divided according to the nature of the refracting medium; and so on. Eventually an aggregate of *differentia* was formed which specifically defined the rainbow itself: 'colours of the spectrum produced by the differential refraction of sunlight in spherical drops in large numbers, the refracted colours emerging at approximately 42° to the incident light and forming part of a circle, etc.'

The definition reached by 'resolution and composition' showed the cause of the phenomenon under investigation, in the sense that it showed the conditions necessary and sufficient to produce it. This was the formal definition, or formal cause, of the phenomenon; it showed what it was. It led immediately to a further question: How do the elements described in the formal definition bring the phenomenon about? To explain this, Grosseteste said, we must consider not only the formal cause (defining what the phenomenon is), but also the material, efficient, and final causes. 'Thus', he said in his *De Statu Causarum*, 'we have four genera of causes, and from these, when they exist, there must be a caused thing in its complete being.'

In natural science, except to characterize the biological function of organs, Grosseteste did not include consideration of final causes. Material and efficient causes he introduced into the explanation by showing the rearrangements of material parts that would have to take place in time, in order to bring about the consequences required by the formal cause. In the case of the phenomenon 'having horns', Grosseteste described the movements of 'earthy matter' taking place in the head in order to produce teeth in some animals, horns in others. A fruitful device which he and his successors adopted to explain the formation of a rainbow was to construct, on the basis of the discovered relations between the limited number of elements defining the species to which the rainbow belonged, a theoretical model from which this phenomenon could be deduced. The purpose of the model was to show in detail how the elements were related, for example exactly how the light behaved in passing through the drops where a rainbow was seen; in this manner it provided the 'demonstrated knowledge' which was the goal of the inquiry.

The special significance of this use of theoretical models in an investigation was that it made it possible to bring a remote and intractable phenomenon like the rainbow down, so to speak, from the clouds and into the laboratory, where it could be studied by

deliberately arranged experiments. Grosseteste constructed a theoretical model in which he tried to deduce the appearance of a rainbow
from independently established laws governing the refraction of
light at the junction of two transparent media. He supposed that
the rainbow was produced by the refraction of sunlight through
successive layers of moist atmosphere forming a cloud, which acted
as a single compound lens; he thought the rainbow was seen on
a second cloud, acting as a screen on to which the colours were
thrown. In his analysis of refraction Grosseteste gave an account of
the behaviour of light passing through a spherical glass flask full
of water. Albertus Magnus, taking Grosseteste's explanation of the
rainbow as his point of departure, used such a flask as a model to
show the action of a cloud acting as a single lens. Roger Bacon,
Witelo, and, finally, Theodoric of Freiberg, departing radically from
Grosseteste's theory, showed that the rainbow was produced, not
by the whole cloud acting as a single lens, but by the *individual* drops
of water of which the cloud was composed. Witelo and Theodoric
built up their theories of the rainbow by using spherical glass flasks
full of water as model raindrops.

A problem encountered in the construction of a theory that took
account of material and efficient causes, as well as the formal cause
(or definition), was fully appreciated by Grosseteste. This was that
such a theory, or theoretical model, could not be reached by a con-
tinuous inductive argument in the same manner as the conclusions
of a theory could be demonstrated by a deductive argument. He
asked in his commentary on the *Posterior Analytics*:

> Can the cause be reached from knowledge of the effect with the same
> certainty as the effect can be shown to follow from its cause? Is it possible
> for one effect to have many causes? If one determinate cause cannot be
> reached from the effect, since there is no effect which does not have
> some cause, it follows that an effect, when it has one cause, may have
> another, and so that there may be several causes of it.

After the resolutive-compositive method had done its work of
separating, describing, and classifying the elements of a phenomenon, there was a logical gap to be crossed only by the investigator's scientific imagination. On the basis of the facts discovered
by induction, the investigator tried to construct a theory from
which those facts could be deduced. This was Grosseteste's scientific
interpretation of Aristotle's νοῦς, which may perhaps be translated
as 'intuition'. Having thought of possible theories, the next step

was to test them and separate true from false, or complete from incomplete. Grosseteste seems to have been the first writer to make systematic use of a method of experimental verification and falsification; certainly this is one of the most striking aspects of his logic of science. His procedure was to deduce from a theory consequences that could be tested by observation or experiment; if these were confirmed, he continued to use the theory; if not, he rejected the theory, at least in the form given, and cast round for another.

Two metaphysical assumptions on which Grosseteste based his procedure for choosing between possible theories were long to play a role in discussions of the use of experiment in science. Both he derived from statements by Aristotle. The first was the principle of the uniformity of nature. As he said in *De Generatione Stellarum*: 'Things of the same nature are productive of the same operations according to their nature'; 'the same cause, provided it remains in the same condition, cannot produce anything but the same effect.' The second assumption was of the principle of economy. 'Nature operates in the shortest way possible', he said in *De Lineis, Angulis et Figuris*. And in his commentary on the *Posterior Analytics* he said: 'that demonstration is better, other circumstances being equal, which necessitates the answering of a smaller number of questions for a perfect demonstration, or requires a smaller number of suppositions and premisses from which the demonstration proceeds . . . because it makes us know more quickly.' This pragmatic form of the principle of economy has become consecrated in the logic of science under the name 'Ockham's Razor'. It was widely used in the thirteenth and fourteenth centuries, especially in astronomy.

An important consequence of Grosseteste's analysis of the logic of experimental science, a consequence of which he was himself aware though it was fully discussed first by Ockham, was to give a special significance to the principle of economy. It followed, from the fact that the same observations could be deduced from more than one theory and that it was impossible to discover all the possible theories from which given observations could be deduced, that the experimental verification of a particular theory did not exclude the possibility that another theory might be 'true' in the same sense. Moreover, the experimental verification of a theory was no guarantee that it would not one day be falsified. Therefore, experimental science showed, as it was put, that some theories were sufficient to 'save the appearances' and others were not; it did not show that a theory was necessarily true in the sense of being a necessary conclusion from the analysis of the observed facts, a unique and final statement of how nature was actually constructed. A theory could be shown to be probably true to a greater or less degree; it could not be shown to be necessarily and ontologically true. Demonstrations in natural science, Grosseteste said in his commentary on the *Posterior Analytics*, were 'probable rather than strictly scientific. . . . Only in mathematics is there science and demonstration in the strictest sense.' In his use of the principle of economy Ockham showed that the choice between two theories, both of which were logically coherent and fitted the facts, could only be a matter of convenience, and that it was convenient to use the simpler.

In the work on the rainbow done between Grosseteste and Theodoric of Freiberg, use was made both of experimental tests, and of the principle of economy, to reject false theories and construct true ones. After the theories of Grosseteste, Albertus Magnus, Roger Bacon, and Witelo had all been shown to be inadequate, Theodoric eventually hit upon one which gave the right results. Before him, investigators had been led astray by the analogy of the rainbow colours seen when sunlight passes through a spray or through a single spherical flask of water and falls on to a screen; they thought that in the rainbow itself the light was refracted right through each raindrop, acting as a spherical lens, and was reflected back to the eye by other drops behind. Theodoric showed that this model would not produce anything like the observed rainbow; for example, the colours would be in the reverse of the order seen. He hit upon the original idea that each part of the sunlight, sent back from the raindrops to be seen as a rainbow, was refracted and reflected within the *same* individual drop. This model, he said, had the additional advantage over the previous one of being simpler. From it he built up and tested, by means of a classical series of experiments with crystals and glass flasks, a theory which explained both the primary and the secondary rainbow. His work completed a line of research which Grosseteste began; above all it is an example of the fruitfulness of a conception of scientific method. All these writers on the rainbow conceived of the investigation of this particular problem as an opening into an indefinitely extended inquiry of which the purpose was to construct a general theory giving 'demonstrated knowledge' of all the phenomena produced by light. Grosseteste himself put forward the earliest known form of the 'wave' theory of light. Witelo, Theodoric, and the mid-fourteenth-century French writer, Themon Judaei, acting on a suggestion by Grosseteste, first stated that each of the colours seen in a spectrum produced by passing sunlight through a prism or hexagonal crystal was a different species of ray, generated by the modification of white light by differential refraction. This work was not forgotten; it led straight into that of Huygens and Newton.

A detailed illustration of Grosseteste's method of scientific procedure is given in the translation of one of his short treatises printed as the Appendix to this chapter. Before coming to this, it will be convenient to discuss briefly the second heading under which his scientific methodology is being considered: mathematical physics.

(3)

Of the means whereby 'demonstrated knowledge' could be obtained of the physical world, Grosseteste gave special importance to mathematics. He had two main reasons for this, one methodological, the other metaphysical.

The method by which Grosseteste used mathematics to provide 'demonstrated knowledge' of observed facts was Aristotle's principle of 'subordination'. Some sciences, Aristotle said, were logically 'subordinate' to others, in the sense that statements made in them could be shown to be particular consequences of more general statements made in a 'superior' science. For example, particular statements made in astronomy about the observed movements of the heavenly bodies could be deduced from a purely geometrical theory; statements made in optics about the behaviour of light could be deduced from geometrical laws; statements about musical harmony could be deduced from arithmetical laws. This relationship of subordination could hold only between sciences making univocal statements about the same subject, 'as number-related sound is number-related' as Grosseteste put it in his commentary on the *Posterior Analytics*. He went on:

> With such sciences, of which one is under the other, the superior science provides the reason (*propter quid*) for that thing of which the inferior science provides the fact (*quia*).
> But one must know that an inferior science always adds the condition by which it appropriates to itself the subject and also the characteristics of the superior science, and they are in the conclusions of the subordinate science like two natures, namely, the nature which it receives from the superior and its own nature which it superadds of itself. And so the

superior science does not speak of the causes of the theory that is super-
added, . . . but treats of the causes of the subject which the inferior science
receives from it. And so the subordinating science treats of the causes of a
conclusion that has been appropriated into the subordinate science, and
it does this not in itself but in its universal, for the conclusion of an inferior
science is in the superior science only in its universal. For this reason
mathematicians very often know the reason for a conclusion of an inferior
science, but they do not know the fact, because they do not know the
cause of the conclusion in itself but in its universal and from the mathematical aspect. And these sciences are subordinate to mathematics which
consider forms existing in the subject, but not as being in the subject but
as abstract. The inferior sciences appropriate these forms in some way to
the subject; just as a science sometimes subordinates, sometimes is subordinated, so the same science may be subordinated to one and subordinate
another to itself. For example, optics falls under geometry, and under
optics falls the science concerned with the rays of the sun refracted in a
concave watery cloud. It is optics that provides the causes of the rainbow
simply speaking, that is according to the condition of radiation which
optics appropriates over and above the geometrical subject.

Precisely how he regarded the relationship between mathematics
and the subordinate, physical sciences, in explaining the observed
phenomena described by the latter, Grosseteste made clear in his
discussion of the law of reflection of light. Having given what he
regarded as a satisfactory geometrical demonstration of the law, he
said in his commentary on the *Posterior Analytics*:

Yet the cause of the equality of the two angles made on a mirror by the
incident ray and the reflected ray is not a middle term taken from geometry,
but is the nature of the radiant energy generating itself according to the
rectilinear progress, which, when it is generated on an obstacle having in
itself this kind of spiritual nature, becomes there as a principle regenerat-
ing itself along a path similar to that along which it was generated. For,
since the operation of nature is finite and regular, the path of regeneration
must be similar to the path of generation, and so it is regenerated at an
angle equal to the angle of incidence.

Geometry could provide 'the reason for the fact' in the sense that it
could describe what happened; it could provide the formal cause.
But it could not provide the material and efficient causes, from which
it was explicitly an abstraction. The material and efficient causes
were the 'nature' which the inferior science, optics, 'superadds of
itself'. 'This is more physical than mathematical', Grosseteste said
in his commentary on the *Physics*, 'and perhaps astronomy in

certain parts of its conclusions is like this.' In discussing astronomy Grosseteste pointed out that the geometrical theory of epicycles and eccentrics, with which Ptolemy 'saved the appearances', could not provide the material and efficient causes of the heavenly movements; for these he relied on Aristotle's 'physical' cosmology. From the embarrassment he was one of the first to feel at the contradictions between the two theories, later astronomers were to begin the reform of the whole subject completed by Copernicus, or, indeed, by Newton.

Grosseteste's second, metaphysical reason for giving special importance to mathematics in attempting to provide scientific explanations of the physical world was based on an ontological theory about the nature of physical reality. He held that the fundamental physical substance, the ultimate identity persisting through all change and the original physical cause of all change, was light. In his short treatise, *De Luce seu De inchoatione Formarum*, he described how in the beginning of time God created unformed matter and a point of light, which, propagating itself in a sphere, produced the dimensions of space and, subsequently, all other physical beings. By its expansion light gave corporeal form to the unformed primitive matter. Into the complicated derivation of this Neoplatonic theory from Greek, Arabic, and Latin sources, and into the details of Grosseteste's 'cosmogony of light', it is impossible to enter here. The importance of the theory for the history of science is, first, that it convinced Grosseteste himself that optics was the fundamental physical science; and secondly, because optics could not be studied without mathematics, that Grosseteste's influence committed a growing body of scientists to the use of mathematical theories, not only in optics but in all possible branches of science. 'All causes of natural effects have to be expressed by means of lines, angles and figures', Grosseteste said in *De Lineis*, 'for otherwise it would be impossible to have knowledge of the reason (*propter quid*) concerning them.' He went on, in *De Natura Locorum*: 'these rules and principles and fundamentals having been given by the power of geometry, the careful observer of natural things can give the causes of all natural effects by this method'. These phrases echo through the writings of later 'careful observers' on whom Grosseteste's influence can be proved: Roger Bacon, John Pecham, John of Dumbleton in Oxford, Albertus Magnus, Witelo, Themon Judaei on the Continent, and many others. In the achievements of modern experimental physics, in which Grosseteste's writings were an early essay, they echo still.

(4)

Grosseteste's influence on later generations of scientists was greatest in his own University of Oxford. He established in the university a tradition of scientific inquiry which gave it the leadership of Western science for over a century. Among the first to show his influence was his friend, and successor as lecturer to the Franciscans, Adam Marsh. Other scientific writers influenced by him in his lifetime were the Franciscans, Thomas of York, Thomas Docking, and Bartholomew the Englishman, and the Dominican, Robert Kilwardby. Most prominent among his immediate disciples was Roger Bacon, who got to know him probably about 1247, when Grosseteste was Bishop of Lincoln. Bacon's discussion of the use of induction, experiment, and mathematics in science, and his detailed work on optics and the calendar, directly and explicitly followed the lines of inquiry laid down by Grosseteste. Among later Oxford writers, the unknown author of the *Summa Philosophiae* formerly attributed to Grosseteste himself, John Pecham, John of Dumbleton, and Simon Tunsted continued his work on optics; Duns Scotus, Walter Burley, and William of Ockham cited him on scientific method; Thomas Bradwardine, Henry of Harclay, William of Alnwick, and Robert Holcot took up his discussions of measurement and of the summation of infinite aggregates; John of Eschenden cited him in connexion with weather prediction, Thomas Werkwoth in connexion with astronomical observations. On the Continent Albertus Magnus, the first important scientific teacher in Paris, quoted at length from Grosseteste's writings on scientific method and on optics; Witelo began his treatise on optics with an account of the theory of 'multiplication of species' by which Grosseteste and Roger Bacon had explained the propagation of light; Giles of Lessines quoted him on comets, Themon Judaei on the rainbow. Directly, and indirectly through Roger Bacon, he also influenced the Parisian astronomers of the late thirteenth century. From the end of the fifteenth century several editions were printed of his commentary on the *Posterior Analytics* and of his astronomical writings. Editions of his optical tracts were published in 1503 and 1514. In the second half of the sixteenth century Dr. John Dee made a collection of manuscripts of works by Grosseteste and Roger Bacon as an explicit part of a programme for reviving science in England; Robert Recorde, in his *Castle of Knowledge*, recommended him in a list of astronomical books among 'Dyvers Englyshe menne [who] have written right well in that argument'. All this shows that Grosseteste was remembered as the founder of an enduring scientific tradition.

A good example of Grosseteste's persisting influence is that of his work on the reform of the calendar. On this subject he wrote four separate treatises: a *Canon in Kalendarium* and a first *Compotus* probably before 1220; a *Compotus Correctorius* probably between 1215 and 1219, to correct the two previous works; and a *Compotus Minor* introducing further corrections in 1244. The theoretical astronomical basis of these writings Grosseteste expounded in the *De Sphaera*, which may be dated between 1215 and 1230, perhaps about 1220.

The inaccuracy of the calendar used in the West was noted at the end of the eleventh century by a chronicler who pointed out that the paschal new moon was falsely predicted. About a century later Roger of Hereford tried to get an accurate reckoning of the mean lunar month. By the beginning of the thirteenth century a fuller knowledge of Greek, Jewish, and Arabic systems of chronology brought to the fore the need to reform the Latin calendar and provided the knowledge by which this could be done.

The basic difficulty in the Latin calendar was the need to combine reckonings based on the length of the solar year with those based on the movements of the moon, since the day, the lunar month, and the solar year are incommensurable. No number of days can make an exact number of lunar months or solar years, and no number of lunar months can make an exact number of solar years. An accurate calendar must therefore include a system of *ad hoc* adjustments.

The immediate practical interest in the reform of the calendar was that its inaccuracy produced gross errors in the date of Easter and thus in the whole series of movable feasts of the Church. Moreover, it was obvious to the eye that the calendar was wrong. In the Julian calendar, long established in the West, the length of the year was reckoned as $365\frac{1}{4}$ days. The relationship between the lunar month and the solar year was determined by means of the nineteen-year cycle, according to which nineteen solar years were considered equal to 235 mean lunar months. But these times were not exactly equal, and an error remained even after further systems of adjustment had been introduced. Grosseteste showed that, with the system in current use, in every 304 years the moon would get 1 day, 6 minutes, 40 seconds older than the calendar showed. He pointed out, in the tenth chapter of the *Compotus Correctorius*, that by his time the moon was never full when the calendar said it should be, and that this was especially obvious during an eclipse. As Roger Bacon, who continued Grosseteste's work for calendar reform, scathingly put it in the fourth part of his *Opus Maius*: 'every computer knows that the beginning of lunation is in error 3 or 4 days in these times, and every rustic is able to see this error in the sky'.

Easter Day was always the first Sunday after the full moon on or after the spring equinox. Grosseteste pointed out that in the contemporary reckoning of Easter there were two errors. First, because the solar year was not exactly 365¼ days, the true equinox then fell on an earlier date than that indicated by the Julian calendar; this is clear, he said, from observations with instruments and from the more accurate *Toletan Tables* made by the Arabs. The second source of error was the inaccuracy of the nineteen-year cycle for the moon. It was generally supposed that the current method of reckoning Easter had been laid down by the Council of Nicaea. Though appreciating the understandable conservatism of ecclesiastical authorities, Grosseteste said that there was an undoubted need for reform.

Grosseteste's plan for reforming the calendar was threefold. First, he said that an accurate measure must be made of the length of the solar year. He knew of three estimates of this: that of Hipparchus and Ptolemy, accepted by the Latin computists, that of Al-Battani, and that of Ibn Thebit. He discussed in detail the systems of adjustments that would have to be made in each case to make the solstice and equinox occur in the calendar at the times they were observed. Al-Battani's estimate, he said in the first chapter of his *Compotus Correctorius*, 'agrees best with what we find by observation on the advance of the solstice in our time'. The next stage of the reform was to calculate the relationship between this and the mean lunar month. For the new-moon tables of the *Kalendarium* Grosseteste had used a multiple nineteen-year cycle of seventy-six years. In the *Compotus Correctorius* he calculated the error this involved, and proposed the novel idea of using a much more accurate cycle of thirty Arab lunar years, each of twelve equal months, the whole occupying 10,631 days. This was the shortest time in which the cycle of whole lunations came back to the start. He gave a method of combining this Arab cycle with the Christian solar calendar and of calculating true lunations. The third stage of the reform was to use these results for an accurate reckoning of Easter. In the tenth chapter of the *Compotus Correctorius*, he said that even without an accurate measure of the length of the solar year, the spring equinox, on which the date of Easter depended, could be discovered 'by observation with instruments or from verified astronomical tables'.

Grosseteste's writings on the reform of the calendar, especially his correction of the lunar calendar, inspired subsequent work for two centuries. Sacrobosco's *Computus*, written probably a few years after Grosseteste's, gives the same (erroneous) figure for the difference between the earlier calendars of Gerland and of Dyonisius. Roger Bacon, in his *Computus* and in the sections on the calendar in the *Opus Maius* and *Opus Tertium*, repeated Grosseteste's criticisms of the contemporary calendar and his remedies, though he also offered new ones based on the Jewish method of reckoning. John Campanus of Novara relied directly on Grosseteste for his *Compotus Major*, copying parts of his section on the moon almost word for word. Cardinal Pierre d'Ailly based his *Exhortatio ad Concilium Generale Constantiense super correctione kalendarii* almost entirely upon Grosseteste's writings. Institutional conservatism blocked these early attempts at reform; nevertheless, Grosseteste can be said to be the original architect of the Gregorian Calendar of 1582, a calendar, ironically, not accepted in his own country for another 170 years.

Grosseteste can truly be claimed as the first great English scientist and philosopher of science. At a time when guidance was essential, he provided England's young university with a creative understanding of science that made it for a time the leading scientific centre in Christendom, and enabled it to contribute to the modern world something entirely new. Stern and intellectual by nature, he called his disciples to high intellectual tasks, yet at the same time inspired a strong personal devotion. He was 'the true teacher who interiorly illuminates the mind, and shows the truth'. In his writings are found to a high degree those characteristics of empiricism, inspired by the imagination and guided by the reason, that have marked the English achievement not only in science, but in many other aspects of practical and intellectual life.

APPENDIX

THE modes of argument used by Grosseteste in his method of experimental verification and falsification are called, respectively, the *modus ponendo ponens* and the *modus tollendo tollens*. The first takes the following syllogistic form:

> If A is B, it is C,
> A is B,
> ∴ A is C.

The second takes the form:

> If A is B, it is C,
> A is not C,
> ∴ A is not B.

We have a good illustration of his use of these forms of argument in his treatise, *De Calore Solis*. As in every period of the history of science, he worked within a framework of existing theory, for example of Aristotle's cosmology with its distinction between natural and violent motions and its assertion that bodies in the inferior, sublunary region could undergo all kinds of change, whereas the heavenly bodies, composed of the fifth element, could change only by local motion. The book, *On Mirrors*, to which he refers, is Euclid's *Catoptrica*. Though not remarkable for its observations, *De Calore Solis* contains the essential elements of the logical procedures used in experimental verification and falsification. The following is a translation from the Latin text printed in Baur's edition of his philosophical writings (pp. 79–84).

On the Heat of the Sun

As our main purpose is to discuss whatever may be the principle of generation of the heat of the sun, we may ask universally: How many principles of generation are there? Since there are three principles from which heat is generated, namely a hot body, motion and a concentration of rays, we should realise that the heat in these is of a single nature (*univocum*); from this single nature an effect of a single nature is produced in them. And since they have an effect of a single nature, it follows that in all these principles there is a cause of a single nature: for, of every effect of a single nature there is a cause of a single nature. That the heat in all of them is of a single nature is clear, because, from whichever of them it is generated, it has the same powers and produces the same effects. Therefore it is univocally, not equivocally, named.

Let us, then, look for this univocal cause. In all of them the proximate cause of heat is scattering (*disgregatio*). Whence, since a hot body generates heat, this is by the scattering of materials. But how this explanation fits motion and a concentration of rays it is difficult to see.

Local motion, from which heat is generated, is divided into natural and violent motion, natural motion again into rectilinear and circular motion. First let us discuss violent motion, or a heavy body violently moved. A heavy body can be moved violently in three ways, up, down, or down but not directly towards the centre of the earth. In all cases it is clear that in the violent motion there is scattering because of the motion. For in violent motion there is a two-fold motive power, one part natural, the other violent, and these move every part of the moving body in different directions. As a result of this tendency to go in different directions, scattering takes place. Because of the violent motion, the moving body must be scattered part from part, and so heat results. Since, in the first way of moving violently, there is the greatest amount of opposition between the tendencies of the moving powers (they are moving in completely opposite directions), this produces the most scattering and the most heat; the second and third ways produce only moderate heat. This is in the highest degree clear from both theory (*ratione*) and from observation (*experimento*).

The same thing is shown in the case of natural motion. For heat is generated during motion in anything moving naturally downwards. Acting on every part there is actually a two-fold motive power, partly natural, partly violent. It is obvious that a natural power is operating here. That a violent power is also operating I show as follows:

Everything that is heavy and is moved downwards not directly towards the centre of the earth, is moved violently. But all heavy parts are moved downwards not directly towards the centre. Therefore all heavy parts are moved violently. The minor premiss I prove thus: The parts of a heavy body always keep the same distance apart in the whole. Therefore, since they are moved downwards with the motion of the whole, they move along lines which remain a constant distance apart. But lines which remain a constant distance apart when extended to infinity in either direction never meet. Therefore the parts of a naturally moved heavy body are moved downwards along non-intersecting lines. Therefore they are not moved directly towards the centre of the earth, because, if they were, they would be moved along lines running directly together there. So the principle is evident, namely that acting on every part of a body moved naturally down there is a two-fold power tending in different directions. But the opposition between these tendencies is weaker than the opposition between the tendencies of the parts in violent motion; so, of all agencies generating heat, natural motion generates the least natural heat in motion. Thus it is plain that from natural rectilinear motion, and from violent motion, heat is generated, and from a hot body heat is generated by a univocal cause.

The same can be shown, by similar reasoning, of the third principle of generation of heat. That some heat may be generated, from a univocal cause of heat, by the concentration of rays is shown by *On Mirrors*; rays from a concave mirror directed towards the sun produce combustion, and this is on account of scattering. A ray in a denser transparent medium is more incorporated than in a less dense one (and we are not speaking of total incorporation, like heat, but of a certain partial incorporation). Because of this incorporation, the incorporated parts of the air fly apart when the rays are concentrated at one point, each part, at the point itself, going along its own straight line. As a result there will be, round this point, the greatest dispersion of the air into different directions, and so there will be a scattering and heat will result. Thus it is evident that in these three genera heat is present from a cause of a single nature.

If, then, the sun generates heat, it will do so either as a hot body does, or as motion does, or as a concentration of rays does. That the sun does not generate heat in the manner in which a hot body does is evident from the following: It is proved in the seventh book of the *Physics* that an agent producing a change of quality, and the subject undergoing change, must be in immediate contact. Hence, if there were a medium between the original agent of change and the ultimate changed subject, that medium would first have to be changed by the heat of the hot sun, rather than the ultimate subject; otherwise the original agent and the first subject to be changed would not be in immediate contact. Therefore, since there are several media between the sun and the air, and next to the sun (which produces change according to the heat it possesses) is the fifth element or part of the fifth element, it must follow that the heat of the sun must first bring about a change of heat in the fifth element, rather than in the air. But this is impossible, because if the fifth element can undergo change of quality, it is corruptible. Therefore the first premiss is impossible, namely that the sun generates heat in the manner in which a hot body does. Perhaps some would say that heat is present in the sun virtually, as it is in pepper. But this is not to the point, because, in so far as heat is present in pepper virtually and not actually, it cannot produce movement unless it is moved by something else, nor qualitative change unless it is changed by something else. And similarly for the sun. But this is impossible; so therefore is the first premiss.

That heat is not generated from the motion of the sun is shown as follows. Now motion does not generate heat, unless there are, in every part of the moved thing, different tendencies moving the part in different directions. But in everything that is moved circularly and not violently, any part has the same tendency as the whole; there is no difference: the tendency of every part is to move in a circle. Therefore no heat is generated by circular motion. You might perhaps say that although there is no intrinsic cause of heat in anything moving in a circle, nevertheless there is an extrinsic cause, as there is with inferior bodies from the resistance of the medium. But this is false for two reasons: one reason is that in these inferior bodies the resistance of the medium is not the source of the heat produced by motion. If it were, since the medium resists equally things moving with natural and with violent motion, the same amount of heat should be generated by violent and by natural motion. But this is false, as observation shows; therefore so is the first premiss. The other reason why it is false is that the sun and stars have no resistance to their motion, because they are not moved by motors of their own. But since they are fixed in their spheres, they are moved by the motion of their spheres, like a ship in a river, which is moved by the motion of the river, as the Philosopher [Aristotle] shows in the second book of the *De Caelo et Mundo*.

There remains therefore only the theory that the sun generates heat by the concentration of rays. This is shown as follows: The sun's rays in the transparent medium of the air are, through the nature of the dense body, to some extent incorporated in it. Rays falling downwards on to the plane, concave, or convex surface of the earth are reflected at equal angles, as shown by the last of the principles taught in *On Mirrors*. Therefore, if they fall perpendicularly, they are reflected perpendicularly; and so the incident and the reflected rays go along the same line in totally opposite directions, and there is a maximum of scattering. This is the case on the equator, when the sun is at the zenith of this region, and at any place south or north of the equator at a distance from it less than that of the tropic of cancer or of the tropic of capricorn. In these regions the sun's rays must fall perpendicularly twice a year. But at a place on the tropic of cancer or the tropic of capricorn, the sun can reach the zenith only once, and only once send rays perpendicularly to this place. When this happens there is a maximum of scattering and of heat in these places. This is a violent scattering, such as is brought about by a concentration of rays refracted through a spherical body or reflected from a concave mirror, though in it the rays go in totally opposite directions, whereas in the case of the spherical refracting body and the concave mirror they do not.

In regions at greater distances from the equator than the tropic of cancer, since the sun does not come north far enough to reach the zenith, the rays fall at an angle less than a right angle, and are reflected at the same angle and so not in a totally opposite direction. The further the place from the equator, the more obtuse the angles at which the solar rays fall and are reflected, and the less opposed the directions in which the incident and reflected rays go, the less the scattering, and the less the heat generated. This is shown by observation.

If it is asked why heat is not generated from the rays of the sun in the fifth element, two replies can be given: first, that reflected rays do not intersect there; secondly, even if they did intersect after being reflected in a totally opposite direction [to the incident rays], heat would not be generated. For, since in this transparent medium there is no dense nature, the solar rays are not in any way incorporated in it, and so cannot scatter the parts of matter. In the uppermost layer of air, where the air is thinnest, the least amount of heat is generated, as observation shows. For there are more clouds on the summit of mountains, where the solar rays are brightest, than in valleys, though, nevertheless, rays are reflected there, just as they are in a valley; but, because of the thinness of the air there, the density of the air is small, so is the incorporation of light with it, and hence so also is the scattering of the parts of the air in the concentration of rays. In a valley there is a greater incorporation of rays and therefore more scattering and more heat.

A. C. CROMBIE.

The Library of Robert Grosseteste

N O catalogue of the books belonging to Robert Grosseteste
has survived, but, in spite of this lack, there are other
sources of information available. Books annotated by him
are extant and others, now lost, are known to have been preserved in
the library of the Franciscan convent at Oxford. His letters contain
a few scattered allusions to books. Thomas Gascoigne, the fifteenth-
century Oxford theologian, has left us valuable evidence. These
sources will not provide us with a complete picture, but they are
enough to justify an attempt to put together the facts that are
known.

A marked feature of Grosseteste's work is the number of notes
and annotations by him that have come down to us, and a consideration of the different types of his notes is the best method of approach-
ing the question of his library. They are well illustrated in two
manuscripts containing annotations in his own hand, one of Augustine *De Civitate Dei* and Gregory *Moralia in Iob* (MS. Bodley 198),
and the other of Boethius *De Consolatione Philosophiae* (MS. Trinity
College, Oxford, 17). The two manuscripts are strongly contrasted
physically. The Boethius is a small book written in an undis-
tinguished hand of the twelfth century. It had no rubrication, and
to make it usable for study Grosseteste added running titles with the
number of the book and chapter. The Augustine and Gregory is a
large quarto finely written on thin parchment in a hand contemporary with Grosseteste, and we may reasonably suppose it to have
been executed at his order. It is an early example of a type of manuscript of works of the Fathers, which only became common in the
latter part of the thirteenth century. The development of the com-
pressed Gothic script and the availability of thinner parchment made
it possible to bring within the compass of a single volume works
which in the twelfth century would have occupied three or four.
The manuscript is manifestly designed for study, not for reading
aloud. The annotation in both these volumes is similar. Grosseteste
to some extent corrected the text, particularly by supplying in the margins passages omitted by the scribe and occasionally by adding variant
readings. He put in cross-references and many short notes drawing attention to subject-matter. In the Boethius a dozen references

are added to various works of Augustine; in the Augustine and Gregory many scriptural passages are identified by giving book and chapter numbers. In both there is a little Greek, in the Boethius without breathings or accents,[1] in the Augustine and Gregory with.[2] In the Augustine he occasionally amuses himself by writing Latin words in Greek characters; for instance in the passage (De Civ. Dei, vii. 12) where Augustine is quoting the contrast drawn by Cato the Censor between the virtues of the ancient Romans and the vices of the Romans of his day, Grosseteste has written αγγλικοι (the English) against the latter.[3] There are no long notes in either.[4]

On other patristic texts we know from the evidence of Thomas Gascoigne that there were more extensive annotations. Gascoigne quotes a long note from the margin of Grosseteste's copy of Jerome's Letters, the substance of which is incorporated in the De Cessatione Legalium.[5] He also quotes extensively from the marginalia in Grosseteste's copy of the Pauline Epistles with the gloss. The annotation of such a book was a common practice. It had become customary to make copies of glossed books of the Bible set out with wide margins so that teachers and students could add their own comments. Further evidence of notes in patristic texts is supplied by a manuscript in the Bodleian Library (MS. Bodley 785), which has not been noticed in this connexion before.[6] The main body of the manuscript, which was written c. 1300, contains Gregory's Cura Pastoralis and texts of scholastic theology, all with annotations by a contemporary hand. Prefixed to these treatises are two quires (fols. 1–16), and on fol. 1 the annotator wrote the following inscription: 'Omnia scripta in hac pecia (et sequenti interlined) extrahuntur de libro magistri R.

---

[1] MS. Trinity College 17, fol. 7. In the text of Bk. I, pr. v, p. 158 Stewart-Rand, the quotation of the Iliad was only given in Latin 'Unus dominus et unus rex' (cf. Trivet's comm. ad loc. 'Ista sententia in veracioribus et antiquioribus libris in verbis grecis ponitur', MS. Bodl. Auct. F. 6.4 (S.C. 2150), fol. 100). Grosseteste wrote in the margin εις κιριος εστγγ [και cut off] εις βασιλεος. The reading κύριος for κοίρανος is found in other English twelfth-century manuscripts in various disguises; see MS. Bodl. Auct. F. 6.5 (S.C. 1856), fol. 9ᵛ.

[2] MS. Bodley 198, fols. 189 (quoted Thomson, Writings, p. 28), 190, 218ᵛ, 219, 260ᵛ.

[3] MS. Bodley 198, fol. 20; cf. fols. 1, 148 (quoted Thomson, op. cit., p. 28).

[4] The only ones which are more than subject heads are on fols. 19, 22ᵛ, 23ᵛ, 24ᵛ.

[5] See below, p. 136, and Smalley, above, p. 93.

[6] S.C. no. 2624. Nothing is known of the history of the volume before 1447, when it was pledged in the Nele chest at Oxford by Magister Petrus Borowghe, who, as Mr. A. B. Emden kindly informs me, was Principal of Neville Inn in Sept. 1446 and subsequently held various benefices. Soon after it came into the library of the Dean and Canons of Windsor, who presented it to the Bodleian in 1612.

Grosseteste et scribuntur ibi de manu sua.' The contents of these two quires are notes on Augustine *Super Genesim ad Litteram,* a copy of a set of *exceptiones* from Augustine *De Trinitate* (fol. 2ᵛ) with marginal notes and the indexing signs, of which we shall speak shortly, written in the same hand as the text, notes on Augustine *De Civitate Dei,* lib. 19 (fol. 11ᵛ),[1] notes 'Prope finem Anselmi de conceptu virginali', a copy of Prosper[2] *Catholica confutatio falso sibi obiectorum* (fol. 13), notes 'Post finem libri Soliloquiorum', and finally (fol. 16) notes from 'Tractatus post librum Catholice confutationis Augustini Augustinus super Genesim', which turns out to be another copy of the beginning of the first item. The second note, 'Near the end of Anselm *De Conceptu Virginali*', is one that Grosseteste incorporated in his *Dicta.*[3] Its appearance in the present context is a welcome support for the correctness of the ascription of the notes to Grosseteste, and fits in well with his own description of the *Dicta* as 'brief notes which I wrote down roughly, while I was in the schools, to preserve them'.[4]

Whether 'the book of Master Robert Grosseteste', from which the scribe of these two quires made the extracts, contained complete copies of all the works mentioned, it is not possible to say; but the type of note corresponds to the two types we have discussed: the subject heads and the references to other works, with the index signs, found in MS. Bodley 198 and the Boethius, are in the margins of the Exceptiones de Trinitate, and the longer note in the Jerome quoted by Gascoigne is paralleled by the piece 'Near the end' of Anselm's work.

So far only passing mention has been made of another kind of annotation which at once catches the eye in his books. It consists of symbols of all sorts—mathematical signs, letters of the Greek alphabet, conventional designs—written in the outer margins close to the text. Gascoigne remarked on them in MS. Bodley 198 and noted that where the same sign recurred the subject-matter of the text was the same.[5] But it was reserved for Professor S. Harrison Thomson to discover their full significance. He found prefixed to a Bible at Lyons a 'Table of Master Robert, Bishop of Lincoln, with the addition of brother Adam of Marsh; and there are nine divisions,

---

[1] They are not in MS. Bodley 198.
[2] Here anonymous, and wrongly ascribed to Augustine below.
[3] No. 140, Thomson, *Writings,* p. 231.
[4] Thomson, op. cit., p. 214.
[5] Fol. 107, quoted by Thomson, op. cit., p. 27.

of which the first concerns God'.[1] The table consists first of a list of some 400 signs with the subject denoted by each. This is followed by a list of fifty-four additional topics without signs. Then come thirty-eight pages on each of which five to ten of the subjects with their signs are set out. Each subject is followed by a string of references, first to the Bible and then to the writings of the Fathers. Under some subjects additional references to other writings are placed in the right-hand margin. An example taken from dist. V will make plainer the way in which the table worked.

℘ Quomodo philosophia accipienda sit a nobis.
Deut. 20, 21.

Ieronimus ep. 104, 109; super ad Galat. c. 2, 3; Contra Iovin. c. 21; Augustinus ep. 9, 11, 15, 20, 38, 50, 57; De civ. dei li. 10, 11, 12, 13, 15, 18, 19, 21, 22; Enchirid. 11, 20; Retractat. li. 1, c. 1, 3; De doctrina christiana 4; Ad Januarium li. 2; De trinitate 4. Gregorius Moralia li. 9, 14, 18, 26, 29; Ioh. Crisostomus De compunctione cordis l. 1. Ioh. Damascenus Sent. c. 20, 21, 85. Dionisius Ierarchia l. 1. c. 2.[2]

The purpose of the signs is now quite clear. They were used to build up a theological subject index to books which were available to the two men. The references given to Augustine *De Civitate Dei* and to Gregory *Moralia* in the extract just quoted can be checked in MS. Bodley 198. They correspond exactly.[3] Unfortunately the *Tabula* is incomplete in the Lyons manuscript, and we are deprived of the opportunity of seeing the dossier on cosmological subjects.[4] As far as Grosseteste is concerned, Professor Thomson has argued that, since the works quoted do not include some which he translated as bishop, the compilation of the index dates from his period as teacher at Oxford or from the early years of his episcopate; and this argument is not invalidated by the phrase in the title 'with the addition of brother Adam of Marsh', because Adam was so closely associated with Grosseteste that, if the table were later, we should still expect to find references added to some of the translations from the Greek, such as that of the *Ethics* of Aristotle. But the introduction of Adam's name does constitute an obstacle to using the list of works quoted as a list of books actually owned by Grosseteste. With

---

[1] *Speculum* 9 (1934), 139–44; *Writings*, pp. 122–4.
[2] Lyons, MS. Bibl. municipale 414, fol. 31ʳ.
[3] It will be noticed that usually only book, and not chapter, numbers are given.
[4] There is a note at the beginning in a later hand, 'Ista tabula scribitur usque ad dist. vi et parum plus'.

the evidence at our disposal we cannot isolate the contribution of Adam, and we must use the evidence of the table with this limitation in mind.

The works to which references are given[1] cover a wide range of the writings of the four great Latin Fathers, Augustine, Ambrose, Jerome, and Gregory, to whom we may attach Isidore and Bede. The Greek Fathers are represented by Origen's *Homilies*, Basil, *Hexaemeron*, works by or ascribed to John Chrysostom, John of Damascus, and pseudo-Denis the Areopagite. The only Carolingian writers are Florus and Rabanus Maurus.[2] For the eleventh to twelfth century we find Anselm of Canterbury, Hugh of St. Victor, and Bernard of Clairvaux. The writings quoted in the right-hand margin are the Latin classical authors Cicero, Horace, and Seneca the Younger, certain writers of later antiquity, Prudentius, Sedulius, Solinus, Chalcidius, and Boethius, and translations of works of Aristotle, of Ptolemy's *Almagest*, of Algazel, Alhasen, and Avicenna.

Grosseteste and Adam Marsh were not the only scholars at this time to feel the need for such indexes. To give only one example, their friend, Thomas Gallus, Abbot of Vercelli, made a subject concordance of the Bible to help him in his work of commenting on pseudo-Denis,[3] but it is a measure of the influence of Grosseteste and Adam Marsh that the complicated set of index signs continued to be used by the English Franciscans in the second half of the thirteenth century. A dozen manuscripts containing them have so far been identified.[4] To deal with them all here would take us too far from Grosseteste, and it is only possible to comment on three which bring us most closely in touch with him and his circle. The first, which was in the library of the Franciscan convent at Lincoln, is a manuscript of works of Anselm and Augustine.[5] Several of them are supplied with analytical chapter-headings in the margin. The first of the works of Augustine so dealt with is the *De Doctrina Christiana*. The analysis is headed 'Secundum fratrem Adam de Marisco'[6] and concludes with the note: 'Distinctio librorum de doctrina christiana

---

[1] A list of the works cited will be found below, pp. 141–5.

[2] In fact one of the works ascribed to him is by Paschasius Radbertus.

[3] G. Théry, 'Thomas Gallus et les Concordances bibliques' in *Aus der Geisteswelt des Mittelalters*, Beiträge zur Gesch. der Philosophie und Theologie des Mittelalters, Suppl. Bd. iii. 1, 1935, pp. 427–46.

[4] I have discussed them in *Bodleian Library Record*, iv (1953), 241–55.

[5] Cambridge, MSS. St. John's College 17 and 47.

[6] MS. 47, fol. 1ᵛ bottom margin.

secundum capitula superscripta non est autentica, sed ad adiuvandam dictorum librorum intelligentiam per ista capitula singulos ⟨libros⟩, prout mee visum est insufficiencie, sum partitus.' Some of the marginal notes on the same work breathe the spirit of the circle of Grosseteste and Adam Marsh, for instance one on 'the almost unavoidable necessity of a knowledge of Greek and Hebrew for the understanding of the sacred scripture, and especially of Greek'.[1] The second is a copy of Rabanus Maurus *De Natura Rerum*, written towards the middle of the thirteenth century.[2] There is evidence to show that it was in the library of the Franciscans at Oxford. The exemplar from which it was copied was defective, and evidently lacked book- and chapter-headings, for they are added in another hand. The concept for them is written in crayon in the bottom margin as far as fol. 35ᵛ, where the writer notes 'Here I left off'. The corrector had access to another copy of the work, which belonged to Grosseteste. Six times he notes the place where a new book began 'according to the bishop's book' (*secundum librum episcopi*).[3] We know that the work was in Grosseteste's possession since it is frequently quoted in the *Tabula*. There is reason to think that the annotation in this manuscript may be in the hand of Adam Marsh. The third manuscript[4] is remarkable for the range of its contents. Besides works of Augustine, John of Damascus, pseudo-Denis with the paraphrase of Thomas Gallus, Jerome, *De Hebraicis Questionibus*, it contains Seneca, *Quaestiones Naturales* and *Epistolae*, and extracts from Cicero, *De Divinatione*. This is a very unusual collection of texts to find in a single volume, and the fact that all of them (except Thomas Gallus) are works cited in the *Tabula* can hardly be a coincidence.

The notes to which modern scholars have paid most attention are those which Grosseteste made on certain of his translations from the Greek, the Ignatian Epistles, works of John of Damascus, the scholia of Maximus the Confessor on pseudo-Denis, the *Nicomachean Ethics* with the commentaries of Michael of Ephesus and others, and on the *De Caelo et Mundo* with the commentary of Simplicius. With

---

[1] MS. 47, fol. 6ʳ top margin. Note on *De Doctr. Christ.* ii. 11: 'Nota quod ex hiis que hic dicuntur et in sequentibus patet quasi inevitabilis necessitas agnicionis ligue [*sic*] Grece et Hebree ad intelligentiam scripture sacre, et precipue Grece.'

[2] Bodl., MS. Laud misc. 746.   [3] Fols. 19ᵛ, 22ᵛ, 26, 27, 29ᵛ, 34ᵛ.

[4] British Museum, MS. Royal 5 D. x. The notes on John of Damascus, which are not referred to by Thomson, deserve investigation in connexion with the *notulae* of Grosseteste; see Callus, above, p. 48.

the partial exception of those on the *Ethics* these are notes of a translator giving explanations of Greek words and discussing their etymology, and occasionally calling attention to variant readings. The notes on the *Ethics* which are found in varying numbers in the margins of some copies of that work include also comments on the arguments of particular passages. That they derive from Grosseteste's own copy is suggested by one reference to the *liber episcopi*.[1]

We have further evidence of marginal annotations from a disputation held at Oxford in 1316–17.[2] The chancellor, Henry of Harclay, put forward a passage from Grosseteste on Aristotle's *Physics* to support one of his arguments. In his reply William of Alnwick, the regent-master of the Franciscans, said:

> It should be known that Grosseteste (*dominus Lynconiensis*) wrote the words with his own hand in the margin of his copy of the *Physics*, which he did not comment on systematically or completely, as he did on the *Posterior Analytics*. But when some noteworthy thought occurred to him, he wrote it down there so that it should not escape his memory, just as he also wrote many slips of parchment (*multas cedulas*),[3] which are not all authentic. What he wrote disconnectedly (*dissute*) in the margin of his copy of the *Physics* is of no greater authority than the other slips of parchment he wrote, which are all kept in the library of the Friars Minor at Oxford, as I have seen with my own eyes.

One other reference to these slips of parchment is known. A copy of a note by Grosseteste *De Quadratura Circuli* at the end of a manuscript at Oxford[4] concludes with the words: 'Hanc demonstracionem inveni Oxonie in quadam cedula domini Lincolniensis.'

The correspondence of Grosseteste and Adam Marsh adds disappointingly little, but there are a few allusions to the buying and copying of books. In a letter to Master John of Foxton,[5] written in answer apparently to one of congratulation and exhortation on his elevation to the bishopric of Lincoln, Grosseteste says that he has been told that John intends to sell the books of Holy Scripture which he possesses and to convert the money to pious uses. Grosseteste goes on to say that he has need of them and offers to pay the price named to the bearer of the letter. John of Foxton is otherwise known

---

[1] Thomson, *Writings*, p. 69; cf. also p. 49 above.
[2] See Callus, 'Oxford Career', p. 46.
[3] i.e. *schedulas*.
[4] MS. C.C.C. 251. This note was printed in *Coxe's Catalogue* (1852), but attention was first called to it by Marshall Clagett in the forthcoming *Essays in Honor of A. P. Evans*.
[5] *Ep.* 33, p. 120.

from a passage in Matthew Paris under the year 1244,[1] where he relates that miracles were performed at his tomb and at that of Roger North, Bishop of London (d. 1241). A list of the books of John of Foxton is entered in a copy of the Commentary on the Psalms by Peter Lombard at Lincoln Cathedral Chapter Library (MS. 139).[2] It consists of theological works, largely glossed books of the Bible. The handwriting of the list would fit Grosseteste's correspondent, and there can be little doubt of the identity. The volume contains no sign that it was ever in the hands of Grosseteste, nor is there any record of the way in which it came into the Cathedral Library.

The purchase of second-hand books was then, as now, one of the main ways of building up a collection, but to obtain new books it was necessary either to make copies oneself or to employ scribes. As a young man Grosseteste might have had time to make copies himself, and one manuscript has survived containing mathematical and astronomical works probably written in his own hand, which can be dated c. 1215–16.[3] It is hard to imagine that he would have had time for such work later, when he would, in any case, have had the means to pay scribes, whose presence in Oxford is well attested. When Adam Marsh sent him some pieces from the various expositions of Abbot Joachim, which had been brought to him by a friar from the Continent, he told him to have the pamphlet read aloud in his room in the presence of his secretaries, and to return it when he had had a copy made.[4] In another letter written in 1251 Adam speaks of a copy Grosseteste has had made of his translation of the *Ethics* and of the elaborate arrangements made for sending it to Provence.[5]

We have so far implicitly assumed that Grosseteste had to depend on his own resources to obtain books, and, in the lack of any information about the store of books available in Oxford in the early thirteenth century, we can hardly do otherwise. It was not until much later that the University had a library, and there is nothing to suggest that the religious houses in Oxford had considerable collections in

---

[1] *Chron. Mai.* iv. 378. The passage is corrupt, and it is not clear where his tomb was.

[2] Printed in R. M. Woolley, *Cat. of the MSS. in Lincoln Cath. Chapter Library*, 1927, p. 98. Woolley wrongly read the name as John of Sexton, and dated the list fourteenth century. The correct reading is due to Dr. J. H. Srawley.

[3] Bodl., MS. Savile 21; see below, pp. 133 f.

[4] *Ep.* 43, *Mon. Franc.*, p. 146.

[5] *Ep.* 26; see Powicke, *Rob. Grosseteste*, pp. 18–20.

his day—a contrast to the position in Paris. There is fortunately one piece of evidence to show that he could draw on the resources of other monastic libraries. MS. 7 at Pembroke College, Cambridge, containing reports of lectures on books of the Bible delivered at Paris, has an inscription stating that it was 'a pledge (*memoriale*) of Master Robert Grosseteste for the *Hexaemeron* of Basil'. It was a normal regulation that when a volume was borrowed a pledge of equivalent value should be left in its place.[1] The manuscript also carries the later pressmark of the Abbey of Bury St. Edmunds, whence the Basil was no doubt borrowed and to which it was presumably never returned. It is a work cited in the *Tabula* and much used in the *Hexaemeron*.

The evidence here collected does not cover all Grosseteste's interests. Natural science is barely represented, and there are hardly more references to theological or Biblical works of the twelfth century. On the other hand, the *Tabula* suggests that he had a considerable library of patristic works and some Latin classical texts and translations from the Greek. We know also that he possessed a certain number of Greek manuscripts and a Hebrew Psalter.[2]

It is obviously out of the question to make a numerical estimate of the size of his collection, but it is worth asking how many books a man in his position might be expected to have. Twenty to forty volumes was a good collection: Master Robert of Edington deposited thirty-eight volumes at the Abbey of St. Victor at Paris in the late twelfth century,[3] a certain M. de Cumtune bequeathed nineteen volumes to his brother R. some time early in the thirteenth century,[4] and the list of Master John of Foxton's books runs to about thirty-four volumes. Grosseteste's collection was probably larger than any of these, and perhaps the list of books belonging to Bernard, Archbishop of St. James of Compostella (1226), which contains ninety-two items, may form a standard of comparison.[5] There is nothing to

---

[1] See the Durham regulation of 1235: 'Item statutum est per eosdem [the Prior and chapter] ut nullus liber accomodetur alicui per librarium vel per alium, nisi receperit memoriale aequipollens; nisi fuerit ad instanciam domini episcopi' (*Catal. veteres librorum eccl. cath. Dunelm.* (Surtees Soc. 1838), p. 121; and the regulation for the canons of Chichester (1226) in *Hist. MSS. Commission, Reports on various collections*, 1901, i. 192.

[2] For Greek manuscripts see below, pp. 134 f., and for the Hebrew Psalter see Smalley, p. 77.   [3] R. A. B. Mynors, *Durham Cathedral Manuscripts*, 1939, pp. 78 f.

[4] Bodl., MS. Digby 108, fol. 1.

[5] Printed by H. Omont in *Bibl. de l'École des Chartes 54*, 1893, pp. 327–33. I have said items rather than volumes, because no. 77 is 'Quidam saccus ligneus cum libris sermonum philosoforum ystoriographorum'. See Addendum, p. 145.

suggest that it approached the very large collection of some 300 volumes which Gérard d'Abbeville left to the Sorbonne in 1271.[1]

II

Grosseteste's will has not survived, and the only contemporary allusion to the disposition of his books occurs in a letter written by Adam Marsh to Richard of Gravesend, Dean of Lincoln, 1254–8. Adam says that he will meet the laudable wishes of the dean about the disposition of the writings (*scripta*) of Grosseteste, both published and translated (*tam editis quam translatis*) after consultation with the provincial of the Franciscans.[2] Nothing can be certainly inferred from this statement except that the Franciscans had some interest in their disposition. It is not until we come to the Chronicle of Nicholas Trivet, written in the early fourteenth century, that we have definite information. He says that 'out of affection for him [Adam Marsh] Grosseteste bequeathed in his will all his books to the convent of the Friars Minor at Oxford'.[3] Trivet is likely to have been well informed on such a point, and the evidence of Thomas Gascoigne shows, as we shall see, that books belonging to Grosseteste, other than his writings, were in the possession of the Oxford Franciscan house and that they were given by him.

We are indebted to the enthusiastic devotion of Thomas Gascoigne for most of our information about the later history of Grosseteste's books. He not only incorporated many extracts from his works in the *Liber de Veritatibus collectis* but also jotted down details about him and his books in the margins of manuscripts which he owned. From these notes we learn that there were in his day two collections of books in the Oxford Franciscan House, the library of the convent and the library of the students, and that Grosseteste's were in the former.[4] An unusual feature of some of the references of Gascoigne is that they give the actual pressmark of some of the books in the following form:[5] 'Psalterium . . . registratur Oxonie inter fratres minores Episcopus Lincolniensis. d.' There are no surviving books from the library of the Oxford Franciscans with pressmarks, but the same form was used in other English Franciscan houses.[6] Take,

---

[1] L. Delisle, *Cabinet des manuscrits*, 1874, ii. 148 f.

[2] *Ep.* 76, *Mon. Franc.*, p. 185.   [3] *Ann.*, p. 243.

[4] See below, p. 136.   [5] See below, p. 136.

[6] N. R. Ker, *Medieval libraries of Great Britain*, 1941, under the Franciscan convents of Bristol, Cambridge, Chester, Coventry, Norwich, and Shrewsbury. Mr. Ker collected the facts together in the typescript addenda, of which a copy is in the Bodleian Library.

for instance, a copy of Josephus from the Coventry Franciscans now in the British Museum (MS. Harley 5116). It has the inscriptions 'De communitate fratrum minorum Coventrie' and 'Et registratur sic Josephus A.' The pressmark is one which consists of an author's name or a subject title followed by a letter[1] to distinguish the various volumes bearing the same title. In the series 'Episcopus Lincolniensis' Gascoigne refers to volumes with the letters D, E, F, I, T,[2] from which we may fairly conclude that there were at one time nineteen volumes in it at least. How many of these came from Grosseteste himself we cannot be certain. D, E, F, and I did, but T was a copy of his letters, which would be a later accession. This series did not comprise the whole of Grosseteste's bequest. Gascoigne quotes from 'Epistole Pauli glosate A' and 'Jeronimus L', both of which contained annotations by him, but nothing more can safely be inferred about the extent of the bequest from them.

Gascoigne sometimes adds a date to his notes. The earliest is 1433 in MS. Bodley 198. He refers to visits paid to the library in 1434, 1455, 1456.[3] One of Grosseteste's books was still in the library at the end of the fifteenth or beginning of the sixteenth century. A copy of the Gospels in Greek (now MS. Gonville and Caius College 403) with the Oxford Franciscan *ex libris*, which had belonged to him, was lent to Richard Brinkley, the Cambridge Franciscan,[4] and has probably survived because it was never returned. The later history of the library is a melancholy one. At the time of the suppression (1538) the convent 'was wretchedly poor and in a ruinous condition'.[5] Leland had visited the library shortly before and notes:[6] 'At the Franciscans there are cobwebs in the library, also cockroaches and wood worm, more than this—whatever others may

---

[1] At Worcester and York, where the libraries were presumably larger, the letter is replaced by a number, e.g. Biblia 13 at Worcester. This system was also used at Oxford in some sections, since Gascoigne mentions a copy of Augustinus Contra Maximinum 'et est ille liber Oxonie inter fratres minores in libro registrato in dorso libri Augustinus 37us' (MS. Lincoln Coll. lat. 117, p. 448a). This, with other references, was collected by W. Pronger, *E.H.R.* liii (1938), 621; but it should be noted that the quotations which she gives from MS. Oriel College 30 are to the library of the Dominicans and not to that of the Franciscans.

[2] For details of the books referred to see below, pp. 135-8.

[3] *Loci*, ed. Rogers, pp. 129, 126, 138, 127.

[4] J. R. H. Moorman, *Grey Friars in Cambridge*, 1952, pp. 155 f. The latest known date in his career is 1526.

[5] A. G. Little, *The Grey Friars in Oxford* (O.H.S. xx, 1891), p. 116.

[6] *Collectanea*, 1715, iv. 60, quoted Little, p. 62. Leland's account in the *Comm. de scriptoribus*, 1709, p. 286, is a later elaboration.

boast—nothing, if you have regard to learned books. For, in spite of the unwillingness of all the friars, I carefully looked over all the bookcases.' In a letter written to Thomas Cromwell, Leland refers particularly to the disappearance of Grosseteste's books: 'All the books of bishop Robert and the copies of his works were stolen by the Franciscans themselves, moving, or to speak more truly, wandering at the command [of their superiors].'[1] If this account is true, there may well be other books waiting to be identified in scattered collections, but perhaps it is nothing more than an echo of the loan to Richard Brinkley.

Many of the facts collected together in this chapter are minutiae of little significance in themselves, but taken together they are important both for the glimpses they give of Grosseteste's method of work and as an illustration of his posthumous fame. More books containing autograph notes by him have perhaps survived than of any medieval writer of comparable eminence. Their survival was in the first place due to the fact that they were kept at the Franciscan convent at Oxford, and may have been further ensured by their being regarded as relics of a man whom many regarded as a saint. With the books were preserved his episcopal sandals made of rush.[2] It was as a relic that the autograph manuscript of the *Summa contra Gentiles* of St. Thomas Aquinas was long preserved in the Dominican convent at Bergamo.[3] But it is only in modern times that the scientific importance of the autographs of St. Thomas has been appreciated. Grosseteste's notes were consulted and copied in the Middle Ages. They had an intrinsic value for medieval scholars because they contained material not contained in his finished writings, and they remained a living force in the University he so dearly loved.

APPENDIX A

(i) *Extant manuscripts containing autograph notes by Grosseteste or once in his possession*

In this and in section (iii), MS. Bodley 198 (no. 2) is taken as the touchstone for the identification of Grosseteste's handwriting. We have the evidence of Dr. Thomas Gascoigne that he obtained it from the Oxford

---

[1] Quoted by Little, op. cit., p. 62, n. 1.
[2] *Loci*, ed. Rogers, p. 141.
[3] M. Grabmann, *Historisches Jahrbuch*, lx (1940), 523 f.

Franciscans and that the indexing symbols in it and other notes are in Grosseteste's hand.

1. Oxford, Bodleian Library, MS. lat. th. c. 17, fols. 158–243.

R. Grosseteste, *De Cessatione Legalium, Hexaemeron* (190).

The text of both works is corrected in the hand of Grosseteste, who has also occasionally added indexing symbols (fols. 195^v, 196^r, 214^r, &c.). Greek words and a phrase from John vi. 45 on fols. 159, 192^{r-v}, 193. Plates of parts of fols. 192^v, 199 in *Bodleian Library Record*, 2 (1948), facing p. 226.

The history of this manuscript is not known. It is bound up with William of Auvergne, *De Universo*. On fol. 155^v is the draft of a letter by Rogerus de Plimp[ton], rector of Enborne, Berks. Mr. A. B. Emden has suggested that he is to be identified with the Rogerus de Plumpton, who was one of the proctors of the University of Oxford in 1267 (S. Gibson, *Statuta antiqua Univ. Oxon.*, 1931, p. 27).

2. Oxford, Bodleian Library, MS. Bodley 198 (S.C. 1907).

Augustine, *De Civitate Dei*, Gregory, *Moralia in Iob* (107).

Subject notes and indexing symbols added by Grosseteste *passim*. For Greek and longer notes see above, p. 122. Biblical quotations identified by book and chapter, fols. 4^v, 11^v, 13^r, 14^v, &c. References to works of Augustine, fols. 2^v, 47^v, 56^r, 57^r, &c., and to Bernard, fol. 26^v. Many cross-references. Towards the end of the *Moralia* the subject notes often call attention to dist(inctiones), e.g. fol. 269: 'dist(inctio) de predicatoribus'. Facsimile of part of fol. 139 in Thomson, *Writings*, facing p. 26.

Given by the Oxford Franciscans to Thomas Gascoigne, who gave it to Lincoln College, Oxford. Came into the possession of Thomas Allen, who gave it to the Bodleian in 1607.

3. Oxford, Trinity College, MS. 17.

Boethius, *De Consolatione Philosophiae* (1–42, 90–98).

Subject notes, fols. 25^v, 30, 39^v, 96^v. Indexing symbols *passim*. References to works of Augustine, fols. 4, 5^v, 7, 31, 36^v, 42, and to Seneca *Ep*. 10, fol. 98^v.

The fifteenth-century list of contents on fol. iii^v shows that the present contents of the volume were then bound together. At the foot of the first page of the last of them (fol. 143) is a thirteenth-century inscription 'Iste liber est de Oxon' //////'. Probably from the Oxford Franciscan convent.

4. Oxford, Bodleian Library, MS. Savile 21 (S.C. 6567).

Algorismus Jordani and other mathematical and astronomical tracts and tables (143–160^v), for which see *Summary Catalogue of Western Manuscripts in the Bodleian Library*, 1937, II. ii, pp. 1106 f. and Thomson, *Writings*, pp. 30–32. One of the tables is reckoned for the years 1215–16, and this is probably the year in which they were written. The same hand has added some notes at the end of a copy of the *Experimentarius* attributed to Bernardus Silvester (fols. 200ᵛ–201ʳ).

The evidence for attributing this manuscript to Grosseteste is purely that of the resemblance of the script to that in MS. Bodley 198, and it is accepted by Mr. N. Denholm-Young in the *Summary Catalogue*, loc. cit. The resemblance is certainly striking, but it would be more satisfactory if the contents of this part of the manuscript could be connected with Grosseteste's known work. They would then provide a valuable fixed point of chronology. Facsimile of part of fol. 158 in Thomson, *Writings*, facing p. 26.

5. Cambridge, Pembroke College, MS. 7.

Collection of glosses on the Psalter, Isaiah, Jeremiah, Daniel, XII Minor Prophets (incomplete), and Mark (incomplete), all anonymous. Late twelfth century.

The gloss on Mark is known to be by Petrus Comestor. The collection is described by B. Smalley, *Cambridge Hist. Journal*, vi (1938), 103–13. For the 'Memoriale' inscription see above, p. 129. Facsimile in Thomson, *Writings*, facing p. 23.

6. Cambridge, University Library, MS. Ff. 1. 24.

Chronicles; Josephus Christianus, *Hypomnesticon*; two short pieces; Testamenta XII patriarcharum. Greek. Late tenth century.

The manuscript used by Grosseteste for his translation of the *Testamenta XII Patriarcharum*. Running titles mostly cropped by the binder. Those of the *Testamenta* on fols. 203ᵛ–204ᵛ, 207ᵛ–208ʳ, 229ᵛ are in Grosseteste's hand. Note by him on fol. 107ᵛ (reproduced in Thomson, *Writings*, facing p. 22). On fol. 42ᵛ are the following marginal glosses on 2 Paralip. iii. 4–5: Deauravit [e]am auro mundissimo. Nomen katha[r]os sumitur hic pro mundo et obrizo. In Latino habetur [p]almas set non sunt manus hominis sed palmas i.e. arbores quia hic habetur phoinicas [*corrected from* phenicas] i.e. arbores palmarum. Nam phoinix [*corrected from* phenix] grece est arbor et latine phenix proferimus, sicut comedia pro comoidia propter rationem diphthongi.

There are two leaves at the end of this manuscript, not fully described in the printed catalogue, which promise at first sight to throw light on its earlier history. They contain (pp. 517–19) the end of a commentary on the Oracles of Leo the Wise (kindly identified by Professor P. Maas) in a much abbreviated script which is unlikely to be as early as the beginning of the thirteenth century. On p. 520 are various *probationes pennae* in Greek and in the middle a short inscription in Arabic, of which the end is rubbed. It reads 'Book of poetry . . .' (Kitâb ash'ār . . .), and is written in a script resembling the Ottoman script of the fifteenth century (information kindly supplied by Dr. A. F. L. Beeston). Presumably the two leaves are strays from another manuscript.

7. Cambridge, Gonville and Caius College, MS. 403.

Gospels in Greek. Late twelfth century.
Running titles in Grosseteste's hand. Note by him at fol. 130ᵛ.
Belonged to the Oxford Franciscan convent. Lent to Fr. Richard Brinkley in the early sixteenth century.

8. Leiden, Vossianus, fol. 2.

Suidas, *Lexikon*. Twelfth century.
Two copies of this manuscript are known to have been made in England in the fifteenth century. Its text agrees with that used by Grosseteste for his translations from Suidas. It is therefore likely to have been his copy, as both M. R. James (*The Library*, 2nd ser., viii (1927), 342) and A. Adler in her edition of Suidas (pars. v, 1938, p. 231) have pointed out. I have not seen the manuscript.

9. Oxford, Corpus Christi College, MS. 108.

Aristotle: De partibus animalium and other works. Ninth to tenth century.
This manuscript has not hitherto been associated with Grosseteste, and I include it with hesitation because the only evidence for so doing is the list of contents on the bottom of the last page. It is very close to the script of Grosseteste in MS. Bodley 198. Other scraps of English writing are on fol. 62ᵛ (thirteenth century) and 177ᵛ (fifteenth century).

(ii) *Manuscripts given by Grosseteste to the Franciscan convent at Oxford*

In a note to the section on Seneca from Jerome, *De Viris Illustribus*, which is prefixed to a copy of the apocryphal correspondence between St. Paul and Seneca in Oxford, Balliol College, MS. 129, fol. 8 (*olim* 7), Gascoigne comments:

Hunc prologum habet S. Jeronimus doctor magnus in libro qui dicitur Liber virorum illustrium, qui ab ipsomet Ieronimo fuit editus. Qui liber est in armario fratrum minorum Oxonie, et continet idem liber plures alios bonos libros. Et nota quod in illo armario sive libraria sunt optimi libri et specialiter ex dono domini Roberti Grostete Lincolniensis episcopi, qui fecit plures libros ibi existentes.

In his *Liber de Veritatibus collectis* Gascoigne quotes from the following books written by or containing annotations of Grosseteste:

1. Pauline Epistles glossed.

Dominus Lincolniensis in expositione sua propria et propria manu sua scripta super epistolam b. Pauli iiª ad Corinthios caᵒ iiijᵒ, et est inter fratres minores Oxonie et registratur Epistole Pauli apostoli a; et est ille liber in libraria conventus, sed non in libraria studencium, due enim sunt ibidem librarie inter fratres minores Oxonie. (*Loci*, p. 103.) Et expositio domini Lincolniensis in illo libro scribitur in margine illius libri, et ibi exponit certos textus b. Pauli apostoli, sed non omnes, et etiam glose communis seu exposicionis communis. (*Loci*, p. 142.)

2-3. Commentary on the Psalter and text of the Psalter.

Et scripsit idem doctor super Psalterium usque ad psalmum centesimum inclusive, ut patet in opere suo super Psalterium scripto manu sua propria. Quod idem opus ego vidi Oxonie pluries anno Christi MᵒCCCCᵐᵒ quinquagesimo sexto et antea. (*Loci*, pp. 126 f.) Et Psalterium expositum et scriptum manu sua propria registratur Oxonie inter fratres minores Episcopus Lincolniensis d, et Psalterium suum, quod non scribitur propria manu domini Lincolniensis, registratur ibidem Episcopus Lincolniensis F. (*Loci*, p. 177.)

4. Dicta and De luxuria.

Dominus Lincolniensis scripsit illud scriptum Contra luxuriam manu sua propria in libro post Dictum domini Lincolniensis xxiij, et tamen illud scriptum domini Lincolniensis cum manu sua propria Contra luxuriam non est in numero Dictorum suorum, sed est opus per se distinctum ... et illud scriptum ... est inter fratres minores Oxonie in hoc registro Episcopus Lincolniensis i, scil. folio vicesimo quarto, ut vidi anno Christi 1455. (*Loci*, p. 138.)

For the identity of the Contra luxuriam see Thomson, *Writings*, p. 181.

5. Letters of Jerome.

Nota Lincolniensem in margine super 20 epistolam b. Ieronimi in libro Epistolarum suarum regestrato Ieronimus l inter fratres minores Oxonie quod b. Ieronimus et Augustinus numquam fuerunt contrarii in exposicione sacre scripture, et ubi aliqui putabant eos esse inter seipsos contrarios in materia de observacione legalium et seremoniarum, in hac materia fuerunt concordes et idem sensientes, et illa que in hac materia videbantur in scriptis b. Ieronimi esse contraria scriptis b. Augustini non fuerunt dicta b. Ieronimi, sed scripta Origenis super Epistolam b. Pauli ad Galathas, et illa scripta Origenis de observacione legalium posuit b. Ieronimus in Commentariis suis super Epistolam Pauli ad Galathas, super quam tres libros scripsit, et in predicta epistola 20 testatur b. Ieronimus se nichil in illa materia dixisse ex propria sentencia. (Lincoln College, MS. lat. 117, p. 473ᵇ.)

In his copy of Grosseteste's Letters (MS. Bodley 312, S.C. 2123) Gascoigne mentions two more books.

6. Letters of Grosseteste.

Episcopus Lincolniensis. t. inter fratres minores continet epistolas domini Lin[colniensis] (fol. 126). In a note to ep. 25 (fol. 135ᵛ) Gascoigne says: 'Copia istarum epistolarum Lincolniensis est inter fratres minores Oxonie (non Exonie *written above*), et ibi sunt omnes eius epistole et sunt optime.'

The corrections which Gascoigne made in the copy of his text of epp. 25 and 127 were no doubt taken from this copy, but there is nothing in Gascoigne's words to imply that this copy was anything more than a copy of the vulgate collection, and Luard is surely wrong when he interprets the passage to mean (R. Grosseteste, *Epist.*, p. xcvi) that Gascoigne's corrections in epp. 25 and 127 were taken from Grosseteste's own autographs in the library of the Franciscans at Oxford.

7. Sermons (?).

In his note to ep. 127 (De Cura Pastorali) Gascoigne says (fol. 172ᵛ): 'Item idem doctor et episcopus fecit sermonem tangentem illam materiam et incipit *Natis et educatis*, etc. Et vidi illud opus correctum manu propria ipsius domini Lincolniensis.' This is Serm. 34, Thomson, *Writings*, p. 177. A similar note is in the *Liber de Verit.* (Lincoln College, MS. lat. 117, p. 403ᵃ), where the reference is given 'Lincolniensis E'.

In a note in his copy of Higden's *Polychronicon* (Balliol College, MS. 235, fol. 181ᵛ) Gascoigne refers to another sermon in the same way: 'ut patet in sermone suo de Levitis scripto manu propria ipsius domini Lincolniensis.' For the identity of this sermon see Callus above, p. 5.

In a manuscript containing sermons of Grosseteste (London, British Museum, MS. Lansdowne 458, fol. 139) Gascoigne noted against one of them (no. 33 in Thomson, *Writings*, p. 176): 'Sermo domini [Lincolniensis] de eo quod op[. . . . .] deum fieri, et vidi is[tum sermonem] propria manu [Lincolni]ensis sc[riptum et] correctum.' The words in square brackets have been cropped by the binder. See N. R. Ker, *M.A.R.S.* ii (1950), 163.

To these references in Gascoigne may be added one in the *Doctrinale* of Thomas Netter. The passage occurs in the discussion on Eucharistic accidents.

Ne autem circa expositionem istam dentur erronee glose, certi doctores magni citeriores eos (scil. Basil and John of Damascus) convenire dicunt in accidente sine subiecto. Unde in libro quodam de studio magni Lyncolniensis quem vidi inter minores Oxoniarum habebat notatum in margine de manu magni Lyncolniensis 'Nota quod dividi possunt accidentia a subiecto et lux a calore' cum longo tractu et in fine eius stellam signatam. Unde et Lincolniensis in sua expositione super Genesim *Fiant luminaria* [i.e. the Hexaemeron]. (*Doctrinale*, ii. 5, c. 77, ed. Venice, 1571, ii. 131B, collated with MS. Bodley 261, fol. 126ᵛᵃ). Attention was first called to this passage by Brian Twyne (Bodleian Library, MS. Twyne XXI, p. 496), whence part of it was printed by Little, *Grey Friars*, p. 58, n. 6. Twyne adds: 'v. opinionem Wiclefi etiam de accidente sine subiecto p. 502 [of MS. Twyne XXI] ubi agit etiam in trialogo de hac nota Lyncolniensis.' This is a reference to *Trialogus* iv. 6, fol. cixᵛ in the edition of 1525 and p. 265 in Lechler's edition, Oxford, 1869: but Wyclif refers there, not to this note, but to a passage in Grosseteste's Commentary on pseudo-Denis, *De Divinis Nominibus*.

It is unfortunate that Netter does not give the title of the book in question, but it is likely enough that he had seen a book 'from the study' of Grosseteste at the Oxford Franciscan convent. The reference to the marginal symbol is a note of genuineness. His description of the long stroke with a 'signed' star at its end may be intended for Grosseteste's symbol 'De eucharistia', which consisted of a long stroke with a circle, flanked by two points, at its end.

(iii) *Manuscripts with notes wrongly said to be in Grosseteste's handwriting*

1. Cambridge, Corpus Christi College, MS. 480.

Psalter in Greek.

The reasons for rejecting this manuscript are given by Thomson, p. 30.

2. Cambridge, St. John's College, MSS. 17 and 47.

Works of Anselm and Augustine (originally bound in one volume); see above, pp. 125 f.

Marginal signa, according to Thomson (*Writings*, p. 124), 'in the heavy black ink characteristic of Grosseteste'. Comparison with MS. Bodley 198 shows that they are not in Grosseteste's hand.[1]

3. Durham, Cathedral Library A. III. 12.

Works by Grosseteste and others, mainly anonymous.

The identification of the works of Grosseteste in this manuscript was one of Professor Harrison Thomson's most valuable discoveries. It contains part of the beginning of the Commentary on the Psalter (fols. 2ᵛ–13ᵛ) later incorporated for the most part in the *Dicta*, Sermons and other *dicta*,[2] together with several pieces by other writers.[3]

---

[1] I am indebted to the Master and Fellows for depositing the manuscripts in the Bodleian Library.   [2] Thomson, *Writings*, pp. 182–91.

[3] Fols. 70–77 is a quire from another manuscript containing theological *quaestiones*,

The approximate date of the manuscript is fixed by the entry in plummet in the bottom margin of fol. 130 of a penance dated 27 Feb. 1231/2. The text is as follows:[1]

Pe(nitentiales) ps(almi) omni die quoad uixerit. Diceret xxii Pater noster propter vii horas, vii propter septiforme donum Spiritus Sancti, v in honore v vulnerum Christi, 3 in nomine Patris et Filii et Spiritus Sancti. Eodem modo l Ave Maria quolibet die tocius vite mee. Item quolibet anno dicam 20 psalteria in propria persona et non per alium. Item quolibet anno durante septennio abstinebo a carnibus tantum [added between the lines] die Mercurii et Sabato auibus autem et caseo et huiusmodi vescibus. Item quolibet anno durante septenio ieiunabo 20 dies Veneris in pane et aqua. Item recipiam a septem [written over quolibet anno crossed through] durante vi unam disciplinam a sacerdote vel a me ipso. Item pascam centum pauperes per quemlibet annum durante septennio. Item abstinebo a carnibus per Adventum totum, sed si opus fuerit, licebit bis comedi in die. Item providebo aliquod ornamentum ad honorem beate Marie, eodem modo ad honorem beatorum Thome et Keterine. Item dicam cotidie infra septe(nnium) septem psalmos penitenciales vel quindecim pro benefactoribus meis. Hec penitencia iniuncta est michi iiii Kalendas Marc. anno ab incarnacione domini M°CC°XXXI°.

In the same hand, on fol. 122,[2] are notes of expenses of a journey from London to South Wales, in which the name [C]adwallader occurs, and of debts on fol. 137[v] partly for parchment and binding.[3] The names of Helias Walensis and Magister Ricardus de Sancto Yltuto point again to a connexion with Wales. The notes of expenses suggest that the person concerned was in the household of a bishop, and the terms of the penance that he held a not inconsiderable benefice, since he was to feed 100 poor men and women for every year during the period of seven years. A connexion with a cathedral is indicated by some further notes on fol. 121.[4]

With so many clues available, it is disappointing not to be able to identify the man, but we may reasonably infer that he had been a student at Oxford and had brought away with him this record of Grosseteste's lectures on the Psalter, notes of his sermons, and a collection of what may

saec. xii/xiii. The incomplete 'work on the sacraments of the church' (Thomson, *Writings*, p. 191) on fols. 194–219 is part of a *Summa* on the Decretum, apparently not otherwise known.

[1] Thomson, op. cit., pp. 14 f. I have revised the text from the manuscript and have attempted a more complete punctuation.

[2] Ibid., p. 15. For 'In duobus aneis 4d.' read 'In duabus aucis 4d.' and for 'reccandos' read 'recreandos'.

[3] Ibid. For 'in soldis cremonensibus' read 'in solidis turonensibus', and for 'Ade mercatori castellorum' read 'Ade mercatori cultellorum'.

[4] 'Summa commune xlv marce et v sol. / Taxacio beneficiorum et obvencionum canonicorum de Land' (?), followed by sums allotted to dignitaries and others.

turn out to be Oxford sermons of *c*. 1229–30.[1] Professor Thomson thought that a part of the Commentary on the Psalter and the following matter (fols. 4ᵛ–15ʳ) was in Grosseteste's hand, though 'more calligraphic and gothic than the other and authentic examples of his writing'.[2] It is always difficult to compare a formal with a cursive hand, but I find it very hard to believe that this part of the Durham manuscript and the notes in MS. Bodley 198 were written by the same hand. Further, if the account of the origin of the manuscript just given is accepted, it is improbable that Grosseteste wrote any of it.

Given to Durham by Bertram de Middleton, prior 1244–58.

4. Lincoln, Cathedral Chapter Library, MS. 144.

Peter Lombard, Gloss on the Psalter. Twelfth century.

There are copious marginal annotations, which Professor Thomson ascribes to Grosseteste. He comments: 'The pen used in making these notes was less flexible than Grosseteste usually used.'[3] The difference here noted is so marked as to make it certain that the notes were not written by the annotator of MS. Bodley 198, whom we identify as Grosseteste. There is nothing in the manuscript to connect it with him.

5. Oxford, Bodleian Library, MS. Laud lat. 105, fols. 257–312.

Priscian, *Institutiones Grammaticae*. Twelfth century.

On fol. 258 'is, in writing which I take to be Grosseteste's "Maius volumen Prisciani"'.[4] There are no other notes in this hand in the volume. It seems to me different from Grosseteste's. The manuscript was one which Archbishop Laud obtained from Germany in 1637.

6. Oxford, Corpus Christi College, MS. 43, fols. 21ᵛ–15ʳ.

Bede, *De Schematibus et Tropis*, 'written in a hand probably that of Grosseteste in his last years'.[5] The characteristics of the hand which Thomson then proceeds to enumerate are those of the typical scholarly hand of the period. They can all be matched, for example in the hand-writing of Alexander Nequam.[6] Compared with MS. Bodley 198 it seems to me a different hand. There is nothing in the manuscript to connect it with Grosseteste. It comes from Lanthony.[7]

[1] They include three sermons of Jordan of Saxony printed by A. G. Little and D. Douie in *E.H.R.* liv (1939), 9–19.

[2] Thomson, *Writings*, p. 35.

[3] Ibid., p. 34; see also pp. 77 f.

[4] Ibid., p. 33.   [5] Ibid., pp. 35 f.

[6] See the marginalia in the copy of his Gloss on the Psalter in MS. Jesus College, Oxford, 94.

[7] N. R. Ker, op. cit. Typescript *addenda* in the Bodleian Library.

7. Shrewsbury School Library, MS. I.

Wisdom and Ecclesiasticus glossed. Thirteenth century.

It contains added notes, which Thomson ascribed to Grosseteste,[1] but comparison with MS. Bodley 198 does not support this opinion. This manuscript and MS. XXXV in the same collection (Luke glossed) both belonged to Alexander of Stavensby, Bishop of Lichfield (d. 1238), who gave them to the Dominican convent at Chester, with which he is known to have had connexions (Grosseteste, ep. xxxiv). It seems probable that Alexander was the annotator.[2]

APPENDIX B

LIST OF WORKS CITED IN THE *TABULA*: LYONS, BIBLIOTHÈQUE MUNICIPALE, MS. 414, FOLS. 17–32

Titles are given in the form in which they are found in the *Tabula*, with the abbreviations expanded. Current titles are added in brackets where necessary for identification.

It may be useful to prefix a list of the *distinctiones* into which it is divided.

i De deo.	vii Same continued.
ii De verbo.	viii De futuris (incl. natural
iii De creaturis (incl. virtues).	phenomena).
iv De ecclesia.	ix De anima et virtutibus eius
v De sacra scriptura.	(incl. parts of the body).
vi De viciis	

I. *Latin Patristic Writers*

AMBROSIUS

De eucharistia.
Exameron.

AUGUSTINUS

(*a*) *Genuine works*

Contra adversarios legis et pro-phetarum.	De bono coniugali.
De agone Christiano.	De civitate dei.
De beata vita.	De concordia evangeliorum (De consensu evangelistarum).
De blasfemia in Spiritum Sanctum (Serm. 71).	Confessiones.
	De cura pro mortuis agenda.

---

[1] Thomson, *Writings*, pp. 34, 72.

[2] I am indebted to Mr. N. R. Ker for allowing me to see his unpublished descriptions of the Shrewsbury School manuscripts.

De deo diligendo.
De disciplina christiana.
Ad Dulcitium (De octo D. quaestionibus).
Enchiridion.
Epistole.
De fide et operibus.
De Genesi contra Manicheos.
Super Genesim ad litteram.
De immortalitate anime.
Ad Ianuarium (Ad inquisitiones Ianuarii).
Super Iohannem (Tract. in Iohannis evangelium).
Super Iohannis primam (Tract. in epistolam Iohannis).
Contra Iulianum.
De laude caritatis.
De libero arbitrio.
Unde malum.
De mendacio.
Contra mendacium.
Musice (liber) 6.
De nuptiis et concupiscentia.
Ad Probam de orando deo (ep. 130).
De orando deo (ep. 131).
De prescientia (presentia) dei ad Dardanum (ep. 187).
Super psalmos (Enarrationes).
De retractationibus.
Super ad Romanos.
In sermone de assumptione.
De sermone domini in monte.
In sermone de simbolo.
De timore (dei).
De trinitate.
De vera religione.

(*b*) *Spurious works*
Catholica confitatio (Prosper, Responsiones ad capit. obiect. Vincent.).
De conflictu virtutum et viciorum.

Super ad Colosios.
Super ad Corinthios.
De differentia spiritus et anime.
De fide ad Petrum.
Yponosticon.
De igne purgatorio (CAESARIUS Serm. 173).
De mirabilibus divine scripture.
De penis purgatoriis.
De penitentia.
Soliloquia.

(*c*) *Unidentified works*
De bono virginali.
Dialogus contra Manicheos.
De predestinatione contra Pelagium.
Contra reprehensores nuptiarum.
In scripto suo ad Marcell.

GREGORIUS MAGNUS
Dialogi.
Super Ezechielem.
Moralia.
Pastoral'.

IERONIMUS
Epistole.
De hebraicis questionibus.
Contra Iovinianum.
De mansionibus filiorum (Israel).
Super Apocalipsin.
Super ad Ephesios.
Super ad Galathos.
Super Marcum.

ISIDORUS
Ethimologie.
De summo bono.

PRUDENTIUS
iii de fide (Psychomachia) cited fol. 24; see also below, p. 144.

II. *Greek Patristic Writers*

ATHANASIUS
(Ps. Vigilius Thapsensis De trinitate.)

BASILIUS
Exameron

pseudo-DIONYSIUS AREOPAGITA
Usually quoted simply as Ierarchia. On fol. 23 (De angelis) 'Ierarchia angelica per totum et commentum (Hugonis q.v.) per totum'.

IOHANNES CHRYSOSTOMUS
De reparacione lapsi.
De compunctione cordis.
De nemo leditur nisi a seipso.
De cruce.
De latrone et iterum de cruce.
De ascensione.
Super In principio.
Super Matheum omelie.
Super Io(hannem) omel. iii^a.

IOHANNES DAMASCENUS
Sententie.

ORIGENES
Omelie de Iohanne.
Omelia de transmigratione domini.
De mundo leproso.
De curato leproso.
Omelie super Num.
Adamantius super Iosue.

III. *Medieval Writers*

ANSELMUS CANTUARIENSIS
De casu diaboli.   Monologion.
De concordia.   De originali peccato.
Cur deus homo.   Proslogion.
De incarnatione verbi.   De similitudinibus.
De libero arbitrio.   De veritate.

BEDA
De penitentia.
De templo.
De temporibus.
De triginta questionibus (in libros Regum).
Super Apocalipsim.
Super Iohannem (perhaps a mistake for the next item).
Super Iohannis primam.
Super Lucam.
Super Regum.
Super Ad Ephesios, Thess., Hebreos, Coloss. (by FLORUS).

BERNARDUS CLAREVALLENSIS
In dictis.
Epistole.
Ad Eugenium (De consideratione).
De libero arbitrio.
Super Missus est Gabriel.
Parabole.
De precepto et dispensatione.
Sermones.

HUGO DE S. VICTORE
Super Ierarchiam (Ps. Dionisii).

RABANUS MAURUS
De cruce.
De natura rerum.
De corpore et sanguine domini (by PASCHASIUS RADBERTUS).

IV. Works Cited in the Marginal Column

A. *Latin Writers*

BOETHIUS
Consolatio.

CALCIDIUS

CICERO
De divinatione.
De immortalitate anime.
De natura deorum.

HORATIUS
Epistole.
Sermones.

PRUDENTIUS

SEDULIUS

SENECA
De beneficiis.
Epistole.
De naturalibus questionibus.

SOLINUS

B. *Greek Writers*

ARISTOTELES
De animalibus (in nineteen books).
Metaphysica.

PTOLOMAEUS
Prohemium Almagesti (cited without author's name).

C. *Arabic Writers*

ALGAZEL
Metaphysica.

ALHASEN
Perspectiva (cited without author's name).

AVICENNA
Metaphysica.

R. W. HUNT.

ADDENDUM

Mention should have been made on p. 129 of the collection of some 100 volumes which Cardinal Guala Bichieri bequeathed in 1227 to the Augustinian Canons of St. Andrew, Vercelli; see A. Hessel and W. Bulst, 'Kardinal Guala Bichieri und seine Bibliothek' in *Hist. Vierteljahrsschrift*, N.F., xxvii (1932), 772–94.

Grosseteste's Administration of the Diocese of Lincoln

GROSSETESTE's predecessor in the see of Lincoln, Hugh of Wells, died on 7 February 1235. He had been closely associated with Grosseteste, who in one of his letters[1] speaks of the ties of affection which existed between them. To him Grosseteste owed his preferment to the archdeaconry of Leicester and the prebend of Leicester St. Margaret, the church of which was part of the endowment of the prebend. He had also held for a short time the benefice of Abbotsley (Hunts.) on the presentation of Hugh of Wells by lapse. By the time of Hugh's death, however, he had surrendered all his preferments except his Lincoln prebend of Leicester St. Margaret.[2] These close associations with his predecessor and with the University of Oxford, then in the diocese of Lincoln, together with his great reputation, help to explain the action of the Lincoln chapter who by a free vote elected him as bishop. Their choice being approved by the king he was consecrated at Reading in June 1235. He was at the time more than sixty years of age[3] when he entered upon an episcopate of rather more than eighteen years, marked by an overpowering sense of the obligations of the pastoral charge and a fearless determination to root out the abuses which prevailed. It was no light task to which he was called. Since the death of St. Hugh in 1200 diocesan administration had twice been hampered by the delays in filling up the vacant see. St. Hugh's successor had only been appointed three years after his death, and another vacancy of three years followed on the death of William of Blois in 1206. Hugh of Wells was appointed in 1209 during the papal interdict, and was ordered by King John to obtain consecration from the Archbishop of Rouen, as Stephen Langton was in exile in France. But instead of this he joined Stephen Langton and was consecrated by him and made his profession to him, whereupon the king had

---

[1] *Ep.* 44. [2] *Ep.* 8.
[3] *Mon. Angl.* v. 191. A confirmation of the grant of churches to the monks of St. Andrew's, Northampton, before 1192, includes among the witnesses *magister* Robert Grosseteste and *magister* William de Monte, who became Chancellor of Lincoln by 1192. Grosseteste must have been about twenty-four years of age when he took his master's degree.

retaliated by seizing the revenues of the see. After the king's sub-
mission to the Pope Hugh returned to England with other bishops
who had gone abroad and his name appears in Magna Carta. The
civil war and invasion of England by Louis of France occupied much
of the years 1216 and 1217 and created further disorganization, until
the final rout of the French following the battle of Lincoln in 1217,
and the restoration of peace. The disorders of the time, leading to
crime and licence and the lack of effective administration in the
shires, had presented serious problems to church leaders, and with
these Hugh of Wells had to deal especially as they affected the clergy.
The low state of morals, the illiteracy of many of the parochial
clergy, the lack of reverence, and many other social abuses are
indicated in the Articles of Enquiry[1] issued by Hugh of Wells to
be made by his archdeacons. Grosseteste owed much to the initiative of his predecessor who had been one of the first to carry out
on a comprehensive scale the provision of vicarages for churches
whose advowsons were in the hands of monasteries or non-resident
rectors. In his *Liber antiquus de ordinationibus vicariarum*, written
for the most part in 1218, there is a list of some 300 vicarages
ordained by him.[2] He had also begun a visitation of the monasteries, as his Rolls indicate, and he had taken steps to deal with the
illiterate clergy and to improve the standard of learning among
them generally.

One of Grosseteste's first measures was to secure the help of
capable and learned men to assist him in the work of his diocese.
On the pastoral side he sought to utilize the evangelistic and preaching gifts of the two new Orders, the Dominicans and Franciscans,
with whom he had been so closely associated at Oxford. Here a
difficulty arose when the superiors of both Orders found some of
their best men being withdrawn from their service at the request of
various prelates. To meet this a series of papal bulls between 1246
and 1255 enjoined that Friars Minor were subject to the jurisdiction
of their superiors and were not to attach themselves to prelates
without their permission or a special mandate from the Pope.
Several of Grosseteste's letters show the difficulty he experienced
in getting his requests granted. In one of his letters, in which he
complains of delay in sending two Dominicans to attend him and
expresses his hope that they will be changed less frequently,

---

[1] Wilkins, *Concilia Magnae Britanniae et Hiberniae*, London, 1737, i. 627 ff.
[2] Edited by A. Gibbons, 1888 (privately printed).

he states that he has a papal privilege and concession in this matter.[1]

Soon after his consecration he wrote to the Provincial Prior of the Friars Preachers (the Dominicans) asking that John of St. Giles and two others, skilful in canon and civil law, may be with him for at least a year,[2] and in a letter to John of St. Giles he asks him to come as soon as possible to help him in 'dispensing the bread of the word of life'.[3]

Preaching

In another letter[4] to the Master General of the Dominicans he again asks for the help of John of St. Giles, and explains the needs of the Lincoln diocese, 'the largest and most populous in England'. He needs help in preaching the word of God, in hearing confessions and enjoining penances, and also he has need of 'wiser counsel in the various and new occasions which daily arise, and of sane and salutary decisions showing an understanding of the Scriptures', and he knows of no one so effective in helping him as John of St. Giles. For similar reasons he asks the Minister General of the Franciscans for two or four friars to be with him as valuable in helping to supplement his own deficiencies,[5] and a like request is made to Adam Marsh. Both John of St. Giles and Adam Marsh played an important part in Grosseteste's career. The former remained a constant adviser and intimate friend throughout. His skill as a physician was of service to the bishop and he was with him in his last illness.

Adam Marsh had been educated at Oxford and had lectured in the Franciscan school there, being the first member of the Order to undertake that office. His letters[6] supply valuable information on many sides of Grosseteste's career, as also does his correspondence with the bishop, who found him a valuable and at times critical counsellor, though throughout a devoted friend.

For help in the administrative side of his work Grosseteste found a valuable recruit in Thomas Wallensis, who had also been a reader in the Oxford Franciscan school, and whom the bishop appointed Archdeacon of Lincoln. Later Robert Marsh, apparently brother of Adam Marsh, appears as bishop's official on two occasions during the bishop's absence[7] from England, and also as Archdeacon of

---

[1] *Ep.* 100. I am indebted to Dr. R. W. Hunt for directing my attention to some of the matters here treated of, and also to the dissertation of W. A. Hinnebusch, O.P., *The Early English Friars Preachers* (Rome, 1951).

[2] *Epp.* 14–15.   [3] *Ep.* 16.

[4] *Ep.* 40.   [5] *Ep.* 41.

[6] *Mon. Franc.* i.   [7] *Rotuli Gros.*, pp. 330, 498.

Oxford. In 1250 he went with the bishop and other clerks to the Council of Lyons.

It was usual for some of the canons to be in constant attendance on the bishop and some of them lived in his household. Robert of Cadney and John of Crakenhall, both canons of Lincoln, are constantly found as witnesses at institutions. The former was appointed precentor after having been the bishop's official. The latter somewhere between 1247–53 appears as 'seneschal' (or steward) in the bishop's household,[1] and accompanied the bishop to the Council of Lyons in 1250.

Among the clerks who were constantly present with the bishop as witnesses to institutions are Roger de Fretewell, Roger de Raveningham, and Roger Blund, who all became canons of Lincoln. The second of these, who became Archdeacon of Huntingdon in 1256, is definitely described as 'Clerk of the bishop' as also are three others, Peter of Stamford, John of Reston, and G. of Leicester.

As Archdeacon of Leicester Grosseteste had been required to carry out the Articles of Enquiry which Hugh of Wells had ordered the archdeacons to deal with, and with the knowledge thus acquired he was prepared to face many of the current abuses. In his letters to the archdeacons in 1236[2] he refers to some of the undesirable social customs of parish life which throw a light on the conditions of the time, and were productive not only of irreverence, but of drunkenness and worse evils. Such were the holding of markets in sacred places,[3] the drinking bouts (*scotales*), the abuses attending the night vigils and the funeral feasts at the exequies of the dead, games in churchyards, the quarrels for precedence in the annual processions to the mother church,[4] clandestine marriages, which are forbidden, and a warning to mothers and nurses of the dangers of overlaying their children. He also deals with the corrupt custom of some priests who required Easter offerings to be made at the time when Mass was being celebrated, a serious hindrance to the devotions of the people and a source of scandal, as though only those who brought offerings were entitled to receive the Sacrament—an evil condemned by

---

[1] *Reg. Ant.* ii. 315, 321.
[2] *Epp.* 21–22.
[3] In 1236 a papal mandate bade him end this custom. *C. Pap. R.* i. 155.
[4] Stevenson (p. 128) assigns these to the annual visitations of the archdeacons. But it seems more probable, owing to the reference to 'the mother church', that they refer to the Pentecostal processions to the cathedral church enjoined by St. Hugh. (*Liber Niger*, Bradshaw and Wordsworth, *Cathedral Statutes*, pp. 307 ff.)

the canons and conciliar decisions. By preaching and by warnings and prohibitions the archdeacons are to guard against these evils.

To the dean and chapter[1] he writes prohibiting the Feast of Fools held on 1 January, an old custom which had degenerated into an irreverent and licentious orgy 'hateful to God', and in a later epistle[2] he claims papal authority for this prohibition.

In a letter[3] to Robert Hayles, Archdeacon of Lincoln, Grosseteste now prepared the way for his coming visitation and also issued Articles of Enquiry, embodying many found in those of his predecessor, Hugh of Wells, but with additions of his own.[4] On this duty of visitation he said:[5] 'I, as soon as I became bishop, considered myself to be the overseer and pastor of souls, and lest the blood of the sheep should be required at my hand at the strict Judgement, to visit the sheep committed to my charge.' That such visitations should be a normal part of a diocesan bishop's duty had been strikingly illustrated by the saintly bishop of Worcester, Wulfstan, in the eleventh century, whose thorough visitation of his diocese is described in the *Vita Wulfstani* of William of Malmesbury.[6] But the growing employment of bishops in affairs of state had often resulted in its being either neglected or delegated to the archdeacons or other officials. The fourth Lateran Council had dealt with one abuse connected with such visitations, the costly procurations demanded of the parishes by bishops, archdeacons, and papal legates on their visits, and had enjoined that these were not to be exacted unless such visits were made in person.[7] The two popes, Honorius III and Gregory IX, had shown concern for the condition of the English Church. The former in 1222 had ordered Stephen Langton to make a visitation of his province, 'so that the profits which the Pope hopes for may come from it, the archbishop having neglected this part of his office'.[8] Gregory IX in 1236 had ordered suffragans of Canterbury to visit, correct, and reform the clergy both regular and secular in their dioceses,[9] and the Council of London under the legate, Cardinal Otto, in 1237[10] had directed that archbishops and bishops

[1] *Ep.* 32.   [2] *Ep.* 72.* Luard, p. 161.
[3] *Ep.* 50, in 1238.   [4] Pegge, App. V, pp. 312 ff.
[5] *Angl. Sacr.* ii. 347 ff.
[6] *Vita Wulfstani* (ed. R. R. Darlington, 1928), introd., p. xxxiii. I owe this reference to Miss K. Major.
[7] J. D. Mansi, *Sacrorum Conciliorum . . . collectio*, xxii. 1019–22.
[8] *C. Pap. R.* i. 86.   [9] Ibid., p. 150.
[10] Wilkins, *Concilia*, i. 654.

at fitting seasons should go round their dioceses by way of correction and reform, or for the consecration of churches and 'sowing the word of life in the Lord's field'. These directions point to the need of reform in the matter of visitation. C. R. Cheney adduces evidence that there were some episcopal visitations in England before that of Grosseteste, and refers, for example, to that of the Bishop of Norwich in 1233 'by command of the Pope'.[1]

Documentary evidence for Lincoln diocese, so far as we know at present, is lacking. The Rolls of Hugh of Wells and of Grosseteste are mostly limited to notices of institutions and licences for private chapels and provide little or no evidence for other forms of episcopal activity. The former record two visitations by Hugh of Wells of Dunstable Priory, one in person, the other by deputy.[2] He had, as we have seen, issued Articles of Enquiry, but how far during his episcopate there was a formal and personal visitation of the parochial clergy we cannot say.

Cheney[3] says that Grosseteste's regularity in visiting his diocese and the strictness of his inquiries made him famous throughout England.

The fullest description of his procedure is given in the *Propositio de visitatione dioecesis suae*.[4] The clergy are to be summoned by deaneries, the people are to be present to hear the word of God and to bring their children to be confirmed. The bishop will preach to the clergy and some friars are to be chosen to preach to the people and hear confessions. After this inquiries are to be made about the administration of the parishes and the necessary corrective measures given. To those who told him that his action was novel and unaccustomed he replied that 'every new thing which instructed and advanced a man is a new thing fraught with blessing'. In his letter to the archdeacon he had also directed that churches as yet unconsecrated should be made ready for consecration in accordance with the directions of the legatine Council of London. The Annals of Dunstable[5] sum up the character of the visitation in the words

he visited the monasteries and the archdeaconries and deaneries. In each he held general chapters, and preached and published constitutions. He suspended many rectors of churches, some he allowed to clear themselves; from others he took bonds binding them to forfeit rank and benefices if

---

[1] *Episcopal Visitation of Monasteries*, Manchester, 1931, pp. 32 ff.
[2] *Rotuli Welles*, ii. 51; iii. 132.   [3] Op. cit., p. 35.
[4] *Angl. Sacr.* ii. 347 ff.   [5] *Ann. Mon.* iii. 147.

they should fail to observe continency. In the same year he dedicated many churches and monasteries.

At some period subsequent to this, probably between the years 1240–3, he issued his series of constitutions for the better ordering of parishes. These embody decrees of the Lateran Council of 1215, and of the legatine Council of London referred to above, as well as various papal rescripts which Grosseteste had received, and they also show considerable use of the statutes put forth about 1240 by his friend Walter Cantilupe, Bishop of Worcester. So far as can be judged, these constitutions had a wide circulation in the Middle Ages, and their influence is seen in the synodical statues of the dioceses of Norwich, Winchester, Ely, and Durham.[1]

Some of the injunctions given in the constitutions had already been dealt with in the bishop's letters to the archdeacons referred to above.[2] Others deal with the religious ministrations of the clergy. They are to teach their people and expound the commandments— for 'without their observance there is no salvation of souls'—also the seven deadly sins and the seven sacraments, and priests are to explain in the common tongue what is necessary for a true confession, and penitence. Directions are given as to reverence in celebrating the Eucharist and in carrying the Sacrament to the sick. Care is to be taken that the canon of the Mass is correctly transcribed and where necessary corrections made. The bishop's care for the devotional life of the priest and for his instruction of the young, as embodied in these constitutions, will be dealt with later.[3] Other sections deal with moral evils and social habits which are inconsistent with the clerical vocation, and the employment of the clergy in judicial and other civil offices is forbidden. Pluralities are forbidden by apostolic authority[4] unless a papal dispensation is given.

Marriage of the clergy is forbidden and strict continency is required of them. Clergy may not take fees in enjoining penances or for any other sacred ministrations, and beneficed clergy must take the orders of ministry which their cure requires. By apostolic authority all rectors and vicars are to keep residence in their benefices, unless for reasonable cause dispensation has been given.

---

[1] For the date and sources of the Constitutions see Cheney, *English Synodalia in the Thirteenth Century* (Oxford, 1941), pp. 119 ff.: and for their later influence, ibid., pp. 124 ff. The Constitutions are printed in Luard's edition of Grosseteste's epistles (*Ep.* 52*) and in a more convenient form, numbers being given, in Pegge, *Life of Grosseteste*, App. VI, p. 315.   [2] p. 149 above.

[3] See pp. 168–71 below.   [4] *C. Pap. R.* i. 178 (1239).

The object throughout Grosseteste's constitutions is to raise the standard of the clergy alike in their preaching and teaching as well as in their moral conduct.

The visitations of the parochial clergy were continued regularly throughout Grosseteste's episcopate. Before the last of his visitations, writing from Lyons in 1250, he had still to bewail the low standard of the people, due to the negligence and bad example of their pastors. The archdeacons are to publish his letter throughout the diocese. In it he solemnly reminds the clergy of the Judgement to come when they will have to give an account of the cure of souls committed to their charge, and he urges them to arise and watch over themselves and their flock, and to feed them by the example of their lives and with the sacrament of life.

A visitation of the monasteries had already been begun by Grosseteste's predecessor, Hugh of Wells, who had visited Dunstable Priory and Tickford in 1220, Dunstable in 1233 by deputy, and Brook Priory in 1234.[1] Hugh had also come into conflict with the monasteries by his requiring religious houses to provide vicarages for those benefices of which they had secured the patronage[2] and appropriated the revenues, and he had already been termed *omnium religiosorum malleus* by monastic opponents of his policy. But in this respect he was far outdistanced by Grosseteste's more drastic and extensive activity.

The huge diocese of Lincoln had shared in the great extension of monasticism in England during the period which followed the Norman conquest. The problems which faced Grosseteste differed in some respects from those which he encountered in dealing with the parishes. There is little trace of flagrant moral delinquencies, which are only recorded in two cases, St. Frideswide at Oxford and the priory of Minting in Lincolnshire, the latter being a dependant of the abbey of Fleury. In the case of the great Benedictine foundations, whose learning and culture had rendered such service to the Church, their great wealth and social qualities had led to a slacker observance of their rule. There were cases in which members had been simoniacally introduced into their houses. Again, such was the attraction and popularity of the monastic life that some men had abandoned their wives in order to enter a monastery. In both such cases Grosseteste procured papal faculties[3] to enable him to deal with these abuses.

---

[1] See C. R. Cheney, *Episcopal Visitation of Monasteries*, p. 33.
[2] See p. 147. [3] *C. Pap. R.* i. 178, 229.

Bad administration was the defect which led on three occasions to Grosseteste's visits to the Dunstable Priory of Austin Canons.[1]

The bishop's object throughout was to secure a strict observance of the monastic rule. By the other Benedictine houses this was regarded as an invasion of their rights. Matthew Paris, though his own house of St. Albans was exempt, out of *esprit de corps* supported them in their opposition alike to the visitation and to Grosseteste's insistence on the establishment of vicarages in the parishes dependent upon them. Exaggerating the bishop's attitude he represented him as a sworn foe to monasticism as a whole. This was far from being the case.

Grosseteste was ever ready to appreciate those monasteries where religion was well kept, and he had his own ideal of the monastic life. In a letter[2] to the abbot and monks of Bury St. Edmunds,[3] with whom he had close relations and who could appreciate his scholarly interests, he sends a translation of a Greek work on the monastic life 'as a small mirror and miniature reflection of the form of the monastic life'. In his will he left bequests to several religious houses including also legacies to some of the poorest of them.

The visitation was, however, severe. In 1236 seven abbots and four priors were removed and replaced. Where priors had been removed on account of age or infirmity provision was made for a pension[4] and the same provision it may be assumed was made in similar cases for abbots.

Grosseteste's intervention in the affairs of the great abbey of Bardney in Lincolnshire had a different origin. A secular priest had sought in vain to procure the payment of a debt due to him from the Abbot of Bardney and had appealed to the Archdeacon of Lincoln, who summoned the abbot to appear before him. He had refused, and the bishop's intervention was invoked. This also was resisted, as also were the visitors whom the bishop had sent to inquire into the matter. The bishop in consequence excommunicated the abbot for disobedience, and eventually, with the concurrence of three Benedictine abbots, deposed him for contumacy. This led, however, to a further controversy with the monks of Canterbury, who, owing to the death of Archbishop Edmund, claimed the right of

[1] In 1240, 1249, 1250. *Ann. Mon.* iii. 152, 178, 181.
[2] *Ep.* 57.
[3] Not Peterborough as Luard and Stevenson suggest. See Thomson, *Writings*, p. 203.
[4] *Ann. Mon.* iii. 143 ff.

the Canterbury chapter to hear appeals *sede vacante*. This opportunity to appeal had been seized by the Abbot of Bardney. Grosseteste and some other bishops had rejected this claim of the Canterbury monks and in consequence he and some other bishops were excommunicated by them. Grosseteste ignored this action of theirs, and the new Pope, Innocent IV, on his accession in 1245 ordered the monks to withdraw their excommunication, while leaving the other issue undecided. Grosseteste now addressed a letter[1] to the former papal legate Otto, setting out the grounds of his opposition to the claims of the monks, and asking him to induce the Pope to give more explicit directions and to safeguard the rights of bishops. The accession to the see of Canterbury of Boniface in 1245 removed for a time any claim of the Canterbury chapter to jurisdiction, and the Abbot of Bardney's deposition remained.

The severity of Grosseteste's visitation had provoked a protest from the Abbot of Leicester, who accused him of having 'a heart of iron and lacking in kindliness'. In his reply[2] the bishop distinguishes between two kinds of hardness. One is that which refuses to be broken by the terrors of the wicked or softened by the blandishments of those who would seduce. The other, as in Ezekiel's words about the house of Israel, is that which is full of cruelty and malice. If his own heart is of this latter character, he bids the abbot pray for him to the Lord that He will take it away and grant him His gentleness. But if his heart is that of the prophet, whose countenance was stronger than theirs, and whose brow was like adamant and flint (Ezekiel iii. 7), he asks that even a modest share may be granted him by Him who is the true Rock, Christ Himself.

The problems connected with patronage had engaged the mind of Grosseteste's predecessor, Hugh of Wells. The rights of lay patrons had arisen out of ownership of the land, and it was the land to which the advowson of the benefice belonged. Bishops, unlike their modern representatives, had no patronage other than that belonging to them as lords of the particular manors in which the churches lay, though in the case of livings where the patronage was unknown or where the living had been vacant for more than three months the Lateran Council of 1215 had given the right of presentation for that turn to the immediate superior, the bishop. Many of the Norman landowners had rebuilt the churches on the estates assigned to

---

[1] *Ep.* 110.   [2] *Ep.* 55.

them and had often presented the advowson of the living in such cases to monasteries founded by them or in which they had some special interest. The pastoral duties in such churches were discharged either through some member of the monastic community or through a secular priest appointed by that body. Neither was really satisfactory. The tenure of a monk in such a cure could not be permanent without affecting his full observance of the monastic rule. Nor had the stipendiary priest any assured permanence. He was often ill-paid and drawn from a class of clergy often ill-equipped and illiterate. One further result of the acquisition of churches by monasteries was that it often resulted in the severance of the advowsons from the manors with which they had originally been connected.[1]

A further development was the practice of 'farming' churches. A monastery presenting a rector would often exact either a 'pension', a fixed payment from the incumbent payable to the monastery, or alternatively a 'portio', a percentage of the yearly income. In the twelfth century it has been estimated that more than a third of the parish churches in the country had passed into the hands of the monasteries. A synod held by Archbishop Anselm at Westminster in 1102 had enacted a canon that parish churches should not be appropriated to monasteries without the consent of the bishop, and that an adequate stipend should be assigned from the revenues to the clerk who served the church. A further check was provided by the Lateran Council of 1179, which gave the bishops the right to ensure the proper pastoral care of parishes thus appropriated.

Hugh of Wells[2] had shown, as we have seen, considerable activity in the establishment of permanent vicarages. The Rolls of Grosseteste's episcopate exhibit a continuance of this policy, and some fresh 'ordinations' of such vicarages were made by him. His attitude to the farming of churches appears in a letter[3] addressed to John Romanus, subdean of York. The subdean was a non-residentiary incumbent of the benefice of Chalgrave, in the bishop's diocese. The papal nuncio, Boetius, had written to Grosseteste asking him to permit the subdean to grant him the free disposal of the church. The bishop points out to the subdean that the farming of a church is not a free disposal of the same, but is more truly described as 'the reduction of the free Bride of Christ to a servile condition', and he

---

[1] On this see Phillimore's introduction to the *Rotuli Hugonis de Welles*, Lincoln Record Society, iii, and Canterbury and York Society, xx–xxiii.
[2] See p. 147 above.   [3] *Ep.* 18. Luard suggests a date *c.* 1235.

appeals to a decision of the provincial Council of Oxford which required that this could only be done for some just reason approved by the bishop, and farmed out to a worthy ordained person on condition that the fruits of the benefice were devoted to good use with the consent of the diocesan. What just reason the subdean had for putting his church to farm Grosseteste says that he does not know. The necessity for him to reside elsewhere does not prevent him from appointing a wise and faithful deputy. 'One worthy ordained person', such as the Council of Oxford required, cannot be interpreted to mean 'religious bodies'. Such bodies are bound by all their works to preach contempt of the world, whereas by farming of churches they evidently preach the contrary to the great danger of religion and at the expense of many souls. By consenting to such farming the bishop would not only be disobeying the Council but would be betraying the souls which he ought to save. He implored the subdean not to consent. He adds that Boetius in his letter had said that many were surprised at the bishop's action in revoking the farming of churches, and he had even used threatening language. But the bishop declares that he feared not man but God alone. Finally in 1250 according to Matthew Paris[1] he obtained a bull from Innocent IV requiring the monasteries to augment from their revenue the meagre provision for vicarages notwithstanding any exemptions, apostolic privileges, or indults by which such action might be impeded or delayed.

With regard to lay patronage the papal lawyers regarded it as falling outside the common law of the Church, and the right of laymen to present had been a matter of toleration rather than of official recognition, and patrons could not complain if the privilege were revoked.[2] Grosseteste had a profound sense of the *plena potestas* of the papacy and its right freely to dispose of benefices.[3] While in one letter[4] he incidentally remarks that it is contrary to right that laymen are held to be patrons of churches, yet in actual practice he had to admit their rights while watching with a critical eye the manner in which they were exercised. In the letter referred to he contends that the bishop in rejecting a presentation does not

---

[1] *Chron. Mai.* v. 300.

[2] In canon 17 of the Lateran Council 1179, the word *sustinuit* is used of the practice. See on this subject Powicke, *King Henry III and the Lord Edward*, i. 261, and the reference to Mary Cheney 'Compromise of Avranches, 1172, and the spread of Canon Law in England' in *E.H.R.* lvi. 190 ff.

[3] See, for example, his letter to Cardinal Otto quoted p. 160.   [4] *Ep.* 72*(p. 228).

prejudice their right of presentation. Bishops reject, he says, those who are illiterate, illegitimate, and of unsatisfactory morals, and also those appointed to a church not then vacant.

The Rolls of his episcopate show that his methods of dealing with presentations followed in some respects those of his predecessor, Hugh of Wells. The institutions recorded are not always unconditional. While rectors who might be absent in the service of bishop, king, or Pope could obtain exemption from residence, vicars were bound to reside. Hence we find in the records it is constantly added that the institution is given *cum onere et pena vicariorum*.

Thus Walter de Houton, deacon, is instituted to the perpetual vicarage of Sixhills *cum onere et pena vicariorum*, and with the further proviso, accepted by the presentee, that if he is found either by being convicted or on his own confession, guilty of immoral conduct, or if he neglects to learn and on a second examination is found to have made little progress in learning, he will be deprived of the said vicarage.[1] In another case William of Careby, subdeacon, instituted rector of Careby in lay patronage, has his induction postponed for a year, in order that it may be known meanwhile how he has advanced in learning.[2] In another instance Reynot, a foreign chaplain presented by a lay patron, is found by the bishop to be entirely ignorant of the English language. He is instituted rector, but a perpetual vicar is appointed who will have the whole church with all the obligations and charges on it, and shall pay to Reynot, so long as he conducts himself worthily as a secular priest and obtains no other benefice, five marks a year, in token that he, Reynot, is rector.[3] Similarly, Master Hervey[4] is instituted rector of Taynton on condition that he presents to the bishop a suitable vicar, because he is a Frenchman and does not know the English language.

Grosseteste had no hesitation in rejecting presentations to benefices, if those who were presented lacked the qualifications which he considered necessary for the cure of souls, whoever were the patrons, whether laymen, friends of his own, monastic bodies, the king, papal officials, or even in the last resort, as time went on, the Pope himself. In his efforts to secure this adequate cure of souls he had to face both the abuses of patronage and the need to defend the Church against aggression from civil authorities, and the abuses in the

---

[1] *Rotuli Gros.*, p. 41.
[3] Ibid., p. 499.
[2] Ibid., p. 88.
[4] Ibid., p. 444.

exercise of papal provisions, a right which in its proper use he was prepared to accept as involved in the plenitude of papal power.

Some examples of his treatment of particular cases will illustrate his attitude.

1. His friend, William Raleigh, treasurer of Exeter Cathedral, had written to him, probably in 1235, to ask him to institute a mere boy, still learning his letters, William de Grana, to a cure of souls, and had expressed indignation at the bishop's refusal. The bishop writes to him a friendly letter[1] and states the grounds of his refusal. By accepting this presentation he would be transgressing alike the demands of Scripture and the prescriptions of the Holy Fathers, and would involve both himself and the boy and those who supported him in the severest condemnation, and at the grave risk of the souls to be committed to his charge. At the same time he is prepared to offer a modest allowance to the boy to enable him to be educated until he obtains a better living or some other suitable provision is made for him. Similarly he writes to the Chancellor of York, John Blund, and expresses the hope that he will not be indignant, in spite of their bonds of friendship, that he has refused to admit a clerical relation of his to a living on the ground of total illiteracy, and he sends to him in evidence of this the answers given at the examination. The claims of friendship cannot justify such a wrong action.

2. Philip de Kyme, steward to Gilbert de Gant, had instituted a prior to Kyme. Grosseteste writes to him[2] and hopes that he will not be annoyed because the bishop has regarded the appointment as unfitting, and acting on the authority of the Council and in accordance with canonical authority, and without violation of any right, has appointed a worthy person who had not sought, but had been pressed, to accept it. He explains that he has similarly quashed other elections in monasteries in the king's gift, and by the authority of the Council[3] has made fresh appointments which the king has graciously accepted.

3. While he was still bishop elect and before his actual consecration a monk had presented to him for institution to a benefice a deacon, who by his whole bearing and manner of dress resembled a foppish layman, or a knight. Contrary to canonical and conciliar requirements he was without the tonsure, with rings on his fingers and arrayed in red garments. His answers showed him to be entirely

[1] *Ep.* 17. [2] *Ep.* 30.
[3] i.e. the Lateran Council of 1215.

illiterate. Grosseteste's wrath was aroused, and both the monk and the deacon received a severe castigation, the monk more especially for daring to present for the cure of so large a number of souls a man who was more likely to slay souls than to heal them. The severity of this rebuke had reached the ears of his friend Michael Beleth, who had remonstrated with him on his immoderate language. In a letter Grosseteste[1] thanks him for his rebuke, which he knows proceeds from true affection, and he willingly accepts it. At the same time he proceeds to show the justice of his action, not by way of excusing, however, the excessive and immoderate language of his censures, but in order that Beleth and others may be enabled to form a true judgement of the case, the facts of which he recounts as above. A wise physician, he says, does not cast out a deadly poison by gentle remedies. Such censure as he pronounced proceeds from the love of souls and fear of their loss. He urges his friend and other critics to join him in condemning what he has censured, and to consider whether in the sight of God and of those who have a zeal for souls such censure is as reprehensible as they have supposed.

4. The papal legate, Cardinal Otto, had nominated his clerk, Atto, to a prebend at Lincoln, and had informed the bishop of this. Grosseteste replies[2] that before he received the legate's letter he had himself already made an appointment to that prebend. Though nothing would prevent him from obeying the holy Roman Church when a charge was laid upon him that tended to promote faith and charity, yet he cannot but be troubled when such a charge is destructive of charity. And as according to the Gospel precept[3] he has to fear God rather than man, no fear of the legate's power will restrain him from speaking the truth. He knows that the lord Pope and the Roman Church have the power freely to dispose of all benefices, but he also knows that whosoever abuses that power is building for the fires of hell, as also is he who does not use it for the promotion of faith and charity. To confer benefices without first obtaining the assent of the patrons can only lead to scandal. He declares that he has been ready to make liberal provision for the legate's people, not under coercion but of his own free will for the promotion of charity, and he begs the legate to withdraw his collation to the prebend.

Another letter of the bishop[4] deals with a similar request of Otto, made through the latter's clerk, that the bishop would confer a

---

[1] *Ep.* 11.

[3] Matt. x. 28.

[2] *Ep.* 49.

[4] *Ep.* 74.

prebend on Atto. The bishop had told the clerk that he would deliberate on the matter and give his answer to the legate on his arrival in England. This he now does. Three things, he says, had weighed upon his mind. One was the fear that in granting the request, favouritism or fear might be mingled with the motive of charity. The second was that Master Atto, who, as he has learned, is eminent in science and of the highest moral character, had at one time told him that he had no dispensation to hold a cure of souls along with a plurality of benefices. The bishop states that he himself had at one time held a prebend of this kind together with a parish church, but his conscience had troubled him, and he had sought the Pope's advice through a wise and God-fearing man. The Pope's reply had been that a prebend of the kind could not be held along with a parish church without such dispensation. A third difficulty was that he did not consider Lincoln a suitable sphere for Atto in spite of his many good qualities. At the same time he leaves the case to Otto's judgement. What the result of both letters was is uncertain. There is no official record at Lincoln of Atto's appointment to a canonry, nor is it mentioned in the Patent Rolls, which record his presentation to the prebend of Norton in Durham diocese.[1] But in the Rolls of Grosseteste his name appears among the canons of Lincoln as witness to an institution.[2] He may have obtained some such preferment not otherwise recorded.

A similar example of the bishop's attitude to Otto's requests is found in Epistle 52. Otto had asked him to admit Thomas, son of Earl Ferrers, to the benefice of Rand, in spite of the fact that he is too young and not in holy orders. Grosseteste begs him to persuade the Earl to present some other fit person. Otherwise, if Thomas has the living the bishop hopes that a vicar will be appointed or a proper pastor, some provision being made out of the benefice for Thomas, without, however, the cure of souls.

In his diocesan administration Grosseteste was confronted with the problem arising from the exercise by the Pope or his agents of the claim to provide incumbents for English benefices. The practice had begun in the twelfth century, originally as a request to some ecclesiastic to provide with a benefice or cathedral preferment a clerk whom

---

[1] *Patent Rolls, 1232–47*, pp. 208, 217.
[2] *Rotuli Gros.*, p. 173. In the printed text of the roll the name of Atto appears in the form 'attone [*sic*]'. Miss D. M. Williamson has kindly examined the original and informs me that the letter *a* printed as a small letter is merely an unusual but not by any means isolated example of the capital A.

the Pope wished to help, or to whom he wished to show favour. But the practice became extended and systematized,[1] especially under Pope Innocent IV, in whose pontificate the struggle with the Emperor Frederick II had involved the papacy in serious financial difficulties, and the Pope found in this system of provisions a useful means of providing for and rewarding those who had rendered him service. Grosseteste's attitude in the earlier years of his episcopate was that it was a natural outcome of the papal plenitude of power that he had the right freely to appoint to all benefices. So he asserts in the letter to the Cardinal Legate Otto.[2] Nor did the system at first in itself awaken much controversy among the English prelates, whatever criticism it might arouse from individual patrons. What did excite criticism was the growing number of foreigners, largely Italian, who were being appointed to English benefices.[3]

In Grosseteste's Rolls we find during the whole of his episcopate not more than ten examples which are expressly stated to have been due to papal mandates or provisions. All except two fall within the first five years of his episcopate, the two remaining ones, being the appointments of the same person, Master Rolandinus, chaplain and physician of the Pope, first to Whissendine in the tenth year, and to the rectory of Tathwell in the eleventh year. Master Nicholas of Hereford is appointed to Brocton, on the ground, as the papal provision states, that he had for several years held the master's chair in Grosseteste's diocese and for two years had studied in the theological faculty and that the Apostolic see is accustomed to favour those who have laboured usefully in study. Moreover, he is a poor clerk, and the bishop is asked to find him a benefice as soon as possible.[4]

Three others bear English names. R. Hanybald, of whom it is said, after inspecting letters of the Pope, at the command of J. Romanus, subdean of York, the rural dean of Gainsborough is written to, bidding him to induct him to the church of Scotter.[5] The second is Richard Nevill, clerk, whom the Archdeacon of Leicester by the authority of the Pope is to induct to the church of Prestwold.[6] The third is G. de Insula (English, Delisle) subdean and chaplain of the Pope.[7] Four others are of foreign extraction. They include Adenulfus,[8] nephew of the Pope, Thomas de Treb,

[1] See Powicke, *King Henry III and the Lord Edward*, i. 274 ff.
[2] Quoted on p. 160.
[3] See Powicke, op. cit. i. 78, 356.
[4] *Rotuli Gros.*, p. 390.
[5] Ibid., p. 137.
[6] Ibid., p. 387.
[7] Ibid., p. 268.
[8] Ibid., p. 394.

canon of Fulginatis,[1] John, son of a citizen of Anagni,[2] and Ottovian, subdeacon and chaplain of the Pope.[3] Master Rolandinus may also have been a foreigner.[4]

Other presentations by monastic houses may have been due to papal requests which tended to be treated as papal commands. The *Acta Stephani Langton* record the presentation by the Priory of Lewes, acting under a papal provision, of an incumbent to Compton.[5]

But though Grosseteste recognized the papal plenitude of power, his letter to Cardinal Otto in 1238[6] shows that he had begun to have misgivings as to the manner of its exercise. So too does a letter of his to Walter Grey, Archbishop of York,[7] written after his return from the Council of Lyons in 1245. The Pope had directed him to urge the archbishop to favour the business of the aged and venerable Bishop of Cervia, who through no fault of his own had been driven from his home in Italy and was in great poverty. Grosseteste begins his letter by saying: 'Out of obedience we are often compelled to do what we do with sadness, and would gladly refrain from doing.' The extensive use of provisions and the abuse of them by papal agents had led to protests from English representatives, and had induced the Pope to agree to limit the number of English benefices to be given away, though this concession had been rendered inoperative by the insertion of the clause *non obstante* into nominations to benefices, and the way was thus opened to further abuses. It was this which provoked Grosseteste's famous protest at the Council of Lyons in 1250 and led finally to his refusal to obey the Pope's mandate in 1253 to admit his nephew, Frederick de Lavagna, a mere boy, to a canonry at Lincoln, 'in spite of any privileges granted by the papal see[8] and threatening those who opposed it with ecclesiastical censure'.[9]

In 1240 Grosseteste came into conflict with King Henry III over the appointment to the church of Thame in Oxfordshire, which formed part of the endowment of a Lincoln prebend. Though the bishop had already made his own appointment to that church, John

[1] Ibid., p. 401.
[2] Ibid., p. 267.
[3] Ibid., p. 353.
[4] Ibid., p. 225.
[5] Canterbury and York Society, l, pp. 134-5.
[6] See p. 160.
[7] *Ep.* 116.
[8] On Grosseteste's previous exemption from accepting papal provisions see p. 164.
[9] The Pope's letter is quoted by Luard in note 1 to *Ep.* 128. On the authenticity of the letter see Powicke, op. cit. i. 285 ff. and Thomson, *Writings*, pp. 212-13.

Mansel, a king's clerk, had been put in possession of it by the favour of the king, and with the help of a papal provision. Thereupon Grosseteste sent two of his archdeacons to the king, who was in Wales, to congratulate him on his victory and at the same time to urge him out of gratitude to God to make amends for his violation of the liberties of the Church. The king replied that the matter was still *sub judice* as an appeal had been made, and also that he had acted with papal authority. One of the archdeacons, probably John of Basingstoke, who was Archdeacon of Oxford, then called his attention to the privilege granted by Pope Gregory IX in 1239, that 'the Bishop of Lincoln shall not be bound by papal letters to make provision to anyone unless special mention is made of this licence'.[1] But it was urged that in this papal mandate no such reference had been made. Moreover, Mansel had got possession of the church against the will of the bishop, and without consultation with him, and the bishop had previously justly assigned it to another person. The bishop's emissaries, acting on his behalf, had further said that in view of Mansel's high character and learning the bishop would be prepared to bestow on him a better living, but that if he persisted in his present course he would be excommunicated. Mansel had the good sense to resign the prebend, and the king presented him to the living of Maidstone.

On two occasions the bishop's zeal for the reform of the morals of both clergy and laity brought him into conflict with the king, and in these he would seem to have exceeded his legal rights. A clerk in Rutland had been deprived of his benefice for incontinence. He had refused to surrender his benefice and was excommunicated by the bishop. The bishop thereupon called on the sheriff of Rutland, who happened to be a friend of the culprit, to imprison him. The sheriff refused, whereupon he too was excommunicated. The king appealed to the Pope, Innocent IV, and received from him a letter forbidding the king's bailiff to be summoned before ecclesiastical courts in secular matters.[2] The action of the Pope followed the injunction of the 42nd canon of the Lateran Council of 1215, which asserts that clergy are forbidden, under the pretext of the liberty of the Church, to extend their jurisdiction to the prejudice of secular justice, but they are bidden to be content with the written constitutions and customs already approved, and to render unto Caesar

---

[1] *C. Pap. R.* i. 178.
[2] Paris, *Chron. Mai.* v. 109 ff.; *Ann. Mon.* (Burton), i. 423.

the things that are Caesar's, and to God the things which rightly belong to God.[1]

Another incident arose in connexion with the bishop's visitation of his diocese. In his efforts to reform the low state of morals among the laity, he had given instructions to his archdeacons and rural deans on the matter. Matthew Paris seems to indicate that these instructions were of a general character.[2] But the actual procedure led to serious complaints. In 1249 the sheriff of Lincoln had served a writ on the bishop requiring him to show on what grounds lay persons of his diocese are required to take an oath, when they are unwilling to do so.[3] As a result of the complaints which reached him the king wrote to the sheriff of Hertfordshire, directing him not to allow any laymen to appear before the bishop in order to answer any inquiries on oath, or make statements on other matters than those concerned with marriages and wills (these falling within the province of the Church) against the customs of the realm and to the prejudice of the Crown.

But to Grosseteste this action of the king appeared to be an interference with the rights and liberties of the Church and impeded it in enforcing its own discipline. Another incident involving, as Grosseteste held, not only interference with the pastoral duties of the clergy, but also danger to the clergy of subjection to civil authorities, was the issue in 1236 by the king of a mandate to the Abbot of Ramsey requiring him to act as an itinerant judge along with others in the counties of Buckingham and Bedford. Matthew Paris sees in the king's project of extending the number of justices his desire, under the pretext of administering justice, to enable him to collect by their means sums of money for the use of the king himself, who, he says, 'squandered everything'.[4]

The bishop accordingly wrote to Archbishop Edmund,[5] pointing out that this was contrary to Scripture and to the canons of the Church, and was unlawful for the clergy, much more for a Benedictine abbot who was bound by the vow of his profession as a monk,

---

[1] Grosseteste's direct order to the sheriff to imprison the clerk naturally provoked the king to anger, as it was contrary to long-established procedure in such matters. He should have sent a letter to the king informing him of his need for royal assistance in dealing with a contumacious and excommunicated clerk and the writ *de excommunicato capiendo* would have been issued from the chancery ordering the sheriff to seize the man in question. (I am indebted to Miss K. Major for this note.)

[2] *Chron. Mai.*, iv. 579 ff.

[3] Powicke, op. cit. i. 282, n. 2. There is no indication of the character of the oath.

[4] Paris, op. cit. iv. 34.   [5] *Ep.* 27.

and he asks the archbishop to write to the king to warn him and to induce him to recall the mandate. In appealing to Scripture and the Canons of the Church Grosseteste had in mind canon 12 of the Lateran Council of 1179, which forbids clerks from subdeacons upwards to undertake secular jurisdiction under princes or secular persons so as to become justiciars. This, it declares, is contrary to Scripture, and the canon quotes 2 Tim. ii. 4, which in the Vulgate runs 'nemo militans Deo implicat se negotiis saecularibus',[1] and involves neglect of the clerical office. More severe punishment still is enjoined for 'religious' attempting to do these things.

Grosseteste goes on to say that if the king does not recall the mandate in spite of the archbishop's counsel, and the abbot, whose soul is in the bishop's care, were to persist in exercising the office of justiciar, it would be a danger to his soul and a scandal to the Church and to the detriment of the liberty of the Church. In a second letter[2] to the archbishop he says that the king has threatened him for his opposition, and that the archbishop has twice suggested that it is better to wait till a Council has discussed the matter. But this temporizing policy was foreign to Grosseteste's convictions, fearless courage, and reforming zeal. For him this was a matter of conscience. He urges that if such action as that of the king is contrary to the statutes of the supreme pontiff and to the regulations of the Canons, which all are bound to obey, those who disobey are guilty of sin, and he quotes Heb. xiii. 17 and his favourite text 1 Sam. i. xv. 23. It is likewise a sin for prelates to permit it, and he appeals to the archbishop to come forward as a 'leader in the camp of Israel, fighting the Lord's battle as Judas Maccabeus had done'.

In this matter Archbishop Edmund was faced with a complex situation. The practice against which Grosseteste protested had long been current. Many ecclesiastics had vested interests in the matter, and previous kings had found in the higher clergy some of their most valuable sources of help in filling important civil positions. Hence Grosseteste's attitude found little support from the prelates, and some of his closest friends, such as William Raleigh, did not share his views on this question. But for Grosseteste the supreme aim of the Church's policy must be the adequate cure of souls, and this was endangered in his view by such invasions of the liberty of the Church as the king's action involved, withdrawing, as it did, the

---

[1] The quotation *Militans Deo* appears in Grosseteste's letter, in Luard's edition, p. 106.
[2] *Ep.* 28.

clergy from their pastoral duties. In this attitude he was supported
by Pope Gregory IX who in 1236 authorized him to proceed
against clerks who discharged the offices of justiciar or sheriff,
while at a later date Innocent IV in 1247 granted him a mandate to
exercise his office without fear against rectors who exercised the
office of justiciar, sheriff, bailiff, or notary in secular courts.[1]

The question was still more fully dealt with by the bishop in a
letter addressed to Archbishop Edmund in 1239.[2] It is really a mani-
festo on the grievances of the Church. In it he not only refers to this
matter of the king's appointment of abbots and other ecclesiastical
persons to the office of justiciar, but also to other infringements of
the liberties of the Church, such as the compelling of ecclesiastics to
submit to lay tribunals, the king's prevention of ecclesiastical judges
from deciding causes which are known to be purely ecclesiastical,
and his hindering their decisions. Prelates too have been required
to give account to secular tribunals for their refusal to institute
persons presented to benefices, a right which properly and intrinsic-
ally belongs to the office of a bishop. By these and similar violations
of the Church's rights the king is in danger of committing the sin of
Uzzah,[3] who usurped to himself the office of priest. Finally, he
points out that the provincial Council of Oxford in 1222 excommunicated all who presume to deprive the Church of its rights and liberties and that the king himself had accepted that principle as laid
down in the Great Charter of 1215.

The bishop in his usual forthright manner proceeded to act upon
the principles which he had set forth. In a letter addressed to the
Cardinal Legate Otto in the latter part of 1239[4] he begs him to
intervene to prevent the Abbot of Croyland, who as a Benedictine
is subject to the bishop's jurisdiction, from acting as an itinerant
justice, and later on about 1245 he refused to admit R. Passelew to
the church of St. Peter, Northampton, to which he had been presented by the king, on the ground that he was a forest judge, and by
reason of the bishop's concern for the souls of the said parish and
out of zeal for the king's honour. So he states in a letter to the king.[5]
Hearing that the king was vexed with him he writes a second letter[6]
to him in which he seeks to remove any grounds of offence which he
may have caused, but instead of seeking to justify his action he

<hr>

[1] C. Pap. R. i. 155, 230.　　[2] Ep. 72*.
[3] 2 Chron. xxvi. 18 f.　　[4] Ep. 82.
[5] Ep. 124.　　[6] Ep. 125.

appeals to the king's clemency and expresses the hope that they may discuss the matter together, and that the king, who desires all things to be directed to the honour of God, the salvation of souls, and the liberty of the Church, which is the bishop's own object, will enable them by a short and friendly discussion to reach a cordial agreement.

But the incident brought him also into conflict with Archbishop Boniface. Passelew had appealed against Grosseteste's decision and had procured from the archbishop a mandate for his institution by the archbishop's official within eight days. This provoked an indignant remonstrance from the bishop,[1] who in a letter pointed out, as he had done some years earlier to Archbishop Edmund, that such an appointment was contrary to apostolic teaching and the canons of the Church, and would bring scandal on the Church and on the archbishop himself, who would be acting not out of zeal to do what was right, but from fear of the king. The bishop had constantly warned Passelew against exercising such an office, as it involved imprisonment both for clergy and laity, and he implores him not to allow his official to hinder and do wrong to the archbishop's suffragans, whom it was his duty to protect. The only record in Grosseteste's Rolls of an institution to St. Peter's, Northampton, is that of Master John Houton, Archdeacon of Northampton, who was instituted in the eighth year of the episcopate.[2]

From these conflicts in which Grosseteste was constantly engaged in order to secure better provision for the pastoral care of his flock and to defend the liberties of the Church, it is a relief to turn to the more positive measures which he took to promote in the minds of his clergy a higher conception of the pastoral life and its obligations. The opening clauses of his constitutions deal with some of these.

1. Since the observance of the ten commandments is vital to the salvation of souls parish priests are firmly bidden to know them and frequently to expound them to the people.(1)[3]

2. In church the divine office is to be recited in its entirety with devout attention of mind to the meaning of the words, lest instead of a complete and living offering there be offered one that is mutilated and dead.(10)

3. All pastors after reciting the offices in church are to give themselves diligently to prayer and reading of Holy Scripture, that

---

[1] *Ep.* 126.   [2] *Rotuli Gros.*, p. 212.

[3] The numbers are given as in Pegge, *Life of Grosseteste*, app. vi. 315 ff.

by understanding of the Scriptures they may give satisfaction to any who demand a reason concerning hope and faith. They should be so versed in the teaching of Scripture that by reading of it their prayer may be nourished, as it were, by daily food.(11)

4. Parish priests are to be ready by day or night to visit the sick when required to do so, lest by their negligence they die without confession, communion, and unction.(8)

5. Parish priests and rectors are to see that the children of their parishioners are diligently taught to know the Lord's Prayer, the Creed, the Salutation of the blessed Virgin, and how to sign themselves with the sign of the Cross, and adults who come to confession should be examined as to the knowledge of these, and be instructed as far as is fitting.(12)

6. All pastors should have, at least in a simple form, an understanding of the faith as contained in the Creed and in the *Quicunque vult* which is recited at Prime.(4)

Concern for the better education of the clergy had already engaged the attention of Grosseteste's predecessor, Hugh of Wells. In the latter's Rolls several examples of this are found. Hugh of Carleton could not be instituted to Barnack, as he was studying in the schools of Paris, until the bishop had received a satisfactory report of him from the Masters there. His institution is recorded later.[1] Walter, parson of Stoke (Oxon.), is granted permission to attend the schools 'beyond the seas'.[2] Hugh of Scalby on account of inadequate education is required to attend the schools (Phillimore suggests at Lincoln) under penalty of forfeiting his benefice.[3]

Grosseteste, as we have seen, had frequently rejected nominees to benefices on the ground of illiteracy, and on one occasion had offered a contribution to a boy thus presented and rejected, in order to enable him to procure a proper education.[4] More positive evidence is supplied by two entries (1247) in Bliss, *Calendar of Papal Registers*, which show that he obtained papal permission for Robert de Melkeley, rector of Clothall, to receive the proceeds of his living while he attended the school of the theological faculty provided he is teachable and apt to learn,[5] and a like privilege for the Archdeacon of Buckingham for the same purpose.[6]

Grosseteste's Rolls show that during his episcopate clergy

[1] *Rotuli Welles*, i. 82, 110.
[2] Ibid. i. 108.
[3] Ibid. i. 147.
[4] See p. 159 above.
[5] i. 238.
[6] i. 241.

instituted to parochial cures with the title 'Magister' prefixed to their names, indicating that they were graduates, represent between 13 and 14 per cent. of the whole number instituted.

Grosseteste assigned a high importance to the ministry of preaching. Among his works is one entitled *The Art of Preaching*. In it he deals with the various classes addressed, knights, judges, princes, cloistered persons, priests, those who are married, widows, virgins, and for each class he sets out the injunctions of Scripture applicable to them.[1]

Grosseteste's ideal conception of the pastoral life was set out plainly and unmistakably in his famous 'sermon' at the Council of Lyons in 1250. After denouncing the abuses of patronage and of papal provisions with their evil results in the appointment of bad pastors, he proceeds:

> The pastoral charge does not consist merely in administering the sacraments, saying the canonical hours, celebrating masses, but in the truthful teaching of the living truth, in the awe-inspiring condemnation of vice and severe punishment of it when necessary. It consists also in feeding the hungry, giving drink to the thirsty, covering the naked, receiving guests, visiting the sick and those in prison, especially those who belong to the parish, who have a claim upon the endowments of their church. By the doing of these things is the people to be taught the holy duties of the active life.[2]

Matthew Paris, who had so often criticized Grosseteste especially for his dealings with the monasteries, has an appreciative verdict on his work as a bishop, speaking of him as 'a director of priests, the instructor of clerks, the supporter of scholars, the persecutor of the incontinent, and the unwearied student of the Scriptures, in his episcopal office sedulous, dignified and unwearying'.

Of his personal relations with clergy who had gone astray there is a touching picture in a letter written, however, before he became bishop.[3] It is addressed to a cleric who was living a luxurious and vicious life, and whom he had known in his earlier and better days. Though denouncing in stern language his present evil courses, and speaking of him as no longer 'in Christ', he yet says that though he had been accustomed to love him as 'in Christ', which he no longer can do, yet he cannot cease to love him 'for Christ's sake', for 'love never faileth', and as his severe reproof is written in all charity and

---

[1] Thomson, *Writings*, p. 121.   [2] Brown, *Fasciculus*, app. ii. 253.
[3] *Ep.* 10.

humility, he looks forward to his restoration and points out to him the only way in which this may come to be. He concludes with the words 'farewell into Christ, that some day I may boldly say, farewell in Christ'.

Impetuous as he was in his righteous zeal against evil things, his wrath would break out at times with bursts of hot temper, but behind this there is the steadfast purpose of seeking to bring both clergy and people to a fuller knowledge and experience of the love of God and of the Christian way of life.

Grosseteste's Relations with the Dean and Chapter of Lincoln

In the course of the visitation of his diocese Grosseteste was faced with the problem of the visitation of the chapter of his cathedral church.

A cathedral chapter was in its origin a body of clergy closely associated with the bishop and forming his Council. But in the lapse of time and in a huge diocese such as Lincoln, where the bishop was constantly absent from the cathedral city, the chapter came to acquire an independence of its own. As the endowments of the cathedral body in lands and churches grew, the bishops, in this as in other dioceses, in order to foster their sense of responsibility, had conferred on their chapters considerable privileges and powers. Thus Bishop Chesney in a charter (c. 1160) had accorded the chapter of Lincoln the same privileges as the chapter of Salisbury had been granted by their founder. The charter exempts the prebends of the church of Lincoln from all episcopal rights and demands.[1] Similar immunities had been granted from time to time by other bishops and confirmed by popes, until by the time of Grosseteste any attempt by the bishop to exercise his ordinary duty of visitation was regarded as an invasion of their rights.

But this independence of outside discipline and control was now becoming a serious matter. In a large diocese such as Lincoln with some fifty-five prebends and other manors with their churches forming part of the *Communa* or common property of the canons, it involved a serious limitation of the bishop's exercise of jurisdiction and pastoral care. But the claim of the bishop to exercise such jurisdiction was stoutly resisted not only by his own chapter but by other secular chapters who supported the protest of their Lincoln brethren by sending copies of their statutes in which their privileges

[1] *Reg. Ant.* i. 249 ff.

were set forth, and Matthew Paris,[1] who had bitterly opposed the bishop's visitation of the monasteries, gives his full support to their action. The deans of Salisbury, Lichfield, and Wells had succeeded in the assertion of their claims to exercise the right to visit their cathedral clergy and their lands and churches, and at Lincoln the same claim was being made.

Grosseteste's action was in a way a novelty. In taking it he claimed that he was winning for all English bishops their lapsed rights,[2] and he was indeed the first English bishop to secure for them the right to visit their cathedral chapters. To him with his zeal for reform, it seemed clear that he could effect little in the way of improvement if his right of canonical visitation was denied him. To that effect he wrote to Pope Gregory IX,[3] requesting his help against the opposition of the dean and chapter, and asking him to grant no letters against him to the judges in England until his proctor had arrived in Rome. On 17 January 1239 the Pope issued a mandate to the Bishop and Archdeacon of Worcester and the Abbot of Evesham bidding them to admonish the dean and chapter to obey their bishop. Failing this they are to hear and decide the case if the parties are willing. If not, it is to be remitted to the Pope.[4] Some days later, on 23 January, the Pope issued a licence to Grosseteste 'to exercise his office in regard to the visitation of the chapter of Lincoln, which had not been hitherto visited by himself or any other, without paying attention to vexatious appeals'.[5] From a letter of Grosseteste[6] written about November of the same year we learn that the Pope had dismissed empty-handed the proctor of the dean and chapter. In spite of the Pope's support of Grosseteste the dean and chapter stood their ground and the controversy dragged on for six years.

Grosseteste's correspondence with the dean and chapter includes many letters covering the whole period of the dispute. In one of the earliest[7] he assures them of his sincere affection for them and asks them to tell him clearly and in detail in what way he has done wrong, instead of denouncing him and appealing to the Pope, and he will correct all injuries that he knows of. Love of truth must replace love of ourselves. He implores them by Him who laid down His life for the sheep and taught His pastors to do the same, that for the

[1] *Chron. Mai.*, iii. 528.

[2] *Ep.* 80 (Luard, p. 256).

[3] *Ep.* 77.

[4] *C. Pap. R.* i. 185.

[5] Ibid., p. 178.

[6] *Ep.* 82.

[7] *Ep.* 71.

effecting of the salvation of souls they will set aside all that is precious to them, and as sons will faithfully and actively help him in his ministry, not placing obstacles or procuring any, that 'we all may be one in Christ our peace, who makes both one'.

In a longer letter[1] he discusses in detail and with many appeals to Scripture the right of a bishop to exercise supervision and discipline. The fact that he delegates in ordinary cases his authority to others does not annul the bishop's right to pass judgement and correction. He must see that his delegates do their duty. Nor can the canons think themselves too great to be visited. 'If we have no sin we deceive ourselves.' The greatest men are the humblest. Scripture shows us that none have sinned more than priests and high-priests. We owe obedience to the fathers of our flesh, much more to our spiritual fathers. He knows not how to rule who knows not how to obey. The fact that previous bishops have not visited does not constitute a custom, which is not created by a negative. Turning to the dean's claim to be visitor of the cathedral church he emphasizes the difference between *visor* and *visitator*. The dean may supervise, but being always resident in the church he cannot be its visitor, for that implies an external and independent approach.[2]

In another letter[3] written in November 1239 to his proctor at Rome, he describes the course of the struggle with the chapter. He states that he had suspended the dean, precentor, and subdean from entering the church because, though frequently warned, they had refused to recall a mandate directing vicars and chaplains ministering in the prebends and churches of the common not to obey the bishop when he wishes to visit in the aforesaid places. On 7 September he had given notice to the dean and chapter that not only by his ordinary authority but by that of the Apostolic See he would visit the chapter on the Thursday after St. Luke's day, and he had begun to visit certain prebends. But on 7 October all the canons had been summoned by the dean and chapter in the chapter house and on the

---

[1] *Ep.* 127.
[2] On this see p. 151. The replies of the chapter are found in MS. Bodleian 760, fol. 160ᵛᵃ (kindly furnished by Dr. R. W. Hunt). The important points are: (1) It is foolish to do over again work already done by the dean; (2) the bishop's responsibilities to his flock include instruction, preaching, admonition, not jurisdiction, which he has granted to lesser officials; (3) where the dean is at fault it is the custom of the cathedral churches of England for the whole chapter to correct him. These objections were formulated by the chancellor, Nicholas of Wadingham. I am indebted to Miss D. M. Williamson of the Lincoln Diocesan Record Office for transcribing the document and for the above brief summary of its contents.   [3] *Ep.* 80.

following Sunday after a public statement from the pulpit of the cathedral church they had received from the people leave to appeal to Rome, and had sent messages to all the other chapters in England, and many of the canons had started on their journey to Rome. On the day appointed for the visitation Grosseteste says that he found no one in the church, and being summoned on urgent business by the archbishop he had gone to London. There the dean and other canons waited for him with a view, as they said, to suggesting terms of peace. Two proposals were made by the bishop, but rejected by them. Finally they agreed to the proposal that before Christmas they should send to the Pope to ask his consent to submit to the Bishop of Worcester (Walter Cantilupe) and the Archdeacons of Worcester and Sudbury the determination of the issue in dispute. Meanwhile things were to remain as they were at the time of the bishop's consecration. In a letter to the Pope (in November) Grosseteste, after stating that the chapter have resisted his authority even when supported by that of the Pope, begs him to agree to the proposals made for a settlement.[1] It was not till 24 April 1240 that the Pope issued a mandate to the persons mentioned above to hear and, with consent of the parties, bring to an end the dispute. If they do not consent they are to remit it by proctors to the Pope within two years.[2] From a later mandate of Pope Innocent IV it appears that the dean and chapter had appealed from the verdict given by the Bishop of Worcester and the two archdeacons to the new Pope, who on 22 December 1243 issued a mandate to the priors of Ely and Warter and to the Archdeacon of Rochester to deal with the matter.[3] The dispute, however, dragged on. At one time the chapter went so far as to obtain from the king a prohibition forbidding the bishop's judges to act in any matter affecting the bishop's relations with the chapter, whereupon the bishop wrote[4] to remind them of the excommunication pronounced by the provincial Council of Oxford against those who 'maliciously disturb the liberties of the Church'. The question could only be settled by an ecclesiastical and not by a secular tribunal.

Sometime before this, probably late in 1239, the dean, William of Tournai, who had previously been suspended, was now deprived by the bishop for his continued contumacy. He was succeeded, on the bishop's appointment, by Roger de Weseham, an intimate friend

---

[1] *Ep.* 81.
[3] Ibid. 203.
[2] *C. Pap. R.* i. 189.
[4] *Epp.* 91-92.

of Grosseteste and one of his successors as lecturer to the Franciscans at Oxford. This action of the bishop has been much questioned.

The election of a dean was one of the privileges of the chapter. On this matter Pegge's suggestion has found much acceptance.[1] The chapter had not agreed to the deposition of William of Tournai and refused to take part in the election of a successor, so that the choice of such a successor devolved upon the bishop, who thereupon collated his friend and had him installed.

In 1241 the chapter took the further step of putting forward a document purporting to be a settlement made in the time of William Rufus by two papal legates, eight archbishops, and sixteen bishops. This was intended to support their claim that the dean had disciplinary powers over the canons. Matthew Paris quotes this and appears to treat it as genuine, but its absurdities are exposed by Pegge.[2] The appeals to the king and to a spurious document show the straits to which the chapter were driven and reflect unfavourably on their candour and intelligence.

The prolongation of the dispute led to serious disquiet. Adam Marsh, the intimate friend of Grosseteste, ventured to suggest to him a compromise which the bishop was unable to accept, and also further urged that he should act in a fatherly way and seek to be loved rather than feared.[3] A similar letter from the dean and chapter of Salisbury had also urged upon him a peaceful settlement, and he had replied that he, too, was anxious for peace, but it must be a true peace and not a false one.[4]

Finally the summons of Pope Innocent IV to the Council of Lyons in 1245 brought this, among other questions of more than local importance for the Western Church, before its notice. The Council was to meet on 26 June. Grosseteste, however, started for Rome in November of the previous year, and the Dean of Lincoln and some of the canons also made their way thither. Before his departure Grosseteste had written to his archdeacons.[5] Quoting the parable of the man who going to a far country entrusted his servants with his goods[6] and bade them 'trade until he come',[7] he urged them faithfully to discharge the care of the household over which they

[1] *Life of Grosseteste*, pp. 85 ff.
[2] Op. cit., app. xiii.
[3] *Mon. Franc.*, p. 146.
[4] *Ep.* 93 (1241).
[5] *Ep.* 112.
[6] Matt. xxv. 14.
[7] Luke xix. 13.

were placed, by preaching unceasingly the word of life in his absence, and by precept and example and by prayer, with charity and zeal for the salvation of souls, exercise their office with justice and equity, remembering that they are engaged in the work of God.

On his arrival at Rome he wrote to his friends, William Raleigh, Bishop of Winchester, and Walter Cantilupe, Bishop of Worcester, telling them of his reception with fitting honour by the Pope and cardinals. The way for a settlement was prepared by the Pope, through the influence of Grosseteste, appointing by papal provision Roger de Weseham to the see of Coventry and Lichfield and consecrating him at Lyons on 19 February 1245.

This action of Grosseteste has been much criticized by Pegge, Luard, and others. But the relations of Roger de Weseham and the chapter do not appear to have been harmonious. Apart from the fact that they had not recognized the deposition of the dean's predecessor, there is the evidence of a letter of Pope Innocent IV which says that the present dean, with the concurrence of the precentor, chancellor, and treasurer, had sought to adjust the dispute with the bishop without, however, first obtaining procuratorial letters, and the chapter had not accepted the arrangement made by them. The Pope's letter is a dispensation rehabilitating the dean and his three colleagues on the ground that they had acted not maliciously, but in simplicity.[1] Grosseteste may well have hoped to bring about better relations with the chapter by giving them the opportunity to elect a successor more acceptable to them than one who had been appointed over their heads. Matthew Paris makes no criticism of the appointment, though he was opposed to the bishop in the matter of his dispute with the chapter, but on the contrary speaks highly of Roger de Weseham's eminent fitness for the post.[2] Nor is it true to say, as Luard asserts, that almost immediately after the consecration of the new bishop, the Pope gave a decision in Grosseteste's favour. The papal decision was not given till six months later, on 25 August.

The decision,[3] while asserting the bishop's right as ordinary to visit the dean and chapter, showed a careful consideration for the rights and customs of the cathedral church. The members of the chapter are to show canonical obedience and reverence to the bishop and his successors, but are not to be required to take an oath to that

[1] C. Pap. R. i. 202.
[2] Chron. Mai., iv. 425.
[3] See Bradshaw and Wordsworth, Lincoln Cathedral Statutes, i (Liber Niger), 315 ff.

effect. In accordance with the customs of the church the chapter itself is to correct irregularities of the canons, and failing action on their part, the bishop may correct them by ecclesiastical censure. Nothing is said in the award about Grosseteste's contention that the dean cannot be visitor, but only supervisor, of the cathedral body, and in the subsequent period and even in post-Reformation days the dean continued to visit both the cathedral church and the prebends and lands of the common property of the church, though the chapter in 1314 secured the right to appoint some of the residentiaries to act as his assessors. Finally in 1421 Bishop Fleming issued an award, in the king's presence, allowing the dean to visit triennially, and his assessors were reduced to two, of whom the dean might choose one.[1]

From two letters of Grosseteste[2] it appears that resentment on the part of some members of the chapter had not quite died down. A misunderstanding had occurred over the order in which the visitation of the chapter and the prebends was to take place. With this the bishop dealt satisfactorily. In his second letter he notes that some of the canons by words and looks still showed their displeasure, and he urges them to put aside all memories of the past and their own feelings about it, and seek to do God's will rather than their own. Then by God's grace both he and they will become fellow counsellors and fellow workers. This letter seems to have borne good results, for in writing to offer the archdeaconry of Huntingdon to a certain cleric, who had previously refused a prebend, he is able to assure him that there is now no ground for refusal, as peace and tranquillity between the bishop and the chapter have been attained.[3]

JAMES HERBERT SRAWLEY.

[1] See Kathleen Edwards, *English Secular Cathedrals in the Middle Ages* (Manchester, 1948), p. 149.
[2] *Epp.* 121–2.   [3] *Ep.* 118.

The writer of this paper, Dr. Srawley, to whom Lincoln studies owe so much, unfortunately did not live to see it in print. He died on 6 January 1954.   *The Editor.*

Grosseteste's Relations with the Papacy and the Crown[1]

ROBERT GROSSETESTE is an outstanding example of a very important type of thirteenth-century bishop, namely the schoolman-bishop, the man who first made his name in the schools and as a result was promoted to a bishopric. This type was the product of the rise of the universities and of the reform movement which culminated in the Lateran Council of 1215. It was the type of bishop that reformers like Innocent III wanted to see filling the bishoprics, and it is to this type that belong Langton and St. Edmund before Grosseteste, and Pecham and Winchelsey after him. In earlier centuries the predominant type had been the monk-bishop, the man who had been called out from a life of contemplation to a life of action, a Gregory, a Dunstan, or an Anselm. The new type was a man called out from a life of study to a life of action. Both types in different ways correspond to the ideal put forward by the Mendicants: 'contemplari et aliis contemplata tradere', and to Langland's life of 'Do-Best', the life of the good bishop, which crowns both the active and the contemplative life. In dealing with a man like Grosseteste, therefore, it is of the utmost importance to try to see how he uses the doctrine which he learnt and taught in the schools and applies it to the practical problems of his episcopal career. We must examine Grosseteste's theories about the constitution and function of the Church and the papacy, and about the relations of the Church to the State, and see how these governed his relations with Papacy and Crown. There was nothing of the escapist or introvert about a schoolman like Grosseteste; he was agonizedly aware of contemporary society, and convinced that his doctrine could be applied to it. He was prepared to apply a suitable dose of scripture allegory, or Aristotle, or cosmology, or the pseudo-Denis to almost any problem.[2]

[1] The various documents or memoranda put forward by Grosseteste at Lyons in 1250 are referred to as 'Lyons (1)', 'Lyons (2)', &c., as numbered in Thomson, *Writings*, pp. 142 ff., where the manuscripts are given. Of these documents, Lyons (1) is printed in Brown, pp. 250–7; Lyons (2) in *Epp.*, pp. 432–7; and Lyons (5) in H. Wharton, *Anglia Sacra*, ii (1691), 347–8.

[2] Although Grosseteste applies his academic doctrine to practical and topical problems, he does not seem to do the converse, i.e. introduce practical or topical themes into his academic works, in the way that Langton and other members of the 'biblical-moral'

His public life is a commentary on his intellectual interests: *abeant studia in mores*. In contrast to some other medieval scholar bishops, Grosseteste's scholarly career and episcopal career were not two separate and successive stages of his life; they overlapped, and some of his most important scholarly work was done while he was bishop. Consequently when we find him quoting the pseudo-Denis and Aristotle's Ethics at the Papal Curia in 1250, these were not reminiscences of distant Oxford days, but the outcome of quite recent studies, undertaken since he became bishop. His work on the pseudo-Denis dated from *c*. 1239–43, and on the Ethics from 1245–7.[1]

The most fundamental of Grosseteste's ideas is the supreme importance of the cure of souls; this is the key to all the rest. At first sight this looks like a pious platitude, to which everyone would agree, but Grosseteste applies it with most searching and devastating logic, so that it has a direct bearing on his attitude towards papal provisions, or the holding of secular office by ecclesiastics, or the exaction of excessive visitation fees, or the advisability of the Bishop of Worcester's accompanying the king across the sea, or the inquiries into the sins of laymen which brought so much opposition.[2] Grosseteste felt about the diocese of Lincoln as a great missionary would feel about the peoples of Asia or Africa; here were thousands of souls, in constant danger of perishing, 'for the life of each one of whom the Son of God was willing to die a most shameful death'.[3] It was the salvation of souls that had caused God to become man, to suffer, and to institute the sacraments and the hierarchy of the Church and the whole economy of redemption. Grosseteste sometimes defines this economy of redemption in terms of the care of sheep, sometimes—and this is very characteristic—in the language of the pseudo-Denis: the pastoral care aims at the purgation and illumination of souls, at their 'deification', their assimilation and union as far as possible with God, their 'perfect and inconvertible recession' from what is evil.[4] As he pointed out in a well-known passage of his memorandum to the Pope at Lyons in 1250,[5] the

---

school had been fond of doing; one will look in vain for references to the problems of ecclesiastical politics in his commentary on the Ecclesiastical Hierarchy of the pseudo-Denis.

[1] Cf. Callus, 'The Date . . .', *R.T.A.M.* xiv (1947), 186–210.

[2] See below, pp. 193–6, 181–2, 211–13, 202–3. For the Bishop of Worcester's case, see *Ep.*, p. 302.   [3] Lyons (1); Brown, p. 252; Stevenson, p. 287.

[4] Lyons (1); Brown, p. 254; Lyons (7); *Ep.*, p. 435.

[5] Lyons (1); Brown, p. 253; Stevenson, p. 287.

work of the pastoral care does not only consist in administering the sacraments, saying the canonical hours and celebrating masses—and even these are rarely performed by mercenaries—but in the teaching of the living truth, in the 'terrific' condemnation and castigation of vice—and this mercenaries can rarely dare to do. It also consists in feeding the hungry, giving drink to the thirsty, clothing the naked, receiving guests, visiting the sick and prisoners, and ministering especially to the parishioners, who have provided the temporal goods of the churches—and this mercenaries cannot afford to do. It is clear then that the pastoral work cannot be adequately carried out by mere mercenaries, middlemen, *mediatores*, as Grosseteste calls them, cheap and inferior substitutes; it needs highly qualified men. The abuse or neglect of the pastoral care by unworthy pastors is the equivalent to spiritual murder or worse and may wreck God's plan of redemption; hence the terrific responsibility both for the candidates for benefices and for the patrons and bishops who appoint them.

Grosseteste was convinced that to appoint an unworthy candidate to any cure of souls was a mortal sin. In one of his statements to the Pope at Lyons in 1250, he explains very vividly how he examined candidates:

It is my custom when anyone is presented to me for a cure of souls, to explain and as far as I can to make plain to the presenter, what kind of man the pastor of Christ's sheep should be, and that anyone who abuses the pastoral office is in himself, according to scripture, spiritually dead, and the slayer of souls committed to him, and in as much as Christ's principal work on earth is to give life to souls, he truly becomes the opposite of Christ and thus Antichrist; and since the power of the pastoral care is a power and force that generates unto eternal life, and in proportion as eternal life is better than temporal life, this force is better than the force that generates unto temporal life, and its abuse is proportionately worse, so whoever abuses this spiritually generative force is proportionately worse than any sodomite. This and the like I try to make plain to them, as well as I can, lest I should seem to speak to them in jest.[1]

This extremely severe and scrupulous standard of pastoral care Grosseteste applied ruthlessly to himself and to others. It was a sense of his own inadequacy that led him, after an illness in 1232, to give up voluntarily all his benefices save one[2]—an act which must have been rare if not unique among the secular clergy of his time,

[1] Lyons (9).   [2] *Ep.*, p. 43 ff.; Stevenson, p. 106.

for most men who felt called to that kind of self-abnegation would
have entered religion. For the same reason he was constantly rejecting candidates for benefices or prebends as unsuitable, on the
grounds of youth or ignorance and so forth,[1] and this among other
things brought him in conflict with papal provisions, as we shall see.
He also objected to ecclesiastics holding secular offices incompatible
with the cure of souls, such as the office of itinerant justice or forest
judge (involving the judgement of blood) or secular stewardships and
the like.[2] 'Nemo militans Deo implicat se negotiis saecularibus',[3]
he was fond of quoting. To reject unsuitable candidates for the cure
of souls sounds commonplace enough, but as Grosseteste applied
it, it brought him into conflict with powerful vested interests and the
accepted, conventional standards of his time. No doubt some of the
candidates he rejected were scandalous by any standard, and their
patrons irresponsible. But some of those whose presentations or
advancement he opposed were certainly not monsters of iniquity.
They included men like William Raleigh,[4] the judge, who became
Bishop of Norwich, and the treasurer, Hugh Pateshull,[5] later Bishop
of Coventry, men whom Sir Maurice Powicke puts among 'the most
stable and helpful, as it was the most intelligent, element in the
State at this time';[6] Master John Blund, one of the leading Aristotelian scholars;[7] the legate Otto;[8] and the chancellor, Ralph Nevill,
Bishop of Chichester.[9] These were not ecclesiastical drones, they
were active, serious, responsible men, and some of them personal
friends of Grosseteste. The same can be said of Walter Cantelupe,
Bishop of Worcester, who made a spirited defence of pluralism in
1236.[10] Where these men differed from Grosseteste was, I think,
that they, like most other men in the later Middle Ages, accepted
the system of the exploitation of ecclesiastical benefices, whereby
the cure of souls could be carried out by paid substitutes, while the
surplus revenues could go to support important persons in the
service of Church and State, wardrobe officials, cardinals, 'sublime
and literate persons', younger sons of the nobility, and so forth.
It would be a mistake to regard this system simply as an abuse; it
must have seemed to contemporaries the only way of supporting the

[1] *Epp.*, pp. 50, 63, 68, 102.   [2] *Epp.*, pp. 105, 108, 158, 205, 262, 349.
[3] 2 Tim. ii. 4.   [4] *Ep.*, p. 63.
[5] *Ep.*, p. 97.   [6] Powicke, p. 143.
[7] *Ep.*, p. 68; cf. Callus, *Aristotelian Learning*, pp. 15–26.
[8] *Epp.*, pp. 144, 241.   [9] *Ep.*, p. 188.
[10] Paris, *Chron. Mai.* iii. 418.

necessary bureaucracy in Church and State.[1] As a fourteenth-century pluralist put it: 'Both he who resides and he who does not reside are understood to serve the altar, so long as the man lives a good life and expends well the income he derives.'[2] Where Grosseteste showed his originality and clear-sightedness was in seeing this system of exploitation as one of the root causes of spiritual inefficiency. To him it was unreal and perverse; it reduced the pastoral care to a thing of secondary importance, whereas in his view only the best brains and energy available were good enough for the work of saving souls. To Grosseteste one of the most objectionable features of this exploitation was, as we have seen, the employment of ecclesiastics in secular office. Throughout the Middle Ages the English civil service was largely peopled with clerics and financed by ecclesiastical benefices large and small. Here again Grosseteste showed his clear-sightedness. The disappointing mediocrity in the high places of the English Church in the fourteenth and fifteenth centuries, the lack of men of the calibre of Langton, Grosseteste, or Pecham, may have been partly due to the way in which the scholar-bishops were crowded out by the civil-servant bishops. To a modern observer Grosseteste seems obviously right. And yet if he had had his way, and had established a clean-cut division between the servants of the Church and the servants of the State, we cannot be sure that it would have been all to the good. It is always difficult to weigh the advantages and disadvantages of the entanglement of the Church in contemporary society. The ecclesiastical civil servants, the king's clerks, were themselves conscious of their importance as good mediators between Church and State, the true hinge on which the social order turned.[3] They did in fact help to bind Church and State together, and to make impossible in England that particular kind of anti-clericalism that flourished in France under Philip the Fair. There was indeed anti-clericalism in England among the lay magnates and gentry, but the one place where it could not exist was in a clerical civil service. How far Grosseteste would have admitted such prudential considerations is another matter.

One point over which Grosseteste was at cross purposes with his contemporaries was his attitude towards prebends in cathedral

[1] For the whole question of pluralism, see A. Hamilton Thompson, 'Pluralism in the Medieval Church', in *Associated Architectural Societies Reports*, xxxiii. 35 ff.

[2] A. Hamilton Thompson, *The English Clergy and their Organization in the later Middle Ages* (1947), p. 246.

[3] Cf. Powicke, pp. 715–16.

chapters. He seems to have regarded them as benefices with cure of souls, they as sinecures. It was over the appointment to prebends that some of his most spectacular rejections of candidates took place, including his rejection of the Pope's nephew in 1253.[1] Cathedral prebends were much sought after by pluralists and non-residents, and they were in fact the field in which these could do least harm; by this time the convention was already established that the majority of canons were non-resident; their liturgical functions were performed by vicars-choral; and canonists held, reasonably enough, that ordinary prebends (in contrast to such offices as deaneries and archdeaconries) were not benefices with cure of souls.[2] Grosseteste on the other hand seems to have regarded prebends, at least in some cases, as involving the cure of souls, and objected on these grounds to unsuitable candidates as endangering souls.[3] This was probably because, in certain cases, prebends were endowed with an appropriated church. But even in such cases, provided that a vicarage was properly established, and still more in the numerous prebends that were endowed with manors, it is difficult to see how the appointment of even the most ill-qualified alien could in practice jeopardize souls. Such an appointment might deprive the bishop of the means of rewarding and retaining a more valuable assistant and counsellor, but that is another matter, and is not the same as the ruin of souls, which Grosseteste took so much to heart. In objecting to the exploitation of other benefices, Grosseteste was on firm ground; but he seems to be spoiling a good case by taking an over-scrupulous line over prebends.[4]

The most striking feature about Grosseteste's theory of the constitution and function of the ecclesiastical hierarchy is his exaltation of the papacy. He was probably the most fervent and thoroughgoing papalist among medieval English writers. In one sense he may perhaps be regarded as belonging to a tradition of English ultramontanism that went back to Anglo-Saxon times, or as a product of the ecclesiastical centralization of the eleventh and twelfth centuries,

[1] See below, p. 194; and his rejection of a Roman noble, described in Lyons (9), see below, p. 214.

[2] See K. Edwards, *The English Secular Cathedrals in the Middle Ages* (1949), pp. 33 ff.

[3] *Epp.*, pp. 241-2, 432-7; Lyons (9).

[4] It is only fair to say that opinions were divided on this matter, and that as late as the time of Boniface VIII there were some who held that a prebend endowed with a church had a cure of souls; Pope Boniface by implication ruled the contrary, following the Lateran Council of 1215. Cf. Sext. Decretal. III. tit. iv, c. 6. *Super eo*; A. Hamilton Thompson, 'Pluralism in the Medieval Church', p. 66.

but his papalism is also strongly coloured by the learning of the schools and by his own favourite studies. He is fond of comparing the Pope and the hierarchy in general to Old Testament figures, or to the angelic hierarchy as expounded by the pseudo-Denis, or to his scientific theory of the sun as the source of life and power in the universe. As the sun is to the moon and stars, so is the Pope to the bishops, and so is the bishop to his inferiors. Thus in about 1236, soon after he became bishop, he wrote to his friend Cardinal Gil de Torres:

As in the visible world the conspicuous sun by its preeminent light, purges the darkness of the world, and in a singular manner lights up the world, and by its own most ordered movement (as the learned men of the world hold) orders and regulates the other natural bodily movements; so in the universe of the Church, the supreme pontiff takes the place of the sun, by the excellent light of his teaching and good works purging the world from the darkness of error, and by a singular prerogative illuminating it unto the knowledge of truth, and by his disposition ordering, regulating and governing all the movements of actions in the universal Church. Therefore just as (so the seekers after the prudence and intelligence of this world hold) the state, beauty and order of the world are due, next after the world's Creator and the angelic spirits that minister at the Creator's command, to the visible sun and to the hinges of the world (*mundique cardinibus*); even so (as they hold who know the things that are above), after the world's Creator and Redeemer and the heavenly court of the blessed spirits of angels and saints, the state, the beauty and order of the universal Church are due to its sun and its hinges, that is, to the supreme pontiff and his assistants the cardinals. And so to the Holy Roman Church is due from all sons of the Church the most devout obedience, the most honoured reverence, the most fervent love, the most subject fear. And these and the like are the more strictly and strongly owing from those who, by the sublimity of their ecclesiastical degree, adhere more closely to the summit of the Church, that is to the supreme pontiff and the cardinals.

And as in the heavenly hierarchy, every inferior order of angels, in so far as it approximates more closely to its head, God, and to the supreme order most immediately attending on Him, receives from Him more limpidly the light of intelligence, more fervently the ardour of charity, more firmly steadfastness in attendance, and more nobly the act of ministering; and therefore, according to the degree of greater approximation and of sublimer illumination received from the Father of lights, it rises more strongly and more completely to unceasing praise and thanks to that Father, and to the obedient, prompt and effective carrying out of all actions commanded; so in the ecclesiastical hierarchy, those who do not desert the order of sacred government and the unity of the universal Church, the higher they are in the degrees of ecclesiastical rank, for that reason, receiving from the supreme pontiff and the cardinals closely attending him the light of the teaching of the faith and the guidance (*moderamen*) by which they ought to live in the house of God, the more closely do they pay back spontaneous devotion of mind and the more effectively the execution of enjoined action. Because therefore I, although unworthy, have been raised up to the degree of episcopal dignity, I confess I have become a more strictly bound debtor in subjection and obedience to the supreme pontiff and the Holy Roman Church, in proportion as I have gained a higher degree.[1]

In 1239, in the course of a long discourse on the ecclesiastical hierarchy addressed to the Dean and Chapter of Lincoln, he wrote:

For this reason, after the pattern of the ordinance made in the Old Testament, the lord Pope has the fullness of power *over the nations and over kingdoms, to root up and to pull down, and to waste and to destroy, and to build and plant.*[2] And he can of his own power judge all the affairs, greater and smaller, both of communities and individuals, greater and smaller, and can correct and reform what needs to be corrected and reformed. But because, for the multitude of his subjects, he cannot by himself do in act, what he nevertheless can do in power, namely bear the burden of all and sundry, there are chosen to share in his solicitude the prelates of churches, namely the bishops, so that drawing on the fullness of his power, they may help him to bear his burden . . . there being reserved to him certain greater things, which he alone can do, and which no bishop can do by the episcopal power derived from the apostolic power. For the order of reason and nature demands that the influencing power (*virtus influens*) should be able to do more than the recipient of influence (*recipiens de influentia*) and that which has power only by reason of what it receives from influence. For the Seraphim can do more than the Cherubim, and the sun can do more in giving light and heat than can the moon and stars, which only derive their light from the sun. And as the lord Pope is with regard to the Church in the fullness of his power, so is the bishop with regard to his diocese in the power which he has received from the apostolic power. . . . Except therefore for those things reserved to the Pope alone, the bishop can do all things in his diocese that belong to the cure and saving of souls and the decision of ecclesiastical causes. . . .

Samuel was like the sun of the people, among the people of Israel, just as the lord Pope is in the universal Church, and every bishop is in his

[1] *Ep.*, pp. 126 ff.   [2] Jer. i. 10.

diocese. For since the sun cannot by immediate presence (*presentialiter*) give light everywhere on earth at one and the same time, for the purging of darkness and for the vegetation of things growing on the earth, lest however any part of the earth should at any time lack the solace of light, it (the sun) out of the fullness of its light, without suffering thereby any loss itself, gives light to the moon and the stars, that in its absence they may shine in the firmament of heaven and give light to the earth; and when the sun comes back and shows its presence to the earth, the lesser luminaries, hidden by the rays of the sun, give place to the sun's light. Just so the lord Pope shows his presence, in respect of whom all other prelates are like the moon and stars, receiving from him whatever power they have for the illumination and vegetation of the Church; he has the power by the regard of his presence (*presentiali intuitu*) of dissipating the darkness of all evil and fostering and vegetating the seeds and plants of all goodness; the other powers in his presence give way to him, as the light of the moon and stars gives way to the sun's rays. In the like manner every bishop, although in respect of the Pope he is like one of the nocturnal luminaries, yet in his own diocese is like its sun; and the inferior prelates under him, who receive from him what ecclesiastical power they have, are in respect of him like the moon and stars, to give light in the bishop's absence.[1]

And in the course of his statements to the Pope at Lyons in 1250, he said:

And although commonly all pastors are one pastor in the first pastor Christ and bear His type and person and office, yet by a special prerogative those who preside in this Holy See, the most holy Popes, in a most special way bear the type and person and office of Christ. And the most venerable fathers of this most Holy See, the cardinals, in a most special way bear the person and type and office of the apostles, and the other pastors bear those of the first holy fathers. . . .

This most Holy See is the throne of God and like to the sun of the world in His sight. Whence just as there exists causally in the sun the whole illumination of this world, its vegetation, nutrition of sensible life, augmentation, consummation, conservation, beauty, and grace; and just as the sun is always causing all these things to flow (*influit*) into this sensible world, and so makes and keeps this world sensible and perfect; so this most Holy See ought to have all these things, spiritually understood, within itself causally, and ought to cause all these things to flow unceasingly into that whole spiritual world of which it is the spiritual sun, and so save that spiritual world. Otherwise, just as, if the causal reasons (*rationes causales*) in the visible sun should fail and the influences from it upon the

[1] *Ep.*, pp. 364 f., 389 f.

world, straightway this whole sensible world would perish; even so if there
should fail in this spiritual sun the spiritual causal reasons, which correspond to those of the sun, and from it the corresponding influences upon
the spiritual world, this world, of which it is the sun, must needs perish,
and it must be the cause and be guilty of this perdition, especially since
these causal reasons and the influences therefrom are in its free power. But
God forbid, God forbid that this sun, altogether shining in its intelligence
and always straight in its justice, should at any time be turned into darkness and turn black like a piece of sackcloth or turn backwards.[1]

What more can I say? [he concludes his last address to the Pope at
Lyons]. Any amount of time would be insufficient to relate the sensible
and material symbols by which in holy scripture is signified the super-
eminence of the power of this Holy See, and the shining clarity of its
wisdom and holiness and most divine works, glorifying and enlightening
the whole world. . . . But the names of immaterial things, by which your
eminence is signified most plainly and fully, are 'angel' and 'god'. For
while priests in general, by transcending all material things to the point
of 'deiformity' as far as is possible for human infirmity, are called angels
and gods, and since you are raised up to the highest priesthood, you are
the angel of angels and the god of gods; no power can be more excel-
lently named. Lest therefore your naming be empty and in vain, it is
necessary that you among all mortals be most highly assimilated and conformed to the angels and to God, that there may not be or appear anything
in you except what is angelic and divine, and so you must be the light and
sun of the world, shining most clearly without any darkening or remission
of light or of vital heat, vegetating and vivifying the world.[2]

According to Grosseteste, then, the Pope is the centre and source
of spiritual life in this world; like the sun, he illuminates, he purges,
he gives life ('vegetates'), he controls movement; if he failed, the
spiritual world would wither away.[3] Spiritual gifts flow down from
God through the orders of the ecclesiastical hierarchy, as through
those of the heavenly hierarchy; the higher in rank and nearer to
the source one is, the more one receives, the more one has to give.
In theory, the Pope could carry on the whole work of the Church
single-handed, he is in the fullest sense the 'universal ordinary', but
in practice he needs to call in bishops as his delegates and assistants.
The bishops derive a reflected power from the Pope, as the moon and
stars do from the sun; they are so many miniature and derivative

---

[1] Lyons (1); Brown, pp. 251, 254; cf. Lyons (9).
[2] Lyons (9).
[3] For Grosseteste's 'Lichtmetaphysik' and his theory of the sun's influence, cf.
Baur, *Die Philosophie*, pp. 76 ff., 160 ff.; cf. also Grosseteste, *De Sphaera* (Baur, *Die
Werke*), p. 29, on the moon's reflected light.

popes. All this is not simply the language of exaggerated compliment or far-fetched allegory, nor does it simply mean that Grosseteste welcomed a strong papacy as a practical expedient, as a useful potential ally in the reform of the Church, though that consideration no doubt counted for something with him. For Grosseteste the *plenitudo potestatis* is an essential part of his theological and scientific scheme of things; he believes in it, because he is convinced that that is the way in which the spiritual and physical universe is constructed. The comparison between the papacy and the sun is the more convincing, because to an Aristotelian like Grosseteste, the physical universe is presumably not simply a divine cross-word puzzle (as it might have appeared to earlier generations) but something that works according to rational and natural laws, which are analogous to moral and spiritual laws.

One implication of this theory of papal power is the necessity of obedience. We are bound by God's commandment to honour and obey our spiritual parent even more than our earthly parents.[1] Grosseteste is fond of quoting the text, that the *sin of disobedience is as the sin of witchcraft*,[2] though he admits that obedience may sometimes be very repugnant; 'by obedience we are sometimes forced to do what we do with sadness and what we would omit with gladness if we could'.[3] Another implication is that the greater the power the more awful the responsibility and the worse the effects of any abuse of power, as St. Bernard had pointed out a century earlier in the *De Consideratione*. Grosseteste was much concerned with this implication. Thus when writing to the legate Otto (*c.* 1237), objecting to the appointment of a clerk of the legate's to a prebend in Lincoln, he says:

I know and I truly know, that the lord Pope and the Holy Roman Church have this power, that they can freely dispose of (*ordinare*) all ecclesiastical benefices. I know also that whoever abuses this power, builds for hell-fire; I know also that whoever does not use it for the promotion of faith and charity, is abusing this power; I know furthermore that when ecclesiastical benefices are conferred *auctoritate potestativa*, without first asking the consent of the patrons, especially when this might easily be asked, those who confer call down on themselves the most terrible hatred of all, besides the hatred of those to whom collation is made, and who hate the patrons of benefices thus conferred. . . . By this way therefore the Church is not built up, but destroyed.[4]

[1] *Ep.*, p. 341.
[3] *Ep.*, p. 337.
[2] I Reg. xv. 23.
[4] *Ep.*, p. 145.

In his memorandum to the Pope at Lyons in 1250, he writes:

Those who preside in this most Holy See are most principally among mortals clothed with the person of Christ, and therefore it is necessary that in them especially the works of Christ should shine, and that there should be nothing contrary to Christ's works in them. And for the same reason, just as the Lord Jesus Christ must be obeyed in all things, so also those who preside in this see, in so far as they are clothed with Christ and are as such truly presiding, must be obeyed in all things. But if any one of them (which God forbid) should put on the clothing of kinship and the flesh or of the world or anything else except Christ, and for love of such things should command anything contrary to Christ's precepts and will, anyone who obeys him in such things manifestly separates himself from Christ and from His body which is the Church and from the president in this see, in so far as he is clothed with the person of Christ and as such truly presiding. And when obedience is commonly given in such matters, a true and perfect falling away has come about and the revelation of the son of perdition is at hand. But God forbid, God forbid that this most Holy See and those who preside in it, who are commonly obeyed in all their commands, by commanding anything contrary to Christ's precepts and will, should be the cause of a true falling away. God forbid that to any who are truly united to Christ, not willing in any way to go against His will, this see and those who preside in it should be a cause of falling away or apparent schism, by commanding such men to do what is opposed to Christ's will. Let them not therefore command anything nor do anything discordant with the will of Christ, to Whom nothing is more abominable and hateful than the losing of souls and the handing over of souls to those who are not pastors but destroyers.[1]

Finally, Grosseteste states his views in the famous letter to Master Innocent, the papal notary, refusing to admit Pope Innocent IV's nephew to a canonry in Lincoln in 1253. To cause the destruction of souls by depriving them of pastoral care is the worst of all sins, comparable to the sin of Lucifer and Antichrist; to command such a thing cannot be a genuine exercise of the apostolic power:

It is not possible that the most holy apostolic see, to which has been handed down by the Holy of Holies, the Lord Jesus Christ, all manner of power, according to the Apostle, for edification and not for destruction, can command or in any way attempt anything verging upon this kind of sin, which is so hateful to Jesus Christ, detestable, abominable, and pernicious to the human race. For this would be evidently a falling off and corruption and abuse of its most holy and plenary power. . . . No faithful subject of the Holy See, no man who is not cut away by schism from the

[1] Lyons (1); Brown, p. 255.

body of Christ and the same Holy See, can submit to mandates, precepts or any other demonstrations of this kind, no, not even if the author were the most high body of angels. He must needs repudiate them and rebel against them with all his strength. Because of the obedience by which I am bound to the Holy See, as to my parents, and out of my love of my union with the Holy See in the body of Christ, . . . as an obedient son I disobey, I contradict, I rebel. You cannot take action against me, for my every word and act is not rebellion, but the filial honour due by God's command to father and mother. As I have said, the Apostolic See in its holiness cannot destroy, it can only build. This is what the plenitude of power means; it can do all things to edification. But these so called provisions do not build up, they destroy. They cannot be the work of the Blessed Apostolic See, for 'flesh and blood', which do not possess the Kingdom of God, 'hath revealed them', not 'the Father of Our Lord Jesus Christ who is in Heaven'.[1]

There seem to be two lines of argument here. The first is that since the *plenitudo potestatis* exists for the purpose of edification and not destruction, any act which tends to destruction or the ruin of souls cannot be a genuine exercise of the *plenitudo potestatis*. This is perhaps connected with the notion that since evil is something negative ('sin is nothing'),[2] the possibility of doing evil is not an addition to our power or liberty, but the reverse. It also resembles Bracton's interpretation of the maxim that the king can do no wrong: 'since the king is the minister and vicar of God, he can do nothing else on earth, except that which he has a right to do by law'.[3] Grosseteste makes the same point in a letter to Henry III: he cannot believe that certain pernicious commands have emanated from the royal conscience, 'for the royal power, since the king is named from right rule (*cum rex a recto dicatur regimine*), has no power to do anything except command what is right'.[4] He seems to apply much the same principle to the Pope.[5]

The second line of argument is that if the Pope, or anyone else,

---

[1] *Ep.*, pp. 435 ff.; Stevenson, p. 310; Powicke, p. 286. The authenticity of this letter has been questioned, but, it seems, without sufficient reason. It contains some of Grosseteste's characteristic ideas about the cure of souls and about 'deification', and it appears in some of the earliest manuscripts of his letters; cf. Thomson, *Writings*, p. 213.

[2] Cf. Grosseteste's argument that since 'sin is nothing', a sinful act cannot constitute possession, *Ep.*, p. 224.

[3] Bracton, *De legibus et consuetudinibus Angliae*, bk. iii, pt. i, c. 9.

[4] *Ep.*, p. 308.

[5] Perhaps cf. also the statement of Innocent III, that the vows of poverty and chastity are so bound up with the monastic rule, that the Pope himself cannot grant a licence against them: *Decretal.* iii, tit. xxxv, c. 6, *Cum ad monasterium*.

should command anything contrary to Divine law, then it will be wrong to obey, and in the last resort, while protesting one's loyalty, and indeed because of one's loyalty, one must refuse to obey. The fundamental problem was that while the Church's teaching is supernaturally guaranteed against error, the Church's ministers, from the Pope downwards, are not impeccable, and are capable of making wrong judgements or giving wrong commands. The problem of obedience had been dealt with in an earlier generation by Peter the Chanter[1] and Langton,[2] and in Grosseteste's own day by St. Thomas.[3] The problem of an unlawful command might seem to many a hypothetical or academic one; to Grosseteste, with his conviction that any unworthy appointment to a cure of souls was a mortal sin, it appeared very real.

Grosseteste's views invite some comparison with those of Wyclif, who admired him and frequently quoted him; for instance he quoted and commented on Grosseteste's letter to Master Innocent *in extenso* in the *De Civili Dominio*.[4] Grosseteste's argument that a papal command is invalid when contrary to the Divine law bears some resemblance to the doctrine of dominion by grace and still more to the theory that he who abuses a privilege, deserves to forfeit it. This doctrine of forfeiture can be traced back to a remark of St. Gregory the Great, quoted in the *Decretum* of Gratian;[5] it was applied by Fitz-Ralph to the Mendicants, and by Wyclif more drastically to the ecclesiastical hierarchy as a whole. The difference between the position of Grosseteste and that of Wyclif seems to be this: Grosseteste, I think, envisaged an unlawful command as a temporary aberration, which deprives the superior's command of

---

[1] Petrus Cantor, *Verbum abbreviatum*, *P.L.* ccv. 315–16; Peter comes very near to Grosseteste's own dilemma over papal provisions: 'Item it is asked whether I, being a bishop, a dean or the like, am bound to fulfil my ministry for the Lord Pope who commands it, to have some unworthy person ordained by me, or given a prebend, or the like? . . . Item Gregory answers, *Moralium*, lib. xxxv, c. 10: Know that evil ought never to be done by way of obedience, though sometimes something good, which is being done, ought to be discontinued, out of obedience.'

[2] F. M. Powicke, *Stephen Langton* (1928), pp. 16, 158.

[3] *Summa Theologiae*, iia, iiae, q. 104, art. 5: 'Utrum subditi teneantur suis superioribus in omnibus obedire?'; cf. ibid., q. 33, art. 7, ad 5; *Quaestiones quodlibetales*, Quodl. I, qu. viii, art. 1, 2. St. Thomas does not specifically touch on the question of papal commands.

[4] *De Civili Dominio*, ed. Poole, i (1885), 384 ff., cf. *Ep.*, pp. 432 ff. For other references to Grosseteste see ibid. i. 392 ff.; *De Potestate Papae*, ed. Loserth (1907), pp. 190, 256, cf. *Ep.*, p. 125.

[5] *Decretum*, ii pars, causa xi, qu. iii, c. 60; cf. the monk of Malmesbury in *Chronicles of the Reigns of Edward I and Edward II*, ed. Stubbs, ii (Rolls Series, 1883), 198.

validity *pro hac vice*, but does not permanently destroy the superior's authority or the office that he holds. The papacy remains absolutely necessary; if it should founder (which God forbid) then the whole Church would founder. Wyclif on the other hand, at least in his final stage, seems to regard reprobate popes and prelates (i.e. those 'fore-known' to damnation) as permanently lacking authority; the Church must if necessary carry on without them. While he quotes some passages from Grosseteste with approval, he explicitly rejects the latter's statement that subjection to the Holy See is altogether necessary for salvation to the whole human race.[1] Again, according to Grosseteste anyone, from the Pope downwards, who acts or commands contrary to Christ's will is playing the part of Antichrist, a phrase that sounds ominous to modern ears; but what he has in mind is a moral, not a doctrinal failure, and he does not envisage the possibility of the papacy or the Church erring in doctrine. To Wyclif, on the other hand, the Pope and the worldly prelates and the friars were to be identified with Antichrist not only because of their moral delinquency but also because of their false doctrine, on the subject of the Eucharist for instance.

Two of the ways in which papal authority would impinge upon an English prelate were papal taxation and papal provisions. With regard to the first, Grosseteste's principles would make it impossible for him to refuse the duty of supporting the papacy in its necessity, though he might protest against the methods employed and the amounts demanded;[2] and he was bound to press this duty upon others. In 1245–6 Henry III, with the support of the magnates and prelates, for a time held out against the demand for a papal subsidy; he was, in Pope Innocent's words, 'playing the Frederick'. In the end, the king gave in, and it seems that the 'persuasive words' of Grosseteste, in an interview which he had with the king on his return from the Council of Lyons, played a part in bringing the king round.[3] In contrast, he felt justified in opposing taxation for temporal purposes. In the Council of 1244 he took a leading part in opposing an aid to the king, though the aid had the backing of the Pope; he rallied the opposition with the words: 'Let us not separate ourselves from the general resolve, for it is written, Divided we perish.'[4]

---

[1] *De Potestate Papae*, p. 258, cf. *Ep.*, p. 123.
[2] *Chron. Mai.* iv. 599–600.
[3] *Ep.*, p. 338; Powicke, pp. 288, 358.
[4] *Chron. Mai.* iv. 366; Stevenson, p. 221; Powicke, pp. 299–300.

And in 1251 and 1252 he opposed the levy of a crusading tenth to the king, backed by papal authority, unless it was freely granted by the prelates.[1] To a grant for the use of the king, constitutional opposition was possible; to a grant to the Pope, it was not.

Papal provision was the exercise of the Pope's right of appointment to benefices, great or small.[2] An increasing number of benefices were thus affected in the thirteenth century. It was essentially the growing principle of centralization as applied to ecclesiastical appointments, just as the centralization of judicial business in the Church had been the great feature of the twelfth century. Such centralization was not in itself an abuse; it was a system that could be used for good or ill. Provision was potentially an instrument of reform and improvement, by the promotion of good men who could not rely on local patronage, and some of the best bishops, like Pecham and FitzRalph, owed their promotion to this means. And it was not by any means confined to aliens. But in general, provision tended to become simply part of that system of the exploitation of benefices for the support of important persons, already referred to. It must have seemed an inevitable way of providing for the officials and protégés of the Roman Curia, who had to be supported if the central government of the Church was to be carried on. It is unfortunate that the more honest and realistic method of providing a permanent income, levied on the whole Church, for the needs of its central government, though several times proposed during the Middle Ages, was never adopted.[3]

Grosseteste, as we have seen, recognized that the Pope had the power to dispose freely of all benefices. He could, therefore, have no objection to papal provision as such, and on one occasion we find him recommending a papal provision.[4] What he objected to was the provision of unsuitable clerks to benefices in particular cases, to the detriment of the cure of souls; this was part of his general objection to the exploitation of benefices. The fact that papal provision respected lay patronage (of which Grosseteste did not

---

[1] *Chron. Mai.* v. 324 ff.; Powicke, pp. 368–9. Cf. also the objection to a subsidy to the king without the restoration of church liberties, put forward in 1250 in Lyons (4).

[2] For papal provisions, see G. Barraclough, *Papal Provisions* (1935); Powicke, pp. 274 ff.

[3] For the schemes put forward by the Emperor Henry VI and again in 1225 by Honorius III, see F. M. Powicke, *Stephen Langton*, pp. 83, 158. The canonist Johannes Andreae put forward another scheme in the Council of Vienne (1311), J. Haller, *Papsttum und Kirchenreform* (1903), p. 54.

[4] *Ep.*, p. 316.

approve), and operated at the expense of ecclesiastical patrons, did not improve it in his eyes. One must not picture Grosseteste as being continually bombarded with papal provisions; his Rolls only contain ten examples of provisions, of which eight belong to the first five years of his episcopate.[1] We do not know how many provisions he may have succeeded in parrying. Matthew Paris says that Grosseteste 'hated like poison the dishonest Romans who had the Pope's precept for obtaining a provision. He was in the habit of saying that if he were to hand the cure of souls over to them, he would be acting Satan's part. Consequently he often threw away letters sealed with the papal bulls, and acted directly in contravention to such commands.'[2] This, like much of Matthew Paris's language, is probably exaggerated, though the remark about the cure of souls sounds like an echo of Grosseteste's thought. As early as 1239 Grosseteste had obtained a papal privilege, exempting him from providing anyone at the Pope's command, unless special mention was made of that privilege,[3] but this was defeated by the hated *non obstante* clause, used in later provisions. The crucial case came in January 1253, when Grosseteste was ordered to provide the Pope's nephew, Frederick of Lavagna, with a prebend in Lincoln. He refused, on the grounds that the man was unsuitable; we have already seen how he justified his refusal in a famous letter to Master Innocent.[4] Matthew Paris professes to tell us what happened when this letter was sent on to the Pope. Beside himself with rage Pope Innocent threatened to have the bishop imprisoned by his vassal, the King of England; he was only restrained by Cardinal Gil de Torres, Grosseteste's old friend, who broke out into a panegyric of him:

You must do nothing. It is true. We cannot condemn him. He is a catholic and a holy man, a better man than we are. He has not his equal among the prelates. All the French and English clergy know this, and our contradiction would be of no avail. The truth of this letter, which is known to many, might move many against us. He is esteemed as a great philosopher, learned in Greek and Latin literature, zealous for justice, a reader in the schools of theology, a preacher to the people, and active enemy of abuses.[5]

Grosseteste died within the year, but his protest may have impressed the Pope more than would at first sight appear, for in

---

[1] See above, pp. 189-90.   [2] *Chron. Mai.* v. 257.
[3] *C. Pap. R.* i. 178.   [4] *Ep.*, p. 432.
[5] *Chron. Mai.* v. 393; Powicke, p. 287.

November 1253, a month after the bishop's death, he issued a bull freeing all patrons, clerical and lay, from any restriction on the exercise of their patronage.[1]

It is instructive to compare Grosseteste's attitude towards papal provisions with that of his contemporaries. Grosseteste did not share in the strong feeling against aliens, which was felt by so many Englishmen, then and later, from a monastic chronicler like Matthew Paris to Robert Tweng, the Yorkshire knight who had led a band of armed and masked agitators against the Italian clerks in 1231.[2] The Franciscan chronicler Eccleston tells us that Grosseteste did not object to alien provisors merely because they could not speak English, but because they only sought profit; he would have been glad to benefice good aliens, even if they could only preach by example.[3] Again Grosseteste did not entirely agree with the grievances and protests put forward, for instance, by the Berkshire rectors in 1240,[4] and by the magnates, prelates, and abbots in 1245 and 1246.[5] He would agree with the complaints as to the practical evil effects of unsuitable provisions on the cure of souls, the upkeep of churches, alms, and hospitality in the parishes concerned. He would be less concerned about the financial loss involved; on at least two occasions he was prepared to offer a pension to compensate a candidate whom he felt compelled to reject.[6] He would have even less sympathy with the complaint that provisions blocked the promotion which the magnates' clerical kinsmen had a right to expect, or with the Berkshire rectors' lament for the good old days when the English clergy were rich pluralists.[7] One point which is stressed in these protests, as in the later protests in the fourteenth century, is the rights of patrons, based on the principle of the *Eigenkirche*. Lords who have founded and endowed churches and monasteries will not endure to see these defrauded, impoverished, and made ineffective on account of papal provisions and papal exactions; if the aim of their benefactions is thus defeated, they will reclaim the endowments they gave.[8] It was the principle of *De donis conditionalibus* applied to church endowment. Grosseteste would not have much sympathy with this; while he admits that papal provision may cause scandal to patrons, he regards lay patronage as a tolerated

---

[1] *Ann. Mon.* i. 314–17; Powicke, p. 281.
[2] See Powicke, p. 78.
[3] Eccleston, pp. 91–92.
[4] *Chron. Mai.* iv. 38 ff.
[5] Ibid. iv. 441 ff., 527 ff., 531, 533.
[6] *Epp.*, pp. 65, 145.
[7] *Chron. Mai.* iv. 442, 42–43.
[8] Ibid. iv. 41, 532.

abuse, fundamentally unjust.[1] The idea of using the threat of lay intervention would have been repugnant to Grosseteste, with his ideas of the complete subordination of the lay to the spiritual power.[2] Much as he disliked the misuse of papal provisions, nothing would have shocked him more than the later expedient of the Statute of Provisors, which simply handed so much ecclesiastical patronage over to the Crown. The difference between Grosseteste and his contemporaries can be summarized thus: while others were concerned with their legal and economic rights and grievances, Grosseteste was quite genuinely concerned with spiritual efficiency alone. As Sir Maurice Powicke has put it: 'Grosseteste was not an Englishman with a grievance; he was a bishop with an ideal.'[3]

In his attitude to the papacy Grosseteste was at once loyal and critical. It was just because he believed so passionately in the papal power that he hated to see it misused. This combination of loyalty and criticism came quite naturally to Grosseteste as to other men of his age—to St. Louis, for instance,[4] but it is a position which modern historians have sometimes found hard to understand. Grosseteste has been criticized[5] as illogical and ineffective, because he believed in the Pope's *plenitudo potestatis* and yet opposed the Pope's wishes; because he could not take the same constitutional stand with regard to the Pope as the barons could with regard to the king; according to this view he should have been either more compliant or more defiant. This picture of him as a lost leader, as an antipapalist *manqué*, misunderstands him. So does Matthew Paris's description of him as the 'hammer and despiser of the Romans';[6] that is too negative and one-sided. His papalism and his criticism were both essential parts of his intellectual make-up. Nor was he in fact so ineffective; his protests impressed Innocent IV into making

---

[1] *Ep.*, p. 228.

[2] This is one of the reasons against the authenticity of the letter supposed to be addressed by Grosseteste to the magnates, commons, and citizens of London, calling on them to resist papal provisions, &c. (*Ep.*, pp. 442–4), which is found in a fifteenth-century manuscript.   [3] Powicke, p. 287.

[4] For St. Louis's protest in 1247, see *Chron. Mai.* vi. 99–112; Powicke, p. 359 n.

[5] For example by Maitland, *Canon Law in the Church of England* (1898), p. 66; cf. Smith, *Church and State*, pp. 147–8, on St. Louis, and p. 175, on Matthew Paris. For a more sympathetic understanding of Grosseteste's position, see Barraclough, *Papal Provisions*, pp. 166 ff.

[6] *Chron. Mai.* v. 407. Matthew Paris gives a long account of Grosseteste's conversation on his death-bed, denouncing papal exactions and other abuses; it is difficult to know how much of this is Grosseteste, and how much Matthew Paris (ibid. v. 400 ff.; cf. Stevenson, pp. 320 ff.).

at least a temporary concession. If there had been more loyal and disinterested critics like Grosseteste, it would have been better for all concerned. 'Corripiet me justus in misericordia et increpabit me, et oleum peccatoris non impinguet caput meum', as Grosseteste himself quoted, when inviting criticism of his own work.[1]

In Grosseteste's theory of the relations of Church and State, the fundamental doctrine is the superiority of the spiritual over the temporal power. This no doubt follows from his conviction, which we have already seen at work, of the absolute primacy of spiritual interests, of the salvation of souls, and his belief in a centralized and hierarchical universe. He seems to stand in the line of development between St. Bernard and Hugh of St. Victor on the one hand, and writers like James of Viterbo and Giles of Rome on the other.[2] He believes that the two swords, spiritual and material, both belong to the Church, the spiritual to be wielded directly by the Church, the temporal to be wielded by the hand and ministry of temporal princes, but at the nod and disposition of the princes of the Church.[3] Whatever authority temporal princes have from God, they receive it through the Church; here we have an embryonic form of dominion by grace.

Writing to William Raleigh to persuade him to bring the secular law into line with the Church's law over the question of bastardy, he says:

Let not anyone deceive himself by believing that secular princes can decree anything, and observe it or cause it to be observed as law, which goes against the divine law or the constitutions of the Church, except at the cost of dividing himself from the unity of the Body of Christ and of the Church, and of throwing himself for ever into hell-fire, and of the just overturning of his own rulership. For the princes of this world receive from the Church whatever they have of power and dignity ordained by God; whereas the princes of the Church receive nothing of their ecclesiastical power or dignity from any secular power, but immediately from God's ordinance; nor is it possible for one who receives to rebel against him from whom he receives, by means of that which he receives.[4]

Again, writing to the Archbishop of Canterbury about the encroachments of the royal jurisdiction upon the ecclesiastical, he says:

All judgment is, properly speaking, by authority of the priesthood and

---

[1] Smalley, *Study of the Bible*, p. 344.
[2] Cf. H. X. Arquillière, *Le Plus Ancien Traité de l'Église* (1926), pp. 60 ff.
[3] *Ep.*, p. 91.   [4] *Ep.*, p. 90.

the clergy. The priesthood however retains for itself the power to exercise judgment by its own ministry, over ecclesiastical crimes and cases, by divine and ecclesiastical laws, for the peace of the sinner; but it hands over to the princes of the world the power to carry out judgment, by their ministry, in secular and transitory matters, by civil and temporal laws, for temporal peace. All judgments therefore belong to the Church, in so far as they belong to wisdom, by proprietary right and authority; but all ecclesiastical judgments belong to the Church by administration, just as all secular judgments likewise belong to the princes and powers of this world by administration. Nor should the one kind of judges invade the territory of the other kind in the ministry of judging, unless by chance unavoidable necessity forces them. For because all judgments belong to the Church by authority, the princes of this world, since they have no superior secular judge, even in secular matters require judgment from the Church. . . . And what wonder, if they (the clergy) are reserved for the judgment of God alone, since they are called in Holy Scripture 'gods' and 'angels'? Whereas the laity are there often compared to 'beasts of burden' (*jumenta*). And so they (the clergy) are to be honoured by laymen, and not to be judged even by kings. For who can even listen with patience to the idea of gods and angels being judged by beasts of burden?[1]

On one occasion, in 1245 or early 1246, perhaps soon after his interview and 'persuasive words' with the king after his return from the Council of Lyons, Grosseteste wrote the king a letter in which he sets out his theory of kingship. This was in reply to a letter from the king, in which the latter had apparently felt obliged to point out to Grosseteste that there were after all two powers, spiritual and temporal, that these were meant to help each other, and that the bishop seemed to be causing discord between them.[2]

As the letter which your Royal Highness wrote to us suggests, there are, we know, two principles of government in the human race, that is to say the priesthood and kingship; of which the one directs all the powers of its government towards eternal peace, the other towards temporal; so that by means of that peace which is temporal, there may be an easier passing over to that which is eternal. Each is helpful to the other, as your letter mentions; from which it clearly follows that neither is a hindrance to the other, and for this reason that each promotes the duties and ministrations of the other, and by no means impedes, diminishes or retards them. For the priestly power does not prevent the royal power from stoutly defending the commonwealth by arms, ruling it with just laws and adorning it with noble conduct; nor conversely does the royal power prevent the priestly

[1] *Ep.*, pp. 217–19.   [2] *Ep.*, pp. 348–51.

power from working unceasingly for the eternal salvation of its flock . . . which cannot be done by those who are entangled with secular business. Wherefore the royal power, which is meant to help the priesthood, can by no means entangle those charged with pastoral care in secular business; for this would be equivalent to turning the sun's light into the moon's, shutting off the sun's rays from giving life (*vegetatione*) to the things that grow on the earth, prohibiting the soul from giving life to the body, and even pulling down heaven to earth. . . . But we desire that all things be done by both parties decently and according to order; so that spiritual things be dealt with by ecclesiastical and spiritual men, secular things by secular men; namely military things by military men, and corrections and reforms of excesses and defects in those things that touch the commonwealth of the kingdom to be dealt with by secular persons skilled and exercised in the just laws of the kingdom; and we are not trying, as has been suggested to your excellency, in any way directly or indirectly to bring about discord between your government (*imperium*) and the priesthood.

Grosseteste is here clearly concerned in justifying his well-known objection to the use of ecclesiastics in secular offices; and he goes on to explain that he cannot admit Robert Passelew to the church of St. Peter, Northampton, because he is a forest judge. He ends his letter by explaining, at the king's request, what the 'sacrament of anointing' would seem to add to the royal dignity, seeing that there are many kings who are not anointed. The royal anointing is the sign of the king's receiving the sevenfold gifts of the Holy Ghost, in accordance with which an anointed king is bound more specially than unanointed kings to direct his actions; that is to say, 'not commonly, but eminently and heroically', by the gift of fear he must restrain himself and his subjects from all that is unlawful, and so forth. 'So that after the pattern of the order of the world and of the angelic order, according to the eternal laws written in the eternal reason of God, by which He rules the whole of creation, he (the king) also may rule in orderly fashion (*ordinabiliter*) the commonwealth subjected to him.' He goes on to point out that 'this prerogative of anointing by no means places the royal dignity above or even on a level with the priestly, nor does it give it the power of any priestly office'. King Ozias (Uzziah), who tried to usurp a priestly function, was struck with leprosy. It is clear that Grosseteste had no sympathy with those who, like the Anonymous of York, thought that anointing made the king something more than a mere layman and gave him some superiority over churchmen. Another aspect of Grosseteste's theory of kingship has already been referred to,

namely his doctrine that the king has no power to command anything except what is right.[1]

What were the practical implications of Grosseteste's high theories
of the relations of Church and State? The way in which these theories
would chiefly be tested in the thirteenth century would be over the
overlapping jurisdictional claims of the ecclesiastical and secular
courts. Grosseteste felt very strongly about what he regarded as the
encroachments of the king's courts upon the business of the Church's
courts, especially by means of writs of prohibition. To Grosseteste
this is not just a matter of injured prestige or legal rights flouted;
the Church's jurisdiction is concerned with eternal interests, 'the
peace of the sinner', and interference with it may amount to spiritual
sabotage and spiritual murder, just like the exploitation of benefices.
Lay encroachments on the Church's rights and liberties are the
subject of a long letter or treatise which he addressed to the Archbishop of Canterbury, St. Edmund, c. 1237.[2] Grosseteste's first
point in this letter is that the king appoints abbots as itinerant
justices. This is contrary to canon law, and abbots or other ecclesiastical persons who take such office sin grievously. The laws of
princes cannot prevail against the natural and Divine law, against
ecclesiastical law or the decrees of the Holy See. Even if it is argued
that ecclesiastical tenants-in-chief owe the duty of performing
justitiariae ministerium by reason of their baronies, they need not
perform this in person, any more than they perform their military
service in person. Secondly, ecclesiastical persons are compelled to
submit to lay courts, when impleaded in personal actions, especially
when they are said to have acted against a royal prohibition or a royal
mandate.[3] Here both judges who compel and clergy who submit sin
grievously. Thirdly, secular judges 'add sin to sin' by encroaching,
when they decide whether certain cases belong to the lay or ecclesiastical courts. It is for the ecclesiastical judges, not the secular ones,
to decide to which jurisdiction doubtful cases belong; 'the judicial
power of the ecclesiastical judge extends even to secular matters,
since all judgment belongs by authority and doctrine to the Church,
though not all by ministry'. Fourthly, secular judges go so far as to
deal with cases which are purely ecclesiastical, such as tithes or
burial or baptismal rights of churches or chapels. If it is argued that

---

[1] See above, p. 190.   [2] *Ep.*, pp. 205–34.
[3] For the use of prohibitions, see G. B. Flahiff, 'The use of Prohibitions by Clerics
against Ecclesiastical Courts in England', *Mediaeval Studies*, iii (1941), 101 ff.

the king can judge clerks in certain personal actions, as when, for instance, a clerk has seized a lay fee, then a distinction must be made: the question whether the occupation of a fee is just or unjust, is a matter for the lay court; the question whether the clerk has been guilty of violent spoliation, is a matter for the ecclesiastical court. Fifthly, the king prevents ecclesiastical judges from dealing with purely ecclesiastical cases, such as whether a particular church or chapel is a chapel dependent upon a mother church somewhere else, or whether the tithes of some piece of land belong to this or that church, and this is done on the grounds that the patronage of the church is involved. This is not true; a man is not less patron, because he is patron of a lesser church, just as a man is not less a father, because he is father of a smaller man; and to cut away unjust possessions does not diminish but improves a church. Sixthly, secular courts encroach in the following way. There may be prolonged litigation in the king's court over the patronage of a church; after a lapse of six months, the bishop himself collates a priest to the church, as he is bound to do by canon law, and he then has to refuse to admit the presentee of the successful litigant. In consequence the bishop is cited to answer before the king's justices *quare non admisit*. Thus a bishop is compelled to answer to a secular judge for an episcopal act. The king has no power to command a bishop to perform or not to perform his episcopal and spiritual duty. All these violations of the rights and liberties of the Church are made worse by the fact that the English Church's freedom is guaranteed by the Great Charter, under pain of excommunications pronounced in the Council of Oxford in 1222 and again at Westminster in 1237.[1] This letter of Grosseteste's seems to be the forerunner or first draft of the more elaborate list of grievances which the clergy asked the legate Otto to press upon the king.[2] Possibly Grosseteste was disappointed with the effect of his letter to the archbishop, and hoped for better results from the legate's intervention.

The most serious clash between the two jurisdictions, secular and spiritual, occurred over Grosseteste's methods of parochial visitation. The regular visitation both of parishes and monasteries was one of the most important features of the reform programme set in motion by the Lateran Council of 1215, and Grosseteste, with his strong sense of pastoral duty, was bound to be active in this respect.

---

[1] *Ep.*, pp. 230–1; Powicke, pp. 153–4.
[2] *Ann. Mon.* i. 254–7; cf. also the grievances compiled by Grosseteste, ibid. i. 422–5.

Earlier bishops, such as Grosseteste's own predecessor Hugh of Wells,[1] were concerned in their Articles of Enquiry with the conduct and morals of the clergy, the administration of the sacraments, the upkeep of church fabric, and so forth. Grosseteste was not content with this; he regarded himself as responsible for the souls of the laymen as well as of the clergy of his diocese. He describes his method of parochial visitation, with himself preaching to the clergy, and a friar preacher or minor preaching to the people; four friars were engaged in hearing confessions; then confirmations, followed by 'inquisitions, corrections and reforms'; it was as much a travelling mission as an administrative overhauling.[2] He did not merely make inquiry about the conduct of the clergy; he also made inquiries about the private morals of laymen, about their sins of incontinence and the like,[3] and this he did by putting laymen on oath to report the sins of their fellows. This was the new canonical procedure of *inquisitio*, which had been introduced by Innocent III; it is the ecclesiastical equivalent of Henry II's jury of accusation.[4] Grosseteste's innovations, putting laymen on oath to reveal the sins of laymen, aroused strong opposition from the king and others. According to Matthew Paris this first arose in 1246; he quotes a writ from the king to the sheriff of Hertfordshire, forbidding laymen to make recognitions on oath at the will of the Bishop of Lincoln, except in matrimonial or testamentary cases.[5] Another writ of May 1249 summons Grosseteste to answer for having forced laymen to take oath against their will, 'to the grave prejudice of our crown'.[6] Yet another writ of June 1252, addressed to Grosseteste, is worth quoting:

We have learnt from the complaint of many, both magnates of your diocese and others, that by means of certain of your clerks and certain deans, you cause to be cited everywhere and indiscriminately poor men of your diocese, and certain freemen, whosoever men they be, and you draw them from various places to various places, and force them under pain of excommunication to come before the said clerks and your subordinates, at various places burdensome to them, when they ought to be attending

---

[1] Wilkins, *Concilia*, i. 627.   [2] *Angl. Sacr.* ii. 347–8.
[3] Grosseteste was perhaps the author of the visitation articles printed in *Ann. Mon.* i. 307 ff., cf. M. Gibbs and J. Lang, *Bishops and Reform* (1934), pp. 160–1; the first fourteen articles are concerned with the morals of laymen.
[4] Cf. Pollock and Maitland, *History of the English Law*, ii. 656 ff.
[5] *Chron. Mai.* iv. 579–80.
[6] *Close Rolls of Henry III*, 1247–51, pp. 221–2.

to the tilling of the fields and other necessary temporal duties, whereby they are unduly impoverished and enormously harassed; and moreover, what is an unheard of thing, your said scrutators compel them to swear concerning the private sins of others, which are not, as it is said, liable to be purged with public coercion, whereby many Christians, perhaps undeservedly, are foully defamed; and because vexations of this kind have been invented against the long custom of our realm, and a double peril hangs over the people by reason of them, both because of the omission of necessary work, and because of the oath made about the private deeds of others, in which men are deceived, whereby they can easily incur the guilt of perjury; we forbid you henceforward to cause to be made any convocations of people in your diocese contrary to the custom of our realm and longstanding usage; nor have we ever heard that the Church was wont to compel any to give witness except in certain cases and unless anyone withheld from giving witness out of favour, hatred or fear; and know that unless you desist from these unwonted and undue vexations of the people, we will not bear with you any longer but will apply our royal hands to this matter.[1]

The king's objections explain themselves; he objects to both the method and the subject-matter of the inquiries. To Grosseteste, on the other hand, this must have seemed the very worst kind of lay interference with the Church and its work of saving souls; the sins of Oza and Ozias were mild in comparison. This incident, like the later struggle between Pecham and Edward I over the constitutions of Reading and Lambeth, shows how easily a matter of pastoral discipline could arouse a constitutional storm. It looks as though Grosseteste stood his ground and won his point, at any rate posthumously, because parochial visitations of the later Middle Ages certainly do include presentments on oath about the morals of the laity,[2] and continued to do so long after the Reformation.

In his protests against lay encroachments on ecclesiastical jurisdiction, and in particular against the machinery of royal prohibitions, Grosseteste showed his characteristic clear-sightedness and far-sightedness. He anticipated, by over a generation, the struggle that was to be taken up later by Pecham, and which ended in the compromise of *Circumspecte agatis*.

Very early in his episcopate Grosseteste had to face what was not so much a conflict of jurisdictions as a conflict of legal doctrine. This

---

[1] Ibid., 1251–3, p. 224, cf. p. 226.
[2] e.g. the Hereford visitation of 1397, *E.H.R.* xliv (1929), 279, 444; xlv (1930), 92.

was over the question of bastardy.[1] According to canon law illegitimate children were made legitimate by the subsequent marriage of their parents. The English secular law of the king's courts refused to accept this doctrine. Though marriage was recognized as belonging to canon law, the question of legitimacy was important for secular lawyers because of its bearing on inheritance and so forth. Grosseteste wrote a long letter to his friend William Raleigh,[2] arguing that the English secular law on this subject was contrary to Divine and natural law, to civil law, and even to old English custom, and urging him to try to bring the English secular law into line with canon law. But Raleigh was not impressed. Similarly at the Council of Merton in 1236, when the prelates asked the magnates to bring the secular law into line with canon law, the magnates refused, with the famous answer: *Nolumus leges Angliae mutare*. The divergence of laws was extremely embarrassing to the bishops for a practical reason. The secular judges, in order to establish legitimacy according to their own rules, were in the habit of asking the bishops whether a given person was born before or after marriage; and conscientious bishops had to refuse to answer, knowing that their answer would be used in a sense contrary to canon law. Grosseteste himself got into trouble with the king's court over such a refusal to answer.[3] The difficulty was eventually got round by the judges referring the matter to a jury.

The ruling class of thirteenth-century England was a small and intimate body, and the personal relations of a man like Grosseteste with his contemporaries therefore played an important part in the relations of Church and State. One does not get a very clear picture of his personal relations with the king. It does not seem that they were on such easy and affectionate terms as his predecessor St. Hugh had been with Henry II and Richard I. But Henry III was prepared to consult Grosseteste and to be lectured by him, even if they did not always see eye to eye.[4] With the king's sister, Eleanor Countess of Leicester, as with her husband, Simon de Montfort, Grosseteste was on very friendly terms; on one occasion he borrowed her cook.[5] For another great lady, the Countess of Lincoln, Grosseteste composed the treatise on estate and household management, which afterwards went by the name of 'the rules of Saint Robert'. This

---

[1] Cf. F. W. Maitland, *Roman Canon Law in the Church of England*, pp. 53 ff.; Powicke, pp. 150–1.

[2] *Ep.*, pp. 76–94.   [3] *Ep.*, p. 104.

[4] *Epp.*, pp. 338, 348.

[5] Letter of Adam Marsh, in *Mon. Franc.*, p. 170.

shows a very practical and business-like side of the bishop, which might otherwise be little suspected; it also shows him a strict disciplinarian, inculcating a strong sense of responsibility. 'Say to all, small and great, and that often, that fully, quickly and willingly, without grumbling and contradiction, they do all your commands that are not against God.' 'If any of them [the servants] speak back or grumble, tell them that you will be lord or lady, and that you will that all serve your will and pleasure, and whoever will not do so, send away, and get others who will serve your pleasure—of whom you will find enough.' 'And you yourself always be seated at the middle of the high table, that your presence as lord or lady may appear openly to all, and that you may plainly see on either side all the service and all the faults.' 'And as far as possible for sickness or fatigue, constrain yourself to eat in the hall before your people, for this shall bring great benefit and honour to you.'[1]

When we come to Grosseteste's relations with Simon de Montfort, we are on more important and more difficult ground. He was undoubtedly a close personal friend of Simon's, perhaps in some sense his spiritual director, and it was to him that Simon entrusted the education of two of his sons.[2] But how far did Grosseteste share in or influence Simon's political views? It has sometimes been supposed that they were joint leaders of a constitutional party, and that the earl learnt his political principles from the bishop. But we have remarkably little to go on. Grosseteste's treatise on kingship and tyranny, which was apparently lent to Earl Simon,[3] seems almost certainly to be identified with one of the memoranda that the bishop produced at Lyons, Lyons (6); this does not deal with secular politics, but with the alleged 'tyranny' of the Archbishop of Canterbury in demanding excessive procurations. The letters of Adam Marsh contain a number of deliberately enigmatic and tantalizing phrases; he speaks of Earl Simon's zeal for the salvation of souls and his efforts for the 'purging, illuminating and sanctifying' of the Church by suitable government (*per idoneum regimen*); he also speaks of Simon's enthusiasm for Grosseteste's 'most salutary project for liberating souls'.[4] This must mean that Simon supported, in a way that was unusual for a lay magnate, some aspect of Grosseteste's

---

[1] *Walter of Henley's Husbandry*, ed. E. Lamond (1890), pp. 133, 137, 141; cf. Thomson, *Writings*, pp. 158–9, cf. 149, 150–1.

[2] *Mon. Franc.*, pp. 110, 129, 163.

[3] Ibid., p. 110; cf. Thomson, *Writings*, p. 145.

[4] *Mon. Franc.*, pp. 111, 225, 264, 271.

programme for the reform of the Church; most probably it refers to his well-known rejection of unsuitable candidates for the cure of souls; possibly Simon, unlike the king, may also have sympathized with Grosseteste's efforts to reform the morals of the laity. It is clear that de Montfort was much interested in ecclesiastical reform; what is less clear, is how far Grosseteste, on his side, was interested in political reform, and what part he would have been prepared to play, if he had lived, in the baronial plan of reform. After his death, de Montfort's followers were certainly admirers of Grosseteste, and rightly or wrongly identified their cause with the aims of Grosseteste and other reforming bishops. The last remnant of baronial opposition, the 'disinherited' at Ely in 1267, when called on to return to the faith of the Holy Church, replied that they 'firmly held the same faith which they had learnt from the holy bishops, that is to say, St. Robert and St. Edmund and St. Richard'.[1] It does not, of course, follow that Grosseteste would necessarily have approved of the course taken by his admirers. There is, however, one incident which seems to be in his tradition. In the negotiations before the battle of Lewes, Simon de Montfort sent his friend the Bishop of Chichester to the king, suggesting that they should submit to the arbitration of sound theologians and canonists. This led to an outburst of anti-clerical resentment from the royalists, on the grounds that it would mean subjecting knights to the decision of clerks.[2] For precisely the same reason, one may suppose, the proposal would have greatly appealed to Grosseteste.

This essay began by considering Grosseteste as an example of the scholar-bishop. How far can we regard him as a successful example of that type? Does he fulfil the hopes of ecclesiastical reformers like Innocent III? Of his learning and his pastoral zeal there can be no doubt. It is more difficult to assess his statesmanship and his success in dealing with other men and other authorities. I do not think that

---

[1] William Rishanger, *Chronica*, ed. Riley (Rolls Series), p. 53. Rishanger, ibid., p. 36, says that Simon did everything by the advice of Grosseteste, and that the bishop enjoined upon him, *in remissionem peccatorum* (as a penance?), that he should take up the cause for which he strove unto death, saying that the peace of the English Church could not be secured without the material sword (cf. *Chron. Mai.* v. 407), and constantly affirming that all those who died for it would be crowned with martyrdom. But it may be doubted whether Simon can be said to have formulated or taken up a 'cause' before the death of Grosseteste in 1253, unless the cause meant is not a political one, but Grosseteste's programme of Church reform.

[2] *The Song of Lewes*, ed. C. L. Kingsford (1890), pp. 7, 8, ll. 193 ff., 243 ff.; Powicke, p. 464.

he was interested in the problems of secular government in the way that Langton and Winchelsey were. I suspect that he was interested in secular politics just in so far as they could be related to his primary interest, 'the peace of the sinner'. It would be tempting to criticize him as too much of the scholar-bishop, as too doctrinaire and unbending. And indeed, if the whole bench of bishops had consisted of men like Grosseteste, it is difficult to see how the working of Church and State could have gone on. If the later exclusion of scholars from bishoprics was a disaster, we must not suppose that the packing of bishoprics with scholars would necessarily have solved all difficulties. Nevertheless, it would be a great mistake to dismiss Grosseteste as an over-rigid scholar. His single-mindedness, intransigence, and inability to compromise were in themselves extremely valuable. One of the tragedies of the later Middle Ages was not that churchmen were too exorbitant in their relations with the State, but that they were too compliant, too ready to compromise and 'make a deal', to let the king's servants take their bishoprics while the cardinals get their deaneries and archdeaconries. In contrast to all this, Grosseteste ˙ is always determined to put first things first. A very good example of his clear-sightedness and salutary intransigence is, as we have seen, his opposition to the employment of ecclesiastics in secular office. Such employment, on the face of it, seems reasonable enough, and has not lacked apologists. The chronicler Ralph de Diceto, in a well-known passage, speaks of King Henry II turning to God's sanctuary to find trustworthy judges,[1] and Maitland has written that Henry II's greatest, most lasting triumph in the legal field was this, that he made the prelates of the Church his justices.[2] Whether such a system was in the true interests of the Church, especially in the later Middle Ages, is more doubtful. An ecclesiastical statesman like Wykeham or Wolsey was not a churchman grasping at temporal power; he was a secular official masquerading as a churchman, for the financial convenience of the Crown. The great power and influence of such a man was not therefore an indication of the Church's triumph, but rather the measure of the extent to which the Church was being subordinated, controlled, and exploited by the State. To Grosseteste belongs the great credit of seeing this clearly. Above all, the thing that makes Grosseteste, for all his intransigence, one of the most attractive and lovable figures in English Church history, is

---

[1] R. de Diceto, ed. Stubbs, i (Rolls Series, 1876), 434–5.
[2] Pollock and Maitland, *History of the English Law*, i. 132.

his overmastering zeal for the cure of souls. He cared deeply and individually for the human beings in his charge, 'for each one of whom the Son of God was willing to die a most shameful death', and he never for a moment forgot them.

In conclusion, if we want a summing up of Grosseteste, this may be given in the words of Sir Maurice Powicke:

Grosseteste was not an Englishman with a grievance; he was a bishop with an ideal. Too often he has been held up to view as an anti-papal leader in a fight for some indefinable liberties of the Church in England. As a reformer he was the clearest and most vigorous exponent of a tendency in contemporary thought which, while it was expressed by Langton and his friends, had become clear in the time of Archbishop Grant and was developed, later in the century, by Archbishop Pecham. The conviction that the cure of souls directed by a responsible and single-minded episcopate must be the aim of ecclesiastical policy was shared by all reformers; but Grosseteste stood almost alone in his longing to separate the clergy from secular cares and interests and in his mystical veneration for the plenitude of papal power. His closest friends and allies among the bishops of his time did not follow his lead in all things. Walter Cantilupe of Hereford disagreed with him about the evils of pluralism; William Ralegh of Winchester did not share his horror at the sight of ecclesiastics in secular office. And he in his turn had taken no part in the opposition to papal taxation. He had no wish to see the king and clergy combined in a struggle with the papacy. He took occasion, after he returned from the Council of Lyons in 1245, to explain to Henry 'in a few gentle persuasive words' how great the royal obligation was to support the Church and be obedient to the Holy See. He wished to have as king a man who would not put forward unsuitable candidates for benefices nor allow interference with ecclesiastical discipline. He put sharp practice or pedantry in English common lawyer and in canonist alike under the same anathema. He brought to bear in his work all the interests of a full, rich mind—his experience as a diocesan, the belief in clear and articulated function, as taught by Aristotle, the sense of mystical order in the celestial and ecclesiastical hierarchy, as it had been elaborated by the pseudo-Areopagite. The result was a reasoned idealism far too intense to be shared, though it was applauded, by most of his associates. It is hard to imagine what he could have done if he had been Pope.[1]

[1] Powicke, p. 287.

APPENDIX

Grosseteste at Lyons, 1250

The series of documents that Grosseteste presented to the Pope at Lyons in May 1250 are so important and illustrate so well the way in which his mind worked and the way in which he dealt with problems of Church government, that it is worth analysing them, especially as most of them are still unprinted. He went to the Curia accompanied by two of his archdeacons, Robert Marsh, Archdeacon of Oxford, and John de Crakehall, Archdeacon of Bedford; one of his chief aims was to protest against the excessive demand for visitation fees from the Archbishop of Canterbury, when visiting his province, and in this he also spoke for his episcopal colleagues; he was also concerned in the struggle with monastic houses in his diocese, though this does not figure much in these documents. There were in all eight documents presented by Grosseteste to the Pope at Lyons, and these were afterwards collected by Robert Marsh, and survive in varying degrees of completeness in some ten manuscripts. The majority of these documents were presented in writing and read out, but numbers (5) and (8), and probably (9), were delivered orally. The proceedings were spread over several days. The whole composes a formidable mass of closely reasoned and sometimes rather abstruse matter, which must have taken a couple of hours or so to deliver. It says much for the intellectual stamina of those present at the Curia that they followed sufficiently closely for some of them to formulate objections, which Grosseteste proceeded to answer (e.g. in no. 7). But men of that period must have been prepared for such intellectual exercise by experience in the schools, in the courts, or in the council chamber. It was the possibility of this kind of thing happening that could make a visit to the Curia on business an exciting intellectual experience, and the Curia itself an important clearing-house of ideas. Half a century earlier law students had gone to hear Innocent III giving judgements, and a century later visitors to the Curia could hear Fitz-Ralph preaching or the discussions about the Beatific Vision. So these scholastic discourses of Grosseteste's were not so out of place as they might seem. Grosseteste seems to have had some success in putting the case against the archbishop's demand for visitation fees, for two years later, in June 1252, Pope Innocent IV issued letters exempting the parish churches of the province from paying procurations to the archbishop.[1]

1. The first and longest of these documents was delivered to the Pope in the presence of the cardinals on 13 May; it is sometimes referred to as Grosseteste's 'sermon', but in fact it was delivered in writing, in quadruplicate, one roll being given to the Pope and the others to three of the

---

[1] I. J. Churchill, *Canterbury Administration*, i (1933), 290; *Ann. Mon.* i. 302.

cardinals. One of these, a cardinal deacon, proceeded to read it out. The document falls roughly into four more or less equal parts. In the first part, Grosseteste deals with the rise, spread, and subsequent contraction of the Christian religion. The purpose of the Incarnation was the saving of souls. Christianity had spread through the labours of the Apostles and early fathers and martyrs; it was the business of the Pope, the cardinals, and the other prelates to carry on their work. But alas, the spread of Christianity has nowadays been narrowed; part of the world is cut off from Christ by unbelief, another part by schism, another part by heresy, and yet another part by sin. The cause of all this is the lack of good pastors and the multiplication of bad ones. Bad pastors are slayers of souls, and therefore are doing the work of Antichrist; they are in effect heretics, since they teach error by their bad life and example, and are worse than sodomites. What is the cause and fount of this evil? It is the Roman Curia, because not only does it not prevent abuses, but by its dispensations, provisions, and collations it multiplies bad pastors, whereby precious souls are handed over to destruction. This leads on to the second part, where he discusses the right use and abuse of pastoral care. It is no excuse for the exploitation of benefices and the neglect of pastoral care to say that it serves the common good, nor to say that bad pastors look after their parishioners by means of middlemen, for the pastoral care is such that it cannot be carried out by middlemen or mercenaries (see above, p. 180). The situation is still worse where churches are appropriated to monasteries, for then the use of mercenaries becomes permanent—Grosseteste seems to have little confidence in the vicarage system. In the third part he deals with the function of the Church in general and of the Holy See in particular. After the pattern of the Church triumphant, the work of the Church militant is to bring about purgation, illumination, and deification (here he is following the pseudo-Denis); the Holy See is like the sun, the source of life in the spiritual world, and the effects of its failure will be disastrous (see above, p. 186); and he concludes by discussing the problem of obedience and its limits (see above, p. 189). The fourth part deals with certain practical grievances. The pastoral power of bishops is being limited, especially in England, in various ways. First by monastic exemptions, a disastrous privilege—there are no exemptions in the Church triumphant. Secondly by interference from the lay power, which prevents inquiry into the sins of laymen (see above, p. 202). Thirdly by tuitorial appeals. Fourthly, when a pastor tries to correct the vices of his subjects, he is worn out by the subtleties and solemnities of the civil law in the archbishop's court. It is particularly dangerous for a prelate to try to remove from the pastoral care unsatisfactory clerks who are in royal service. The work of the bishops is being frustrated by legal subtleties. This is as though military strategy were directed by the subordinate art of the armourer. The art of saving souls must be given absolute primacy. It is the duty of the Holy See to get rid of such evils. But in fact the whole world is crying out against the impudence of the Curia's servants, against the Curia's use of the material sword, against the prevalence here of bribery, and, to come down to particulars, against the Curia's granting the first-fruits of benefices to the Archbishop of Canterbury. It is no excuse to say that the days are evil and one must ignore or put up with many things for the common good of the Church; the worse the days are, the more one must fight against evil. The troubles which the Holy See now suffers (for instance its exile) are a punishment for past misconduct. It will be seen that this is not simply a denunciation of the vices of the Curia, though that may well have seemed the most sensational part; it covers Grosseteste's whole theory of the functioning of the Church.

2. At this point in some of the manuscripts there is inserted the letter concerning the Pope's nephew (1253), which does not, of course, belong to the visit to the Curia in 1250, though its relevance is obvious.

3. The next document, apparently produced at Lyons, is addressed by the bishops to the Archbishop of Canterbury. It begins with Grosseteste's parable: a certain rich householder (Christ) has ten pastures, each containing 10,000 sheep. He entrusts these groups of 10,000 sheep to certain principal shepherds (the bishops), giving each full power, and he gives one of these principal shepherds (the archbishop) power to supervise the others. Seeing that the principal shepherds cannot carry out their work unaided, he orders them to appoint a special shepherd (rural dean or parish priest ?) over every 100 sheep, and one superintendent (archdeacon ?) over every ten special shepherds, but he does not thereby take away from the fullness of power given to the principal shepherd. The bishops go on to beg the archbishop to help them in their ministry, and not to hinder them by encouraging tuitorial appeals and hearing frivolous complaints. The superintendent (archbishop) ought to have some confidence in his fellow shepherds, and not to call them up at the bleating of every scabby and infected sheep, and weigh them in the balance with their own sheep; this only gives the sheep boldness in sinning, wears out the bishops, and discourages them from doing their duty. Let them all be united to do battle against the world and the worldly things that disturb and hinder the pastoral office, and let the archbishop take the lead in resisting the disturbances and violation of the liberties of the Church and of the kingdom and the ruin of souls.

4. After a few days interval, Grosseteste presented the next document on behalf of the English clergy, protesting against the exaction of unaccustomed procurations by the Archbishop of Canterbury on account of his provincial visitation. The clergy say that in the past they have been much oppressed, both by the Crown which has disturbed and diminished

the rights and liberties of the Church, and by exactions made by the authority of the Holy See; but these things are small in comparison with what they fear is coming. In the first place, the archbishop proposes to levy procurations by reason of his visitation, and this will be imitated by the other bishops, and so a new and unsupportable burden will be laid upon them. The rectors of churches are already burdened with the annual procurations payable to the archdeacon; this is tolerable, because they are accustomed to it and because they realize that procurations form part of the archdeacon's stipend. But the procurations of the archbishop and bishops are something new and unjustified, for they already have large endowments given to their sees by kings and magnates. If the apostle refused to take the reward of his labours for fear of giving scandal (1 Cor. ix. 15), how much more so should the bishops avoid taking their reward twice over? In the second place, the clergy fear that they will be compelled by the authority of the Holy See to pay a heavy subsidy to the king, who has taken the cross, and this will be done without the king restoring the Church's rights and liberties, which have been disturbed and diminished, contrary to the Gospel and canon law, and contrary to the king's coronation oath and to his charters, which are enforced by excommunications pronounced by Stephen Langton and St. Edmund. These things are likely to produce hatred against the Holy See, and to remedy them would therefore be pious and make for safety.

5. Grosseteste then proceeded to explain verbally his own method of visitation (see above, p. 202). He himself has no intention of making himself a burden to his subjects; but unless the Holy See provides a remedy, his successors will exact new and unwonted procurations, causing scandal and a stumbling-block to the Gospel.

6. In the next document, a written one, Grosseteste puts forward philosophical arguments in reply to those who say: 'It is the common law that a visitor should receive procurations.' This is his celebrated discussion *de regno et rege, tirannide et tiranno*. According to Aristotle the best form of government is monarchy, and its perversion is tyranny. The tyrant seeks his own profit, the king that of his subjects, and the king shows friendship towards his subjects. We ought to let reason govern rather than man, because man is liable to seek his own good and so become a tyrant.[1]

---

[1] Grosseteste quotes these passages as though they came from the *Politics*: *sic ait philosophus politicorum* (or *in politicis*); but in fact they are from the *Nicomachean Ethics*, bk. viii, cc. xii and xiii, and bk. v, c. x. The passages quoted by Grosseteste run as follows: 'De regno et rege, tirannide et tiranno, sic ait Philosophus politicorum (*or* in politicis): "Optima quidem regnum, transgressio autem regni tirannis. Differunt autem plurimum. Tirannus enim sibi ipsi conferens intendit, rex autem quod subditorum." Et paulo post: "Tirannus autem ex contrarietate regno; sibi autem bonum prosequitur, et manifestius in hac quoniam pessima. Et pessimum enim contrarium optimo." Et iterum post pauca ait: "Regis quidem ad subditos est amicicia in superhabundancia beneficii. Benefacit enim subditis, quidem bonus ens curam habet ipsorum ut bene

According to Scripture, royal government (*regia potestas regitiva*) is a type of the government of souls (*potestas regitiva animarum*); and therefore a spiritual king, that is to say a prelate, who has power over rational spirits and is a spiritual father, is even more bound to put his subjects before himself, and any lapse into tyranny is so much the worse. Hence anyone placed *in potestate regitiva spirituali*, if he abounds in temporal goods, cannot extort anything unwonted from his subjects, without acting *supersumme tirannice*; and the Bishop of Lincoln and still more the Archbishop of Canterbury would be *supertirannicus et supersatanicus*, if he extorted unwonted visitation procurations. It is no excuse to say that this is justified by common law; because the natural law, that is the Divine law, is more common than the positive common law. If the two disagree, we ought to adhere to the natural and Divine law, as more certain, infallible, and circumspect than human law.

7. Because certain of the cardinals still adhered more to the positive law and its glosses (*et eius apparatibus*) than to the natural and Divine law, Grosseteste answered them in the following written document. Those who prefer the positive law and its glosses to the Divine and natural law are honouring God with their lips and not with their heart and preferring the traditions of men to the commandments of God, and so they come under the condemnation of the prophet (Isa. xxix. 13) and of the Gospel (Mark vii. 6, Matt. xv. 8) and of the Apostle (Gal. i. 8). And the Archbishop of Canterbury and the Bishop of Lincoln will come under the same condemnation, if they transgress the law of the Gospel for the sake of the positive law and its glosses, not to say for the sake of insatiable cupidity, by exacting unwonted procurations. He goes on to define the function of the hierarchy according to the pseudo-Denis; its end is the salvation of souls, that is, their assimilation and union with God. If a hierarch oppresses his subjects, he divests himself of the *raison d'être* of the hierarchy, since he is working to the dissimilitude of God. The unwonted exaction of procurations when there is no need is oppressive, scandalizes the weak, and is a stumbling-block to the Gospel. Moses and Samuel oppressed no one; St. Paul was prepared to give up for ever the eating of meat, though it was lawful, rather than scandalize his brother (1 Cor. viii. 13). Therefore let the Pope, in the plenitude of his power, see to it that innumerable souls are not imperilled by these exactions.

8. Grosseteste continues verbally to expand the argument about natural and positive law. Natural law or natural justice is true and equitable, both in itself and in every particular case; thus the maxim that you should do

operentur." Et iterum idem Philosophus ait: "Non sinimus principari hominem sed racionem, quoniam homo principans sibi ipsi plus tribuit bonorum et minus malorum et sic fit tirannus. Racio autem princeps (*or* principans) omnia que regiminis sunt dirigens racione, custos est iusti et equalis, cuius merces solum honor et gloria."' (MS. Merton 82, fol. 102; MS. Royal 6 E v, fol. 129; 7 E ii, fol. 389; MS. Lansdowne 458, fol. 149.)

to everyone what you would wish done to yourself, is true in itself and in all possible particular cases. Legal or positive justice is true and equitable in itself, but not necessarily so in every particular case; thus the legal maxim, that one must return a deposit to its owner when he asks for it back (*depositum reddere repetenti*), is true in itself but not in every particular case, for it would not be right to give back a sword to a madman. A just judge will use the virtue of *epikeia*, preferring natural justice to legal justice, and not condemning those who for the sake of natural justice seem to transgress legal justice; judges who in such cases condemn according to legal justice are called *acribodikaioi*.[1] It may be legal justice to pay procurations, but in this particular case, since the bishops are endowed and payment would cause scandal, payment would be contrary to natural and Divine justice.

9. The final document arose out of the following incident. While the above proceedings were going on in the Curia, a certain Roman noble pressed Grosseteste many times to admit him to a certain prebend in Lincoln having the cure of souls, which he said had been conferred on him by the Pope's authority. Grosseteste according to his custom explained to him what a pastor should be and that an unworthy pastor was spiritually dead and a slayer of souls and Antichrist and worse than any sodomite, and he added that he did not think him suitable, and that if he took on the office, he would fall under these condemnations, and so he should never receive that prebend if he (Grosseteste) could help it. The noble and his friends were extremely indignant and went off crying: 'It is the Pope's act, it is the Pope's act, and you are condemning the Pope's acts.' And they went to the Pope and said: 'This bishop has publicly called you a slayer of souls and Antichrist and worse than any sodomite and so forth, which we are prepared to prove.' Whereupon the Pope and many of the cardinals were much offended. Grosseteste therefore defended himself before the Pope and the cardinals as follows. In the first place he pointed out that it was his custom to explain to candidates for benefices what a pastor ought to be and the dangers of abusing the pastoral power (see above, p. 180), and so he had given his usual warning to this importunate noble, who had taken great offence. When people are offended, they are apt to misrepresent other men's actions, as the Jews misrepresented the actions or the sayings of Christ. So too Grosseteste has been misrepresented and his criticism of bad pastors has been quite falsely applied to the Pope. He appeals to the Pope and cardinals: if matters are rightly understood, they ought not to be alienated from him, but rather drawn to him. He protests his great love for the Pope and the Curia; as he has said before, he would gladly suffer death many times or be handed over to Satan to suffer temporal pains,

---

[1] On *epikeia* and *acribodikaioi*, and on natural and legal justice, and the madman's sword, cf. St. Thomas Aquinas's commentary on the Nicomachean Ethics (ed. Pirotta, Marietti, 1934), s. 1016 ff., 1025, 1078, 1089; *Summa Theologiae*, iia. iiae, q. 120.

like Job or St. Ignatius, for the sake of the exaltation and salvation of the Curia. He concludes with what is at once a panegyric and a warning: the Pope is the light and sun of the world, he is the tree of life in the midst of paradise, he is the fountain of paradise watering the world with the teaching of speculative virtues and with the most divine manifestation of active virtues. Hence any failure in his vital functions will be disastrous. The Holy See is the seat and habitation of God, the heart of the world, the angel of angels and the god of gods (see above, p. 187). 'Being what you are', he says to the Pope and cardinals, 'you cannot help desiring the salvation of this Holy See and through it, that of the world; and feeling thus, since kindly feeling naturally hopes and believes that others feel the same, you cannot be sundered from me, because I have spoken my mind to you out of my affection; and so your heart and your love cannot be turned away from me.'

WILLIAM ABEL PANTIN.

APPENDIX I

The Familia *of* Robert *Grosseteste*

THE present list of clerks is not intended to do more than give the names of those who were in Grosseteste's service, indicating as far as possible the period they were with him, the preferments they held, and their subsequent careers. No attempt has been made to furnish every instance of their attestation of letters or of their other activities. The material in the Rolls themselves is much more copious for the first half of the pontificate than later when letters of institution were not so frequently entered on the dorse.[1] Nor do there seem to be large numbers of surviving original *acta*, and it proved to be entirely impossible to find a single specimen of the bishop's seal in a state fit for photographic reproduction.[2]

An examination of the Rolls for the confirmation or correction of doubtful readings in the printed text has resulted in raising numerous queries of a general nature on the method of enrolment by the clerks.[3] When the Rolls were printed there was less interest in the mechanism of diocesan administration than now, consequently the editor made no observations on changes of hand, which are numerous, nor thought worthy of habitual remark the marginal notes which periodically occur, such as, 'deficiunt littere inquisitionis' or 'non habemus litteras presentationis' or 'et sunt littere presentationis cum negotiis anni decimi', though he has included some from the Oxford Roll.[4]

[1] It is possible that witnessed letters were less frequently issued for institutions in the later years, as a change in the form of such letters is to be noted about this time and was apparently complete by the time of Bishop Gravesend. See *Acta Stephani Langton* (Canterbury and York Society, vol. l, p. xxxv).

[2] The British Museum, the Public Record Office, the Bodleian Library, the Cambridge University Libraries, County Record Offices within the old diocese, archives of colleges possessing lands of monastic houses within the diocese, Lambeth Library, and the chapter records of Canterbury were all tried in vain. A reputed charter with a good seal among the archives of St. James's Abbey, Northampton, proved to be an odd forgery in which the seal of Robert Bishop of Carlisle had been attached to a charter of Robert Bishop of Lincoln, but this was probably an attempt to replace a lost charter of Robert Chesney rather than one of Grosseteste. This is among the Duke of Buccleuch's deposited records in the Northamptonshire Record Office. (Buccleuch Box 7, no. 3/5.)

[3] I am indebted to Mrs. Varley and Miss Williamson of the Lincolnshire Archives Office for verifying certain points for me, and for reading these notes and making many helpful suggestions. It is clear from a comparison of the Rolls with the printed text that the volume needs the same additional notes that Canon Foster and Dr. Hamilton Thompson provided for those of Richard Gravesend in an appendix to the edition. I hope that the archivists may be able to undertake this in the near future.

[4] *Rotuli Gros.*, e.g. p. 489.

It seems that institutions were often enrolled in batches, probably some time after they had taken place, and on one occasion a clerk with a large number overran the pontifical year and found he had entered the first of the seventh year in the Lincoln Roll immediately after the last of the sixth year without leaving space for the usual heading in large capitals LINCOLN. ANNUS SEPTIMUS., which is therefore crowded in the empty half-line of the previous entry.[1]

Apparently the entry of the institution of John of Reston to Ewerby with those of the seventh year was not entered until at least the tenth year, for the note 'Sunt littere inquisitionis cum negotiis factis anni decimi et desunt littere presentationis' is in the same hand and ink as the entry of institution, and the same hand has also added 'et sunt littere presentationis cum negotiis anni decimi' to the preceding entry concerning Gunby, the main part of which had apparently been written earlier.[2] As the institution to Ewerby had been entered in the ordinary course of the ninth year and the letters of institution had been issued in the tenth year it is difficult to see why this late entry was added to the seventh year.[3]

The lack of names of presentees or of their orders is noticeable, but these have sometimes been added in the margin, though they have not been noted in the printed text. For example, *subd.* is in the margin beside the institution of Peter of Stamford to St. Michael's, Stamford, in which the space for orders is left blank and is so noted by the editor who has not, however, added the marginal note.[4]

Any satisfactory discussion of all the problems which have presented themselves in the course of examination of the Rolls would take more than the time available for the purpose of this appendix, but I hope a comparison of these Rolls with those of Hugh of Wells and of the successors of Grosseteste may be made at no very distant date.

One point, however, demands further comment. Bishops usually date their *acta* from the day of their consecration. Mr. J. C. Russell contends that Grosseteste differed in this and instead of dating from 17 June he dated from the time of his election shortly after the death of Hugh of Wells in February 1235, or even from the day of the latter's death, basing this view on three letters of institution printed on pp. 112, 118, and 394.[5] The earliest of these is 'Datum apud Vetus Templum Lond' v kal. Februarii anno gratie mccxxxvi': a contemporary hand has added in the margin

---

[1] The edition does not always contain the full heading as in the original.
[2] *Rotuli Gros.*, p. 65.   [3] Ibid., pp. 72, 78.
[4] Ibid., p. 36; on p. 42 there should be a note against the entry for Birardesdon (? Burreth) *diaconus est et ord*[*inandus*] *in sacerdotem.*
[5] *Harvard Theological Review*, xxvi. 171, and *Dictionary of Writers*, p. 138. Mr. Russell is under the impression that the English kings had already adopted the practice of dating their regnal year from the day of their predecessor's death and that Grosseteste was following their custom.

'pontificatus nostri anno secundo'.[1] This date Mr. Russell has taken to be January 1236, but since 25 March was the normal beginning of the year at this time it should more probably be read as 1237. In any case January 1236 could not be Grosseteste's second year if Hugh did not die until 7 February 1235. Similarly on p. 118 'Datum apud Grenewic nonis Marcii anno gratie mccxlix et pontificatus nostri anno xv' offers no difficulties if the year is reckoned from 25 March, as it will read 1250 and will tally with the consecration date for the beginning of the pontifical year.

The third presents a more difficult problem. 'Datum apud Rinckele kalendis Februarii anno gratie mccxlix et pontificatus nostri anno xiiij':[2] these two elements would agree only if the year of grace were reckoned from Christmas and in that case either the election or consecration date would give the pontifical year as fourteen, the end of the fourteenth year being in the one case on or shortly after 6 February and the other 16 June 1249. If, however, the usual reading of 1250 is taken the pontifical year would not tally in either case.

There seem though to be two pieces of positive evidence in favour of 17 June. On p. 390 the bishop recites a bull of Gregory IX dated 'Perusii id. Junii pontificatus nostri anno nono'. Gregory was elected on 19 and consecrated on 21 March 1227: the date of this bull must therefore be 13 June 1235. Grosseteste dated his recital of it 'in crastino Sancte Trinitatis pontificatus nostri anno primo'. In 1235 the morrow of Trinity was 4 June, therefore it is clear that this bull cannot have been recited until the morrow of Trinity 1236, which was 26 May.

Another document, an agreement made between two canons who were members of his household and sealed by the bishop himself, by Robert Marsh the bishop's official and John of Crakehall his steward, was dated 'Act' apud Dorkescestriam ij idus Junii anno gracie millesimo ducentesimo quadragesimo nono et pontificatus dicti domini episcopi quartodecimo'.[3] This again clearly indicates a reckoning from 17 June.

At least twenty-two of the clerks had the master's degree, and of these Mr. Emden considers that Roger de Burwardiscote, Walter de Bilesdon, Robert Marsh, and John de Offinton can be claimed for Oxford.[4] Robert of Cadney the first official became precentor of Lincoln, Robert Marsh the second official successively Archdeacon of Oxford and Dean of Lincoln. Thomas Wallensis, John of St. Giles, John de Dyham, John of Crakehall, Solomon of Dover, and Roger of Raveningham all became archdeacons within the diocese though not necessarily during Grosseteste's time. Nicholas Tessun and Roger de Burwardiscote became Archdeacons of

---

[1] *Rotuli Gros.*, p. 394.   [2] Ibid., p. 112.
[3] *Reg. Ant.* ii, no. 382.
[4] From notes communicated to the present writer by Mr. Emden, who kindly allowed me to send him the notes on the *Magistri*.

the institution of a chaplain of that name to Offord Darcy in 1244-5, but he is not described as canon.[1]

It may be noted that in the charters of Grosseteste in the period 1237-9 the other person not a *magister* who almost invariably witnesses first is John of St. Giles (q.v.), and since the two are never found witnessing the same document and since John of St. Giles was rector of Banbury as early as 1237 I would point out the possibility of these two being the same man, more especially as the attestations of both as canons seem to cease when John of St. Giles became Archdeacon of Oxford.

BEDINTUN (? Beddington, Surrey) EDMUND DE, accompanied Grosseteste abroad in 1250 when letters of protection with the clause *volumus* were issued to last so long as he should be beyond the sea with the bishop.[2]

BILENDON, WALTER DE, *magister*, appears only once as a witness to letters of institution, at Fingest on 29 September 1247.[3] In the same year he was the proctor appointed by Robert of St. Denis, rector of Mursley, to present a vicar to that church.[4] He may well be identical with the proctor of Oseney Abbey described as *dominus* in 1240,[5] without title on 6 October 1265, but as *magister* on 4 February 1271.[6]

BILESDON, WALTER DE, *magister*, was described by Matthew Paris as 'vir iurisperitus et fide dignus'.[7] He gave evidence that the dean had collated three churches of the bishop's patronage during the vacancy when a dispute arose between the archbishop and the chapter after Grosseteste's death. He witnessed one charter of Grosseteste at Biggleswade 20 November 1246.[8]

BLUND, ROGER, was the son of Robert Blund of Leicester[9] and was probably related to William Blund the precentor whose executor he was in 1244.[10] He is possibly to be identified with Roger Blund of Leicester, chaplain, who witnessed a grant of a rent in Leicester by Henry le Coveror of Leicester to Bishop Hugh II about 1215.[11] He was presented by Croxton Abbey to a portion in Sproxton (Leics.) before the tenth year of bishop Hugh,[12] and held this until his presentation to Galby (Leics.) by the master and brothers of Burton Lazars Hospital in 1231-2.[13] In 1236-7 he presented Hugh of Blaby as perpetual vicar of Galby.[14]

---

[1] Ibid., p. 287.
[2] *C. P. R. 1247-58*, p. 60.
[3] *Rotuli Gros.*, p. 331.
[4] Ibid., p. 376.
[5] *The Cartulary of Oseney Abbey*, ed. by H. E. Salter, iv. 434.
[6] Ibid. ii. 235; v. 264. I owe these last two references to Mr. A. B. Emden.
[7] Paris, *Chron. Mai.* v. 412.
[8] *Rotuli Gros.*, p. 229.
[9] *Rotuli Welles*, i. 73.
[10] *Reg. Ant.* vii, no. 2130.
[11] Ibid. iii, no. 886.
[12] *Rotuli Welles*, i. 73.
[13] Ibid. ii. 320.
[14] *Rotuli Gros.*, pp. 393-4.

He was with Grosseteste as early as 30 September 1235[1] and is usually described as one of the chaplains in the witness lists, following the canons and preceding the clerks. He became a canon between 28 January and 7 April 1238[2] and in 1248–9 was prebendary of Leighton Ecclesia, when he presented Robert de Maperton to the vicarage of the prebendal church.[3] After the sixth year he is by no means so frequent a witness, though he is found with the bishop at Buckden on 21 January 1242,[4] at London in October of the same year,[5] and at Liddington in December 1243.[6] He was present at Lincoln when Baldwin de Charneles resigned a living in Hereford diocese on institution to Wistow (Leics.) 1245–6, but may have been there as a canon rather than as a member of the household of the bishop, for none of the other witnesses are of the *familia*.[7]

In 1249–50 he founded a hospital for poor and sick priests on his estate near the church of Holy Trinity, Leicester, in honour of God, the Virgin, and the holy confessors Edmund Archbishop of Canterbury and Hugh of Lincoln. The charter of the bishop's confirmation and the consent of the Abbot and convent of Leicester are given. Gregory de Milwere was instituted as warden on Roger's presentation.[8] Unfortunately the later history of this foundation is extremely obscure.

BURGO, BENEDICT DE, was as a subdeacon instituted to Slawston Church (Leics.) on the presentation of Owston Abbey in 1231–2.[9] He was with Grosseteste at Liddington on 30 September 1235[10] and witnessed the bishop's charters until 1252.[11] He became a canon after 25 March 1247 but in or before July of that year.[12] He seems to have resigned Slawston by 1238–9 when Robert the subprior of Owston was instituted,[13] possibly when Benedict now a deacon was instituted to Potton on the presentation of St. Andrew's Priory, Northampton.[14] Two years later, as rector of Potton, he was instituted to Carlton Curlieu on presentation of Ware Priory.[15] On 9 May 1252 he was admitted to Dunstable Priory as a canon.[16]

BURWARDISCOTE, ROGER DE, *magister*, does not appear to have entered Grosseteste's household until some years after his consecration. He is found among the *familia* on 5 August 1242 and at intervals throughout the next two years until 9 November 1244.[17] The bishop having the collation of Tackley (Oxon.) by lapse gave it to him in 1243–4, when he was a subdeacon.[18] He acquired some property in All Saints parish, Oxford, which

[1] *Rotuli Gros.*, p. 389.
[2] Ibid., pp. 258, 310.
[3] Ibid., pp. 295–6.
[4] Ibid., pp. 417–18.
[5] Ibid., p. 364.
[6] Ibid., p. 324.
[7] Ibid., p. 425.
[8] Ibid., pp. 435–7.
[9] *Rotuli Welles*, ii. 318.
[10] *Rotuli Gros.*, p. 389.
[11] Ibid., *passim*.
[12] Ibid., pp. 428, 104.
[13] Ibid., p. 402.
[14] Ibid., p. 311.
[15] Ibid., p. 411.
[16] *Ann. Mon.* ii. 185.
[17] *Rotuli Gros.*, pp. 479, 289, &c.
[18] Ibid., p. 482.

he intended to leave to St. Frideswide's Priory but for some reason the gift did not take effect and it was later owned by the Hospital of St. John the Baptist. It was known first as Burwolscot Hall, later as Broadgates.[1] Roger was archdeacon of Wiltshire[2] in 1246 and died probably about 1267.[3]

CADNEY, ROBERT OF, *magister*, was, as a deacon, instituted to Kelstern on the presentation of the Abbot and convent of Thornton in 1227–8.[4] He was already *magister* at this date. He witnessed Grosseteste's charters from the year of the bishop's accession and though he is not often given the title of official in the witness list there is no evidence for any other person holding that post in the first nine years of the pontificate.[5] He was a canon by 25 May 1236.[6]

By 1238–9 he had resigned Kelstern.[7] In 1241–2 he was instituted to the rich rectory of Heckington on the presentation of Bardney Abbey, with the proviso that this was conditional on his being able to hold it with his prebend.[8] As no evidence is found for his supersession the difficulty was presumably overcome by dispensation. By 22 September 1244 he had become precentor of Lincoln.[9] He was alive on 3 February 1251[10] but died not later than 6 November 1257.[11] His successor Peter of Aldenham and other canons were his executors, and established an annual rent-charge of ten shillings from the houses in St. Margaret's parish which Robert had bought from the executors of his predecessor William Blund, to be paid to the provosts of the Common Fund of the canons for distribution on his anniversary.

CAMPDEN, ROGER OF, *magister*, was, as a subdeacon, instituted rector of Epworth on the presentation of the Prior and convent of Newburgh in 1233.[12] He witnessed documents of Grosseteste during at least the first nine years of his pontificate.[13] On 5 November 1237[14] he is given

---

[1] *A Cartulary of the Hospital of St. John the Baptist*, ed. H. E. Salter, ii. 1–4, where an account of the property and its history is given. *Cartulary of St. Frideswide*, ed. S. R. Wigram, i. 292–5. *Medieval Archives of Christ Church, Oxford*, ed. N. Denholm Young, pp. 32–33. For this information and that contained in the two subsequent notes I am indebted to Mr. A. B. Emden.

[2] *Sarum Charters and Documents*, ed. W. H. Rich Jones (R.S.), p. 308.

[3] *Cartulary of the Hospital of St. John the Baptist*, ii. 1.

[4] *Rotuli Welles*, iii. 164.

[5] *Rotuli Gros.*, pp. 135, 389 and *passim*.   [6] Ibid., p. 389.

[7] Ibid., p. 33.   [8] Ibid., p. 61.

[9] *Reg. Ant.* iv, no. 1261.   [10] Ibid. v, no. 1461.

[11] Muniments of the Dean and chapter of Lincoln, Dij/79/1/119; the anniversary is stated to be 6 Nov. The ordinance for the establishment of the payment was witnessed by Richard the dean who was consecrated as bishop on 3 Nov. 1258. The other witnesses preclude a later Richard.

[12] *Rotuli Welles*, i. 235. I am indebted to Mr. A. B. Emden for this reference.

[13] *Rotuli Gros.*, *passim*.

[14] Ibid., p. 257.

the title of canon in the witness lists, but in April, and on 16 May 1239,[1] when the witnesses are carefully divided into canons, chaplains, and clerks, he is placed with the clerks. On 16 September 1239 and 29 July 1240 he is back among the canons.[2] Epworth rectory was filled again in 1244–5 but no reason for the vacancy was given.[3] He was a physician, and Matthew Paris says that Grosseteste owed his life to Roger's skill after an attempt to poison him in 1237.[4]

CAPELLA, THOMAS DE, evidently joined Grosseteste in the bishop's last years. He witnesses 30 March 1251 and 6 June and 3 October in the same year.[5] There is no certainty that he is to be identified with the man of that name who occurs as the administrator of Watton at Stone Chapel (Herts.)[6] in 1261–2 and who apparently was also known as Thomas of Sacombe, as appears from the record of his death in 1274.[7] Nor can it be certain that he was the Thomas de Capella instituted by proxy on the king's presentation to Bletchingdon (Oxon.).[8]

CARLISLE (Karleolo), THOMAS OF, witnessed a few charters from 3 September 1236[9] to 26 June 1237.[10] He does not seem to have held any benefices in the diocese.

CASTELLO, STEPHEN DE, was in the service of Bishop Hugh II at least as early as 9 August 1229.[11] In 1229–30 he was instituted to Oakley (Beds.) on the presentation of Caldwell Priory, being at that time a subdeacon.[12] The date of his successor's institution has not been found. Stephen can be traced with Grosseteste until 10 November 1244.[13]

CONSTABLE, SIMON, *magister*, witnesses frequently in the first four years of the pontificate, less frequently in the fifth, and on 28 July 1240.[14] He was instituted as subdeacon to the rectory of Carlton le Moorland (Lincs.) in 1235–6, on the presentation of the Abbot and convent of Thornton,[15] but the date was not earlier than 11 November 1235, when his predecessor Richard of Rothwell was still in office.[16] He was instituted to Belgrave rectory on the presentation of the Prior of Ware in the fourth year and had letters of institution dated 12 August 1239 (fifth year).[17] It seems

---

[1] *Rotuli Gros.*, pp. 190–1.
[2] Ibid., p. 316: *The Cartulary of Eynsham Abbey*, ed. H. E. Salter (O.H.S.), i. 176.
[3] Ibid., p. 146.
[4] Paris, *Hist. Angl.* ii. 398.
[5] *Rotuli Gros.*, pp. 127, 248, 382.
[6] *Rotuli Grav.*, p. 168.
[7] Ibid., p. 180.
[8] Ibid., p. 235.
[9] *Rotuli Gros.*, pp. 252, 343.
[10] Ibid., pp. 23, 172, 400.
[11] *Rotuli Welles*, ii. 231 and *passim*.
[12] Ibid. iii. 23.
[13] *Rotuli Gros.*, p. 289 and *passim*.
[14] Ibid., p. 58 and *passim*.
[15] Ibid., p. 3.
[16] *Reg. Ant.* vii, no. 2013.
[17] *Rotuli Gros.*, pp. 405, 410.

probable that he died in 1241 as a successor was instituted to one of his livings by 15 November 1240 and to the other before 17 June 1241.[1]

CRAKEHALL, JOHN OF, seems to have entered the service of Hugh II in 1231. From March of that year he is found as a frequent witness to letters of institution[2] and on 9 April he received the collation of Somerton Church (Oxon.).[3] He became a canon before 15 March 1234[4] and was an executor of the testament of Bishop Hugh II.[5] He probably entered Grosseteste's service immediately, for he witnesses, with the title of steward,[6] a charter of the Bishop concerning land at Newark in the first year of his pontificate, and continually witnesses letters of institution in the Rolls as well as charters both by and to the bishop concerning land.[7]

In 1241 he was sent to negotiate with the king over the difficult business of Thame prebend.[8] Adam Marsh addressed several letters to him, sometimes on the affairs of the bishopric sometimes on more personal matters such as urging him to seek absolution from the Nuncio for some sin.[9] By 1240 he held the rectory of Shillington (Beds.)[10] and on 24 April 1245 had a papal indult to hold an additional benefice with cure of souls[11] which may have enabled him to receive Althorpe Rectory in the gift of St. Leonard's Hospital, York, before 17 June 1245.[12] The letters of institution were apparently not issued until 9 January 1250.[13] This rectory he was not holding at the time of his death, though he still had Shillington, Somerton, and the rectory of Brington with Bythorne and Old Weston (Hunts.).[14] Both Shillington and Brington were of the patronage of Ramsey Abbey.

He accompanied Grosseteste to Lyons in 1250 and evidently resigned the stewardship about this time, for references are made to his successor, by name Roger.[15] With the Archdeacon of Oxford and Robert de Wynkele he was appointed to settle a dispute between the men of the Earl of Leicester and those of the bishop in Leicester.[16] John was with Grosseteste when he died at Buckden and from him Matthew Paris learnt of the bells heard ringing at the moment of the bishop's death. Paris describes him as 'episcopi clericus specialis, vir venerabilis et inter omnes episcopales non ultimae auctoritatis'.[17] He was an executor of Grosseteste's testament.[18]

[1] Ibid., pp. 55, 411, 414.
[2] *Rotuli Welles*, ii. 238 ff.
[3] Ibid., p. 35.
[4] Ibid. iii. 32.
[5] *Reg. Ant.* ii, no. 372.
[6] *Rotuli Gros.*, p. 135.
[7] Ibid., *passim* and *Reg. Ant.* iii, nos. 891, 937.
[8] *Patent Rolls, 1232–47*, pp. 257.
[9] *Mon. Franc.*, pp. 252–3, 222, 229, 241.
[10] *Roll of the Justices in Eyre, 1240*, ed. G. H. Fowler. *Bedford Historical Record Society*, ix. 121.
[11] *C. Pap. R.* i. 216.
[12] *Rotuli Gros.*, p. 148.
[13] Ibid., p. 155.
[14] *Rotuli Grav.*, pp. 190, 215, 167.
[15] *Mon. Franc.*, p. 105.
[16] Ibid. i. 110.
[17] Paris, *Chron. Mai.* v. 408.
[18] *Close Rolls, 1254–6*, p. 37.

He became Archdeacon of Bedford not earlier than 1253 but had resigned by 8 July 1259.[1] In 1258 he was appointed by the nobles of the Council to be the king's treasurer and the treasure, rolls, and keys were to be delivered to him on 2 November.[2] This office he only enjoyed briefly, for he died in 1260.[3] He had evidently lent money both to Dunstable Priory and to Newnham Priory, for on his instructions his executors cancelled these debts.[4] Both houses undertook the singing of masses for his soul and Dunstable in 1272 took a blind man into the infirmary in memory of him.[5]

It seems probable that he came from Crakehall in the parish of Bedale, Yorks., where a family of that name inherited part of the fee of Conan son of Ellis in Yorkshire and Lincolnshire.[6]

DEREHAM, RICHARD OF, witnesses letters of institution between 28 January and 21 July 1237.[7]

DOVER, SOLOMON OF, *magister*, was instituted as a subdeacon (already *magister*) to Holdenby (Northants.) on the presentation of Eustacia de Ardern in 1237–8.[8] He was referred to by Adam Marsh as having been ordained by Grosseteste and having carried out his duties at Holdenby well: he was considered by Adam and Robert Marsh to be suitable to become a prebendary.[9] He was not a canon on 30 March 1251,[10] when he attested letters of institution, but was referred to as the bishop's chaplain and canon on 12 May 1251, when he went with letters patent of the bishop to the king asking for the delivery to the bishop of John Aylrich of Hemel Hempstead accused of robbery.[11] He was with the bishop at Nettleham in October 1251.[12] He became Archdeacon of Leicester shortly before 17 June 1252[13] and was one of the envoys of the chapter to the king to obtain the *congé d'élire*, which was issued on 20 November 1253.[14] Although he had a papal dispensation to hold another benefice, which was recited by Grosseteste at Banbury on 26 November 1251,[15] he does not appear to have held another, apart from his prebend, in the diocese. His prebend as archdeacon was St. Margaret's, Leicester, which was usually annexed to the archdeaconry, and Grosseteste quitclaimed to him and his successors

---

[1] For his appointment see under John de Dyham below: Peter of Aldenham had succeeded him by this date: *Cartulary of Oseney Abbey*, ed. H. E. Salter, iv. 47. I owe this reference to Mr. A. B. Emden.

[2] *C.P.R. 1258–66*, p. 1.   [3] *Rotuli Grav.*, p. 215.

[4] *Ann. Mon.* iii. 255; *Rotuli Grav.*, pp. 190–1.   [5] *Ann. Mon.* iii. 255.

[6] For this family see *Early Yorkshire Charters*, vol. v. *The Honour of Richmond*, ed. C. T. Clay, pt. ii. 276.

[7] *Rotuli Gros.*, pp. 15–16, 172, 254, 257, 310, 400, 452.

[8] Ibid., p. 171.   [9] *Mon. Franc.* i. 34–5.

[10] *Rotuli Gros.*, p. 127.   [11] *Close Rolls, 1247–57*, p. 539.

[12] *Rotuli Gros.*, p. 382.   [13] *Reg. Ant.* iii, no. 891.

[14] *C.P.R. 1247–58*, p. 252.   [15] *Rotuli Gros.*, p. 247.

all rights which the bishop had in houses and sites of houses which were of John his predecessor.[1]

In 1263 he resigned the rectory of Holdenby.[2] He died in 1274.[3] Adam Marsh addressed a letter to him asking him to interest himself in the nunnery of Belton.[4]

DUNWICH, LEONARD OF, *magister*, as subdeacon and already *magister* was presented by Sir Hugh of Boothby to Boothby Pagnell rectory and had letters of institution 30 May 1238.[5] He witnesses from 16 September 1239 throughout practically the whole of the pontificate.[6] He is probably to be identified with Leonard son of Alexander who is also found in the household.[7] In 1241 Grosseteste sent a master L. the clerk with others to the king to put his case about Thame prebend.[8] Leonard of Dunwich was instituted on or before 30 April 1243 to Ab Kettleby on the death of Simon de Arderne, this being of the gift of Launde Priory,[9] and had a papal indult to hold a benefice additional to these two with cure of souls.[10] He had become a canon by 21 September 1249.[11] He was no doubt the envoy sent by Grosseteste to the papal court in 1249 to get the bull allowing review of appropriations, which the bishop used with effect in 1250.[12] In 1255 and 1256 he was a prominent spokesman in the discussions with Master Rostand the papal envoy, and on the second occasion, the meeting of bishops and archdeacons on 13 January 1256, is spoken of by Matthew Paris as 'quasi cleri advocatus et prolocutor universitatis'. His argument was remarkably like that of his former master in such circumstances.[13]

DYHAM, JOHN DE, witnesses letters of institution from the first to the ninth year.[14] Before his consecration Grosseteste collated the rectory of Hambleton (Rutland) to John.[15] On 2 January 1239 he had letters of collation to Wheathampstead which Matthew de Stratton, Archdeacon of Buckingham, had resigned.[16] On this occasion he was specifically described as *capellanus noster*. He was ordinarily given the title of chaplain in witness lists.

In 1244 Amaury of Buckden, Archdeacon of Bedford, died and was succeeded by a John.[17] This John the editor of the Rolls assumed to be John of Crakehall, who did in fact become archdeacon about 1253, but it

---

[1] *Reg. Ant.* iii, no. 891.
[2] *Rotuli Grav.*, p. 103.
[3] Ibid., p. xxxvii.
[4] *Mon. Franc.* i. 197.
[5] *Rotuli Gros.*, pp. 22, 26.
[6] Ibid., p. 316 and *passim*.
[7] Ibid., p. 317: also p. 207 where the edition gives the initial H., though it is L. in the original.
[8] *Reg. Ant.* i, no. 242.
[9] *Rotuli Gros.*, p. 420.
[10] *C. Pap. R.* i. 204.
[11] *Rotuli Gros.*, p. 243.
[12] Paris, *Chron. Mai.* v. 96; vi. 152.
[13] Ibid. vi. 533, 539.
[14] *Rotuli Gros.*, *passim*.
[15] Ibid., p. 159.
[16] Ibid., p. 267.
[17] Ibid., pp. 327–39: indexed as John of Crakehall.

appears from an entry in the Eyre Roll of 1247[1] that it was John de Dyham who was Amaury's successor, and from the Newnham cartulary that he was still in office in 1253.[2] John of Crakehall was certainly in office in 1255.[3] The date of John de Dyham's successor's institution to Wheathampstead is not known, but he had been succeeded at Hambleton by John of Yarmouth by 1242.[4] He had obtained a canonry by 28 July 1240.[5]

EASTON, JOHN OF, frequently witnesses letters of institution from 1237 until 18 April 1240.[6] In 1239–40 he received collation of the church of Mursley (Bucks.),[7] but had either died or resigned by Grosseteste's eighth year, 1242–3, when Robert of St. Denis was instituted on the presentation of Nuneaton Priory.[8] An order for the delivery of a clerk of this name from Newgate to Walter, dean of the city of Oxford, for custody in the bishop's prison until trial, was dated 19 January 1240.[9] There is no certainty of identity and the name is not uncommon, but if this does refer to the bishop's clerk his disappearance from the witness list is accounted for.

EXL', THOMAS DE, occurs as a witness among the chaplains at Dorchester on 19 October 1243.[10] Unless he is identical with Thomas of Aylesbury or Thomas the almoner he does not otherwise appear.

FLEET, THOMAS OF, witnesses a letter of institution to Fulletby in which the date is 1 February 1249 according to the episcopal year (fourteen), but the year of grace is given as 1249, which implies calculation from Christmas rather than 25 March which by this time was more usual.[11] He received as a deacon collation of Sacombe (Herts.) shortly before the bishop's death,[12] and apparently held it until 1277, when Laurence of Gisors was instituted on the death of Thomas the previous incumbent, whose surname is not given.[13] Thomas was charged with the payment of four marks yearly to Master Robert Grecus, possibly a relative of Nicholas Grecus (q.v.), until he should be better provived for.

FRITWELL, ROGER OF, witnesses letters of institution throughout the pontificate.[14] As a subdeacon he was instituted to Wing (Rutland) on presentation by St. Neot's Abbey in 1239[15] and received collation of Narborough rectory, the letters of collation being dated 21 January 1242.[16]

---

[1] *Calendar of the Roll of the Justices in Eyre, 1247*, ed. G. H. Fowler. *Bedford Historical Record Society*, xxi. 194–6.

[2] Cartulary of Newnham Priory, B.M. Harl. MS. 3656, fol. 57ᵛ. I owe this reference to Miss Joyce Godber.

[3] *Ann. Mon.* iii. 197.   [4] *Rotuli Gros.*, pp. 208–9.

[5] Ibid., p. 58. Dyham is probably to be identified with Dedham in Essex.

[6] Ibid., *passim*.   [7] Ibid., p. 354.

[8] Ibid., p. 360.   [9] *Close Rolls, 1237–42*, p. 170.

[10] *Rotuli Gros.*, p. 475.   [11] Ibid., p. 112.

[12] Ibid., p. 300.   [13] *Rotuli Grav.*, p. 184.

[14] *Rotuli Gros.*, *passim*.   [15] Ibid., pp. 191, 195.   [16] Ibid., pp. 417–18.

He became a canon between 3 March 1251 and 7 June 1251,[1] though later in the same week he witnesses without title.[2] The dates of the institutions of his successors in these livings do not appear.

GRECUS, NICHOLAS, *magister*, was one of the assistants of Grosseteste in translation from the Greek.[3] He was with the bishop as early as 19 March 1237 and is found witnessing continuously throughout the pontificate.[4] He had become a canon by 14 September 1246[5] though it is not as yet known what prebend he held. He was present in chapter on 26 December 1247, 3 February 1251, and 7 April 1263 and witnessed a charter of Henry Lexington 1254–8.[6] After the death of Grosseteste he was sent to Rome to procure the bishop's canonization.[7] In 1256 he was evidently one of the leaders of the canons who were refusing to contribute to the expenses of the chapter in preserving their liberties and was mentioned by name in the papal mandate on this subject.[8]

In 1258 Robert son of William of Lincoln bound himself on behalf of his father-in-law Robert of Kent to pay Master Nicholas sixty shillings within the quindene of Michaelmas 1258: failing this payment Nicholas was to have fifteen shillings of annual rent from a tenement in the parish of St. Peter at Arches for a term of ten years. The lease ratifying this arrangement was dated Easter 1260.[9] A similar transaction was made with John the skinner of Eastgate and Margaret his wife, to whom Nicholas had lent money in their great need.[10]

He had been instituted to Datchet (Bucks.) as a subdeacon in 1239–40[11] and was still holding this on his death on 4 December 1279.[12] The contention of Mr. Russell that Nicholas of St. Albans, with whom Nicholas Grecus has sometimes been confused, was dead in 1252 is confirmed by a reference to the executors of Nicholas of St. Albans early in 1253.[13]

GROSSETESTE, JOHN, *magister*, witnesses letters of institution from the second to the fourth years, 1236–9.[14] As subdeacon he was instituted to

---

[1] Ibid., p. 248.   [2] Ibid., p. 500.

[3] For an account of his life and literary work see Russell 'Preferments and *Adiutores*' and *Dictionary of Writers*, p. 89.

[4] *Rotuli Gros.*, p. 166 and *passim*. Mr. Russell gives 6 April 1236 as the first date at which he is found, but if the year is calculated from the bishop's consecration this document would be 6 April 1237.

[5] Ibid., p. 92.

[6] *Reg. Ant.* iii, nos. 830, 963; v, no. 1461; vi, no. 1784.

[7] R. E. G. Cole, 'Proceedings relative to the canonization of Robert Grosseteste, Bishop of Lincoln', *Associated Architectural Societies Reports and Papers*, xxxiii. 6.

[8] *Reg. Ant.* i, no. 282.

[9] Muniments of the Dean and chapter of Lincoln, Dij/80/3/24, 27.

[10] Ibid., Dij/82/2/133.   [11] *Rotuli Gros.*, p. 354.

[12] *Gesta Abbatum Sancti Albani* (R.S.), i. 440.

[13] *C.P.R. 1247–58*, p. 181.

[14] *Rotuli Gros.*, pp. 26–27, 164–6, 184, 186, 351, 401, 406–7, 452.

Litchborough rectory on the presentation of St. James's Abbey, Northampton, the letters being dated 6 April 1237,[1] and to Whissendine (Rutland) on presentation of Lindores Abbey in 1237-8.[2] He died before the end of Grosseteste's eleventh year.[3] His successor had already been instituted in 1239-40 to Litchborough which he must have resigned.[4]

HEMINGBOROUGH, WILLIAM OF, was sent by Grosseteste to Rome in 1239 with further instructions to Simon de Arderne the bishop's proctor in the cause against the dean and chapter.[5] In 1241-2 Horkstow Church was collated to him when a subdeacon, the bishop having the presentation by lapse.[6] This he held until his death, which occurred shortly before March 1277.[7] He does not often witness letters of institution but may be found so doing on 21 January 1242, 2 June 1243, 25 March and 20 August 1247, and 1 February 1249.[8] In the sixteenth year he became a canon, certainly before 7 June, when he witnesses with that title,[9] and was also a witness in October 1251[10] and at Stow Park in 1251-2.[11] He held the prebend of Bishop Norton and acquired four cottages in that village which were to be held by successive prebendaries.[12]

HERTFORD, ELIAS OF, has not so far been found witnessing letters of institution earlier than January 1247.[13] He received the church of Scot Willoughby from the bishop, who was patron by lapse, in 1247-8[14] and was certainly with the bishop in January 1250.[15] The next reference to an institution to Scot Willoughby is in 1279 but the resignant is John.[16] It is possible that Elias may be the king's clerk of that name who was sent to the monasteries in the diocese and later throughout the country to ask for assistance with money and horses in 1242,[17] and who after Grosseteste's death reappears in the king's service as the associate of the Abbot of Pershore in the escheator's office with a salary of £20 a year.[18]

LEICESTER, G. DE, appears to have entered the *familia* in 1247, when he is first found witnessing at the end of the list of clerks.[19] He was certainly with Grosseteste as late as October 1251[20] and there is a probability that he was with him to the end and entered Lexington's household, for at least two charters of the latter, one issued at Buckden on 14 March 1255,

[1] *Rotuli Gros.*, pp. 164, 167.
[2] Ibid., p. 172.
[3] Ibid., p. 225.
[4] Ibid., p. 196.
[5] *Ep.* 80.
[6] *Rotuli Gros.*, p. 64.
[7] *Rotuli Grav.*, pp. 73, 80.
[8] *Rotuli Gros.*, pp. 417-18, 365, 428, 293, 112.
[9] Ibid., p. 248.
[10] Ibid., p. 382.
[11] *Reg. Ant.* iii, no. 891.
[12] Ibid. ii, no. 632.
[13] *Rotuli Gros.*, p. 428.
[14] Ibid., p. 100.
[15] Ibid., p. 156.
[16] *Rotuli Grav.*, p. 83.
[17] *C.P.R. 1232-47*, p. 280.
[18] Ibid. *1247-58*, pp. 397, 410.
[19] *Rotuli Gros.*, p. 104.
[20] Ibid., p. 382.

the other at Fingest 3 February 1256, were witnessed in the one case by
Gilbert of Leicester, in the other by G. of Leicester.[1]

MARSH, ROBERT, *magister*, was the brother of Adam Marsh and is often
mentioned in the latter's letters.[2] He was a graduate of Oxford and had
hoped that Grosseteste would attend the ceremonies of his degree. Adam
requested that the bishop would ordain Robert priest.[3] On Robert of
Cadney's preferment to the precentorship Robert Marsh became the
bishop's official and also acted as vicar-general in his absences abroad in
1245 and 1250.[4] He was a canon by 13 October 1244.[5] When Roger de
Weseham became Bishop of Coventry and Lichfield Grosseteste bestowed
the rich prebend of Aylesbury, hitherto held by the dean, on Robert
Marsh.[6] He also held a prebend of Wells and occasionally went there.[7]
In 1249–50 he became Archdeacon of Oxford,[8] and, on the election of
Gravesend to the bishopric, Dean of Lincoln, which office he held until his
death in 1262.[9] He was evidently a supporter of the barons and was one
of their nominees in the negotiations in 1261.[10] A long list of the privileges of the clergy, said to have been drawn up by him on the instructions
of Grosseteste, is placed under the year 1258 by the Burton annalist.[11]

MITON, MYTHON, N. DE, witnesses three charters, on 9 January 1250
and on 3 March and 7 June 1251.[12]

MORA, HENRY DE, witnesses from February 1249[13] and is found on
3 March 1251.[14]

OCCOLD (Acholt, Akholt, Hoch', Hokholt, Okholt), HENRY OF, *magister*,
had been presented to the rectory of Shillington (Beds.) by the Abbot and
convent of Ramsey in 1228–9.[15] He appears as a clerk of Grosseteste from
1237 to 1239[16] and attained to a canonry between 27 August and 20 September 1238.[17] In 1238–9 he acted as the proxy of Master Leonard de
Reate.[18] By 1240 he had been succeeded at Shillington by John of Crakehall[19] and as there is no further trace of him it is possible that he was dead
or had entered religion: the prebend which the legate Otto wanted for his

[1] *Reg. Ant.* iii, no. 832; ii, no. 388.
[2] *Mon. Franc.*, pp. 99, 137, 159, 250.   [3] Ibid., pp. 132, 135.
[4] *Rotuli Gros.*, *passim*.   [5] Ibid., p. 79.
[6] Paris, *Chron. Mai.* iv. 425.
[7] *Calendar of the Manuscripts of the Dean and Chapter of Wells* (H.M.C.), i. 70, 72.
[8] *Rotuli Gros.*, p. 496. Adam Marsh addressed several letters to him as archdeacon.
Mon. Franc., pp. 198, 202.   [9] *Rotuli Grav.*, p. xxxv.
[10] *Ann. Mon.* iv. 129.   [11] Ibid. i. 425–9.
[12] *Rotuli Gros.*, pp. 156 (where his initial is incorrectly given as H.), 248, *bis*.
[13] Ibid., p. 112.   [14] Ibid., p. 248.
[15] *Rotuli Welles*, iii. 21.   [16] *Rotuli Gros.*, *passim*.
[17] Ibid., pp. 406, 37.   [18] Ibid., p. 264.
[19] Cartulary of Newnham Priory, B.M. MS. Harl. 3656, fol. 58ᵛ. I owe this reference
to Miss Joyce Godber.

clerk Atto, and which Grosseteste speaks of as having been that of 'our clerk H.', may have been Henry of Occold's.[1]

OFFINTON, JOHN DE, *magister*, was the Chancellor of Oxford's Commissary in 1231.[2] On 12 June 1234 he had letters of protection without term.[3] In a letter dated? 1246 by the editor of Grosseteste's letters, the bishop in his name and that of Adam Marsh wrote to Master John urging his return to England.[4] It seems that this letter had effect, for by March 1247 he was with Grosseteste at Houghton and accompanied him to various parts of the diocese in the course of that year.[5] He was already a canon by March 1247 and held the prebend of Langford Manor (Oxon.).[6] About this time he acquired Seneschal Hall, Oxford.[7] In 1249–50 he was instituted to Earl's Barton (Northants.) on the presentation of Delapre Abbey, Northampton, being described as subdeacon and papal chaplain.[8]

On 8 November 1247 he had received from Innocent IV a dispensation additional to that already obtained from Gregory IX. The dispensation of the latter enabled him, though illegitimate, to receive a dignity, that of Innocent permitted him to receive a bishopric.[9]

Matthew Paris notes under the year 1251 that there died Master J. de Offintone, canon of Salisbury, than whom there was no more famous clerk in England.[10] There is, however, no trace of him as a canon of Salisbury in the *Sarum Charters*, the *Register of St. Osmund*, or the *Calendar of the MSS. of the Dean and Chapter of Salisbury*. He had, however, been a canon of Wells at least as early as 1236, holding the prebend of Werminster.[11] In 1242–3 he was a proctor in the court of Rome for the chapter at the time of the election of a new bishop.[12]

OLNEY, SIMON OF, occurs as a clerk on 14 December 1238.[13]

POCKLINGTON, REMIGIUS OF, was a frequent witness of letters of institution until the fourth year of Grosseteste.[14] He and William of Pocklington were described in one list as 'carnal brothers'[15] and it is likely that Richard of Pocklington was also a kinsman. Remigius had letters of institution to Ab Kettleby rectory (Leics.) on the presentation of Launde

---

[1] *Ep.* 74.
[2] *The Cartulary of Oseney Abbey*, ed. H. E. Salter, i. 137. I owe this reference to Mr. A. B. Emden.
[3] *C.P.R., 1232–47*, p. 55.   [4] *Ep.* 120.
[5] *Rotuli Gros.*, pp. 428, 92, 103, 293, 328, 331.   [6] *Reg. Ant.* ii, no. 382.
[7] *Oriel Records*, ed. H. E. Salter, pp. 115–16. I owe this reference to Mr. A. B. Emden.
[8] *Rotuli Gros.*, p. 240. On his death the nuns rapidly presented his successor 'for fear of the Romans', ibid., p. 245.
[9] *C. Pap. R.* i. 238.   [10] *Chron. Mai.* v. 230.
[11] *Calendar of the Manuscripts of the Dean and Chapter of Wells*, i. 82, 92.
[12] Ibid., p. 98. I owe these last two references to Mr. A. B. Emden.
[13] *Rotuli Gros.*, p. 352.   [14] Ibid., *passim*.
[15] Ibid., p. 289.

Priory dated 6 April 1237,[1] and on the same day letters to receive Med-
bourne Rectory *in commendam* on the presentation of Owston Abbey.[2]
He must have vacated Ab Kettleby by 13 June 1238 when Simon de
Arderne (q.v.) was instituted to it.[3] On 12 December 1240 he had letters
of institution to Surfleet Rectory on the presentation of Spalding Priory[4]
and his absence from witness lists henceforward suggests that he must
have retired to his livings. He died in 1248–9.[5]

POCKLINGTON, RICHARD OF. Although he was chaplain to Grosseteste
from the second year until the thirteenth of the episcopate[6] Richard of
Pocklington did not attain to a canonry and seems to have retired to the
rectory of Merton near Bicester about 1248. He had been instituted to this
on the presentation of Eynsham Abbey by 13 January 1239[7] and was holding it on his death in 1258 or 1259.[8] He had held for a year the vicarage of
Bonby on the presentation of the Prior and convent of St. Fromund, being
instituted in the third year and presumably resigning on presentation to
Merton.[9]

POCKLINGTON, WILLIAM OF, *magister*, does not seem to have entered
the service of Grosseteste until the ninth year and is found witnessing on
19 September 1243 and appears frequently thereafter.[10] He was described
in one list as 'carnal brother' of Remigius of Pocklington:[11] Richard of
Pocklington, if not another brother, was presumably a kinsman. He was
made a canon in the course of the tenth year[12] and held the prebend of
Langford Ecclesia, in connexion with which he made an agreement with
Master John de Offinton the prebendary of Langford Manor.[13] He was
described by Adam Marsh in a letter to Grosseteste as 'devotissimus filius
vester et secretarius meus amicissimus', when Adam sent William to him
on affairs some of which were to be communicated by word of mouth.[14]
On another occasion William was the messenger whom Adam sent to
discuss with the bishop matters concerning Robert Marsh.[15]

He held the living of Upton, Hunts., to which a successor was instituted
in the seventeenth year on the entry of master William into religion.[16] The
date of his own institution does not appear. The living was in the gift of
the Rand family. In 1251 he entered the Franciscan order at Oxford. A note
on him appears in Dr. Little's *Grey Friars in Oxford*, where like the editor

---

[1] Ibid., p. 395.
[3] Ibid., p. 401.
[5] Ibid., p. 106.
[7] Ibid., pp. 457, 461.
[9] *Rotuli Gros.*, pp. 17, 34.
[11] Ibid., p. 289.
[13] *Reg. Ant.* ii, no. 382.
[15] Ibid., p. 137.

[2] Ibid., loc. cit.
[4] Ibid., p. 56.
[6] Ibid., *passim.*
[8] *Rotuli Grav.*, p. 213.
[10] Ibid., p. 475 and *passim.*
[12] Ibid., p. 325.
[14] *Mon. Franc.* i. 133.
[16] *Rotuli Gros.*, p. 300.

of Marsh's letters he calls him Marsh's secretary though it is perhaps rather early to use this term in any but a general sense.[1]

QUENTIN, QUINTIN, QUANTYN, PHILIP, witnesses as a clerk from the first to the third year but is not found thereafter.[2] He was instituted to Buckminster (Leics.) on presentation of the Prior of the Order of Jerusalem,[3] but had been succeeded there before the end of the third year.[4] No cause for the vacancy is given but it may have been on his death or entry into religion.

RAVENINGHAM, ROGER OF, *magister*, was with Grosseteste probably in October 1235 and certainly in his second year[5] and was evidently regarded as one of the most able clerks, for he was sent on such delicate missions as the negotiations with the legate about a clerk whom the latter had excommunicated and whom Grosseteste had absolved:[6] and the negotiations with the king about the disputed presentation to the prebend of Thame.[7] He became a canon at some date between 7 August and 5 November 1237[8] and may have held the prebend of Sutton cum Buckingham.[9]

He is said to have succeeded William of Arundel as Archdeacon of Huntingdon in 1246–7 and there is no doubt that the office was held by one whose initial was R.,[10] who presumably received it after T., to whom Grosseteste had offered it, had refused.[11] Canon Foster in a note on the archdeacons of Huntingdon says that although Roger occurs from 1246–7 to his death shortly before 24 September 1276 it is doubtful whether he held office all the time.[12] He does not give his reason for this view, but it is probably based on the occurrence of Roger in several witness lists in 1250–1 without the title of archdeacon and in one list of Lexington's time when both the archdeacons of Stow and Leicester are given their titles.[13] An examination of the original roll for Huntingdon archdeaconry seems to settle the question and to show that R. the archdeacon was not Roger of Raveningham in 1249. Master Roger of Raveningham was instituted to Warboys Church on the presentation of the Abbot and convent of Ramsey, after an inquisition had been made by R. the archdeacon, and to R. the archdeacon the induction mandate was addressed.[14] Evidently these

[1] A. G. Little, *The Grey Friars in Oxford* (O.H.S. xx), p. 188.
[2] *Rotuli Gros., passim*.   [3] Ibid., p. 394.
[4] Ibid., p. 399.   [5] Ibid., pp. 392, 137.
[6] *Ep.* 76.   [7] *Reg. Ant.* i, no. 242.
[8] *Rotuli Gros.*, pp. 24, 257.
[9] Muniments of the Dean and chapter of Lincoln, A/2/6, Registrum Magnum, no. 696 (as yet unpublished).   [10] *Rotuli Gros.*, pp. 290 ff.
[11] *Ep.* 118.   [12] *Reg. Ant.* iii, no. 846.
[13] *Rotuli Gros.*, pp. 118, 247: in an inquisition made by him and Master Leonard of Dunwich he is not given the title, ibid., p. 244; *Reg. Ant.* ii, no. 387.
[14] *Rotuli Gros.*, p. 297. The printed text reduces the sentence to 'etc.' and omits the reference to the archdeacon.

are two different persons, though who R. was I am unable to say. Roger apparently obtained the office between 14 October 1255, for he is still 'master Roger' in letters close of that date and 5 June 1256 when he is given the title of Archdeacon of Huntingdon.[1]

He occurs in the Ramsey cartulary as archdeacon in 1256[2] and there are two titles of bulls of Alexander IV against Roger the archdeacon, Berengar le Moigne, and Thomas de Beyvile.[3] Both the latter held land in Wood Walton where the abbey was also a proprietor. In 1259 Roger had a dispensation to hold one benefice in addition to those he already had and on resigning one to accept another.[4] On the death of John of Crakehall, in 1260, Ramsey Abbey presented him to Shillington (Beds.).[5] At the time of his death he also held Great Catworth (Hunts.)[6] in the patronage of the Bekering family and Yaxley (Hunts.) of the patronage of Thorney Abbey.[7] For neither of the last two is the date of his institution known. He had also had Burton Coggles (Lincs.) but had resigned in favour of Master Roger of Raveningham the younger in 1268.[8]

RESTON (RISTON), JOHN OF. It is probable that this man was the clerk of Thomas Wallensis, Archdeacon of Lincoln, for a John of Reston so described made the inquisition before the institution of Ralf son of Simon of Ormsby to Ruckland in 1247–8.[9] He had performed the same duty for the vicar of Grantham Australis prebend in the previous year.[10] He does not seem to have been the official of the archdeaconry for when a mandate to the latter is mentioned he is often, though not habitually, called *magister*.[11]

On 26 July 1248 Thomas Wallensis was consecrated Bishop of St. Davids and it seems that his clerk then entered Grosseteste's service for he is found witnessing from 1249 onwards.[12] He seems later to have been in Lexington's household and he may also have been in Gravesend's as he was present with him at Elsham on 2 May 1265.[13]

He held Ewerby Rectory in the gift of Kyme Priory and record of his institution was made in Grosseteste's seventh year and again in the ninth year, though letters of institution were not issued until 13 October 1244.[14] As rector of Ewerby he had a papal indult to hold another benefice with

---

[1] *Close Rolls, 1254–6*, pp. 228, 313. There are a number of earlier letters close referring to him without the title.

[2] *Cartularium monasterii de Rameseia*, ed. W. H. Hart (R.S.), i. 204.

[3] Ibid. i. 69–70. [4] *C. Pap. R.* i. 363.

[5] *Rotuli Grav.*, p. 190. [6] Ibid., p. 182.

[7] Ibid. [8] Ibid., p. 29.

[9] *Rotuli Gros.*, p. 93. [10] Ibid., pp. 89–90.

[11] Ibid., e.g. pp. 40–42, 103 with title of *magister*; pp. 42–44 without title.

[12] Ibid., pp. 118, 243, 247, &c.

[13] *Rolls and Register of Bishop Oliver Sutton*, ed. R. M. T. Hill (Lincoln Record Society), xxxix. 69; *Rotuli Grav.*, pp. 105, 240.

[14] *Rotuli Gros.*, pp. 65, 72, 78–79.

cure of souls in July 1247.[1] In 1249–50 he had St. Peter's Stamford *in commendam* of the gift of St. Fromund's Priory with letters dated 27 February 1250,[2] and in 1251–2 on the death of Robert of Graveley, canon of Lincoln, he received Wainfleet St. Mary rectory on presentation of the Prioress and convent of Stixwould.[3] All these he held until his death shortly before 17 May 1281.[4] It is not certain that he is to be identified with the John de Reston, clerk, who had letters of institution to Skellingthorpe in 1237.[5] In the note of institution the incumbent (incorrectly given in the printed text as of Biston) is described as deacon, while the rector of Ewerby was described as subdeacon on p. 65 and as clerk on pp. 72 and 99. On the other hand, Skellingthorpe had been vacated by an unnamed clerk just before our John of Reston was instituted to Ewerby,[6] and it must be admitted that the scribe does at times make some errors, so that it would be impossible to assert that he could not have made an error as between deacon and subdeacon in the one case or the other, though a point of this kind was one of importance and therefore one in which a mistake might be noted and corrected.

John of Reston acted as proctor for the Prior and convent of St. Fromund, who had lands and patronage in the diocese, in 1268, 1269 (when he took the opportunity of presenting a kinsman or connexion to St. Paul, Stamford), and 1273.[7] He was himself the patron of Newton by Toft to which he presented William of Kibworth in 1247–8, Robert of Manby on the death of William in 1262–3, and Bartholomew of Bucknall in 1279:[8] on the last occasion he had had a suit against William Modkan to establish his right.

It was probably this John of Reston who on 6 October 1280 gave his houses in the Bail of Lincoln to the Fabric Fund of the cathedral for the benefit of his soul and that of his parents.[9]

RICHARD the bishop's chaplain who witnesses at Liddington on 30 September 1235[10] was also a canon and therefore cannot be identified with Richard of Pocklington. He might be Richard of Wisbech who witnesses as chaplain and canon on another occasion in the first year.[11]

RICHARD THE NORMAN, *magister*, witnesses four times between August 1239[12] and October 1240.[13]

[1] *C. Pap. R.* i. 249.   [2] *Rotuli Gros.*, pp. 117–18.
[3] Ibid., p. 128.   [4] *The Rolls and Register of Bishop Oliver Sutton*, pp. 13, 91.
[5] *Rotuli Gros.*, pp. 16, 24.   [6] Ibid., p. 64.
[7] *Rotuli Grav.*, pp. 27, 36, 54.
[8] *Rotuli Gros.*, p. 102; *Rotuli Grav.*, pp. 12, 84.
[9] Muniments of the Dean and chapter of Lincoln, Dij/77/3/54.
[10] *Rotuli Gros.*, p. 389.   [11] Ibid., p. 448.
[12] Ibid., p. 466.   [13] Ibid., p. 143.

Roger the bishop's steward is referred to by Adam Marsh in a letter to Grosseteste as having gone in company with the writer and John of Crakehall to compose a difference between the men of Oxford and those of the Earl of Cornwall.[1] He succeeded John of Crakehall about 1251.

St. Giles, John of, has been confused with the Dominican of the same name, but their identities were separated by Mr. Russell.[2] He witnesses as canon charters of Grosseteste from 1237 to 1240.[3] He evidently held Banbury as his prebend, for he was rector of the church in 1235–6,[4] but before 10 December 1238 had been given Leighton Buzzard, which was so well endowed as to be known as the golden prebend.[5] He appealed to Rome concerning his rights in this and a settlement was reached in 1242 concerning the chapel of Grove within the bounds of the prebend, which belonged to the nuns of Fontevrault. He became Archdeacon of Oxford in 1240 and continued in office until succeeded by Robert Marsh in 1249–50.[6] His health had been the subject of anxious comment in letters of Adam Marsh to Grosseteste.[7] He was involved in a dispute with Dunstable Priory about tithes at Gledly and also about a tunic of St. Hugh, of which Dunstable ultimately kept the sleeve and restored the rest.[8]

The possibility of his identity with John of Banbury is noted above, p. 221.

Southwell (Sywelle, Siwell, Suthewelle or Suwell, Notts), William of, *magister*, is probably the clerk who as a subdeacon was instituted to Blaby, on the presentation of the Abbot and convent of Leicester, in December 1235.[9] As Master William he witnesses acts of Grosseteste during 1250 and 1251[10] and held the prebend of Asgarby by 1256.[11] He is probably to be identified with the Master William de Sewelle, who with Nicholas Grecus was named as being one of the canons who were refusing to contribute to the expenses of the chapter in preserving their rights and liberties,[12] but Canon Foster's identification of him with the vicar of Timberland instituted in 1233–4 seems less likely, since the latter is described as 'chaplain', which implies priest's orders.[13]

In 1260 he was the bishop's official[14] and in 1267 he presented a vicar to his prebendal church.[15] The next entry concerning it is not until 1289,

[1] *Mon. Franc.*, p. 105.
[2] *Dictionary of Writers*, pp. 73–75.
[3] *Rotuli Gros.*, pp. 24, 26, 184, &c.
[4] Ibid., p. 447.
[5] *Reg. Ant.* ii, no. 648.
[6] *Rotuli Gros.*, pp. 468–96.
[7] *Mon. Franc.* i. 132–3, 172.
[8] *Ann. Mon.* iii. 155.
[9] *Rotuli Gros.*, pp. 386, 388–9.
[10] Ibid., pp. 118 (*ter*), 127, 247–8, 382, 500. He was already a canon by this time.
[11] *Reg. Ant.* ii. 4, no. 498.
[12] Ibid. i, no. 282.
[13] Ibid., ii, no. 498, note.
[14] *Rotuli Grav.*, p. 4.
[15] Ibid., p. 26.

by which time he had been succeeded by Richard of Rothwell as prebendary.[1]

STAMFORD, PETER OF, is a frequent witness from at least November 1240
to June 1251 and may have been with Grosseteste to the end.[2] He does not
seem to have had the title *magister* and therefore is more probably to be
identified with the rector of Little Casterton, Rutland, who died in 1263
and who held Denton, Hunts., *in commendam*,[3] rather than with Master
Peter of Stamford who was rector of St. Paul, Stamford,[4] and resigned it in
May 1269.[5] It may be Grosseteste's clerk who was warden of Lutterworth
Hospital, as he is not described as master in the record of institution:[6]
on the other hand this Peter is called chaplain, which implies priest's
orders, and many of the group who witness as clerks were no more than subdeacons or deacons. Adam Marsh recommended the warden of Lutterworth
as the presentee to Sulby though there is no record of institution at that
time.[7] Possibly this Peter of Stamford was a third of that name. Grosseteste's clerk seems to have passed into the service of Lexington.[8]

STOKES, JOHN DE, *magister*. He probably obtained the degree of master
during Grosseteste's episcopate, as he was instituted to Offley as a subdeacon without the title, letters of institution being dated 19 May 1239,[9]
but he presented John of Shrivenham to the vicarage of the church in
1249–50 as *magister* John de Stokes.[10] The date of his death or resignation
does not appear, as the next entry concerning this living is the death of
John Shrivenham in 1277, by which time Henry de Malolacu was rector.[11]
He is probably to be identified with the Master John de Stok who was
admitted to Twyford (Bucks.), 27 December 1241,[12] and to an unnamed
parish in the archdeaconry of Lincoln in the patronage of Beauport Abbey,[13]
but not with the man of the same name instituted to the vicarage of
Steeping on presentation of Bardney Abbey in 1250–1.[14] He witnesses
from 1241 to 1249 and is sometimes designated master, sometimes not:[15]
the description in the lists at this date is erratic and since some known
masters are not given the title in some acts there is no certainty from these
lists of the date at which he obtained the degree.

TESSUN, NICHOLAS, *magister*, witnesses from the fifth to the tenth years
but does not appear to have held preferment in the diocese.[16] He held,

[1] *The Rolls and Register of Bishop Oliver Sutton*, ed. R. M. T. Hill (Lincoln Record
Society), i. 126.

[2] *Rotuli Gros.*, pp. 55, 500, and *passim*.   [3] *Rotuli Grav.*, pp. 103, 167.

[4] *Rotuli Gros.*, p. 74.   [5] *Rotuli Grav.*, p. 36.

[6] *Rotuli Gros.*, p. 419.   [7] *Mon. Franc.* i. 173, 254.

[8] *Rolls and Register of Bishop Oliver Sutton*, ed. R. M. T. Hill, i. 69.

[9] *Rotuli Gros.*, pp. 263, 267.   [10] Ibid., p. 297.   [11] *Rotuli Grav.*, p. 185.

[12] *Rotuli Gros.*, p. 359. There is no record of his death or resignation.

[13] Ibid., p. 106.   [14] Ibid., p. 123.

[15] Ibid., pp. 65, 111, 222, 319, 417, 475, 479.   [16] Ibid., *passim*.

however, the prebend of Blewbury in the church of Salisbury, where he was apparently in residence on 7 March 1247,[1] and bought a plot of land with buildings in the Close from Solomon, vicar of Salisbury.[2] He evidently had family connexions with the diocese of Salisbury, as Master Henry Tessun had been a canon there as early as 1222[3] and was holding the prebend of Bedminster in 1243,[4] which he retained after he became Archdeacon of Bath,[5] a preferment in which Nicholas Tessun afterwards succeeded him.[6] Nicholas witnessed a grant of Master Roger de Burwardiscote about 1267.[7]

THOMAS THE ALMONER (*elemosinarius*) witnesses two institutions: that of Adam of Dorchester to Rearsby 31 September 1235,[8] and that of Robert of Somercotes to Sibsey 1236–7.[9] He is certainly not identical with Thomas of Ashby who also witnesses the first of these, but he might be identical with Thomas of Aylesbury (q.v.) or with Thomas de Exl' (q.v.).

THOMAS WALLENSIS, *magister*, witnessed a few charters in the first, second, and third years of the episcopate as a canon.[10] In 1238 he became Archdeacon of Lincoln and his activities can be traced through the Lincoln Roll[11] until he was consecrated Bishop of St. Davids on 26 July 1248.

W., canon of Waltham, chaplain of the bishop, witnesses one charter 22 September 1249.[12]

WESEHAM, GERARD DE, *magister*, seems to have entered the household in 1241 and to have continued throughout the pontificate.[13] He was Grosseteste's envoy to the king during the bishop's struggle with the Prior and convent of Canterbury.[14] He held the vicarage of Long Sutton and the rectory of Fleet (Lincs.), both of which were in the gift of the monks of Castle Acre.[15] There is no trace of the date of the institution of his successors in either case. He took his name from Weasenham in Norfolk and probably came into Grosseteste's service through Master Roger de Weseham. He became a canon at some date between 9 November 1244 and 14 September 1246, but it is not known what prebend he held.[16]

[1] *Sarum Charters and Documents*, ed. W. H. Rich Jones (R.S.), p. 314.

[2] Ibid., p. 354. See also Kathleen Edwards, 'The Houses in Salisbury Close in the Fourteenth Century', *Journal of the British Archaeological Association*, 3rd series, iv. 84.

[3] *The Register of St. Osmund*, ed. W. H. Rich Jones, i. 339.

[4] *Sarum Charters*, p. 287.   [5] Ibid., p. 244.

[6] *Calendar of the MSS. of the Dean and Chapter of Wells*, i. 79.

[7] *The Medieval Archives of Christ Church, Oxford*, ed. N. Denholm Young, p. 33. I owe these last two references to Mr. A. B. Emden.

[8] *Rotuli Gros.*, p. 389.   [9] Ibid., p. 165.

[10] Ibid., pp. 392 (21 Oct. 1235) and 165, 252, 343, 291–2.

[11] Ibid., pp. 22–86.   [12] Ibid., p. 435.

[13] Ibid., *passim*.   [14] *C.P.R. 1232–47*, pp. 404.

[15] *Rotuli Gros.*, pp. 75, 79: papal dispensation granted in Feb. 1243, *C. Pap. R.* i. 204.

[16] *Rotuli Gros.*, pp. 289, 92.

WISBECH, RICHARD OF, was a canon and in priest's orders at least as early as 1 April 1236, when he witnessed in chapter in Lincoln.[1] He was with Grosseteste on various occasions in the first two years of the pontificate,[2] but seems to have gone into residence at Lincoln shortly afterwards and is found witnessing a number of transactions relating to chapter property.[3] He bought land at Fillingham c. 1240–50.[4] He seems twice to have been at the papal court, once in connexion with litigation over the prebend of Sutton in 1245[5] and again in 1251 when the Archbishop of York certified the contents of some documents of Hugh II which the chapter did not wish to send in the original to the papal court. The certificate is endorsed *Domino Ricardo de Wysebech uel magistro R . . . . . . de Glo'*,[6] which suggests that he was to produce it in the Curia. He has not so far been found later than the period 1253–8.

WORTHAM, WILLIAM DE, had letters of protection with the clause *volumus* on going abroad with the Bishop of Lincoln. These were to continue so long as he was there or with Simon de Montfort, on 7 March 1250. He is not described as clerk and may have been a layman.[7]

WROXTAN, R. DE, witnesses one letter of institution in 1244–5 and another on 22 September 1249.[8]

WYCOMBE, GILBERT OF, witnesses among the chaplains in 1246 and 1247.[9] He is probably to be identified with the Gilbert of Wycombe instituted to Kettlethorpe Rectory (Lincs.) in Grosseteste's sixth year.[10]

YAXHAM (Jakesham, Norfolk), ROGER OF, *magister*. The collation of Wold Newton to him while Grosseteste was still bishop elect is the first entry on the Lincoln archdeaconry roll.[11] He was with the bishop at Liddington on 30 September 1235.[12] Twice, on 3 September and on 27 November 1236, he was the datary of letters of institution.[13] When a division is made in the witness lists between the chaplains and the clerks, he is usually found with the former. He is not found after August 1237,[14] and since Thomas Sutton was instituted to Wold Newton on the presentation of the king in 1237–8 it seems probable that Master Roger had died or retired into religion.[15]

[1] *Rotuli Gros.*, pp. 163, 391.
[2] Ibid., pp. 165, 252, 343, 448, 452.
[3] *Reg. Ant.* iv, nos. 1216–17, 1220, 1228, 1231; v, no. 1461.
[4] Ibid. iv, no. 1215.   [5] *C. Pap. R.* i. 221.
[6] *Reg. Ant.* ii, no. 357.   [7] *C.P.R., 1247–58*, p. 61.
[8] *Rotuli Gros.*, pp. 221, 336.
[9] Ibid., pp. 92–93, 229, 293, 328, 428.
[10] Ibid., p. 142.   [11] Ibid., p. 1.
[12] Ibid., p. 389.   [13] Ibid., pp. 252, 343, 138.
[14] Ibid., pp. 24, 257.   [15] Ibid., p. 21.

Non-clerical servants of Grosseteste

BAINCTON, ALAN OF, was constable of Banbury Castle.[1]

BELISTON, GILBERT OF, was constable of Newark Castle.[2]

LINCOLN, WILLIAM OF, the marshal (*marescallus*), was referred to by Adam Marsh in terms of high praise.[3]

JENEVE, W. DE, was a messenger (*nuntius*) mentioned by Adam Marsh.[4]

JOHN, reeve of Buckden, was mentioned by Adam Marsh who wrote to John of Crakehall on his behalf.[5]

WILLIAM the bailiff of Buckden was a kinsman (*germanus*) of Adam Marsh, who asked John of Crakehall to discharge him from his duties on account of the state of his health.[6]

KATHLEEN MAJOR.

APPENDIX II

The Attempted Canonization of Robert Grosseteste

THE instinct to venerate departed heroes of the faith showed itself very early in Christian history. When Polycarp, Bishop of Smyrna, was put to death in A.D. 156 his bereaved flock collected his remains and laid them in a suitable place where, as they wrote to the Christian world, 'the Lord will permit us to gather ourselves together, as we are able, in gladness and joy, and to celebrate the birth-day of his martyrdom for the commemoration of those that have already fought in the contest, and for the training and preparation of those that shall do so hereafter'.[7] In subsequent centuries the cult of the martyrs and of those who, though not suffering death for the faith, had yet been conspicuous examples of heroic virtue, assumed an increasingly large place in popular devotion. Pilgrimages were made to the tombs of such persons, their relics were eagerly sought after, and many tales were collected of the miracles wrought by their intercession. The evidence of the miracles in particular was regarded as

---

[1] Ibid., p. 448.
[2] Ibid., p. 135.
[3] *Mon. Franc.* i. 137–8.
[4] Ibid., p. 137.
[5] Ibid., p. 253.
[6] Ibid., p. 252.
[7] *Martyrium Polycarpi*, ch. xviii, trans. J. B. Lightfoot. *The Apostolic Fathers* (1926), p. 209.

demonstrating that they now occupied a privileged state in heaven and could laudably be invoked in the public worship of the Church on earth. These developments were not ignored by the ecclesiastical hierarchy. They afforded a means of focusing the popular mind upon the realities of the world beyond the grave, there was no doubt that the example of the saints inspired virtue in many who were otherwise little touched by the preaching of the Gospel, and the shrines and pilgrimage sites were a welcome source of very considerable revenue. The devotion, however, needed some regulation. There were occasions when persons of very unedifying life were discovered to have become the object of veneration, and there were several unfortunate incidents when more than one community claimed to possess the body of the same saint. From time to time bishops and councils had to intervene to check abuses of this kind, and also to give their special approval to the cult of persons whom they regarded as particularly worthy of veneration. There thus came into being the practice of asking authority for the formal canonization of a saint.

For some time people were content with the approval of their own bishop, or of the provincial council, but gradually they began to appeal to higher and higher authorities until at last the Pope himself was brought in, and having come in, eventually claimed and established an exclusive right of canonization. There are two important dates in this process—the years 1234 and 1634. The first of these, which is the year of the publication of that part of the *Corpus Iuris Canonici* which is known as the Decretals of Gregory IX, marks the climax of a steady growth of opinion in the Western Church that the Pope alone had the right of sanctioning the veneration of any new saint. 'This belief was shared and expressed by the two great lawyer popes, Alexander III and Innocent III, so that after their time there could be no going back, and the lawyers, faced with this situation, found in a letter of Alexander III a text which in their eyes came to be the formal reservation of this right to the papacy.'[1] This text is enshrined in the Decretals of Gregory IX.[2]

This papal reservation of the right of canonization was not, however, at once completely effective. People continued, often with ecclesiastical approval, to venerate their own local saints without always having recourse to Rome for canonization. The papal court was apt to be slow and the expenses of a process in it very considerable. The veneration of unofficial saints had, however, reached such proportions by the end of the sixteenth century that the papal court decided that these abuses must be checked. At length, on 5 July 1634, Urban VIII issued the brief *Caelestis Hierusalem Cives* by which he forbade in the strictest possible terms any form of public veneration of persons who had not been canonized or beatified by

[1] E. W. Kemp, *Canonization and Authority in the Western Church* (1948), p. 106.
[2] C. 1, X. iii. 45.

the Holy See and also prohibited the publication of books recording the miracles and revelations of such persons unless they had been examined and approved by the ordinary and sent by him to the apostolic see.[1]

It will be seen that Robert Grosseteste died at a time when papal canonization had first been established but had not yet driven off the field all local rivals. In the opening years of the thirteenth century four English saints had been canonized by the Pope[2] and two contemporaries of Grosseteste, Edmund Rich and Richard Wych, were to be so canonized before the end of the century. At least three other thirteenth-century Englishmen are reputed to have wrought miracles and been the object of veneration without being canonized.[3]

The chronicles of the time suggest that the veneration of Grosseteste began almost immediately upon his death. Matthew Paris gives the bishop's last discourses, describes the wonders attendant on his death, and has no hesitation about referring to him as 'sanctus Lincolniensis episcopus Robertus secundus'.[4] At the end of 1253 he notes that miracles daily increased in the church of Lincoln, for the works of God performed through Bishop Robert had stirred up the other two saints, Remigius and Hugh, to bestow benefits upon the faithful.[5] Later, under the year 1255, he has more to say on this subject and suggests that the miracles attest the truth of the story that in a night-time vision a voice was heard to say of Grosseteste and Edmund Rich: 'Dilexit Dominus Edmundum in odorem benignitatis, et dilexit Dominus Robertum in odorem fidelitatis.' Paris comments: 'Et datum est in spiritu hoc cognoscere, ut intelligeret haec dicta de beatis Edmundo et Roberto episcopis et confessoribus fuisse.'[6] A few pages later Grosseteste's miracles are set side by side with those of Richard of Chichester.[7]

Other monastic annalists also noted Grosseteste's sanctity and miracles in their account of the year 1255. The Annals of Burton contain, between notices of the death of Archbishop Gray of York and of the capture of an eight-foot-long sturgeon in the Trent, the note: 'Isto anno Sanctus Robertus Lincolniensis episcopus claruit miraculis.'[8] The same annalist, after describing the murder of Little St. Hugh and the burial of the child's body near the tomb of Grosseteste, tells how in that same year the king's brother, Richard of Cornwall, came on pilgrimage to the tomb of 'St. Robert' at Lincoln.[9] The Annals of Tewkesbury, under the year 1257,

[1] C. Cocquelines, *Bullarum Romanorum Pontificum Amplissima Collectio* (1756), v, part v, pp. 318 ff.
[2] Gilbert of Sempringham, 1202; Wulstan of Worcester, 1203; Hugh of Lincoln, 1220; William of York, 1226.
[3] Walter Suffield, Bishop of Norwich; William Button II, Bishop of Bath and Wells; Thomas de la Hale of Dover. Cf. Kemp, op. cit., pp. 117, 118, 123.
[4] *Chron. Mai.* v. 407.
[5] Ibid., p. 419.
[6] Ibid., p. 490.
[7] Ibid., p. 496.
[8] Annals of Burton in *Ann. Mon.* i. 336.
[9] Ibid., p. 344.

contain the statement that 'The lord Robert Grosseteste formerly Bishop of Lincoln, was, on account of manifest prodigies of miracles, canonized at Rome.'[1] That, however, is another story.

The evidence of documents preserved at Lincoln shows that not long after the bishop's death Nicholas Grecus,[2] one of Grosseteste's *familia*, was sent to Rome with the first request for canonization. As the Pope with whom he dealt was Alexander IV the date of his visit must have been between 25 December 1254 and 25 May 1261. The papal Curia did not as a rule act hastily or even speedily in such matters and Nicholas received the reply that the Pope required time for consideration.[3] It is possible that this may have been a polite refusal as the more usual step was to issue a commission of investigation if sufficient prima facie evidence was forthcoming with the original petition.[4] However this may have been no further move was made for some twenty-five years.

Soon after Oliver Sutton had become Bishop of Lincoln in 1280 Canon Simon de Worth was sent to Rome with a further request for Grosseteste's canonization. He brought back the reply that before any commission of inquiry could be issued the suffrages of many more people must be obtained. During the autumn and winter of 1286-7 the Bishop, Dean, and chapter of Lincoln collected some twenty-eight letters in support of their petition.[5] Although the correspondents include the Archbishop of York, and the Bishops of Durham, Worcester, Ely, Hereford, and St. Davids, they are not as a whole very impressive. The twelve letters from religious houses[6] all come from the diocese and most of them from Lincolnshire itself, and apart from Edmund of Cornwall the lay correspondents[7]

---

[1] Annals of Tewkesbury in *Ann. Mon.* i. 159.

[2] Cf. above, Callus, p. 40; Major, p. 229.

[3] These facts are given in Bishop Oliver Sutton's letter of April 1288 contained in the document referred to in note 5.

[4] On the early process of canonization see R. Foreville, *Un Procès de canonisation à l'aube du XIIIᵉ siècle (1201-1202): Le livre de saint Gilbert de Sempringham* (1943), and M. R. Toynbee, *St. Louis of Toulouse and the Process of Canonization in the Fourteenth Century* (1929).

[5] These letters are to be found on a roll preserved in the Lincoln Cathedral Muniment Room, Press D, 1, 20, Box 2a. Cf. R. E. G. Cole in the *Associated Architectural Societies' Reports and Papers*, xxxiii, for 1915, pp. 1–34. The letter of the Archbishop of York dated 6 Jan. 1286 must be 6 Jan. 1286-7, which would bring it into the same period as the other letters. The archbishop was not consecrated until Feb. 1286. The date of John de Kirkby's letter is wrongly given by Canon Cole and should be *vi Non. maii*.

[6] The Benedictine abbeys of Peterborough and Bardney; the Cistercian abbeys of Revesby and Louth Park; the Premonstratensian abbeys of Newhouse and Hagneby; the Augustinian abbeys of Wellow, Thornton, Oseney, St. James Northampton; the Augustinian priory of Markby, and a joint letter from the Augustinian priories of Thornholm, Elsham, Torksey, Nocton, and Kyme.

[7] Robert de Tatersale; Edmund, Lord Deyncourt of Blankney; Thomas de Multon; Philip de Kyme; Robert de Cadworth, sheriff of Lincolnshire, and twelve knights—a letter given in the county court at Lincoln; William de Cressy and William de Bratoft,

are not particularly distinguished. It is surprising that there should be no letter from Archbishop Pecham or the University of Oxford and that the Franciscans, other than the Greyfriars of Lincoln who wrote in 1289, should have been so little active.

On 5 March 1286–7 Canon Stephen Tawell was appointed proctor for the dean and chapter and armed with the twenty-eight letters mentioned above and two covering letters from Bishop Sutton and from the dean and chapter set out for Rome, probably in the summer of 1288.[1] There he presented his letters to two cardinals who had been commissioned to inquire into the truth of the reports of Grosseteste's sanctity. An official copy of the letters, dated 25 May 1289, was made by two Italian notaries public, and four months later three further letters, from King Edward I, the Dean and chapter of Lincoln, and the Greyfriars and Blackfriars of Lincoln were added to them. What happened next we do not know, other than that the case was not successful, and we have no further information until 1307.

Early in that year Bishop Dalderby, who had succeeded Oliver Sutton in 1300, set himself to collect the support of King Edward and Queen Margaret for a new petition for Grosseteste's canonization. Drafts survive of letters which he wrote to various friends in the royal household asking them to use their influence with the king and queen in this matter. About the same time the subdean and chapter of Lincoln tried to enlist the support of the Chancellor and masters-regent and non-regent of the University of Oxford, and the Master and seniors of the Order of Sempringham wrote to the Pope.[2] The proctor for the chapter was now Canon Robert de Killingworth and, by an ordinance of 10 May 1307, he being about to set out for the apostolic see was allowed to count his residence as if personally present during the time that he was prosecuting the canonization of blessed Robert.[3] Again our information breaks off and the last reference we have to these events is in John de Schalby's *Lives of the Bishops of Lincoln*, completed about 1330. He says that the dean and chapter wrote repeatedly to the Apostolic See, supporting their plea with letters from the magnates of the realm both clerical and lay, and with testimony to the many miracles wrought by Grosseteste's merits and an account of his holy life, but why they were unsuccessful God knows—'in nullo, ante confectionem praesentis tractatus, qua de causa Deus novit, proficere potuerunt'.[4] Grosseteste's unsparing criticism of the papal

knights, with the knowledge and testimony of the whole township of Bratoft; William de Vescy, Justice of the Forest, William de Welles and William de Wylgelm or Willingham, knights; the mayor and citizens of Lincoln; the mayor and burghers of Grimsby.

[1] Sutton's letter is dated 23 April and the chapter's 2 May.
[2] These drafts are all in Muniment Room, Press D, 1, 20, Box 2a.
[3] *Registrum Capituli* 1305–13. Lincoln Cathedral Muniment Room A 2/22.
[4] *Works of Gir. Cam.* vii. 206.

Curia and the comparative lack of interest shown in his sanctity outside Lincolnshire are probable explanations of the failure.

The lack of a papal canonization did not, however, prevent people from speaking of him as *beatus* or even *sanctus Robertus*. Oliver Sutton on the occasion of the proceedings about the confirmation of the election of Roger de Wesenham as Chancellor of Oxford in February 1295 referred to 'beatus Robertus quondam Lincolniensis episcopus qui huiusmodi officium gessit';[1] and in the same year an ordinance of that bishop, providing for the establishment of an obit for himself, puts side by side the 'custos capitis feretri beati Hugonis' and the 'custos tumbe beati Roberti'.[2] In October 1314 Bishop Dalderby granted forty days' indulgence to all who should visit the shrine of St. Robert.[3] Six years later the offerings at all the Lincoln shrines had so much diminished that the chapter was compelled to revise the distribution of the money. In their decree, St. Hugh, Grosseteste, and John Dalderby (who since his death in 1320 had had a silver shrine in the south-west transept) are all called *beatus*. St. Hugh, of course, had two feasts of his own, and it was ordered that the distributions of offerings at his shrines should be made on the feast of his translation, 6 October. Grosseteste's distributions were to be on St. Pelagia's day, 8 October, which was the anniversary of his death, and the dawn mass on that day was to be a *missa de reliquiis*.[4] As the general feast of relics at Lincoln was on 14 July this must have been a special commemoration of Grosseteste by a liturgical office which was neither the ordinary requiem mass nor the proper of a confessor bishop—a compromise between law and devotion which has its parallels elsewhere.[5]

ERIC W. KEMP.

APPENDIX III

The Tomb of Robert Grosseteste with an Account of its Opening in 1782

IN his *Itinerary* (ed. Toulmin Smith, v. 122) Leland noted that Grosseteste 'lyethe in the hygheste southe isle with a goodly tumbe of marble and an image of brasse over it'. Sanderson recorded in his Survey (1641): 'In the south end of the isle going into the revestrie, is an antient tomb called Grosthead's. At the feet a chapel, made south to another of the

[1] *Snappe's Formulary* (O.H.S. lxxx), 52.
[2] *Reg. Ant.* ii. 305.
[3] *Assoc. Arch. Society Reports*, xxxiii. 245.
[4] Bradshaw and Wordsworth, *Lincoln Cathedral Statutes, The Black Book*, pp. 335 ff.
[5] Cf. Kemp, op. cit., chap. vi.

same fashion; both semi-circular.' Thomas Sympson made a copy of Sanderson's Survey 'with an account of some monuments erected since' in 1735, and adds at the end of the reference to the tomb that 'there was formerly his effigy in brass' (Notebook in possession of J. W. F. Hill). When John Loveday made his tour in 1732, he recorded that the tomb 'is much ruinated' (*Diary of a Tour in 1732*, Roxburghe Club, 1890, p. 206).

Richard Gough says, 'it appears to have been an altar tomb, with a border of foliage round the table, which was supported by circular pillars at the corners, but now lies broken and disordered on the floor'; and he gives a plate. He continues:

> After the bishop had rested in his grave exactly 529 years and one month, the hand of inquisitive curiosity (*absit invidia sacrilegii*) availing itself of the new paving of the cathedral, and the friendship of the present Praecentor, exposed his venerable remains to view.

He then describes the contents of the coffin, and goes on:

> After a careful examination by the Precentor, Mr. Sympson, Mr. Bradley, the organist, and one or two more members of the church, these respectable remains were carefully covered up again, and as the surface of the coffin is considerably below the level of the new pavement it may be presumed they will rest undisturbed to the end of time. . . .

And by way of postscript:

> These remains could not however escape the penetration of the President of the Royal Society, to gratify which they were again opened about a month after their first uncovering. Sir Joseph Banks took out a small portion of the liquor in which the body was originally laid. (*Sepulchral Monuments in Great Britain* (1786), i. 47–48.)

There is a copy of Sir Joseph Banks's account of this second opening of the tomb among the Dawson Turner Transcripts of his letters at the British Museum (Natural History) (*Sir Joseph Banks' Correspondence*, ii. 234–40). As this seems not to have been published it is here printed in full.

SIR JOSEPH BANKS' CORRESPONDENCE
MS. Vol. II, 1781–1783, pp. 234–40

Dawson Turner transcripts, British Museum (Natural History)

Lincoln, 1782

Grosthead

Being at Lincoln Races in the year 1782, I heard that, the week before, at the instigation of a celebrated antiquary[1] who visited that place, the

---

[1] R. Gough Esq., Director of the Society of Antiquaries (note from MS.).

Tomb of Bishop Grosthead had been opened, and his Ring and Pastoral Staff found in it.

I felt some disapointment at having missed a sight so extraordinary; the Bishop who, in his lifetime, was eminent for learning and piety, highly respected by the Clergy of his times, and at his death enjoyed the Chancelership of the University of Oxford as well as the Bishoprick of Lincoln, was likely to have been interred with all the expense and magnificence of the age he lived in, and he had been buried about 500 years; so that the remains, if any there were, of customs so antient, and the preservation in which those remains might appear after such a lapse of time, promised much gratification to antiquarian curiosity.

My Friend, the Precentor,[1] on being applied to, readily granted the indulgence of a second inspection, which, as the Bishop's remains were left untouched, promised every advantage the first; and I determined, as it had not been done before, to employ a draughtsman to delinate [sic] whatever might be found worthy of remembrance.

Robert Grosthead, consecrated Bishop of Lincoln in 1235, was also chancelor of Oxford, he was excommunicated by Pope Innocent 6th;[2] but, trusting to his purity of manners, his learning which was very extensive and the reverence with which he was regarded by his diocese, he continued his function of Bishop to his death, which happened on the third day of October 1253, in the 75th year of his age.

The dean & chapter of Oxford[3] petitioned Pope Clement the 5 to canonise him as a Saint, alledging as a reason, many miracles said to have happened at his death, but were refused.

A piece of Blue Marble of an oblong square, wrought round the edges with a slight foliage, laying upon the pavement in * * *[3] was traditionally held as the place of his interment; no inscription of any kind was discoverable upon it, but on the Pavement were evident marks of 4 Pillars, which might have supported a Tablet above the Tomb.

This stone being removd, the pavement under it, and about 4 inches of rubbish, we found a large flat stone, 5 inches thick, and somewhat wider in all its dimensions than the coffin of which it was the cover.

This being also removd, we came to a thin plate of lead resting upon the edges of the coffin and 4 slight iron bars laid loose across it: on the part of this lead nearly over the face of the interr'd was a very rough resemblance of a human face emboss'd, for the reception of which a small indenture had been made in the covering stone.

This covering of lead being also removd, the bones appeard, laying in a sheet of lead, the ends cut and turnd together, but in no manner join'd, solder'd, or even doubled in the joint, which servd as a lining to a stone

---

[1] The Rev. Dr. Gordon (note from MS.).
[2] sic: recte Innocent IV.   [3] sic.

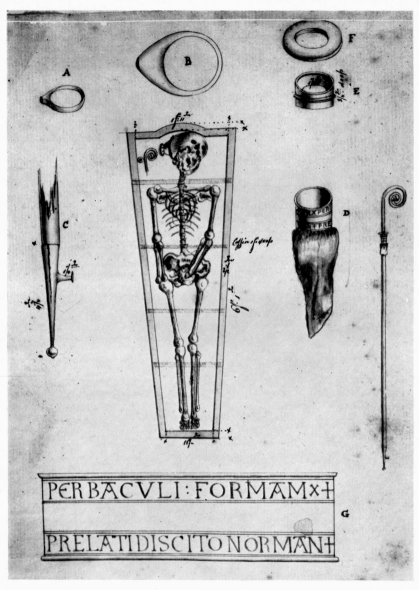

II. THE FINDS IN THE COFFIN OF ROBERT GROSSETESTE

coffin 6 feet 1 inch long, and 1 foot deep (the shape of which is seen by the draught), hollowed out of one stone of the kind found in the quarries near Lincoln, and very roughly hewn, about 2½ inches in thickness, and somewhat deeper in the middle than at either end.

The Head rested on a Chalice bent down in the stalk by its weight; when first opened, the Pastoral staff laid across the body, from the right shoulder to the left leg; and among the bones of the fingers of the left hand, the episcopal ring had been discovered: on the left leg was an appearance of caries, possibly form'd by the iron foot of the pastoral staff which had lain across it.

No traces of shroud or vestment remain'd, except a small piece of gold brocade, which adher'd, when found, to the bone of a finger of his left hand.

All the bones had a damp appearance, but were hard and little decay'd; in the middle of the coffin, where deepest, lay a yellowish fluid, floating upon a soft brown mud, together about ½ an inch in depth; we were told that, since the coffin was first opened the week before, it had considerably wasted; the lead at the head and feet was corroded and crack'd, as if eaten by a menstruum, produced in the course of the dissolution of the body, and the marks of the flesh of the feet were evident on the bottom end of the lead.

That the body had been preserved in some fluid adapted for such purposes seem'd very probable, but what fluid could have remained 529 years?; in any other case, how could a fluid have gotten into this coffin, on the top of a hill and in a dry soil, under cover of the Church. We examined the sides of the stone coffin, expecting to have found them stain'd by the contact of this liquor, which, if the coffin had been full, must have run through the loose joints of the lead; but found them as fresh and clean as if they had not been many days from the hands of the workmen.

Had the body been put in without some means of preservation the stench must have pervaded the small depth of covering, as the lead was not solder'd or the stones cemented together.

Of the Pastoral Staff the head appeared to have been of box or some compact wood, spird, and ending in the form of a lamb's head, in consistence it resembled soft cheese, scarcely bearing to be lifted up; a hoop of wood represented at F, was rather more solid; one of ivory, B, perfectly sound, one of silver, D, but little rusted; under it were the remains of somewhat which might have been leather: the staff was almost annihilated till nearly in contact with the iron bottom, C; the bottom itself by no means destroy'd, the excrescencies had shot out on its side, much resembling rich iron ore, which, in effect I suppose they were.

The inscription on the silver hoop is accurately delineated, G; both for the form of the letters and the remarkable blunder in the lest of them.

The ring also of gold, set with a small sapphire, is delineated in its real size; its weight was ****[1] Mr. Kirwan, an able chymist, whose knowledge is amply testified by his publications in the Philosophical transactions, undertook at my desire to examine chymicaly the liquor found in the coffin; he gave his opinion, founded on such experiments as he could make with the small quantity brought away, that it was merely a fluid produced in the course of the body's dissolution; he found volatile alkali, but no traces of marine salt nor of any of the gums, resins, or other matters which were generally us'd in enbalming or preserving the dead. The liquor, which was void of smell when taken out of the coffin, in a few days contracted a horrible putrid fator; a strong proof, said he, that the air had been much better excluded by the coverings over the coffin than from this small depth at which it was lodged and their loose texture, we who dug it up, were inclin'd to believe.

A. The Ring view'd sideways.
B. The Ring full size, laid flatt upon the paper.
C. Piece of the bottom of the staff with the iron ferule.
D. Silver hoop, gilt, through which the staff went with the drapery fixt to it.
E. Ivory hoop which was fixt above the silver one.
F. Wood hoop, which capt the ivory one.
G. Inscription upon the silver hoop full size.

The last letter of the inscription is an N, not an M: had it been an M there would scarcely have been room for a cross between it and the P of Prelati; a thing that might be thought of consequence.

JAMES WILLIAM FRANCIS HILL.

[1] *sic.*

Chronological Table

c. 1168	Grosseteste's birth.
1186–9	Master in Arts.
1198 (at the latest)	In the household of the Bishop of Hereford.
(?)	The *De Artibus Liberalibus* and *De Generatione Sonorum*.
1200–9 (?)	Master in Arts at Oxford. Commentary on *De Sophisticis Elenchis* and on *Posterior Analytics*.
1209–14 (?)	Theological student at Paris.
c. 1215–21	Chancellor of Oxford. Regent-master in theology. Theological treatises.
1225	Rector of Abbotsley (Deacon).
1229/30–5	Reader to the Franciscans.
1229–32	Archdeacon of Leicester.
Before 1231	Notes on the Pauline Epistles and Psalms i–lxxix; *Moralitates in Evangelia*.
1230–1	Early Greek studies.
1231–5	Commentary on Galatians and on Psalms lxxx–c. *De Cessatione Legalium*. Notes on the *Physics*. *Hexaemeron*.
1232	Resigned all his preferments (except his Lincoln prebend).
1235–53	Bishop of Lincoln.
Before 1239	Translation from the Greek of John of Damascus and the Epistles of St. Ignatius.
1239–41	Translation and commentary on the *Angelical* and *Ecclesiastical Hierarchies* of pseudo-Denis.
1241–3	The *Divine Names* and the *Mystical Theology*.
1242	The *Testaments of the XII Patriarchs*.
1244	*Compotus Minor*.
1245–7	Translation of the *Nicomachean Ethics* and the Greek Commentators.
(?)	*De Vita Monachorum*.

after 1247   *De Caelo* and the commentary of Simplicius.

1250 (?)   The *Superscriptio Lincolniensis.*

1253, October   Death.

Rejected

1210   Archdeacon of Chester.

1214–20   Archdeacon of Wilts. (with the living of Calne).

1221–2   Archdeacon of Northampton (with the prebend of Empingham in Lincoln Cathedral).
De Anima.
Quaestio de Accessu et Recessu Maris, or *De Fluxu et Refluxu Maris.*
Prohemium et Glosae in Libros Sapientiae et Ecclesiastici.
In Ep. ad Romanos.
Notulae in Commentarium Petri Lombardi in Psalmos.

Select Bibliography

In this list only those works are included which are referred to in the footnotes or in the body of the book.

ADLER, A. *Suidae Lexicon*, ed. Leipzig, 1928–38.
ALBERT THE GREAT, ST. *Opera Omnia*, ed. A. Borgnet. Paris, 1890–9.
—— *Opera Omnia. De Bono*, xxviii. Münster i. W., 1951.
ALLAN, D. J. 'Mediaeval Versions of Aristotle, *De Caelo*, and of the commentary of Simplicius', *M.A.R.S.* ii, 1950.
AMBROSE, ST. *Hexaemeron*, ed. C. Schenkl (C.S.E.L. xxxii). Vienna, 1896.
Annales Monastici, ed. H. R. Luard (R.S.). London, 1864–9.
AQUINAS, THOMAS, ST. *Summa Theologiae* (editio Leonina). Rome, 1888–1906.
—— *In Decem libros Ethicorum Aristotelis ad Nicomachum*, ed. A. M. Pirotta. Turin, 1934.
—— *Quaestiones Quodlibetales*, ed. R. Spiazzi. Turin, 1949.
—— *Tractatus de Spiritualibus Creaturis*, ed. L. W. Keeler (Textus et Documenta, ser. philosophica, xiii). Rome, 1938.
Aristoteles Latinus, codices descripsit G. Lacombe in societatem operis adsumptis A. Birkenmajer, M. Dulong, A. Franceschini, vol. i. Rome, 1939.
—— See Lorimer.
ARQUILLIÈRE, H. X. *Le Plus Ancien Traité de l'Église*. Paris, 1926.
AUGUSTINE, ST. *Opera Omnia. P.L.* xxxii–xlvii.
—— *Epistulae*. See Schmid.
—— (Pseudo), *De Spiritu et Anima. P.L.* xl.
AVICEBRON. *Fons Vitae* ex Arabico in Latinum translatus ab Iohanne Hispano et Dominico Gundissalino, ed. C. Baeumker (B.G.P.M. i. 2–4). Münster i. W., 1892–5.
AVICENNA. *Opera*. Venice, 1508.
BACON, ROGER. *Opera quaedam hactenus inedita*, ed. J. S. Brewer (R.S.). London, 1859.
—— *Compendium Studii Theologiae*, ed. H. Rashdall (B.S.F.S. iii). Aberdeen, 1911.
—— *Opus Maius*, ed. J. H. Bridges. Oxford, 1897.
BALE, JOHN. *Index Britanniae Scriptorum*, ed. R. Lane Poole and Mary Bateson. Oxford, 1902.
BARRACLOUGH, GEOFFREY. *Papal Provisions, Aspects of Church History Constitutional, Legal and Administrative in the Later Middle Ages*. Oxford, 1935.
BAUR, L. 'Das Licht in der Naturphilosophie des Robert Grosseteste', *Abhandlungen aus dem Gebiete der Philosophie und ihrer Geschichte, eine Festgabe z. 70. Geburtstag Georg Freiherrn v. Hertling*. Freiburg i. B., 1913.
—— *Die Philosophie des Robert Grosseteste* (B.G.P.M. xviii. 4–6). Münster i. W., 1917.
—— *Die philosophischen Werke des Robert Grosseteste* (B.G.P.M. ix). Münster i. W., 1912.
BIBERACH, RUDOLPH DE. *De septem itineribus aeternitatis*. In S. Bonaventurae *Opera Omnia*, ed. Rome, 1596, vii; Paris, 1866, viii.
BIRKENMAJER, A. See *Aristoteles Latinus*.
BONAVENTURE, ST. (Pseudo). See Biberach.
BRACTON, HENRY. *De legibus et consuetudinibus Angliae*.
BROWN, EDWARD, *Fasciculus rerum expetendarum et fugiendarum*, ii. London, 1690.
BRUNET, A. See Paré.
Bullarum Romanorum Pontificum amplissima collectio, ed. C. Cocquelines. Rome, 1756.
BUYTAERT, E. M. 'The Earliest Latin Translation of Damascene's *De Orthodoxa Fide*, III, 1–8', *Franciscan Studies*, xi, 1951.

CALLUS, DANIEL A. 'Philip the Chancellor and the *De Anima* ascribed to Robert Grosseteste', *M.A.R.S.* i, 1941–3.
—— 'The *Summa Duacensis* and the Pseudo-Grosseteste's *De Anima*', *R.T.A.M.* xiii, 1946.
—— *Introduction of Aristotelian Learning to Oxford*. Proceedings of the British Academy, xxix, 1943.
—— 'The Oxford Career of Robert Grosseteste', *Oxoniensia*, x, 1945.
—— 'The Date of Grosseteste's Translations and Commentaries on Pseudo-Dionysius and the Nicomachean Ethics', *R.T.A.M.* xiv, 1947.
—— 'The *Summa Theologiae* of Robert Grosseteste', *Studies in Medieval History presented to F. M. Powicke*. Oxford, 1948.
—— 'An Unknown Commentary of Thomas Gallus on the Pseudo-Dionysian Letters', *Dominican Studies*, i, 1948.
—— 'The *Tabulae super Originalia Patrum* of Robert Kilwardby, O.P.', *Studia Mediaevalia in honorem R. J. Martin*. Bruges–Louvain, 1948.
—— 'New Manuscripts of Kilwardby's *Tabulae super Originalia Patrum*', *Dominican Studies*, ii, 1949.
CHENEY, C. R. *Episcopal Visitation of Monasteries in the Thirteenth Century*. Manchester, 1931.
—— *English Synodalia of the Thirteenth Century*. Oxford, 1941.
—— *English Bishops' Chanceries*. Manchester, 1950.
CHENU, M. D. 'Notes de lexicographie philosophique médiévale, *Antiqui, Moderni*', *Revue des sciences philosophiques et théologiques*, xvii, 1928.
Chronicles of the Reigns of Edward I and Edward II, ed. W. Stubbs (R.S.). London, 1882–3.
CHURCHILL, IRENE J. *Canterbury Administration*. London, 1933.
COLE, R. E. G., 'Proceedings relative to the canonization of Robert Grosseteste', *Associated Architectural Societies Reports and Papers*, xxxiii, Pt. I, 1915.
—— 'Proceedings relative to the canonization of John de Dalderby, Bishop of Lincoln', ibid. xxxiii, Pt. II, 1916.
COMBES, A. *Jean Gerson commentateur Dionysien*. Paris, 1940.
Corpus Iuris Canonici, ed. E. Friedberg. Leipzig, 1879–81.
CROMBIE, A. C. *Robert Grosseteste and the Origins of Experimental Science*. Oxford, 1953.
DAUSEND, H. 'Johannes Damascenus in der Chronik des Salimbene', *Theol. Quartalschrift*, cxviii, 1937.
DAVY, M. M. *Les Sermons universitaires parisiens de 1230–1231*. Paris, 1931.
DEAN, RUTH J. 'An Anglo-Norman Version of Grosseteste: Part of his Suidas and *Testamenta XII Patriarcharum*', *PMLA*, li, 1936.
DENHOLM-YOUNG, N. *Summary Catalogue of Western Manuscripts in the Bodleian Library*. Oxford, 1937.
D'ENTRÈVES, A. P. *Dante as a Political Thinker*. Oxford, 1952.
DICETO, RADULFUS DE, *Opera Historica* (R.S.). London, 1876.
DONDAINE, H. F. *Le Corpus Dionysien de l'Université de Paris au XIIIe siècle*. Rome, 1953.
[DOUCET, V.]. *Alexandri de Hales Summa Theologica. IV. Prolegomena*. Quaracchi, 1948.
DOUIE, DECIMA L. 'Adam de Marisco, an English Franciscan', *The Durham University Journal*, xxxii, 1940.
—— See Little, 'Three Sermons'.
DULONG, MARTHE. See *Aristoteles Latinus*.
ECCLESTON, THOMAS DE. *Fratris Thomae vulgo dicti de Eccleston Tractatus de Adventu Fratrum Minorum in Angliam*, denuo edidit A. G. Little. Manchester, 1951.
EDWARDS, KATHLEEN, *English Secular Cathedrals in the Middle Ages*. Manchester, 1949.
—— 'The Houses of Salisbury Close in the Fourteeth Century', *Journal of the British Archaeological Association*, 3rd ser., iv, 1939.

EMDEN, A. B. See Rashdall, H.

EYNDE, D. VAN DEN. 'Les Magistri du commentaire *Unum ex Quatuor* de Zacharias Chrysopolitanus', *Antonianum*, xxiii, 1948.

Eynsham Cartulary, ed. H. E. Salter (O.H.S. li). Oxford, 1908.

FLAHIFF, G. B. 'The Use of Prohibitions by Clerics against Ecclesiastical Courts in England', *Mediaeval Studies*, iii, 1941.

Flores Historiarum, ed. H. R. Luard (R.S.). London, 1890.

FOREVILLE, R. *Un Procès de canonisation à l'aube du XIIIe siècle (1201-2). Le livre de saint Gilbert de Sempringham.* Lille, 1943.

FRANCESCHINI, EZIO. *Roberto Grossatesta, vescovo di Lincoln, e le sue traduzioni latine* (Atti del R. Istituto Veneto di scienze, lettere ed arti, xciii). 1933.

—— 'Grosseteste's Translation of the *ΠΡΟΛΟΓΟΣ* and *ΣΧΟΛΙΑ* of Maximus to the Writings of the Pseudo-Dionysius Areopagita', *J.T.S.* xxxiv, 1933.

—— 'Un inedito di Roberto Grossatesta', *Rivista di filosofia neo-scolastica*, xliv, 1952.

—— 'Sulla presunta datazione del "De impressionibus aeris" di R. Grossatesta', ibid.

—— See *Aristoteles latinus.*

FUNK, F. X. *Die Echtheit der Ignatianischen Briefe.* Tübingen, 1883.

GAMBA, U. *Il commento di Roberto Grossatesta al 'De Mystica Theologia' del Pseudo-Dionigi Areopagita.* Milan, 1942.

—— 'Commenti latini al "De Mystica Theologia" del Ps.-Dionigi Areopagita fino al Grossatesta', *Aevum*, xvi, 1942.

GHELLINK, J. DE. 'Patristique et argument de tradition au bas moyen âge', *Aus der Geisteswelt des Mittelalters* (B.G.P.M., Suppl. iii. 1). Münster i. W., 1935.

—— *Le Mouvement théologique du XIIe siècle.* Bruges, 1948.

GIBBS, MARION, and LANG, JANE. *Bishops and Reform 1215-1272.* Oxford, 1934.

GIBSON, S. *Statuta Antiqua Universitatis Oxoniensis.* Oxford, 1931.

GILSON, E. 'Pourquoi saint Thomas a critiqué saint Augustin', *Arch. H.D.L.M.A.* i, 1926.

GILSON, J. P. See Warner.

GIRALDUS CAMBRENSIS, *Opera*, ed. J. S. Brewer, J. F. Dimock, and G. F. Warner (R.S.). London, 1861-91.

GLORIEUX, P. *Répertoire des maîtres en théologie de Paris au XIIIe siècle.* Paris, 1933-4.

GODEFROID DE FONTAINES, *Le Huitième Quodlibet*, ed. J. Hoffmans (Les Philosophes Belges, iv. 1). Louvain, 1924.

GOUGH, RICHARD, *Sepulchral Monuments in Great Britain from the Norman Conquest to the Fifteenth Century.* London, 1786.

GRABMANN, M. *Forschungen über die lateinischen Aristoteles-Übersetzungen des XIII. Jahrhunderts* (P.G.P.M. xvii. 5-6). Münster i. W., 1916.

—— *Mittelalterliches Geistesleben.* Munich, 1926.

—— 'Die Autographe von Werken des Hl. Thomas von Aquin', *Historisches Jahrbuch*, lv, 1940.

—— *Guglielmo di Moerbeke O.P. il traduttore delle opere di Aristotele* (Misc. Hist. Pontificiae, xi). Rome, 1946.

GREGORY THE GREAT, ST. *Moralia in Iob. P.L.* lxxv.

GREGORY OF NYSSA, ST. *De creatione hominis. P.L.* lxvii.

GROSSETESTE, ROBERT, *Epistolae*, ed. H. R. Luard (R.S.). London, 1861.

—— *Rotuli*, ed. F. N. Davis (Canterbury and York Society, x; Lincoln Record Society, xi).

—— *Commentaria in Aristotelis Posteriorum libros.* Venice, 1552.

—— Philosophical and scientific works, see Baur.

—— *St. John Damascene. Dialectica. Version of Robert Grosseteste*, ed. O. A. Colligan. New York, 1952.

—— See Gamba, *Il commento.*

HALLER J. *Papsttum und Kirchenreform.* Berlin, 1903.

HASKINS, C. H. *Studies in the History of Mediaeval Science*. Cambridge (Mass.), 1924.
HEREFORD. 'Visitation Returns of the diocese of Hereford in 1397', ed. A. T. Bannister, *E.H.R.* xliv, xlv, 1929–30.
HILGENFELD, A. *Ignatii Antiocheni et Polycarpi Smyrnaei Epistulae et Martyria*. Berlin, 1902.
HILL, ROSALIND. *Oliver Sutton* (Lincoln Minster Pamphlets, iv). Lincoln, 1950.
—— 'Public Penance: Some Problems of a Thirteenth-century Bishop', *History*, 1951.
HINNEBUSCH, W. A. *The Early English Friars Preachers*. Rome, 1951.
HOCEDEZ, E. 'Les Trois Premières Traductions du *De Orthodoxa Fide*', *Le Musée belge*, xvii, 1913.
—— 'La Diffusion de la *Translatio Lincolniensis* du *De Orthodoxa Fide*', *Bulletin d'ancienne littérature et d'archéologie chrétiennes*, iii, 1913.
HOLCOT, ROBERT. *Comment. in Ecclesiasticum*. Venice, 1509.
—— *Lectiones in Sapientiam*. Basle, 1586.
HUNT, RICHARD W. 'English Learning in the late Twelfth Century', *Transactions of the Royal Historical Society*, 4th series, xix, 1936.
—— 'The Introductions to the "Artes" in the Twelfth Century', *Studia Mediaevalia in honorem R. J. Martin*. Bruges–Louvain, 1948.
—— 'Studies on Priscian in the Twelfth Century', *M.A.R.S.* ii, 1950.
—— *Bodleian Library Record*, ii, 1948, pp. 226–7.
—— 'Manuscripts Containing the Indexing Symbols of Robert Grosseteste', *Bodleian Library Record*, iv, 1953.
ISIDORE OF SEVILLE, ST. *Etymologiarum sive Originum libri XX*, ed. W. M. Lindsay. Oxford, 1911.
JAMES, MONTAGUE R. 'Robert Grosseteste on the Psalms', *J.T.S.* xxiii, 1921–2.
—— *A Descriptive Catalogue of the Manuscripts in the Library of Pembroke College, Cambridge*. Cambridge, 1905.
——'Greek Manuscripts in England before the Renaissance', *The Library* (Trans. of the Bibliographical Society, 2nd ser. vii), 1927.
JEROME, ST. See Schmid.
JOHN OF DAMASCUS, ST. *P.G.* xciv–xcv.
JOHN DUNS SCOTUS. *Opera Omnia*. Rome, 1950.
JOHN THE SCOT. *P.L.* cxxii.
KEMP, ERIC W. *Canonization and Authority in the Western Church*. Oxford, 1948.
KER, N. R. *Medieval Libraries of Great Britain*. London, 1941.
KILWARDBY, ROBERT. *De Natura Theologiae*, ed. F. Stegmüller (Opusc. et Textus, xvii). Münster i. W., 1935.
KUTTNER S., and RATHBONE, ELEANOR. 'Anglo-Norman Canonists of the Twelfth Century', *Traditio*, vii, 1949–51.
LACOMBE, G. See *Aristoteles Latinus*.
Lanercost, Chronicon de, ed. J. Stevenson (The Maitland and Bannatyne Clubs). Edinburgh, 1839.
LANG, J. See Gibbs, M.
LECLERCQ, J. *Jean de Paris et l'ecclésiologie du XIIIᵉ siècle*. Paris, 1942.
LELAND, JOHN. *The Itinerary of John Leland in or about the years 1535–43*, ed. L. Toulmin Smith. London, 1906–10.
—— *Collectanea*, ed. T. Hearn. Oxford, 1774.
LIGHTFOOT, J. B. *The Apostolic Fathers*. London, 1926.
LINCOLN. *The Registrum Antiquissimum of the Cathedral Church of Lincoln*, ed. by C. W. Foster and Kathleen Major (Lincoln Record Society, xxvii–xxix, xxxii, xxxiv, xli–xlii).
—— *The Statutes of Lincoln Cathedral*, ed. Henry Bradshaw and Christopher Wordsworth. Cambridge, 1892–7.

LITTLE, A. G. *The Grey Friars in Oxford* (O.H.S. xx). Oxford, 1891.

—— 'The Franciscan School at Oxford in the Thirteenth Century', *Archivum Franciscanum Historicum*, xix, 1926.

—— *Franciscan Papers, Lists, and Documents.* Manchester, 1943.

—— See Eccleston.

LITTLE, A. G., and DOUIE, DECIMA. 'Three Sermons of Friar Jordan of Saxony, the Successor of St. Dominic, preached in England, A.D. 1229', *E.H.R.* liv, 1939.

LORIMER, W. L. *De Mundo*, ed. (Aristoteles Latinus, XI. i. 2). Rome, 1951.

LOTTIN, ODON. *Psychologie et Morale aux XIIe et XIIIe siècles*, i. Louvain, 1942.

—— 'Saint Albert le Grand et l'Éthique à Nicomaque', *Aus der Geisteswelt des Mittelalters* (B.G.P.M., Suppl. iii. 1). Münster, i. W., 1935.

LOVEDAY, JOHN. *Diary of a Tour in 1732 through parts of England, Wales, Ireland and Scotland.* Edinburgh, Roxburghe Club, 1890.

LUARD, H. R. 'Grosseteste', *D.N.B.*

—— See Grosseteste, *Epistolae.*

—— See *Flores Historiarum.*

MAITLAND, F. W. *Canon Law in the Church of England.* Cambridge, 1898.

MALMESBURY, WILLIAM OF, *The 'Vita Wulfstani'*, ed. R. R. Darlington (Royal Historical Society, Camden 3rd ser. xl), 1928.

MEYER, P. 'Alexander Nequam, *Corrugationes Promethei*', *Notices et extraits*, xxxv. 2.

MINIO-PALUELLO, L. 'Note sull' Aristotele latino medievale', *Rivista di filosofia neoscolastica*, xlii, 1950; xliv, 1952.

Monasticon Anglicanum, by William Dugdale: new enlarged edition by J. Caley, H. Ellis, and B. Bandinel. London, 1817–30.

Monumenta Franciscana, ed. J. S. Brewer and R. Howlett (R.S.). London, 1858, 1882.

MORGAN, MARJORIE. 'The Excommunication of Robert Grosseteste in 1248', *E.H.R.* lvii, 1942.

MUCKLE, J. T. 'The Hexameron of Robert Grosseteste', *Mediaeval Studies*, vi, 1944.

—— 'Robert Grosseteste's Use of Greek sources in his Hexameron', *Medievalia et Humanistica*, iii, 1945.

OXFORD. *A Cartulary of the Hospital of St John the Baptist*, ed. H. E. Salter (O.H.S. lxvi, lxviii, lxix). Oxford, 1914–16.

—— *The Cartulary of St Frideswide at Oxford*, ed. S. R. Wigram (O.H.S. xxviii, xxxi). Oxford, 1894–6.

—— *The Cartulary of Oseney Abbey*, ed. H. E. Salter (O.H.S. lxxxix, xc, xci, xcvii, xcviii, ci). Oxford, 1929–36.

—— *Mediaeval Archives of the University of Oxford*, ed. H. E. Salter (O.H.S. lxx, lxxiii). Oxford, 1920–1.

—— *Mediaeval Archives of Christ Church, Oxford*, ed. N. Denholm Young (O.H.S. xcii). Oxford, 1931.

—— *Oriel Records*, prepared by the late C. L. Shadwell and edited by H. E. Salter (O.H.S. lxxxv). Oxford, 1926.

PAPAL REGISTERS. *Calendar of entries in the Papal Registers relating to Great Britain and Ireland*, ed. W. H. Bliss, i. London, 1893.

PARÉ, G., BRUNET, A., and TREMBLAY, P. *La Renaissance du XIIe siècle.* Paris–Ottawa, 1933.

PARIS, MATTHEW. *Historia Anglorum* (R.S.), ed. F. Madden. London, 1886–9.

—— *Chronica Maiora*, ed. H. R. Luard (R.S.). London, 1872–84.

PAULUS, J. *Henri de Gand.* Paris, 1938.

PEGGE, SAMUEL. *The Life of Robert Grosseteste.* London, 1793.

PELSTER, F. 'Zwei unbekannte philosophische Traktate des Robert Grosseteste', *Scholastik*, i, 1926 (cf. *R.T.A.M.* v (1933), 388, n. 38).

PELZER, A. 'Les Versions latines des ouvrages de morale conservés sous le nom d'Aristote, en usage au XIIIe siècle', *Revue néo-scolastique de philosophie*, xxiii, 1921.
PETRUS CANTOR. *Verbum abbreviatum. P.L.* ccv.
PETRUS LOMBARDUS. *Libri IV Sententiarum*, ed. Quaracchi, 1916.
PHELAN, G. B. 'An Unedited Text of Robert Grosseteste on the Subject-matter of Theology', *Revue néo-scolastique de philosophie*, xxxvi, 1934.
PLATO, *Timaeus interprete Chalcidio*, ed. I. Wrobel. Leipzig, 1896.
POLLOCK, F., and MAITLAND, F. W. *History of English Law* (2nd edit.). Cambridge, 1923.
POWICKE, SIR MAURICE. *King Henry III and the Lord Edward.* Oxford, 1947.
—— *Robert Grosseteste and the Nicomachean Ethics.* Proceedings of the British Academy, xvi, 1930.
—— *Stephen Langton.* Oxford, 1928.
—— *The Medieval Books of Merton College.* Oxford, 1931.
—— ed. *Handbook of British Chronology.* London, 1939.
—— See Rashdall, H.
PRISCIANUS, *Institutiones Grammaticae*, ed. M. Hertz. Leipzig, 1855.
PRONGER, WINIFRED. 'Thomas Gascoigne', *E.H.R.* liii–liv, 1938–9.
RASHDALL, HASTINGS. *The Universities of Europe in the Middle Ages.* A new edition by F. M. Powicke and A. B. Emden. Oxford, 1936.
RATHBONE, ELEANOR. See Kuttner.
RIEDL, CLARE C. *Robert Grosseteste On Light (De Luce).* Translation from the Latin, with an Introduction. Milwaukee, Wisconsin, 1942.
RISHANGER, WILLIAM. *Chronica*, ed. H. T. Riley (vol. ii of the *Chronica Monasterii S. Albani*, R.S.). London, 1867.
ROGERS, J. E. T. *Loci e libro Veritatum.* Oxford, 1881.
RUSSELL, JOSIAH COX. *Dictionary of Writers of Thirteenth Century England* (Bulletin of the Institute of Historical Research, Supplement 3). London, 1936.
—— 'The Preferments and *Adiutores* of Robert Grosseteste', *Harvard Theological Review*, xxvi, 1933.
—— 'Richard of Bardney's Account of Robert Grosseteste's Early and Middle Life', *Medievalia et Humanistica*, ii, 1944.
—— 'Phases of Grosseteste's Intellectual Life', *Harvard Theological Review*, xliii, 1950.
SALIMBENE. *Cronica*, ed. O. Holder-Egger (M.G.H., *Scriptores*, xxxii). Leipzig, 1905.
SALISBURY, JOHN OF. *Opera. P.L.* cxcix.
—— *Metalogicon*, ed. C. C. J. Webb. Oxford, 1929.
SALISBURY. *The Register of St. Osmund*, ed. W. H. Rich Jones (R.S.). London, 1883–4.
—— *Charters and Documents of Salisbury Cathedral*, ed. W. H. Rich Jones (R.S.). London, 1891.
SCHALBY, JOHN DE. *Lives of the Bishops of Lincoln*, translated with Introduction and notes by Canon J. H. Srawley (Lincoln Minster Pamphlets, ii). Lincoln, 1952.
SCHMID, J., ed. *SS. Eusebii Hieronymi et Aurelii Augustini Epistulae mutuatae.* Bonn, 1930.
SCHUM, W. *Verzeichnis d. Amplonianischen Handschriften zu Erfurt.* Berlin, 1887.
SHARP, D. E. *Franciscan Philosophy at Oxford in the Thirteenth Century.* Oxford, 1930.
SINKER, R. *A Descriptive Catalogue of the Editions of the Printed text of the Versions of the Testamenta XII Patriarcharum.* Cambridge, 1910.
SMALLEY, BERYL. *The Study of the Bible in the Middle Ages* (2nd edit.). Oxford, 1952.
—— 'Robert Bacon and the Early Dominican School at Oxford', *Transactions of the Royal Historical Society*, 4th ser. xxx, 1948.
—— 'The *Quaestiones* of Simon of Hinton', *Studies in Medieval History Presented to F. M. Powicke.* Oxford, 1948.

SMALLEY, BERYL. 'A Collection of Paris Lectures of the Later Twelfth Century in the MS. Pembroke College Cambridge 7', *Cambridge Historical Journal*, vi, 1938.

—— 'Hebrew Scholarship among Christians in Thirteenth-Century England, as illustrated by some Hebrew-Latin Psalters', *Lectiones in Vetere Testamento et in Rebus Iudaicis*, n. vi, 1939.

—— 'A Commentary on the Hexaemeron by Henry of Ghent', *R.T.A.M.* xx, 1953.

—— 'Which William of Nottingham?', *M.A.R.S.* iii.

—— 'John Wyclif's Postilla super totam Bibliam', *Bodleian Library Record*, iv, 1953.

SMITH, A. L. *Church and State in the Middle Ages*. Oxford, 1913.

Snappe's Formulary, ed. H. E. Salter (O.H.S. lxxx). Oxford, 1923.

The Song of Lewes, ed. C. L. Kingsford. Oxford, 1890.

SOUTER, A. *The Earliest Latin Commentaries on the Epistles of St. Paul*. Oxford, 1927.

SRAWLEY, J. H. *Robert Grosseteste, Bishop of Lincoln*. (Lincoln Minster Pamphlets, vii). Lincoln, 1953.

—— See Schalby, John de.

STEENBERGHEN, F. VAN. *Siger de Brabant* (Les Philosophes Belges, xii–xiii). Louvain, 1931–42.

STEVENSON, FRANCIS SEYMOUR. *Robert Grosseteste, Bishop of Lincoln*. London, 1899.

SZIGETI, R. L. *Translatio latina Ioannis Damasceni (De Orthodoxa fide, l. III, c. 1–8) saeculo XII in Hungaria confecta*. Budapest, 1940.

THÉRY, G. 'Documents concernant Jean Sarrazin', *Arch. H.D.L.M.A.* xviii, 1950–1.

THOMPSON, ALEXANDER HAMILTON. *The English Clergy and their Organization in the later Middle Ages*. Oxford, 1947.

—— 'Pluralism in the Medieval Church', *Associated Architectural Societies Reports and Papers*, xxxiii.

THOMSON, S. HARRISON. *The Writings of Robert Grosseteste, Bishop of Lincoln*. Cambridge, 1940.

—— 'Grosseteste's Topical Concordance of the Bible and the Fathers', *Speculum*, ix, 1934.

—— 'A Note on Grosseteste's Work of Translation', *J.T.S.* xxxiv, 1933.

—— *The 'Notule' of Grosseteste on the Nicomachean Ethics*. Proceedings of the British Academy, xix, 1933.

THUROT, C. *Extraits de divers manuscrits latins pour servir à l'histoire des doctrines grammaticales au Moyen Âge*. Paris, 1869.

TIERNEY, BRIAN. 'A Conciliar Theory of the Thirteenth Century', *The Catholic Historical Review*, xxxvi, 1951.

TOYNBEE, MARGARET R. *St. Louis of Toulouse and the Process of Canonization in the Fourteenth Century*. Manchester, 1929.

TREMBLAY, P. See Paré.

TRIVET, NICHOLAS. *Annales*, ed. Thomas Hog. London, 1845.

TROILO, S. *Due Traduttori dell' Etica Nicomachea: Roberto di Lincoln e Leonardo Bruni* (Atti del R. Istituto Veneto di Scienze, Lettere, Arti, xci). Venice, 1932.

TROPIA, L. 'La Versione latina medievale del ΠΕΡΙ ΠΑΘΩΝ dello PseudoAndronico', *Aevum*, xxvi, 1952.

USSHER, J. *Polycarpi et Ignatii Epistulae una cum veteri interpretatione*. Oxford, 1644.

VAUX, R. DE. 'La Première Entrée d'Averroës chez les Latins', *Revue de sciences philosophiques et théologiques*, xxii, 1933.

VINCENT OF BEAUVAIS, *Speculum Historiale*. Venice, 1591.

Walter of Henley's Husbandry Together with an Anonymous Husbandry, Seneschaucie, and Robert Grosseteste's Rules, ed. Elizabeth Lamond. London, 1890.

WARNER, G. F., and GILSON, J. P. *Catalogue of Western Manuscripts in the Old Royal and King's Collections* (British Museum), London, 1921.

WEISS, ROBERTO. 'The Study of Greek in England during the Fourteenth Century', *Rinascimento*, ii, 1951.

WELLS, HUGH OF. *Liber Antiquus de Ordinationibus Vicariarum tempore Hugonis Wells, Lincolniensis Episcopi*, ed. A. Gibbons. Lincoln, 1888.

—— *Rotuli Hugonis de Welles Episcopi Lincolniensis*, ed. W. P. W. Phillimore and F. N. Davis (Canterbury and York Society, i, iii, iv; Lincoln Record Society, iii, vi, ix).

WESTERMANN, E. J. 'A Comparison of some of the Sermons and the *Dicta* of Robert Grosseteste', *Medievalia et Humanistica*, iii, 1945.

WEY, J. 'The *Sermo finalis* of Robert Holcot', *Mediaeval Studies*, xi, 1949.

WHARTON, HENRY, ed. *Anglia Sacra*. London, 1691.

WILKINS, D. *Concilia Magnae Britanniae et Hiberniae*. London, 1737.

WINGATE, S. D. *The Mediaeval Latin Versions of the Aristotelian scientific corpus*. London, 1931.

WOOLLEY, R. M. *Catalogue of the MSS. in Lincoln Cathedral Chapter Library*. 1927.

WYCLIF, JOHN. *De Benedicta Incarnatione*, ed. E. Harris. London, 1886.

—— *De Civili Dominio*, ed. R. L. Poole. London, 1885.

—— *De Potestate Papae*, ed. J. Loserth. London–Vienna, 1907.

XIBERTA, B. M. 'De magistro Iohanne Baconthorpe, Ord. Carm.', *Analecta Ordinis Carmelitarum*, vi, 1927.

Index of Manuscripts

PRINTED IN
GREAT BRITAIN
AT THE
UNIVERSITY PRESS
OXFORD
BY
CHARLES BATEY
PRINTER
TO THE
UNIVERSITY

Thin
19 Feb. 1955.